Maryann Opalach

9/78
&
9/79

Reading Instruction

DIAGNOSTIC TEACHING IN THE CLASSROOM

LARRY A. HARRIS
*Virginia Polytechnic Institute
and State University*

CARL B. SMITH
Indiana University

The illustration on pp. 424–425 is reprinted with permission of Macmillan Publishing Co., Inc., from *Who Can* (Level 4, Series r: The New Senior) by Carl B. Smith and Ronald Wardhaugh. Copyright © 1975 Macmillan Publishing Co., Inc. The illustration on p. 184 is reprinted with the permission of the Encyclopedia Britannica Press, Copyright © 1962 by C. Gattegno. Copyright © 1964 Learning Materials, Inc. All rights reserved.

Library of Congress Cataloging in Publication Data:
Harris, Larry Allen, 1940–
    Reading instruction, diagnostic teaching in the classroom.

    Published in 1972 under title: Reading instruction through diagnostic teaching.
    1. Reading.   I. Smith, Carl Bernard, joint author.   II.
Title.
LB1050.H34   1976   372.4   75-28467

ISBN 0-03-089682-7

Printed in the United States of America
  89   074   9876543

Preface

The second edition of *Reading Instruction* reflects changes that have taken place in the teaching of reading during the past five years, changes that emphasize the tremendous importance of the child's language activity, his feelings and interests, and the intellectual clarity needed by the teacher for success in the classroom. Six new chapters have been written to explain those changes. They are: "The Real World," "A Map to Work From," "Language and Reading," "Reading Comprehension: Experiential and Language Factors," "Reading Comprehension: Cognitive and Affective Factors," "Creative Reading," and "Evaluating Progress." The remaining chapters have been considerably revised to show clearly how the classroom teacher can be more effective as a prescriptive teacher. The pressure for accountability, the use of informal diagnostic techniques, and the trend of recent instructional materials all point toward prescriptive teaching for today's classroom teacher. We have written this text for the elementary reading methods course to help teachers conceptualize and design activities that speak directly to the learning needs of all the children in the classroom.

We believe that diagnostic-prescriptive teaching separates effective teachers from teacher technicians. A well-trained technician can make group assignments and carry out group activities. But it takes an analytic teacher to identify the strengths and deficiencies of each child and to plan instruction on that basis so that the child can become an effective reader. Only when the teacher assumes a diagnostic-prescriptive role does learning become personalized for every child in the classroom.

This text, then, is more than a synthesis of ideas about the teaching of reading in the school. It is a commitment to a point of view. We believe that every child needs to succeed in reading every day. He needs to find joy in books as an evident part of that success. The attitudes, interests, and feelings of the child must be considered, as well as his knowledge and skill. Constant observation of and planning for the individual must take place to accomplish those ends.

The order of the chapters in this edition has been drastically altered from that of the first edition. We have attempted to make the reader more aware of classroom dynamics. We start with a description of a language arts classroom activity and end the book by returning to that same classroom to ask how the teacher would evaluate her effectiveness as a classroom reading teacher. The core of the book discusses the development of the language base of reading, the major reading skills, children's interests, children's creativity, organizational considerations for the classroom, and book selection.

Part 1 presents a view of a real world classroom and a definition and model for teaching reading. Thus, the textbook user has an image of a reading class and a schema for analyzing what is happening there.

With the real world of the classroom in mind, as well as a map that gives perspective to reading activities, we want the students to have an understanding of the general principles and underpinnings of reading. The development of language and comprehension are the foundations for all other specific skills. Part 2 considers the language base and the central role of comprehension, or getting meaning. General assessment techniques are discussed here as continuing components of a diagnostic-prescriptive approach to classroom teaching.

Part 3 begins a series of chapters on reading and thinking skills. They are arranged to show the child's movement toward independence and the emphasis those skills typically receive in children's developing learning stages. Because readiness and word skills are described in Part 3, the teacher should not conclude that we recommend exclusive work on those areas during a child's early growth stages. It is only natural for teachers and children to emphasize readiness activities and word skills in the initial stages of reading instruction. For that reason we isolate those activities for discussion in the section on initial reading.

Part 4, "Primary Reading," follows the child's progress toward independence in reading, his search for fulfilling interests, and his need to read critically.

Upon reaching a sense of independence in reading the child can focus on creativity and reading in the content areas.

Part 5 shows how creativity and reading come together. It stresses the need for several specialized skills which must be developed in order to help the child cope with reading content subjects. The child must also learn the study and library skills that will serve him as a life-long reader.

In Parts 2, 3, 4, and 5 we explained the foundations of reading and the skills typically associated with teaching reading. But the classroom teacher has to help a room full of children. In Part 6 we turn to the organization and management of reading instruction in the classroom. The conceptual model, underlying principles, and activities for observing and teaching in specialized areas must now be applied to organizing people and things, and also to evaluating and selecting books and materials.

Part 7 continues the process of fitting all the pieces in place. Special attention is paid to a general evaluation plan for the reading classroom, including a special section on self-evaluation for the reading teacher.

We have constructed a model, or schema, of reading so that the teacher can more easily understand the major reading operations. The model not only helps clarify but also directs the teacher's observations and suggests plans for the child's continuing progress. It serves as a major organizing feature for the discussions of reading skills, interests, and attitudes.

There are several other aids to the reader which will help to organize thinking about the content of this text. Starting with Part 2 each chapter has an introduction and related questions for the reader. In this way the major ideas of the chapter are identified. At the end of each chapter are terms for self-study. These guide the reader in reviewing important concepts. End of chapter discussion questions attempt to trigger group discussion which will apply the main ideas in the chapter.

The index of the book identifies terms that are defined in context, thus serving also as a glossary. This provides the reader with a more accurate picture of the meaning of the term.

Several items frequently used by classroom teachers appear in the appendices: a list of book clubs for children, a list of children's newspapers and magazines, and a special series of lesson plans for teaching various aspects of reading.

This revision has turned more and more toward real-life reading and the observation of a child's competence as he reads magazines and newspapers as well as regular school books. A major section of each chapter is devoted to techniques for observing or assessing the child's progress, regardless of the special focus of the chapter. We feel that a reading methods text should provide practical aids, not simply the general direction of discovering a child's needs. Self-evaluation for the teacher is treated in the same concrete way.

Thus the circle closes. The book starts with a description of a classroom in operation, proceeds with an analysis of various aspects of teaching reading, and ends with recommendations for the teacher who must put the teaching-learning process together—always according to the individual style of the teacher. We hope the book lives up to its theme of being diagnostic-prescriptive both for the learner and the teacher. For these are the two unique and precious persons with whom we are concerned.

One further item relating to another aspect of this text needs to be mentioned. We are very aware that children in the classroom and the teachers and librarians in the school are both male and female. But until the American language comes up with a better substitute for repetition of he and she or himself and herself, we have chosen to use the male pronoun generically; that is, to stand for the human being. This is not a matter of sexist bias, but hopefully a way to make for smoother reading.

Acknowledgments

Many people have prodded our thinking in the development of this edition of *Reading Instruction,* especially the students and teachers, with whom we have worked. The ideas and research of Jean Piaget, Frank Smith, and Kenneth Goodman have been very persuasive in formulating some of our ideas. Longtime guides Theodore Clymer and Mary Austin should not be left out; nor should Richard Owen, our HRW editor, or Louise Waller, our editor and congenial whip on this edition. This is not an exhaustive list of colleagues and researchers who have aided our thinking, but most others are reflected in the bibliography. To all of them we owe a continuing debt.

Blacksburg, Virginia
Bloomington, Indiana   —*L.A.H.*
December 1975   —*C.B.S.*

Contents

Reading in the Classroom

Perspective gives a person knowledge of where he stands in relation to the world around him. Some sort of perspective is needed at the start of a discussion on how to teach children to read. In the first part of this book we step into a classroom to see what is meant by reading and by language activity. Next we outline reading so as to help a classroom teacher prescribe both individual and group needs. Part I sets the stage for the more specific discussions of the rest of this book.

1

The Real
World

The uniqueness of each teacher is precious. So is the uniqueness of each learner. In the best sense, those unique qualities should be preserved—not squelched. A teacher learns to bring individual students and individual learning together so that children are able to read well and the teacher thereby succeeds in his function.

With thirty kids in a classroom? All unique? Yes! those individual differences constitute the continuing challenge and excitement of teaching. In teaching reading those differences are probably more important than in any other area of the school's curriculum. That's what this book is all about— helping teachers think through ways of guiding children to grow toward competency in reading. It starts with the real world of the classroom.

Faces and Spirits

What constitutes a reading class? Wiggling bodies—some that smell like a deodorant soap and some that do not—smiling faces, suspicious eyes, tousled hair. Those are superficial differences, as every teacher knows. Those faces mask an expansive range of abilities, interests, attitudes toward learning, and socioeconomic conditions. All of that is called "background." Each child brings to school his person, his experiences, his spirit, which constitute a hidden curriculum.

The teacher clears paths for those individual spirits in order to construct

3

competency in reading. He arranges opportunities to satisfy the range of competencies, those interests, the attitudes, and the socioeconomic circumstances. What does that mean for the reading class?

A Room Is a Room

Look at any classroom. Many tools of the profession are right there. Books, record players, desks, tables, bookshelves, the library, the audiovisual supply—the teacher manipulates all of those things to accommodate the children. But each room and each library is different. No standardized description fits every classroom. Each teacher mixes and matches tools and children to cultivate learning. And the question persists. how does one teach a class to read and constantly adjust to the varying performances of each child?

The Rule Book

In the teacher's lounge many myths rise from the smoke and the clutter of coffee cups. Usually these myths begin with the phrase—"you can't." In the teacher's lounge it's always "against the rule." *You can't* use different books; *you can't* be yourself; *you can't; you can't.* But teachers are and do. If they want to try something different, they ask a supervisor or check the rule book themselves. They find that most schools have various support personnel to help them and their students with reading. Reading consultants, remedial teachers, and administrators can help with forming new approaches to reading. It is our experience that with proper clearance teachers can do most of the things they want to do for their pupils. But first they must find out what the customs and rules are. Teachers cannot afford to be hampered by teacher lounge myths.

Additional help and resources often can be found in the community. When a teacher needs another pair of hands or a resource, or the children need another lap to sit on, parents, college students, retired people, and business and professional people in the community will frequently help out. To get this kind of assistance, though, the teacher has to reach out, has to think beyond the four walls of the classroom and the school.

Pressure to Individualize

Each pupil in a school must become successful in reading. The climate of the time—if a professional conscience were not enough—alerts teachers to personalize pupil instruction. Many states now legislate that teachers demonstrate pupil progress in the basic subjects of reading, math, and English. Clear learning objectives and a performance record for each child are obvious components for that kind of accountability. More and more parents are asking for personal performance information, instead of a single quality grade from

"A" to "F." Federal and state project monies are frequently earmarked for schools in order to increase individualization.

After decades of discussion about meeting individual needs in the classroom, political and social currents are pushing educators to put their words into action. Reading, more than any other area in the curriculum, is expected to produce results.

Those same political and scoial pressures work in favor of the reading teacher. Reading is important. Parents and children know that success in reading is the most necessary and basic part of education. They may even have careers in mind or day-to-day circumstances where fluent reading ability helps them to gain information, relaxation, or enjoyment. Basically, therefore, teachers have a powerful motive working for their success and the success of children in learning to read.

The teacher's job is helping each child realize he is making daily progress in becoming a competent reader. Exactly how is that accomplished? The beginning of this chapter is concerned with formulating means to that end. They suggest attitudes as a powerful force for change. Each teacher needs to identify instructional strategies and find ways of achieving clear signs of success.

Let us first look at an actual reading and language class. The preceding paragraphs give a sense of direction to our analysis. And the scene that follows should cause questions to sprout—questions that hopefully will be answered in this book and in related classroom discussions.

Regina Clare's Class

What is a reading and language skills classroom like? Here is a description of an operating class, one that we think is within the capability of most teachers. We do not advocate that all classes should look and function alike, but we want to present an example that stimulates thinking about how to work with children in the classroom more effectively. Depending on his personal style and the school where he teaches, each teacher must construct his own "best environment" for success in reading.

Regina Clare—first-grade teacher, warm, smiling, and alert—moves with confidence and purpose around her classroom. She makes sure each group of children knows what to do, and asks her two adult volunteer helpers if they have questions about the children's tasks. Then she returns to a group of six children so that she can work with them.

The classroom, though informal, is clean and bright in appearance, with children's papers and seasonal decorations on two walls. There are several adult-constructed charts and wall hangings which suggest that Regina Clare has an artistic flare and uses it to decorate vocabulary charts, success record charts, and timely poems. There are several centers of reading activity around the room, as well as centers used for other purposes. (*See* Figure 1.1 for a

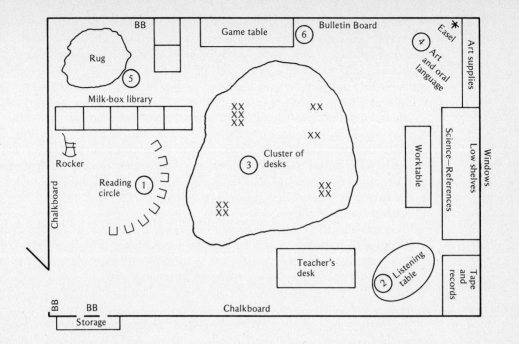

FIGURE 1.1   Regina Clare's room

diagram of the room, which includes a reading circle, library, a place for games, oral language area, listening center, and general work area.)

1. *Reading Circle*   Regina Clare sits in a rocking chair and a small group is seated in a circle on the floor on corduroy-covered cushions. With her teacher's guide on her lap and some work cards for a chart beside her, Regina Clare introduces a story which is in the children's readers. These books are on the floor in front of the children. The teacher reads a couple of pages with the children and then asks them to read a couple of pages silently so they can discuss what is happening in the story. When the silent readings have been completed by everyone, they talk about the words and ideas they have encountered.

2. *Listening Table*   In the tape corner of the room four children sit around the listening table, place headsets over their ears, open their books (these children are on a different level than Regina Clare's group), and wait while one of the volunteers selects a tape and starts the tape recorder. The children read along with the taped voice, occasionally responding by smiling or nodding their heads. Then, using a worksheet, they answer questions according to directions given on tape.

3. *Cluster of Desks*   In the center of the room where desks have been clustered some children take out a workbook and begin to read and answer the questions. From time to time they refer to their readers in order to complete

the workbook exercises. The volunteer who had helped in the listening corner circulates among this group giving each child help with the directions as needed. When each individual finishes, he either goes to the library corner (Area 5) to lie on the floor and read, or to the kit and game table (Area 6) to practice some skill which a volunteer helps him to identify from a folder. These folders for each child are kept in a box near the kits and games. A checklist in the folders details the skills to be emphasized and the kinds of practice materials the child has used. Those skills he has mastered have stars pasted in front of them.

As the children at the listening table finish their tasks they, too, go to the library corner or to the kits and games table. In the library corner they share books and help one another read the stories.

4. *Art and Language*   The group in the art corner works with the second adult volunteer. At first this volunteer reads a brief story and the children assume the roles of the characters and pantomime their actions. Then the volunteer takes picture cards, which the children identify and discuss; they also match word cards to the pictures. (*See* Figure 1.2).

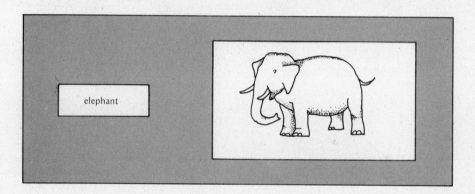

FIGURE 1.2

Each child then takes a picture card and a piece of paper and draws a scene. The children describe one of the pictures as the volunteer writes those sentences which the child artist agrees have meaning for his picture on a piece of chart paper.

The attitude pervading this classroom is one of: "Let's explore a world of ideas." From that attitude follows expression of self, enjoyment of stories, verification of information, and sense of autonomy. Each child seems to feel accepted, for he is willing to express his ideas; and books are evidently valuable resources. This is an excellent atmosphere for learning.

Regina Clare's classroom reflects her teaching philosophy and the kind of person she is. This philosophy is valuable because it works well for her and the children. Another classroom may not look the same, because it will reflect a

(Photo by Carl Smith)

FIGURE 1.3   When they are well-trained and well-organized, adult volunteers can make a substantial contribution to a classroom.

different teacher and different children. *Your reading class reflects you!* That's a rule for creative thought, not for intellectual apathy.

This description of Regina Clare's reading class raises two major questions: Why were those activities included in the general area of teaching reading? How does Regina Clare adjust class activities from day to day to meet the changing needs of the children?

Each center of activity seems to represent an important aspect of Regina Clare's definition of teaching. Some activities are group-oriented and teacher-directed. Some are highly controlled, and some are creative. Some appeal to children's interests and independence. Directed reading, practice reading, creativity, independence—all these are options. Regina Clare feels that frequent contacts with adults promote children's language growth, so she trains adult volunteers to assist her. But those other adults are there because they are part of Regina Clare's philosophy of learning to read. A beginning teacher, for example, might find it overwhelming to organize volunteers in addition to organizing himself. Each teacher must evolve his own philosophy, his own definition of teaching reading.

Regina Clare's first-grade class shows a range in reading performance from some who cannot recite the alphabet to those who can read third-grade books with relative ease. How does she adjust? Her attitude, classroom organization, and materials should aid her decisions.

A teacher in a typical fourth-grade class would find some children who stumble over first-grade selections and others who breeze through seventh- and eighth-grade selections. To benefit all those children each teacher must learn to prescribe reading and language activities for the typical range in the class.

This text devotes itself to answering the proposition that a reading philosophy must be developed by each teacher to prescribe for that range. It suggests ways of doing so through a definition of reading and a description of classroom procedures and practices; through a description of a class where language and meaning are being constructed and where interests and enjoyment are part of the lives of the children and the adults who function there.

2

A Map to
Work From

The classroom scene is set. But what intellectual roadmap charts the activities, the movements, and the adjustments that are made in that classroom? Each teacher has an intellectual map for guiding learning. The clearer the map, the easier the journey.

Concentrate on Learning

Children naturally want to learn. Most children even want to learn to read. The teacher's job, then, is to concentrate on learning. But how is that done?

Marla, a child we know, went to kindergarten filled with Sesame Street and stories that her daddy had read to her. She wanted to learn to read and told her kindergarten teacher of her desire.

"You learn to read in the first grade," said the kindergarten teacher. "Sorry, but I'm not allowed to teach you."

Stop action!

At the start of the first grade Marla asked again "Can I read now?" Instead, the first-grade teacher put her through a series of kindergarten readiness activities.

Stop again! Stop thinking!

At a most impressionable time Marla was told, in effect, "Don't think ahead. Watch what the group is doing and follow along."

Those two teachers were not concentrating on learning. They were not thinking with the child. They were concerned about something else—their grade levels, some artificial rule, a set of books. Without intending to, they conveyed to the child a working attitude about school: "Don't push out; don't explore; squelch your curiosity."

If Marla's learning had been the center of the teacher's attention, both teachers would have encouraged her and tried to find out what she could not do and what she might try next.

Motivation? What higher point of interest is there than when a learner says, "Oh, teach me that!"

Fortunately, Marla's story is a good news-bad news story. The good news is that she and her teachers came to love each other. The teachers were warm, wonderful people. The bad news is that these good people—loving people who should be imitated—had indicated to Marla that she should wait for someone else to tell her when to learn, that her internal learning clock was not keeping "normal" time. Not everyone we know works on standard time.

Observe the Child

To focus on learning means to focus on the individual child. To know what to observe, the teacher must know what to look for. Otherwise, observation is random—perhaps erratic and nonproductive. What is it, then, that the teacher must observe?

Before a doctor operates on you, you hope the doctor has passed the anatomy course. Before a teacher confronts a child, shouldn't he have identified some objectives and know what goals he is aiming for? The teacher is not a physician prescribing for a patient, but he should adjust to the needs of individual learners and proceed in an analytic fashion in prescribing learning activities in the classroom.

The classroom teacher looks for alertness, family environment, language development, attitudes, and some very specific behaviors related to a printed page, for academic learning is related to intelligence, environment, and language development. But a teacher cannot discharge his obligation to observe a child's reading performance by "*generally* observing his *general* characteristics." Those general aspects of learning only form a backdrop and give perspective to the more specific activities of a subject or a tool skill such as reading.

What abilities as a language user does a child have? What are the speech and writing skills that we expect in a child of his age? Are the skills related to vocabulary, articulation, message-oriented utterances? Is this child average in using them? Does he surpass them? For reference, a sample of oral language objectives is presented in Table 2.1 (see page 12).

When a child reads or works with written symbols, does he have an orderly sense of them? Does he have a system for figuring out unknown words? Does he know how to read for various purposes? Can he think systematically about what he reads? Does he read content out of his personal interests? Those

TABLE 2.1   Oral Language Objectives and Activities

---

1. Child should be able to retell the story using his own words.
   a. Use individual filmstrip and tell story to group in his own words.
   b. Read short story; retell to small group.
   c. Prepare individual or small group "book talks" or "commercials."
2. Child should be able to create a story, given a stimulus.
   a. Have a puppet show.
   b. "Story starters"—either objects or pictures—used to prepare a story.
3. Child should be able to participate in a discussion.
   a. "Discussion starter"—slips of paper with children working in small groups to reach a conclusion.
   b. Trips around the school—teacher talks about five senses, things the children feel, see, and so forth. Limit subject to keep discussion relevant.
4. Child should be able to organize ideas orally in a sequence of events.
   a. Explain a hobby or craft.
   b. Pictures (storyboard) or slides; explain why they were put in that order.
5. Child should be able to make introductions.
   a. Role-playing—celebrities, people in the news, people in history, school personalities.
   b. Children arrange for resource persons as guest speakers and introduce them.
6. Child should be able to interpret and restate the main idea of an oral dialogue.
   a. "Magic Circle"—child repeats gist of previous speaker's remarks before making his contribution.
   b. Child tells main idea of a sport—baseball, football, and so on.
7. Child should be able to give verbal descriptions.
   a. Children sit back to back. One must describe an object while the other draws a picture of the object.
   b. Children prepare and teach a lesson to other children—how to tie a shoelace, draw a cat, and so on.
8. Child should be able to formulate relevant questions.
   a. "Press conference"—some children act as people in the news; others ask questions. Can also be used with questions on historical periods.
   b. "Gambit" game—children make up questions to be used in the game. Grab bag is for prizes at the end of the game (first team to reach a score of 21).
9. Child should be able to adjust to different oral situations.
   a. Children make a tape of nursery rhymes or fables in their own versions, complete with sound effects.
   b. Use refrigerator box as a television station for reporting books, commercials, newscasts, weather reports, and so forth.

---

questions should be a permanent part of any teacher's method, because they guide the teacher in making instructional decisions and in helping the child make progress. And for the teacher they indicate the need for goal setting.

Make Decisions

Questions about the child's language, word strategies, and comprehension strategies can be answered when the teacher knows specifically what he is looking for. Indeed, he needs a map of reading—a cognitive map that gives him directions and checkpoints. Cognitive clarity (knowing what is to be accomplished) is the teacher characteristic most highly correlated with learner success (Rosenshine, 1972). Doesn't it seem reasonable that the teacher with a sense of direction is more likely to help his students than one who says, "I don't know much about teaching reading." It follows logically that each teacher should develop a definition of reading and language growth, a definition that will work in the classroom, one that will enable the teacher to solve the major decisions involved with teaching reading. The teacher must decide:

1. the level of the child's reading-language performance
2. the word and comprehension skills he has
3. the attitudes and interests that he brings to reading.

Level of Reading

The child's level of reading performance is tied closely to a reading vocabulary, that is, the printed words that he can identify. General comprehension is also a factor in the level of reading performance. Deciding about the level of performance is similar to determining which book in the school's reading program matches the level from which the child can make comfortable progress. That's the book to begin instruction with.

Word Skills

A fluent reader can use various techniques to figure out unfamiliar words. Suppose the child did not know *grizzly* in the sentence: "The grizzly man scratched his beard." What techniques or skills can the child use to figure out what the unknown word means? Can he use context clues (sense around the word), sound-symbol correspondences (phonics), word structure clues (structural analysis), and visual memory (configuration)? Those word skills that he can't demonstrate should be taught.

Comprehension Skills

What kind of comprehension-thinking operations can the child perform? Given content reasonable for his age and background, can he identify the content? ("Yeah, I known Bushmen are found in Australia.") Can he recall major details? Can he analyze the information and rearrange it to suit his purpose? Can he apply some criterion to judge the content? Can he use the content or extend it? Those thinking operations that he dosen't know, should be taught.

Interests and Motivation

Each person likes to read what appeals to him. Yet, interests are far from uniform. How does one grab the child's attention and hold it, as he participates in reading? Built into each person is a set of reactions to reading and a set of reactions to the particular content. Sometimes subtle and sometimes violent, those reactions stem from the previous experience of the learner and the personal framework he has developed. "Nobody reads at my house," says one child. This set of reactions colors all that the child reads. Often labeled the *affective domain* of learning, attitudes and feelings can work for or against learning. By locating major interests and sources of positive feelings, the teacher develops valuable clues for keeping the child alive to and healthy in reading. Attractive books and reading activites will grab the child's attention. Working through the child's interests and showing him success will keep him on target through the school years.

Define Reading

The teacher's major decision areas in reading are level of performance, word-solving strategies, comprehension strategies, and interests and attitudes. Through these decisions the teacher guides the child toward competency. Armed with a definition of competent reading—that is, with a definition stated in real-life terms or in operational terms—the teacher knows what is important and what has to be emphasized.

Even a brief definition of competent reading helps. For example, reading may be briefly defined as the *reader's interaction with a printed message.* That tells the teacher that reading is not *passive,* that there is intellectual energy to be expended. By enlarging that definition, greater direction can be achieved. *Reading is the reader's interaction with a printed message across a range of thinking operations as guided by a purpose for reading.* This definition can be turned into teaching directions and performance goals for students and parents and a sense of order begins to evolve within the activity called reading.

For the teacher *interaction with the printed message* means that the child's background and attitudes actively mix with the surface meaning of the printed words. Take the word *beard,* for example, "My nice, smiling daddy has a beard." Or "The smelly man down the street has a beard." The word *beard* is not a sterile term for the child.

Interactions *across a range of thinking operations* indicate that the child's intelligence deals with the message through a variety of crucial skills, including analysis and evaluation, as *guided by the child's purpose for reading*—to find information, to compare, to enjoy, and so on.

A teacher's definition of reading is not sufficient. The child's career as a learner and as a person in society suggests a definition that helps him and his parents understand what the teacher is helping him to do. For the benefit of the child, then, reading can be defined in terms of the child's activity.

Reading Performance

The child is able to gain information and pleasure from his schoolbooks and from those items that he reads at home; he is able to figure out unfamiliar words in those books, and can perform typical comprehension tasks; for example, tasks of recalling, analyzing, and evaluating the content (according to his stage of development).

For discussion with parents a teacher may want to break down the definition to show what the major features of reading are. This might be accomplished through a letter, such as the sample which follows:

Letter Form Sample

Dear Parent,

Here is a brief list of what we will help your child accomplish as he learns to read. If you want to discuss any of these goals, please call.

We want your child to work with the following goals in the months ahead:

GOALS

1. Establish an attitude that reading leads to knowledge and to enjoyment.
2. Have content reading skills that enable him to read schoolbooks, magazines, newspapers, and other material outside of school.
3. Use various word skills to figure out unfamiliar words.
4. Develop comprehension—thinking skills and creative reading.
5. Build the child's vocabulary from its present level.

Sincerely,
I. M. Strate

(Examples under each goal area could be provided for the parent at the discretion of the teacher.)

Set the Stage

Grabbing a student's attention and holding his interest of necessity occupies a significant place in every teacher's thoughts. Diverse as interests are, and slippery as motivation is, the teacher needs an approach, a strategy that prevents him from using only a thunderbolt. The thunderbolt approach means employing startling activities or dramatics akin to a flash of lightening or the menacing crash of thunder in order to attract a child's attention. It startles him for the moment, but soon wears off.

The organized teacher acts as a catalyst for learning. He brings together the child, the setting, the content, and the material in a way that engages the child's mind as well as his emotions. The word engage stands in deliberate contrast to the word thunderbolt. Engagement implies involvement, relevancy, challenge, and continuity. It's the difference between a neon highway billboard and a mystery story you can't put aside.

As the teacher designs the classroom, the materials, and the exercises, he appeals to the values and interests of the child. He clarifies the purposes of classroom activities and provides regular feedback on the child's growth and accomplishments. After all, what better motivation is there than knowing that you are succeeding in something that has recognized value—recognized by parents, teachers, and classmates. Reading stands high on almost everyone's list—children included—as a value to be achieved. Kindergarten children, for example, show awe for one of their classmates who can read. For that reason, if for no other, the teacher sets up systematic means for letting the child know about his successes. Whether through star charts, notes to parents, lists of skills to be checked off, or other methods, the child should be told regularly what progress he is making. That kind of feedback often ignites the youngster because he wants to hear again and again that he is doing something that is viewed as important, or something for which he receives praise. To this point, however, the teacher links perseverance, for each child's fuse has a different length and the ignition is not always a brilliant flash.

Promote Interaction

Motivation to learn comes from within and from without. A child wants to learn to read because it satisfies his desire to conquer his world and reading feeds his interests. But he is also motivated by the pressures and the pleasures that adults and his agemates apply. One of the fascinating challenges for the teacher is to combine the intrinsic and extrinsic forces that keep a child moving toward fluency and competency in reading. The word *interaction* can be used by the teacher as a guide to activites: "Let's read this story to see which of you has the best solution to the problem of the missing gem."

There should be an interaction between internal and external forces. The child who delights in reading about the mysterious events on a haunted island should experience an increase in satisfaction when he describes the parts of the mystery that appealed most to him to some of his classmates. Book-sharing time as a regular classroom activity will emphasize the community value of reading and will give the child a stage to perform on. In this way the child interacts with printed material; and he also interacts with people, both adults and children. Some teachers prompt children to think about what they have read by saying: "See if you can outguess the author. Maybe you know what he will say before you read it." This notion of interacting with the author motivates and establishes a mental stance whereby the child acts upon the content, instead of merely trying to absorb it.

Interacting with classmates and adults about reading has always been held in high esteem by alert teachers. Discussing stories in groups not only brings the selections alive for the children but gives each of them a chance to be important. They can tell others what they found significant in the story.

A combination of independence and sharing ideas can be promoted, for example, by having two periods a week during which everyone in the class reads anything that appeals to him—the teacher too. Each could read a story, a magazine, a selection from the science text—whatever is of interest. There would be only one requirement. At the end of the free reading time each person has to be willing to tell a small group what he found interesting or important about the piece he read. The reporting can be done on a random basis by drawing names from a hat or by some other means that involves everyone over a couple of weeks. Given a two to three-minute time limit for telling what's important to them, most children will thrive on the opportunity. Through sharing, they are alerted to many kinds of selections that otherwise might not have been called to their attention.

The value of that kind of personal reaction to reading extends beyond the immediate emotional responses. By asking themselves what is important or what makes a selection "come alive," they begin to examine their own feelings and thinking strategies for reading different kinds of exposition. It may very well be a spark for refining all kinds of reading-thinking skills. The child in his own way, then, asks questions similar to those that the teacher asks him: "What am I interested in reading? Should my interests be expanding? What must I do to read well? What are my reasons for reading one selection that are different from another? How do I improve?"

Internalize a Map

The circle comes back on itself. A definition leads to improvement, which leads to a better definition. Teaching reading includes many aspects of learning and needs to be defined operationally to incorporate skills, interests, and attitudes. These various elements should turn into a definition, a set of terms that a busy classroom teacher can recall and then can use to guide instruction. When a new student arrives, or when children show spurts of growth—as they always do—the teacher needs some framework as a guide for starting instruction and for keeping the children moving forward. After all it isn't following lesson plan directions that create a problem for the teacher. He can carry out a set of instructions for group activities simply by following the teachers' plan book for the basal reader: But teacher expertise equates with teacher adjustment to individual difference in progress—that is, to variation in pupil growth. In order to identify the kinds of differences and in order to have a sense of direction for adjusting instruction, the teacher needs an *intellectual* (cognitive) *map*. Similar to the surgeon's knowledge of anatomy and of operating procedures, the teacher must have knowledge of important components in reading competency and must know procedures for helping children achieve those components.

A cognitive map for reading does not assure success in reading. Teaching and learning are fraught with uncharted twists and swirls, based on environment and genetics, that necessitate ingenuity. Nonetheless, a cognitive map lays out a direction and a series of paths to try. It gives teachers and children a clear focus on objectives.

We intend to outline a concept or a model for understanding the teaching of reading. In succeeding chapters this outline will help guide the discussion of specific aspects of reading and related teaching-learning activities in the classroom.

The model should help a teacher accomplish the following objectives:

1. set objectives for learning
2. diagnose progress
3. prescribe instructional activities
4. observe interests and attitudes.

As an intellectual map, the outline should help the teacher put reading instruction into some sensible pattern. All of us—teachers and students—are searching for ways of putting order into our academic lives. Thus we offer a model for reading instruction.

Harris-Smith Model—An Outline of Reading

Reading never takes place in a sterile box. Stored within every reader are his knowledge, his feelings, his attitudes, his premonitions—some in neat array, some in a clutter—filling the memory with subjective reactions and viewing each new idea within the framework available to the reader at that time in history (J. Piaget, 1952). Reading, like any other learning, is subject to the intellectual and emotional overlays that each individual brings to the task. The teacher watches and listens to the child in order to search out the language, experiences, and thinking operations that a child can apply. For example, has the child developed mental structures wherein he can read history with a perspective of time?

Given a general learning perspective, the teacher then asks: "What is involved in learning to read?" He needs a model that illustrates the major components of reading activity and indicates what direction analysis of the reading act should take. Figure 2.1 presents an outline that has been helpful to many teachers.

The major operations that a reader can perform on a printed message are shown in the figure. It therefore indicates questions a teacher can ask about a child's skill—classroom diagnosis, if you wish. But it also categorizes major teaching-learning activities designed to help the child learn to read. A cursory look at the labels shows that reading includes a wide range of operations, both visual-perceptual responses and analytic-evaluative thinking acts. Teaching children to read involves more than a decoding phase or a simple stimulus-

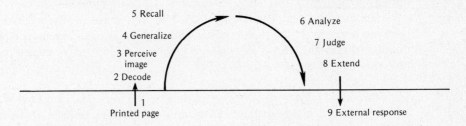

FIGURE 2.1   Operations in learning to read

response bond to a printed symbol. Reading involves an active pursuit of and interaction with the written message.

Items 1 (the printed page) and 9 (the external response) in Figure 2.1 are those things that can be observed in a direct physical sense. We can see the book page and the eye making contact, and we can see or hear responses a reader may make—for example, an explanation, a written summary, a shrug of disgust, a dance, an illustration. There are internal responses, too—for example, placing the information received in a framework of knowledge, a feat we cannot observe in a physical sense. In logical order the reader can proceed through each category in the model.

Decode

The printed page has to be translated and related to spoken language. In the early stages of reading this involves a decoding operation. The letters and patterns of letters are related to the sounds they stand for. A correct translation of symbol into sound provides the reader with a basic recognition of the word, assuming that the word is part of his listening vocabulary.

Perceive Image

The recognition of the word on a sensory level evokes what is sometimes called a perception or a *perceptual image*. This is an image at the threshold of abstraction. It is the learner's first step toward forming a *concept*. The young reader's perception of the word *dog* is a rather specific image of a four-legged creature that barks and answers to the name Hobo.

Generalize

The image of a specific *dog* is then related to animal, pet, or various kinds of dogs. In that way the word dog becomes a generalized concept of dogness.

Recall

As the reader feels that the passage holds some meaning for him, he has a number of options or operations open to him. For example, he can search the message for specific ideas, analyze it, and evaluate it. Given the whole message, the reader can then go back into it to recall details or parts that are important—either to the reader or important because some specific purpose for reading was assigned.

Analyze

To analyze means to manipulate the events or the ideas of a message in order to accomplish a specific end. Analysis includes activities such as categorizing elements, identifying organizational principles, differentiating opinions from facts, and so on.

Judge

Evaluation is an operation which applies selected criteria to a passage to indicate its worth. The reader must develop criteria based upon logic, empirical studies, or the subjective feelings he has about the issue. As he reads, he uses these criteria to judge the value of what he sees in the passage.

Extend

The reader may decide to do something with the knowledge he has gained *(application)*. Depending on his evaluation, he may reject the selection and the author who wrote it; or he may look for a similar work in order to build additional knowledge. His decision may result in an observable response expressed orally, in writing, or through a gesture; or it may be an unobservable decision or response to synthetize or reject what he has learned.

The model in Figure 2.1 is a logical interpretation of part of the reading process. Because it proceeds in numerical fashion, it may appear that these operations are linear. That is not necessarily true. All sorts of crisscrossing within Figure 2.1 is likely in actual reading. For the sake of diagnosis and instructional planning, however, the teacher may find it beneficial to classify the operations from simple (decode) to complex (extend), and use that logic in analyzing children's performances and in organizing records to keep track of their progress.

Figure 2.1 is a skeleton which will be fleshed out in succeeding chapters of this text. But a word of caution is needed here with a reminder of the perspective mentioned earlier. Teaching reading and learning to read are not simply a sum of seven operations or skills such as those in Figure 2.1. Whether the list is eight or eight hundred items long, reading is somehow greater than the sum of its parts. Each learner brings with him a unique set of experiences, attitudes, and interests. These stored memories interact profusely with the mental operations listed in the Harris-Smith model. Even a single word such as *shop* calls up various images and feelings, depending on that unique storehouse of memories. *Shop* may mean a place where mother works or something you do when you go to the grocery. It may evoke pleasant feelings or those of irritation.

Aware of these nuances in the child, the teacher remains flexible in observing and guiding the child's reactions.

Figure 2.2 expands the view of reading presented earlier. It not only shows an "affective dimension" (interests, feelings, beliefs), cutting across the entire range of reading operations or skills but points to the constant interaction between the message, any one operation, and the memory bank of the reader.

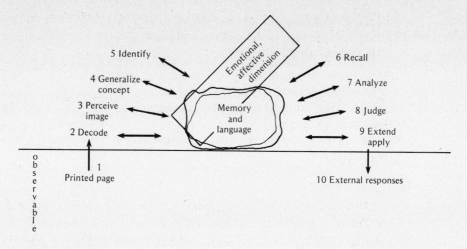

FIGURE 2.2   The reading model

Communicate a Definition

If the teacher defines reading as a type of communication, then he communicates an attitude about reading. Children begin to realize that they are to interact with the printed page, that they not only work on a word but they act on the entire message. They are constructing meaning when they read. Thus the writer and the reader each contribute to the meaning.

The teacher defines reading in terms of the child's construction of meaning with selections that are appropriate for his stage of development and the environment he lives in—usually his schoolbooks and the magazines he reads at home. The teacher further defines reading in terms of word recognition operations and thinking operations that help in observing the skills of the child, and in planning activities that promote continuing progress toward competent reading. That definition is made flexible by the teacher's attempts to utilize the unique experiences and interests of the child in the process of learning to read.

Refine

All that needs to be added to our map of reading is a principle of refinement. From the outset the child constructs meaning in the manner that his intellectual development allows. As the child's intellectual structure changes, and as his experience expands, he is more and more able to construct meaning from a message in the manner of an adult, like a fluent and competent reader. The work of the teacher, then, is to promote a continuing refinement of the operations listed in Figure 2.2.

Since that refinement, that progress in reading rolls along, sometimes fast, sometimes slow; sometimes wobbly, sometimes straight; the teacher observes and adjusts week-by-week and year-by-year. With a cognitive map such as that in Figure 2.2, the teacher helps the child to progress in a spiral fashion.

To accomplish this the teacher:

1. Determines the level of development and what operations or skills the learner can perform.
2. Observes the learner's strategy for solving various word and comprehension problems.
3. Uses interests and background to obtain healthy interaction with written messages.
4. Keeps opening opportunities to move up and refine his skills.

Diagnose

Where the teacher makes decisions about children and the learning environment in the classroom, the Harris-Smith model can be used to guide the child toward efficient, fluent, enjoyable reading.

The reading-communication model gives the teacher a schema with which to diagnose a reader's progress at specific stages in the process of learning to read. The teacher can ask about the reader's skill in decoding, in perceiving, in conceptualizing, in recalling, in analyzing, in evaluating, and in applying. Simply being aware that a reader may experience difficulty at any one of these stages gives the teacher an orientation toward analyzing each student's needs and in assisting his students. Means for testing and teaching arise from an awareness of these aspects of reading.

The Model and the Book

Now that the model has been introduced briefly, where and how does it apply in the classroom? Some perspective is needed to relate the model to teaching and to the rest of this book, for a cursory view of the chapter headings reveal no one-to-one match up with the categories in the model.

The Harris-Smith model is an attempt to describe the reading process in a logically consistent sequence from its simple to complex aspects. The model provides a reasonable outline of how the reader works on the printed message—at his own level of sophistication. But activities in the classroom, and thus books and materials for teaching reading, traditionally have been organized around topics—such as readiness, word skills, comprehension skills, study skills, and creative reading. And those topics provide convenient categories for listing activities in reading instruction. In teacher's guides, for example, the objectives and the exercises are labeled in this way. Therefore these categories are one important aspect of the teacher's knowledge. At the same time that he is teaching a word skill or a comprehension activity, the teacher should know how that activity is used by the reader in the act of reading; he should know where it fits into the reading process. That's why we call the Harris-Smith model a map, and why we will refer to it throughout the book to show where the activities of a given chapter touch on the model.

Below is a list of the categories in the model and the chapters that contain related activities. Due to the complex nature of reading, and therefore the reading activities described in these chapters, some are listed in more than one category of the model.

Decode   Chapters 7, 8, and 9 discuss listening, sound-spelling patterns, and word structure activites.

Perceive image   Chapters 4, 5, and 10 include basic comprehension and word recognition activities.

Generalize   Chapters 3 and 4 on language growth and comprehension deal with the development of concepts and purposeful identification of a message.

Recall   Chapters 5, 8, and 10 on comprehension and memory of words provide recall activities.

Analyze   Chapters 4, 5, 12, and 14 on critical comprehension and content reading show how analysis is applied in reading.

Evaluate   Chapter 12 on critical reading is especially applicable to this stage of the model, as is Chapter 15 on study skills.

Extend   Chapters 11, 13, and 14 discuss creative and utilitarian applications in reading.

Other chapters in this text describe testing, organizing, and selecting materials—concerns that cut across any one skill or any one phase of the reading process. Throughout the book, by means of this recurring model, the reader will be reminded that he must interrelate the model with the discussion of separate classroom practices.

SUMMARY

This chapter describes the need teachers have for a clear intellectual map for teaching reading. A map should give the teacher a design for diagnosing reading performance of students and for planning instruction. The Harris-Smith model is an intellectual outline, or map, that teachers can use. It is a logical description of the reading process, and moves from simple to complex operations. Included in the model are the cognitive operations of decoding, perception, concept formation, recall, analysis, judgment, and extension.

Discussion Questions

1. In what ways do you see that a model of reading will help you observe children as they read?

2. If you accept the Harris-Smith model, how would you define the act of reading? If not, tell why.
3. Parents often ask about their child's progress in reading. Explain how you would use the Harris-Smith model in simplified form to describe reading to a group of parents?

part II

Every Child Reads

Learning to read is a personal undertaking. Each child in a classroom is a unique composite of experiences, abilities, interests, and attitudes. To be effective, reading instruction must accommodate and build on these attributes of the learner. In this part of the book language is presented as the child's first basic resource for learning to read. Reading comprehension is discussed as a process involving the interaction of complex factors that vary from child to child and from topic to topic even for the same child. Procedures and devices for identifying the child's personal state of readiness and unique strengths and needs are also presented.

3

Language
and
Reading

Billy is a bright-eyed six-year-old. Today is his first day of school. He is eager to learn to read, write, spell, add, sing, and do the many other things his older brother can do. Billy enters the classroom on his first day carrying a brown paper bag containing the materials his parents thought he would need for school. This includes pencils, paper, crayons, a ruler, and various other supplies. While these items will be useful, Billy carries the really necessary equipment for learning in his head. Especially important is the attitude Billy carries about school. Also important is his inherited potential for learning—his intelligence. In his brief, but full lifetime he has acquired personal experiences and the language and concepts that have grown along with those experiences.

While all these factors are objects of interest and much research and discussion among educators, the child's language has recently been given special attention. The importance of language in learning to read is better understood as a result.

The student should look for answers to these questions as he reads this chapter:

What language abilities do children bring to school?
How are language abilities important in learning to read?
How do language abilities develop?

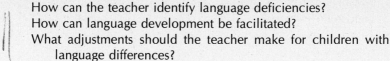

How can the teacher identify language deficiencies?
How can language development be facilitated?
What adjustments should the teacher make for children with
    language differences?

If he is at all typical, Billy, the six-year-old described in the chapter opening, arrives at school with a superb grasp of his native language. Without formal study, and despite the often confusing inconsistencies of the English language, Billy can communicate with and understand others who use the same language. While his speech may still carry some signs of immaturity in the pronunciation of certain sounds, and his usage may indicate a need for further refinement, Billy can converse with a person he has never met before and exchange information effectively. In a relatively short period of time Billy has developed the most important ability that distinguishes humans from animals: language.

Children Develop Language Facility at an Early Age

The typical six-year-old has an impressive vocabulary (usually exceeding 20,000 words), an intuitive understanding of the grammar of English, the ability to hear and pronounce all or nearly all the sounds in the language, and a history of successful verbal interactions with others. He may be shy and confused by the newness of his school surroundings to the point of being temporarily "nonverbal," yet he has excellent control of his language. In fact, he has already learned something far more significant than virtually anything the school may be able to teach him in the next twelve years—how to talk.

Obviously schooling can nurture and expand the child's language skills, but the hard part is already done. For example, the child knows that the order of words in an utterance *(syntax)* is important to meaning. Most English-speaking six-year-olds can tell which of these statements "makes sense": 1. The dog barked. 2. Dog barked the. He can tell whether an event has already taken place or not from the form of a sentence—for example, We *saw* the fireworks. He knows that words have various meanings *(semantics)* depending on their use in a particular sentence—for instance, a *bat* is both an animal and a wooden club used in playing baseball. Many other examples of what is known about language by even an "unschooled" six-year-old could be given. The point, however, is that children bring language skills to school; they are equipped, so to speak, with a basic capacity for learning.

If children do indeed have sufficient language for learning, why make a special point of it here? The explanation is simple: Often classroom activities neglect what the child knows about communicating and how he acquired that knowledge and impose many fragmented, mechanical activities to teach him to write, and, of special concern here, to read. Reading instruction should take advantage of the child's language skills building on what he knows, relating word recognition and comprehension activities to that base of competence. Teachers should also be aware of how language facility is achieved, so that wherever possible reading can be learned in a similar way.

How Language Is Important to Reading

It is almost too obvious to state that reading is a language-based process. At a superficial level this seems evident, because the printed page is made up of symbols that stand for words. Words are combined to form sentences; sentences form paragraphs; and so forth. Words, sentences, and paragraphs are language. Therefore, reading is language-based. But the fuller meaning of this statement requires exploration.

Reading is a form of communication. Information and ideas are exchanged between writer and reader in the act of communicating. The writer expresses his thoughts on paper with language, using whatever skills and style he has developed personally. The reader attempts to retrieve meaning from the printed page. Contrary to common-sense explanations that have persisted over the years, it is not the letters on the page or even the individual words that provide significant cues to the competent, fluent reader. The ability to predict meaning is based on the reader's previous experiences with a topic, his familiarity with key concepts, and his knowledge of how language works. The fluent reader scans the page for cues to meaning. The scanning is not a precise, letter by letter, or even word by word process but rather one of predicting and anticipating meaning.

To illustrate, a reader who has had experience with football can predict what might go into the following blank: "The quarterback passed the ball to the _____." Experience helps the reader predict reasonable alternatives, such as *end, receiver, halfback,* and *fullback.* The reader may predict incorrectly if the written message is unusual or unpredictable (for example, "The quarterback passed the ball to the waiter.") But his experience enables him to reduce the possible number of alternatives and predict with a high degree of certainty.

The reader's knowledge of language is also important in predicting the author's message. The previous example is again useful. Knowledge of syntax enables the reader to predict that the sentence: "The quarterback passed the ball to the _____," will be completed by a noun. Whether he can verbalize that condition or not, the speaker of English knows intuitively that *jump, hop, blue,* and *slowly* do not fit meaningfully into the blank. The reader predicts, using his knowledge of syntax. It is not necessary for him to look at every letter of every word or even to look at every word to make this prediction.

Similarly, the reader's knowledge of semantics enables him to determine that in this case *passed* has a specific meaning. An appropriate synonym here would be *threw. Passed* has various other meanings that are inappropriate in this context. The reader recognizes this fact and predicts on the basis of the meaning that makes the most sense.

Because he is reading for meaning, an unexpected message will cause the reader to retrace his steps to locate the source of confusion. Erroneous predictions are cast aside, new predictions made, and the search for cues to meaning continued. Often the pace becomes slowed and more cues are sampled in an effort to gain understanding following a false prediction. If necessary, individual words and even parts of words may be scrutinized, as the reader attempts to retrieve meaning once again. But this careful study of cues interferes with meaning if it reduces the pace to a word-by-word reading. Understanding occurs best when phrases and sentences can be gulped in large, meaning-bearing units or chunks. This is possible when the reader relies heavily on his knowledge of a subject, syntax, and semantics, and less on his ability to identify individual words.

Frank Smith (1975) describes the reading act as one that involves both visual and nonvisual information. Reading obviously has a visual component in that the reader attends to printed symbols on a page. This information comes from in *front* of the eyeballs. As the reader scans the page the eyes pick up cues that are transmitted to the brain. Reading also involves nonvisual information, or information that comes from *behind* the eyeball. The reader brings concepts, attitudes, and knowledge of how language works to the reading act. This behind-the-eyeball information permits the reader to sample cues as a means of triggering his own nonvisual information. All cues on a page are not, indeed cannot be, sampled, without overloading the brain with information. Meaning is not obtained by identifying the words and adding them up in a left to right summation process. In fact, word identification is very much dependent upon meaning. The human memory simply cannot process all the letters presented on a printed page. Meaning helps the brain organize letters so that they can be processed. To illustrate, *see the locomotive* is readily identified because it refers to a familiar object. In contrast, *rps xta wpraztfgex* contains exactly the same number of letters, but it is impossible to hold in short-term memory because it is too complex; it is unorganized. In addition, the spelling patterns in *see the locomotive* are much more common in English than are those in *rps xta wpraztfgex*. The reader's knowledge of written language helps him predict the types of spelling patterns he will meet. Thus it is often unnecessary to look carefully at the internal structure of words. This further demonstrates that reading is not primarily a visual task. Meaning is important to word identification.

A mechanical view of reading suggests that the reader first identifies letters in words, then whole words, then sentences, and so forth until meaning is obtained. In this view the significant feature of written language is what appears on the page—the surface structure of the language. It follows then, that early reading instruction would begin with those visual elements. This emphasizes the mechanics of reading. Children learn to associate sounds with letters. Words are sounded out letter-by-letter, and sounds are blended to pronounce

FIGURE 3.1   Reading should mean more than the interpretation of printed symbols. It can give pleasure, knowledge, and emotional release.

(Holt, Rinehart and Winston photo by Richard H. Goff, Jr.)

words. With this approach we believe reading may become a word-calling process. Meaning can get lost with this approach, since the task fails to draw on children's language or their background of experience.

Meaning Is Conveyed by the Deep Structure of Language

Meaning is not conveyed by the purely physical aspects of language; that is, sounds or printed symbols. Obviously, meaning of individual words is dependent on the shared understandings of those who speak the language. *Chair* refers to what we sit on only because that is our unspoken agreement; it is not any inherent quality of the object that makes *chair* its rightful label.

The order of words is also important to meaning. (For example, dog bites man versus man bites dog.)

Sounds or printed symbols alone represent only the *surface structure* of a language. Meaning is carried by the *deep,* or *underlying structure*. Syntax, the set of rules underlying language usage, links the surface and deep levels of language to permit the exchange of meaning. The receiver of a message must utilize the set of rules to get the meaning of a message. The words alone can be ambiguous and unclear to one who lacks an understanding of syntax. Fortunately, it is unnecessary to teach the rules of syntax, since children have learned them in the process of acquiring language.

The implications of the child's language competence for learning to read are all too often ignored. Thinking that reading is primarily a visual task, involving the identification of individual words (or letters), we have traditionally presented beginning readers with material that is devoid of the rich syntactic and semantic clues they so badly need to make sense of the printed page. Stark sentences such as, "A fat cat sat," force the child to rely heavily on visual clues to identify words. Teaching strategies that treat each word as a goal to be conquered individually strip the child of his most powerful strategies for dealing with language and meaning—syntax and semantics. Words in isolation or near isolation lack contextual clues that permit the child to use his knowledge of language, his background of experience, and his store of concepts.

Viewed as a process of predicting meaning, reading becomes an act that is only incidentally visual. As has been said, the words on the page are not ends in themselves but rather cues or clues that help the reader search for meaning. Syntax provides the reader with valuable information even if every word cannot be pronounced. As the reader gains experience, and as his concepts grow, he samples fewer cues in order to predict meaning accurately. As his command of language increases, he employs more powerful strategies and understands more complex relationships in print. Instruction that leads the child to predict and anticipate meaning, to draw on his own experiences, and experiment with language contribute to reading competence. Suggestions for accomplishing these objectives will be provided throughout this book.

Words Are Identified More Easily in Context

This description of reading as a process of predicting does not negate in any way the importance of identifying words. Especially in the beginning stages the reader must learn to identify words or he will never be able to put them together into sentences so that he can predict meaning. Therefore, it is necessary to spend some time helping children acquire strategies for decoding word symbols. More will be said about this in Chapter 7. But it is important to take a fresh look at word recognition when reading is considered as a language-based operation.

The major factor to remember in decoding instruction is simply that word identification should be related to meaning. This can be accomplished most easily by always dealing with words in context. It is only in context that words have any specific meaning. The simplest words—*man, store, house, can*—

have various meanings. We can *man* the boats, talk to the *man*, and read the history of *man*. In addition to this semantic consideration, words should be presented in context because of the clues to identification provided by syntax. As was stated earlier, the reader who is gaining meaning from the printed page seldom needs to look carefully at all parts of a word. He predicts words using a minimum of clues. Occasionally he will predict incorrectly and find it necessary to look more carefully at a word. An unknown word, or one predicted incorrectly, requires a systematic attack, and readers need analytic skills to accomplish this (for example, phonics and structural analysis).

The key point to remember is that word identification does not lead to understanding; but understanding leads to word identification. And that is as it should be, since reading is a meaning-getting process not a word-calling process.

How Language Is Learned

The remarkable thing about language acquisition is that no one formally teaches a child how to talk. In a completely natural, self-directed process (which we will describe a little later), the child masters the language of his culture. This process is worth considering for several reasons. First, there are implications for how children might learn to read in the way they learn to talk. Second, the language so necessary for effective reading cannot be taken for granted. Children can and should engage in classroom activities that further develop their language skills and, in the process, their reading skills. Knowing how language develops can be helpful in understanding how and where to begin with further language development.

Reflect for a moment on how a child from birth to five years learns to talk. The descriptions given will make more sense if you can relate them to actual observations. It would be worth your effort to visit a nursery school to gain some personal impressions of child language growth. Even if your observations are informal and unsystematic, watching a child experiment with language can be quite revealing. Described in conventional terms the process is one of gradual expansion and refinement of language.

Initially, the infant produces sounds that are not language but merely random noises. Babies in all cultures make essentially the same sounds, and no single sound is used to signal meaning. Noise gets attention, but any noise does the job in this early babbling stage.

Later (by six months), the infant begins to make sounds intentionally. Sounds foreign to the baby's environment are dropped from the babbling. During this period certain sounds become associated with objects or situations. Parents often urge the infant to produce certain sounds and reinforce their production (for example, da-da-da).

As the infant's sounds become associated with specific needs or situations, recognizable speech begins. At first only single syllables may be produced—or single words. The tendency on the part of many adults is to believe that the

(Photo by Featherkill Studio)

FIGURE 3.2   Toys, interactions with adults and other children, and the child's own body are all serious learning experiences for a six-month-old baby.

child learns a word and then begins to search for ways to use it. In fact, the process is probably just the opposite. The child is a thinking, feeling being with ideas to communicate. Rather than searching for the meaning of words, he searches for words to convey his meaning. Limited physical ability (for example, the ability to articulate), limited vocabulary (What should I call that thing put in my mouth?) and lack of knowledge of grammar (Do I say "me drink" or "drink me" when I'm thirsty?) cause the twelve-month-old child to use *holophrases*, or one word sentences, at first. The simple, single-word sentence represents complex meaning. "Ball" may mean, "Where is the red ball I had before?" Or "Throw me the ball." Or "The red ball just hit me in the head." In other words, the surface structure of the child's language is a rather stark representation of an elaborate deep structure.

Gradually the child begins to produce a more complete surface structure, as he acquires an understanding of the grammar of language. The earliest grammatical rule used by the child is one adults do not use in their own speech. Two- or three-word sentences are produced that clearly communicate meaning; for example, "want down." Parents assist in language development by expanding the child's efforts at communication.

Robin: "want ball."

Parent: "Robin wants the ball. Here, Robin. Catch the ball."

Eventually the child's grammar evolves to that used by the parents.

The growth of the child's grammar is evidently not simply a matter of imitating adults. At various points the child seems to overgeneralize the rules of grammar and apply them in "incorrect" ways. For example, the child who says, "Grandpa comed to my house," has probably never heard an adult use that form of the verb *come*. Yet many verbs are put into past tense by the addition of *-ed*. The explanation seems to be that the child experiments with languages. By testing the system, he learns how grammar works. Smith (1973) likens the acquisition of language to learning about cats. "In order to learn what it is about cats that makes them cats, the child needs to examine positive and negative examples" (Smith, 1973, p. 145). The child learns to generalize about how language operates, but also learns to discriminate among proper and improper applications of his generalizations. It is important that he get feedback about incorrect use of language in order to learn how the system works. The child actually learns as much from being wrong as he does from being right. Simply imitating adult language would fail to help the child learn what features of the language are significant.

Language Learning Holds Implications for Learning to Read

There are obvious differences between learning to talk and learning to read. It would be simplistic to equate the two and argue that children can learn to read in *exactly* the same way they learn to talk. Yet there are interesting parallels between the two that at least deserve consideration in our discussion of language and reading. These are discussed a little later. The authors believe that recognition by teachers of the similarities between these two aspects of communication will provide some guidance for instructional activities.

Errors Are a Necessary Part of Learning

The most significant principle of language learning, insofar as reading is concerned, has to do with the importance of making errors. It has just been pointed out that children make many errors in learning language. Errors are a necessary part of learning how the language system works. Certainly there is an implication here for reading instruction. Whether the activity is one of learning sound-symbol associations or searching for an author's main point, children should be supported by adults when they make errors.

Both teacher and child need to understand that reading involves prediction and that prediction involves error. One way to reduce error in reading is to approach word symbols strictly on a visual level. Careful processing of letters and words with great attention to detail will result in accurate word-by-word reading. But reading for meaning necessarily involves less attention to visual cues or clues, more attention to nonvisual ones. Errors are a natural consequence of a search process involving anything as complex as retrieving meaning from the printed page. Neither the teacher nor the child should expect word-perfect oral reading or letter-perfect word identification.

This statement should not be interpreted to mean that errors are preferred to accuracy in reading. Accuracy in word identification and comprehension are important, but they are the result of effective prediction (which risks error), not the result of precise word-calling. In fact, the real test of a reader's skill is whether he corrects those errors that interfere with meaning, not whether he avoids errors altogether. Just as in learning to talk, the child who is learning to read must be allowed to make errors as a natural consequence of learning the written system of communication.

Language Grows from the Needs and Interests of a Child

The child who grows up in an environment where almost his every need and wish are anticipated and fulfilled typically is retarded in semantic development. In the absence of a need to communicate, children simply don't learn to communicate. In a normal environment the child learns to ask for a drink because he will be thirsty if he doesn't. Language develops around a child's needs.

Carried a bit further, the child who becomes interested in rocks develops an extensive vocabulary and set of concepts around that interest. Or he may be devoid of language and experiences related to ballet if he has no need to learn about or no interest in ballet. Language also develops around a child's interests.

The child's language is personal. It represents his experiences, and in many ways enables him to label and manipulate his environment. His language is adequate to his needs or he learns new language to meet those needs. Remarkably, his language develops without the aid of formal instruction.

Reading instruction might profit from greater attention to the needs and interests of the child. Whereas language develops naturally around an interest, for example, frequently the reading program ignores the child's interests and brings topics to him in the form of stories. Often the language needed for success in learning to read is also missing when interest is lacking in a topic.

Particularly in beginning reading the needs and interests of the child can be seized by the teacher as a point of departure. Stories can be read and discussed on topics children enjoy. This would obviously involve individualization from the outset, since each child has different needs and interests. It is also possible to have the child write (or dictate) his own stories on topics he enjoys. Various techniques for building reading instruction around the child will be described throughout this book.

Language Is Related to Meaning

Most people can remember getting trapped in a situation where language was exchanged more as a matter of custom or ceremony than as a way of exchanging a meaningful message. Even in such cases, words are strung together in a conscious way, not at random. This points up the obvious fact that the use of language always involves meaning.

(Holt, Rinehart and Winston photo by Russell Dian)

FIGURE 3.3   A child who becomes absorbed in an activity learns to talk about the hobby and the pleasure it gives.

The infant who is just learning to talk uses language in an effort to communicate ideas. Emphasis is on the use of whole words in some context that involves meaning. Oral language is not normally broken down and analyzed into its separate elements even by the child who is just learning to use it. To be sure, individual sounds may occasionally be isolated and taught to a child who has difficulty, for instance, saying "rabbit," "Say r-r-r-r." But these instances usually occur in context, and the sounds do not become ends in themselves. Individual sounds are important only as they relate to the pronunciation of a word, which is typically part of a sentence intended to communicate meaning.

By the same token reading activities should always be in context. Meaning should be the overall concern. Words and parts of words should be seen against a backdrop of meaning. Attention to the mechanics of reading should not become an end in itself.

Approached in this way reading will not become an abstract, memorization process with great attention to individual parts. The child who is learning to read is able to use the powerful semantic and syntactic strategies he has already learned in acquiring language. Phonics and other forms of word analysis are taught and learned in a reading program that focuses on meaning, but they are not the starting points and they are not important in and of themselves.

Children with Language Differences

Reading has been presented as a language-based process. The child who speaks a language other than English faces a serious handicap in learning to read. Not only does he lack the necessary vocabulary to read English, frequently the syntax of his native language is different from English, and certain sounds of English may not appear in his tongue. Often economic and physical deprivation accompany his basic language problem, and in some cases he also meets prejudice and discrimination in his community and school.

A detailed discussion cannot be given here of how English can be taught to the non-English-speaking child, nor is that the purpose of this book. Nevertheless it is well established that a second language, in order to make the child bilingual, can best be learned when the child is young. It is also clear that the language-learning process is not substantially different for the young child acquiring a second language than it is for the child learning a first language. Stimulation from the environment, coupled with oral interaction with speakers of a second language and feedback concerning incorrect attempts at using the language, usually enable a child to master language use. Typically the bilingual child occasionally mixes vocabulary and sentence structures of two languages, but maturity and experience normally eliminate this tendency.

From the standpoint of reading instruction, there is little point in even beginning until or unless the child has the ability to express his thoughts spontaneously in English speech. Until the child uses English easily and confidently in conversation, time spent teaching him to read English will be better used teaching him to speak it. Time lost from reading instruction in acquiring facility with the language will quickly be made up once the bilingual child has control of English.

Some programs first teach the non-English-speaking child to read in his native language. The special advantage of this approach is related to the pride the child can acquire in his own heritage. He gains confidence in his ability to succeed at learning to read a native language, which may carry him through the difficult moments of learning to read English later on. Ultimately he must make this transition, however, and in order to do so he must acquire English. Since that is unavoidable, the better approach is probably to delay reading instruction in favor of learning English from the outset. This approach eliminates the often difficult tasks of finding teachers who speak, write, and read the child's native language and finding appropriate materials for the child to read in that language. The wide variety of languages spoken in the United States makes the approach of learning to read in a native language impractical in many classrooms.

Suggestions for improving language skill are offered in a later section of this chapter and in Chapters 4 and 5, "Reading Comprehension." Although directed primarily to English-speaking children, the suggestions given are also appropriate for helping the non-English-speaking child acquire the language skills he needs for learning how to read.

Another Language Difference: Dialects

It comes as no great surprise that the English language is spoken by people who represent a large number of *dialects*.[1] One need not be a linguist to realize that a native Minnesotan speaks a different variety of English than a native South Carolinian. Yet two people who have dialect differences can usually communicate without great hardship, because their English is more alike than it is different.

With only a little analysis of the matter it is possible to conclude that differences in pronunciation and word meaning are usually due to differences in background experience. Someone who grows up in an environment where *pen* and *pin* are pronounced exactly the same (as in southern Indiana) will probably learn to pronounce those words accordingly. Someone else will pronounce them differently, because it is a distinction made by important speech models in his environment. Likewise, the meaning attached to a word such as *dinner* varies from group to group (for example, for some it is a meal at the end of the day, for others it refers to the noon meal).

Differences in grammar are due to variations in background, and may show up in inflections or in syntax. Some groups are inclined to report that "Jimmy *dived* into the water," while others say "Jimmy *dove* into the water." "We could play tag" contrasts with "We might could play tag."

There are some obvious implications for the teacher of reading when dialect differences exist in the speech of children in the classroom or when the teacher's dialect is different from the children's. Certain sound-symbol associations will be different in various dialects. Thus, phonics instruction must reflect the relationships as children speak them. This can be tricky if several dialects are present, but not necessarily difficult. The teacher must also watch for discrepancies in word meaning, so that understanding does not falter due to vocabulary differences. These adjustments, important as they may be, are not really the crucial issue insofar as teaching children with divergent dialects to read is concerned. The greater problem is simply one of attitude. Dialects often tend to evoke negative attitudes if they are not understood as an anthropological phenomenon.

Dialects Are Often Misunderstood

The problem with regard to dialect differences is related to the human tendency to label as wrong, or inferior, traits or characteristics of others that are different from our own. Sociologists have a label for such attitudes; they call it *ethnocentrism*. The teacher must constantly guard against ethnocentristic thinking, especially with regard to language differences. Even teachers who

[1] A dialect is the form or variety of a language spoken in a region, community, social group, or occupational group. Dialects of a language often differ with regard to pronunciation, word meaning, and grammatical rules.

understand that "Southerners (or Northerners) talk as they do because that is the norm in their environment" may have a tendency to add consciously or unconsciously, "but it's wrong" or "it sounds ignorant." Such attitudes interfere with effective teaching by diverting attention from *what* is said to *how* it is said.

The teacher who lets an attitude about "correctness" of language creep into classroom procedures will typically reject the child's "incorrect" attempts at communicating. The rejection may be done kindly, but the consequences are the same: The child begins to wonder about his ability to communicate. Since reading is a language-based process, any reluctance on the part of the child to use language will ultimately interfere with his success at learning to read. The preferred approach in such cases is to accept and reinforce the child's use of language whatever its form, so that he gains confidence in communication skills.

Most teachers can accept this argument where matters of pronunciation and vocabulary are concerned. The most misunderstood aspect of dialect, however, is difference of grammar (including usage). Such differences seem harder to accept probably because dialects are not adequately understood. Many "enlightened" people appreciate that Lyndon B. Johnson's speech was "correct," even if it sounded "different," but do not understand that in the Black dialect, "Momma, she be at the store," is "correct" or grammatical. The ethnocentricity of some people is better concealed, but it exists nonetheless. Teachers should realize any dialect of English is a complete language system having all the elements necessary to permit communication. No dialect is "better" than any other when the purpose of language is considered. Some dialects may have more prestige than others, because of social factors and people's attitudes, but every dialect is linguistically acceptable.

All Dialects Are Functional

Language is an invention of humankind. It is a constantly changing invention that evolves to keep up with the need to exchange ideas and thoughts. Outdated or antiquated features of language die out because they no longer serve a function. Ambiguous or confusing aspects of language usually evolve or change in order to eliminate misunderstanding. Language systems do not harbor or support anomalies because such irregularities do not facilitate sharing of ideas. This is true of dialects as well, since they are simply special forms of language; dialects do not retain features that obscure or confuse a meaningful exchange of ideas.

From the ethnocentric point of view a statement such as, "Momma, she be at the store," may seem incorrect. Against some forms or standards of English it is ungrammatical. But viewed within the context of a subcultural dialect, the dialect of the Black American, it is correct; it is grammatical and it communicates. It communicates more to the speaker of the dialect than is apparent to the unknowing observer. "Momma, she" is effective communication if reduction of uncertainty is the goal. The subject of the sentence is clearly identified twice. Is that necessary? Perhaps. But "standard" English has similar redundancies not characteristic of Black English. (For example, in Black dialect, "three girls," would be said *"three girl."* Why not? *Three* has already indicated the plural condition; the plural marker, *s,* on *girls* is redundant. Black English would economize. So-called standard English economizes in other usages. Who is to say which is right?) "Momma, she be at the store," indicates that Momma is where she usually is. "Momma, she at the store," would indicate that this is an unusual occurrence. Standard English has no parallel use of the verb *is*.

Without exploring any specific dialect further, the point is that no dialect is superior to any other. Differences in dialect exist. Each dialect is complete and functional. Children may actually need to be skilled in using more than one dialect *eventually*. But when children first arrive at school, their dialects represent their cultures, their homes, their self-worths. To reject the child's language is to reject him. To insist that he converse in another dialect is to rob him of his ability to communicate. The six or so years he has spent learning the intonation, syntax, and semantics of his dialect are stripped from him. The language tools needed to talk or read are denied to him.

An example of a common occurrence will help illustrate this point. The child who speaks a divergent dialect will quite naturally translate the symbols on the printed page into his own language. The Black child may read the sentence: "Tom and Mary are out playing" as "Tom and Mary, dey out playing." The teacher who regards Black dialect as inferior language will probably indicate dissatisfaction and regard the reading as inaccurate. Yet the child has drawn on the language that has enabled him to communicate successfully with others for a number of years. Confused, he may then pronounce each word in the teacher's dialect, but will do so haltingly and probably without complete understanding. The child's own language competence is denied, and he is forced to approach reading as a highly abstract decoding task which has no relationship to his own experiences or concepts.

Start with the Child's Language

By accepting the child's dialect the teacher begins with the tools the child needs to acquire more effective communication skills. One goal may be to make the child a skilled user of a more prestigious form of English—a status-conscious culture may leave no other choice. But even that goal is not achieved by insisting that the child speak "proper" English in his discussion of a story or when reading aloud. The standard spelling in his reader will be no handicap if the child is reading for meaning. He will translate the visual symbols into his dialect as his personal language and experience are triggered. And the argument that he will be reinforced for using "poor" language fails to recognize that his language is functional and adequate to his needs.

Often the mislabeled "nonverbal" child is one who has learned that if he cannot speak "correctly" it is best to keep his mouth shut. The teacher may have rejected his dialect as improper. His resulting silence and nonparticipation in school can easily be misunderstood as ignorance or even uncooperativeness. And so the vicious cycle continues as the language-different child fulfills the teacher's prophecy and fails in reading and other language-related activities. How much better it would be if the child felt confidence in his ability to express ideas in his dialect. Armed with the confidence gained from numerous successful attempts at sharing his thoughts, the child can learn to read using his language as a tool for retrieving meaning from the printed page.

Teachers Must Encourage Language Development

It is beyond the scope of this book to present a thorough and complete classroom program for language development. Other sources have addressed this task (Smith, Goodman, and Meredith, 1970). In the context of the present discussion it seems important to recognize that reading instruction cannot occur in the absence of, or separate from, a conscious language program. To do otherwise ignores the significant relationship between language and reading presented in this chapter.

One important aspect of a language program is the continued stimulation of natural language growth. Clearly the school-aged child has mastered the rudiments of his language inductively, but still has much to learn in order to use his language abilities maximally. The school can nurture the more effective use of language in part by creating opportunities for experiences, facilitating interaction with others, stimulating and broadening personal interests, and generally supporting the child in his experiments with language. In other words, many situations which encourage the use of language can be created.

Here are several examples illustrating the kind of opportunities that are appropriate. Children can be encouraged to participate in a regular sharing session. Important personal news, hobbies, topics of local interest, current events, interesting books, class projects, and other similar matters can be discussed. No specific content is organized for study in sharing sessions, nor are any specific aspects of language growth pursued. Children are simply given the opportunity to interact orally with their peers in a free flowing exchange of ideas. Personal philosophy should dictate whether a sharing session includes the presentation of new possessions via the "show and tell." This is not a necessary feature of a sharing period which primarily focuses on stimulating language.

Children can gain in general language growth from excursions. A class walk to a nearby park to search for signs of spring or a field trip to a distant museum provide stimulation and the need to communicate. Inviting a parent or member of the community into the classroom to talk about a hobby, vocation, or personal experience broadens children's horizons and generates language

Sharing stimulates language

(Holt, Rinehart and Winston photo by Russell Dian)

FIGURE 3.4   A field trip widens the horizon for each child and makes a topic for conversation both in and out of school.

opportunities. These and other activities immerse the children in language. From such experiences, continued expansion and refinement of language occurs.

The school has a responsibility for *influencing* language growth to some degree. Whereas many open-ended activities are helpful in continuing the child's inductive language learning, other structured or controlled situations should be created to focus attention on specific, predetermined aspects of language development. Even here evidence suggests that didactic lecturing or drilling on language skills will be largely ineffective. The child needs to generalize for himself from specific exercises and activities which the teacher has planned and structured in keeping with some overall curricular design. Specific examples are needed to help make the point.

One goal might be to sensitize children to the importance of words that describe or qualify. An activity that involves children in expanding basic sentences might be introduced. The teacher can put a statement on the chalkboard; for example: "A tree fell." The children are then invited to discuss how the sentence could be made more descriptive. Questions such as, "What kind of tree fell? What did it look like? Where did it fall?" can be asked to elicit specific details. An expansion like the following could occur.

A tree fell.
A maple tree fell.
An old maple tree fell.
A tall, old maple tree fell.
A tall, old maple tree fell across the road.

Followup activities could be developed to involve children in adding descriptive words to a newspaper article or to one of their own creative-writing efforts. A contest could be held with several small groups trying to add the most descriptive words to a kernel sentence.

Another specific instructional goal might be to interpret figurative language correctly. Expressions such as "lost his head," "mended his ways," "take your time," "stick your neck out," and "none of your lip" can be discussed and explained. Children can record the use of such expressions in daily conversation, on television or radio, and in newspapers over a period of time. A dictionary of figures of speech could be developed by the class.

Communication Skills Must Be Integrated

Just as there is danger of divorcing reading instruction from language, there is equal danger of divorcing language instruction from speaking and writing. All of these communication skills are interdependent. None should be pursued in isolation from the others. It is important to keep classroom language activities closely linked to children's experiences and interests. Language flourishes around experiences, which in turn create and broaden interests. More will be said about the interdependency of all these variables as they relate to reading in Chapters 4 and 5, "Reading Comprehension."

As subsequent chapters deal with various aspects of reading there may be a tendency to think of it as a separate, self-contained curricular area. Nothing could be further from the truth. Reading, once again, is a language-based process.

SUMMARY

This chapter argues that reading is a language-based process. Language is learned inductively by the child as he receives feedback concerning his attempts at communication. Efforts to teach reading should build on the language competence the child brings to school.

Reading involves more than adding up the words in a sentence or page to arrive at meaning. Understanding is important to word identification and helps the reader predict the author's message. Meaning must be emphasized from the outset of reading instruction.

Language differences can interfere with learning to read. The bilingual child must learn to speak English before trying to read it. The child who speaks a divergent dialect must be permitted to translate the printed page into his natural language.

Reading must always be viewed in its proper perspective, as one aspect of communication. Efforts to teach reading should be integrated with instruction in the areas of listening, speaking, and writing.

Terms for Self Study

syntax	deep structure
semantics	bilingual
surface structure	dialect

Discussion Questions

1. How would language that is unnatural and stilted make the child's task of reading a book written in this way more difficult?
2. Ms. Petrie teaches seven-year-olds. She makes a special effort to find books on topics that are of personal interest to her students. What is the basis for her concern? Why is it well founded?

4

Reading Comprehension: Experiential and Language Factors

Have you ever watched a preschooler "read" a book? In an often funny bit of mimicry, two- and three-year-olds sometimes page through a book making up their own stories. At times they use pictures for clues; at other times their "stories" bear no resemblance to the one in the book. The book may even be held upside down! But unlike the preschooler, who can make up meaning for himself, the eight- or nine-year old is expected to get the message from the printed page. How does the teacher help make that happen? This is perhaps the biggest and certainly the most important challenge in the teaching of reading— building reading comprehension.

These questions are addressed here:

Why do some children have difficulty understanding what they read?

What are the major factors affecting comprehension?

How can the teacher help children overcome limited background experiences?

How can the teacher identify the causes of comprehension problems?

The improvement of reading instruction is an important undertaking that has captured the attention of people all over the world. The pursuit of better strategies and techniques for teaching reading has taken different people in a variety of directions. It is probably an understatement to suggest that disagreement may be found on many aspects of learning to read. Despite disagreements on particulars, however, there is widespread recognition of the primacy of comprehension. Even advocates of intensive decoding approaches to reading explain that once a word is pronounced, it will be understood (comprehended) by the reader.

Despite the importance of comprehension, relatively little is known about how it takes place or why some children comprehend well and others don't. It is not lack of attention that causes this state of ignorance about comprehension, for many researchers and theoreticians have addressed themselves to the question. Rather it is the abstract nature of comprehension that makes it elusive. Any mental operation that cannot be observed or measured directly is slippery. Certainly the results of comprehension, the *product*,[1] can be observed and analyzed; but the *process,* the hidden mental operation, cannot.

The consequences of this uncertainty about the process of comprehension are real and far-reaching. Without a clear and accurate model of the process, classroom instructional activities tend to focus on the products of comprehension. Attention is given, for example, to answering questions about a story on a test or in a discussion. Some time *should* be spent with the products of comprehension, since they often involve the application of ideas gained from reading. But attention to only the products of comprehension fails to deal directly with the process itself. The child who has difficulty finding the main idea of a selection, for example, is often given extra practice in discovering main ideas. The hope apparently is that by concentrating on the product, we can somehow positively affect the process. A better approach would deal directly with the process.

What is needed is a better understanding of the reading process and how comprehension occurs in that process, so that classroom instruction can focus on the appropriate factors. Many experts are working on that aspect. While the search continues, we must make some attempt at conceptualizing how comprehension occurs using the evidence available. A model of the reading process was presented in Chapter 2. Review the model again at this time, paying particular attention to how comprehension fits into the total reading act.

The authors believe that a conceptualization of comprehension helps the teacher deal with the process by identifying key components and describing how those components interact. By focusing instructional activities on the key components, the teacher is able to improve comprehension by attention to its basic elements. In this way attention is given to the process as well as the

---

[1] A product of comprehension would be the result of understanding. Some results might be observable (such as a written answer to a question); other results might not be (such as a change in opinion).

product of reading comprehension. With some conceptualization of the basic components of comprehension, the teacher is also much better able to locate the source of any difficulty in comprehension. Rather than attacking an amorphous mass called comprehension, the teacher can deal with recognizable components.

Factors Affecting Comprehension

Figure 4.1 presents the authors' idea of the major factors that enable a person to comprehend the printed page. It is a simplification of a highly complex process, and consequently contains some generalizations. Nonetheless, it depicts a map of comprehension and should be helpful in organizing the information presented in this chapter. It has implications for instructional activities, as well as for the assessment of student needs.

Five factors are identified as the primary determinants of reading comprehension in the figure: background experience, language abilities, thinking abilities, affection (interests, motivation, attitudes, beliefs, feelings), and reading purposes. The reader draws on these resources in order to understand what he reads. To illustrate how these factors interact, consider the following situation. Malcolm has been given this story to read.

Soap Box Derby

Charlie had waited for this day all his life. As he pushed his soap box racer to the starting line memories came flooding back. He had spent days and weeks and months drawing sketches and building models of this red beauty.

When he was only five years old he had watched his oldest brother win the derby. Two years later his cousin won the race. The next year it was his sister who crossed the finish line first.

"Now it's my turn to carry on the Hansen tradition," Charlie thought.

In the last two weeks he had won races in his home town and state. Now Charlie would have a chance to win the national soap box derby.

At last his racer reached the starting line and Charlie pushed it into place. He put on his helmet and adjusted his goggles. The announcer began to tell the large crowd the names of the drivers and their home towns. Charlie climbed into his car and crouched forward.

"Watch the man with the flag," Charlie reminded himself.

They were off! The racer to Charlie's left dropped back slowly, but on his right a green car stayed even with him. This was going to be close. As they coasted down the hill the cars picked up speed. Suddenly Charlie's red racer began to weave. He swayed left and then right. The steering wheel wiggled in his hands.

"Oh, no! This is no time for problems," Charlie whispered.

The green car pulled ahead, and beat Charlie to the finish line.

Putting on the brakes Charlie slowed to a stop. The boy in the green racer smiled

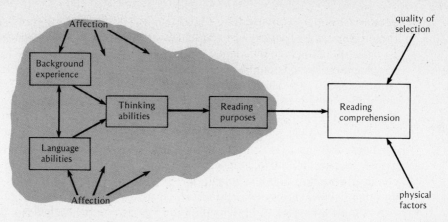

FIGURE 4.1   A reading comprehension model

The major factors affecting comprehension interact to bring about comprehension.

and waved. Tears of disappointment filled Charlie's eyes. A man came forward and helped the winning driver from his car into a wheelchair.

Disappointed as he was, Charlie was glad the green car had won.

Malcolm will understand this story only if certain conditions are met.[2] First, if Malcolm has never seen a race he will find the story hard to follow. If he has never heard of a soap box racer the story will be impossible for him to understand. If Malcolm has never felt compassion for someone less fortunate than himself he will certainly not understand the ending of the story. Malcolm must have experiences in his background that enable him to bring personal meaning to the events and feelings of the story. His understanding will be greater the more his own experiences are like Charlie's. Clearly, not all children can comprehend this or any other story in exactly the same way, because each has different background experiences on which to draw.

A second dimension of understanding this story is related closely to the first. The story involves language that must be meaningful to Malcolm. The most obvious language requirement is one of semantics, or word meaning. Malcolm must know what a *soap box racer* is. He must have the appropriate meaning for words such as *place, even, picked up,* and *race,* as they are used in the context of this story. Expressions such as *crossed the finish line first* and *they were off* must be understood. Understanding of semantics comes from experience with words in various, personally meaningful settings. If Malcolm has built his own racer or discussed racing with other children he has probably

[2]We will assume Malcolm can identify the words. Other chapters of this text discuss that matter in detail.

acquired the depth of semantic understanding he needs to give meaning to these terms. If such personal experiences are lacking, comprehension suffers because of a language deficiency.

Another language ability that Malcolm needs in order to comprehend the story is a grasp of syntax. The order of words has much to do with the message the author intends to share. Malcolm must be able to retrieve the flow of ideas as they are communicated by words working together in a sentence. For example, "Two years later his cousin won the race" involves any number of elements that must be correctly related to each other for accurate interpretation. Malcolm's ability to understand the story depends on his ability to recover the deep structure of the language. This requires that Malcolm have a mastery of syntax, which links deep and surface structure.

A third aspect of comprehending the story concerns Malcolm's ability to think. Depending on his intellectual development, and the opportunity he has had to engage in various types of reasoning, Malcolm will be able to deal with the events and concepts in the story to a greater or lesser degree. For example, if Malcolm has not yet developed the ability to keep a series of events in correct sequence, important aspects of the story may be missed. Charlie's reminiscing on the way to the starting line may confuse Malcolm and interfere with his understanding. Malcolm will be unable to make inferences or engage in critical thinking about the story unless opportunities have been created for him to develop such thought processes in the past. He will also understand the ending of the story better if his own sense of justice, his moral development has progressed to an advanced stage. A self-centered child would be inclined to reject Charlie's defeat on a selfish basis. A more advanced child, who has developed altruistic traits, could relate to the story ending with more understanding.

Another factor that could cause comprehension problems for Malcolm is related to his ability to understand his own emotions. Perhaps the most easily recognized affective factor is Malcolm's personal interests. Common sense suggests that Malcolm will attend better to a story about a topic he finds personally interesting, and in the process will comprehend it better. The cause of greater understanding may also lie in the reader's attitudes and beliefs. Interest, attitudes, and beliefs are usually closely linked. A reader understands material better when it matches his own attitude on a topic. Malcolm will comprehend the soap box derby story more fully if he is interested in the topic and positively inclined toward such competition.

Malcolm could also have problems understanding the story if he reads it with no particular purpose in mind. Or understanding can be a problem if the story is read for one purpose and then analyzed or discussed relative to some other purpose. To illustrate, Malcolm might read the story because it is assigned by his teacher. With no specific purpose in mind to focus his attention, Malcolm will probably wander aimlessly through the story passively processing words. Unless he establishes his own purpose before reading, or commits the entire story to memory, he will recall little if any of what he has read. Most people have the general purpose of following and enjoying the storyline even if no other purpose is established. Yet, in the absence of specific directions that have been consciously established by either Malcolm or his teacher in this situation, subtleties may be missed. The feelings of the handicapped boy driving the green car could easily be overlooked, for example. This would clearly be truer when the selection is longer and more complex than in this story.

This overview contains an attempt to identify the key factors that affect comprehension. Subsequent sections of this and the next chapter deal with each of these factors in more detail. Chapter 4 deals with experience and language factors. Chapter 5 deals with intellectual and emotional factors. Included will be descriptions of ways to assess and develop children's performance in these basic areas. It should be pointed out that there is great interdependence among the factors singled out for discussion here. Because each factor is individually presented, does not mean that they are in fact separate. Indeed, it is impossible to discuss language without discussing background experience, for example. Purposes for reading are closely linked to thinking skills. Thinking and feeling are obviously related, and both grow from personal experiences, and so on. With the caution that the factors affecting comprehension are interdependent, each is now considered.

Background Experiences Build Concepts

In simplest terms, experiences supply the child with the raw material he must organize and manipulate as he goes through life. From infancy onward the child is constantly bombarded with stimuli from the environment. He learns to cope with those stimuli by classifying and cataloging them for future reference. Through a process of noting similarities and differences he develops concepts and an understanding of relationships between and among concepts. As this organization of environment develops, so does the child's understanding of the world and his place in it.

As he reads, the child decodes symbols on the printed page that trigger understandings he has developed about life. Those understandings are the result of first-hand and vicarious experiences. When the printed message relates to experiences he has not had, the child fails to comprehend. He may even be able to pronounce every word on the page, but if the experiences that give personal meaning to the topic or idea are lacking, the child cannot bring understanding he does not have to the reading.

Suppose a group is about to read a story about the circus. Let's say two children in the group have vastly different backgrounds. Tony is the son of a farmer. His home is far out in the country. All members of his family help with the chores, and so there has never been time to see the circus. Sarah has a relative who works for the circus. Whenever the circus is in town she sees every performance. She has also met the clowns, and even eaten with them in their tent. Who will have the best chance of understanding the story? Even if

(Photo by de Villeneuve)

FIGURE 4.2   Adult reading to a child

The data absorbed by the child is classified and organized so that concepts are developed and relationships begin to be understood. Being read to is one experience every child should have.

Tony is the better decoder, Sarah has an enormous headstart. Certainly Tony may follow the series of events in the story and be able to answer basic questions. But obviously his understanding is limited by inadequate experience with circuses.

This does not suggest that one cannot learn by reading. Everything he reads about need not be experienced in order to understand it. But there must be a reservoir of relevant concepts to draw on, or a reader cannot interpret the printed page adequately. If the closest point of reference is a rough ride in an airplane or an automobile ride on a bumpy road, when one reads someone's description of a roller coaster ride, an approximation of the author's meaning can be gotten. But, clearly, the best experience for understanding the description is an actual roller coaster ride.

The really significant point is that children often have rather limited backgrounds on which to draw. Some children have seen and done far more than others, and differences will exist from topic to topic. But if understanding of any given story is to be maximized, the teacher will help children recall whatever experiences they may have had that will help them relate to the events or ideas in a reading selection. Where possible, experiences that build understanding should be provided, ideally at first-hand, but at least vicariously prior to the reading. The discussion of building background will be continued later.

Although a more complete consideration of the matter will be presented in Chapter 5, it is appropriate to point out that a person's experiences have a great deal to do with their interests, attitudes, beliefs, and feelings about a topic. Having tried snow skiing, for example, one is more interested in reading about snowplow turns and stem christies. Later these affective factors will be explored as they relate to comprehension.

Assessing Background Experiences

In order to maximize the chances that a child will understand what he reads, it must be determined what relevant background experiences he has or will need to have before reading a selection. As was stated earlier, no amount of effort will make all children alike insofar as readiness to comprehend a story is concerned. Nevertheless, it is necessary to know how much preparation is needed for a basic level of understanding and which children require such preparation.

The classroom teacher can employ informal assessment techniques to identify specific background limitations. Standardized tests and other formal instruments only generally indicate that a youngster has difficulty with comprehension. To determine whether limited background is the factor particularly responsible for comprehension difficulties, the teacher has several means at his disposal.

Questionnaires Can Provide Information on Background Experience

One of the primary advantages of teacher-constructed questionnaires is that special concerns can easily be incorporated in their design. The teacher can write certain questionnaire items to obtain information relevant to a special topic or theme. For example, suppose a group of second-grade children is about to begin a unit on pets in their developmental reading program. Recognizing that understanding is greatly dependent on familiarity with concepts, the teacher could construct a questionnaire like the one on page 54 to assess his students' backgrounds.

Questionnaires can be developed so that even younger children, who cannot write, can provide the information a teacher needs. In this case a first-grade teacher might read the questions to his students and ask them to draw or find a picture in a magazine for their answers. A questionnaire can also be used individually with a child in a conference, with the teacher jotting down the child's responses.

Questionnaires can be designed to gather general information on a child's travel experiences, hobbies, interests, play activities, or other topics relevant to classroom activities.

Interest Questionnaire

Name _____

1. Do you have a pet? _____
*2. What kind of pet do you have? (Or what kind of pet would you like to have?) _____
3. What other pets have you had before?   _____
4. Where does your pet sleep? _____
5. How do you care for your pet? _____
6. Does your pet get a bath?_____ How do you give the pet a bath?_____
7. What does your pet like to eat? _____

*Note: Children who indicate in Item 1 that they do not have a pet can answer subsequent questions for a former pet or the pet they would like to have. Their answers still provide the teacher with a knowledge of the child's background and understanding.

Observations Reveal Valuable Information on Background Experiences

Classroom discussions and informal conversations before, during, and after school provide the teacher with an excellent opportunity to note a youngster's background and understanding. Contributions and comments that show misunderstanding or general ignorance about a topic should alert the teacher to the possibility of poor background in that area. For example, a first-grade child who does not know the difference between a helicopter and a jet airplane may never have been to an airport or seen a helicopter hovering overhead. This lack of understanding could be troublesome if the child were going to read *Helicopters and Gingerbread* from the Ginn 360 Series.

At the same time a child's unwillingness to contribute to a group discussion might *not* indicate a lack of background. Shyness or boredom can also explain silence, so additional evidence must be obtained in this case.

In time the teacher will learn which students require further background experiences on most school-related activities. It would be dangerous to categorically label a child limited in terms of background; constant assessment is necessary. Nevertheless teacher's observations can be guided to a degree by past experiences with the class.

Conferences Help the Teacher Assess Background Experiences

One of the best means for assessing background experience is through a personal conference with a child. Whether a pupil-teacher conference is structured by the completion of a questionnaire or is simply an informal chat, the alert teacher can gather valuable information about a child's experiences by this means. A technique recommended by Strang (1969), introspection by the child, can be employed in a conference. Strang suggests that the child be invited to describe his thinking process while reading a selection. The teacher may ask the child how he managed to know the meaning of a word or arrive at the meaning of a sentence or paragraph. The child may be asked to explain a specific difficulty as he sees it. Given the opportunity, even young children may be able to explain where their comprehension begins to falter. Breakdowns in understanding due to lack of background can also be revealed with this approach.

Building Background Experiences

The reason for assessing background is to provide experiences the child lacks. This might occur on two levels: The teacher can plan and create numerous opportunities for enriching the child's background generally; or the teacher can often build background for understanding a specific reading selection. Suggestions for dealing with both situations are given below.

Helping Children with Limited Backgrounds

We must be especially careful when talking about children with limited backgrounds. Nearly every child comes to school with a wealth of experiences. However, poverty and lack of mobility often limit some children to a certain type of experience. They may not have had such experiences as visiting Disneyland, the Smithsonian Institute, or Yellowstone National Park. A strong cultural bias can creep into a teacher's thinking if the experiences a child might have had in the inner city or in the hollow of some mountain are disregarded in favor of a typical middle-class experience. Schools and teachers might well respond with more sensitivity to the experiences every child has by building on what he brings to school. The language experience approach (discussed later in this book) attempts to do just that. New curricular materials do a better job of reflecting a variety of backgrounds, so that every child need not fit into a white, middle-class mold.

Limited background, as defined here, does not refer to children from poverty areas alone. For example, children from the inner city or the suburbs may have no conceptualization of events and things on a farm. Their experiences frequently have not exposed them to a tractor, a hayloft, a litter of pigs, or an apple orchard. The word *tractor* may cause some children from suburbia to think of the seven horsepower miniature used to mow the lawn and plow snow. When Farmer Jones uses his tractor to pull a truck from a ditch, their experience may not square with the description.

A person's understanding of a topic can seldom be called complete. Adults as well as children learn daily and broaden already rich concepts. One's concept of a word like *river* is constantly growing as new experiences provide new information. Understanding the role of waterways in the development and settlement of the United States is a complexity not easily grasped. A concept of space is another, more dynamic example of an ever-growing field of study. Except for very simple writing, it is safe to say that understanding of a selection is seldom completed. As the appropriate concepts deepen and expand, greater comprehension of a selection previously read is increased. The point is that no matter how many advantages the child has had, he can expand his concepts to increase understanding of what he reads.

With this broad definition of background it is clear that nearly anything the teacher does to involve children in a world of ideas is helpful as a way of stretching their experiences. This, in turn, contributes to reading comprehension by building concepts needed for ready reference during reading. Obviously some activities are more fruitful than others. Concrete, first-hand experiences nearly always have a more lasting impact than vicarious experiences. Active experiences that involve children are preferable to ones in which they are passive observers. Experiences that relate to personal interests or have relevance to children's lives are especially meaningful.

It is important to remember that differences in cognitive development may permit some children to get more out of a common experience than another, less mature child will.

A specific example might help illustrate the application of these principles. Suppose Judy Crawford, a primary-grade teacher, decides her students need a better understanding of pollution. This decision might be the result of her general observations of the children's lack of understanding, a consequence of some classroom incident, or related to an upcoming unit of study. Ms. Crawford might plan a series of active, first-hand experiences that focus on how pollution affects children's daily lives. This could include a walking excursion to a nearby shopping center to observe littering, a field trip by bus to a water filtration plant, a clean-up hike around the neighborhood, a visit to the classroom by an environmentalist, and individual exploration by children to identify sources of pollution in the community. Discussions can be held, letters written for information and to protest pollution sources, interviews conducted, and so forth. Displays might be arranged, and objects handled by the children. All these activities can be done in such a way as to broaden children's backgrounds and introduce or enrich concepts.

While this example is long term and fairly involved, simple one-time experiences can be valuable. A lesson can be planned, for example, to sensitize children to various textures. Common objects in the classroom environment are touched and compared. Items can be classified into groups and labels found to describe their textures.

These first-hand experiences certainly do not rule out the possibility of vicarious experiences, such as watching a film or listening to a record. These and other, similar activities are more abstract and consequently are not as easy for children to relate to. Nevertheless, concepts and the language related to those concepts can be explored via audiovisual means as ways of building general background.

Building Background for a Specific Reading Selection

In a reading program where the teacher frequently assigns the same selection to a group of children it is feasible to spend some time building background for a single story. If children are selecting their own stories and reading them independently, it is nearly impossible to build backgrounds for every child and every story. In that case the child's interest in the topic has probably guided his choice of the story or book, and so he often has some background experiences that account for his interest and facilitates comprehension. If understanding falters, the teacher should be alert to the need for background experience and supply it if at all possible. The language experience approach automatically builds on the child's background, since in such cases the child usually writes his own stories.

When a group is about to read a story the teacher is obliged to determine what background experiences are basic to understanding the story and supply those experiences wherever possible. Here is an example.

Suppose a group in a second-grade class is about to read "The Airport," a story about two boys who take their first plane ride.

Well in advance of the day the group will read the story, the teacher should begin to assess background experience and gather resources for overcoming limited backgrounds among the children. The teacher can prepare a question-

(Photo by de Villeneuve)

FIGURE 4.3   Sharing a hobby

Besides field trips, experiences with real airplanes, and reading about airports, one other way that a story about "The Airport" can be an enriching experience is an explanation of his hobby by a model airplane fan.

naire that explores each child's familiarity with airports and airplanes. He may have noticed youngsters with a special interest in airplanes, whom he can ask to share a book or models they may have built. If the school district has an instructional materials center that stores or obtains films and other teaching aids on various topics, the teacher can request materials on airports and airplanes. In some instances it might even be profitable to arrange for a trip to an airport as a means of building necessary background. The extent of the teacher's efforts in gathering materials and arranging background experiences depends on the readiness of the youngsters to proceed to read the story without this special preparation. It also depends on the amount of time the teacher can devote to such activities. A balance must be struck between giving adequate time to building background and making an unjustified production out of such activities.

On the day the reading group is ready to begin "The Airport" the teacher can introduce the topic and make use of the resources he has gathered. The teacher can initiate a discussion by asking questions and relating experiences of his own. For example:

> Boys and girls, today we are going to read about Ben and Matt's trip back to their home. How do you suppose they will travel? (Children offer ideas.)
> You will see that they are flying by jet airplane. Have any of you ridden in a jet? Tell us about it. (Sharing takes place.) What was the airport like? What interesting or unusual things did you see there? (Comments by children.) What happens to your luggage at the airport? (Suggestions are given: the teacher tells about losing his luggage on a recent trip.)

The discussion should be guided by the teacher to cover topics that are important in the story (handling of luggage in this case). During this period the teacher can introduce some vocabulary items orally and sometimes on the chalkboard, as well, to be sure they have meaning for the children when they see them in the story. (All "new" vocabulary probably should not be introduced, since children need opportunities to employ their word identification skills.) A model airplane might be shown, and a child asked to tell about her hobby of flying models with her father.

These activities are designed to create interest in reading the story, as well as to build vocabulary and related concepts. The goal is not to guarantee that every child knows the same amount about airplanes but rather to provide sufficient information for every child to predict meaning and understand the story. Because of past experience a pilot's son will find much more personal meaning in the story than another child, George, whose experience with airplanes is negligible. Nonetheless, George will be better prepared to comprehend the story, having heard and seen the planned activities before reading. Keep in mind that on another topic (for example, fishing) George may be the expert and the pilot's son the inexperienced one. The alert teacher will capitalize on student's strengths and try to use stories that are related to their personal experiences.

Comprehension Is Dependent upon Language Abilities

To state the obvious, one must have a basic knowledge of the English language in order to read it. *Semantics* and *syntax* are important to the delivery of meaning. As a reminder, the semantics of a language refers to the meanings of words; syntax refers to the way words word together. Semantics and syntax as they relate to reading comprehension, and suggestions for assessing student language abilities and overcoming deficiencies are given in the next section.

Semantic Meanings Grow from Personal Experience

Teachers and publishers have for decades recognized the importance of semantics in reading instruction. Typically, their concern has been identified as one of controlling vocabulary. When the printed page presents too many "new words" the vocabulary load overburdens the reader and comprehension falters. Try reading this paragraph that contains a high percentage of "hard" words:

> A neoteric car can egress anyplace. This exiguous car has six wheels. It egresses on promontory and in the paludal. Fishermen desiderate this neoteric car. They can egress into the paludal with it. Farmers desiderate this neoteric car, too. They can egress into barnyards and variform lieus without roads.

Put more simply:

> A new minicar can go anywhere. This little car has six wheels. It goes on land and in the water. Fishermen like this new car. They can go right into the water with it. Farmers like this new car, too. They can go into barnyards and other places without roads.

Obviously, vocabulary can interfere with comprehension.

The burden of vocabulary is a relative matter. What is hard for you may not be hard for someone else. A second dimension of this matter has been mentioned previously, for each person is an "expert" on a different topic. You are undoubtedly more knowledgable than your friends in a number of areas and consequently have in your vocabulary many terms they may not know (for example, ballet terms, fencing terms, sewing terms, physics terms, and so on).

The explanation for vocabulary differences is relatively simple. People normally have the vocabulary that accompanies their experiences. Younger children have fewer experiences than older people; consequently their vocabularies are smaller on the whole. The best way to increase vocabulary is to engage in stimulating experiences that are accompanied by language. Thus, each of the activities suggested earlier for building background will also build vocabulary, provided they include discussion, question-asking and answering, and general conversation with people who know the language related to a topic (for example, a teacher, a guide, a visiting expert).

Programs that attempt to build vocabulary by teaching the meanings of selected words are not well founded. Dictionary meanings are not learned by memorizing; they grow from using a word in a context which is important to meaning. Having students look up "new" words in a dictionary before reading a story is typically not productive. Those terms should be embedded in an interesting discussion or activity about the topics treated in the story. In other words, vocabulary must be met in context.

Context is important to word meaning in several ways. First, the clues of surrounding context help readers make specific applications of the intended meaning. To illustrate, if you are told a *gasket* is "a piece of rubber, cork or other material placed around a joint to make it leakproof," you have an abstract description of the item. If you meet the term in this context: "The *gasket* on this dripping faucet needs to be replaced," its meaning becomes much more vivid through application. Second, since most terms have a variety of meanings, context is needed to know which particular meaning applies. For example, the word *rule* can mean (1.) something that usually happens (for example, We eat around 8:00 A.M. as a rule.); (2.) a regulation (for example, one rule we have is no running.); (3.) a measuring device (for example, I'll get a rule and measure it.); (4.) the reign of a government (for example, It was during the *rule* of Queen Victoria.). The intended meaning is clear only in context.

Syntactic Clues to Meaning

When children first learn to read it is the semantics of their language that typically gets the greatest attention. The fact that word meaning varies and in turn affects the meaning of a sentence or paragraph is so obvious it cannot be overlooked.

Just as obvious, but not so readily understood, is the importance of syntax, which refers to the "rules" or sentence structure people use unconsciously when they speak a language. Consider the following sentence: "The jurd sumped dooly to the rem." Most of the words in this example do not have lexical or dictionary meaning. They do have structural meaning, however; that is, they contribute to meaning by their places and function in the sentence. Persons who are familiar with English can readily determine that the subject of the sentence is *jurd*. Furthermore, the structure of the sentence enables us to tell what the jurd did, how it was done, and where it was done.

Meaning is signaled through the structure of English in three ways:

1. by patterns of word order
2. by inflectional endings
3. by function words that have little or no meaning of their own (Goodman, 1963).

The words in the nonsense sentence example follow a common pattern for American English. Even without semantic clues, any speaker of English can specify that this alteration of the previous sentence is not grammatic: "Jurd dooly sumped rem the to the." Word order is one important carrier of meaning.

In this example the inflectional ending *ed* on *sumped* tells us that:

1. *sump* describes an action.
2. whatever action occurred took place in the past.

In the same way *dooly* is evidently an adverb telling how the *jurd sumped.* We also know that only one *jurd* was involved in the action; the inflectional ending *s* would be used to indicate more than one *jurd.* Meaning is also carried by variations in word endings.

Finally, *the* serves as a *function word* in the nonsense sentence, marking *jurd* and *rem* as nouns. Examples of other function words are *very, not, there, when, yes, no,* and *well.*

One does not add word meanings together in a left to right sequence and arrive at meaning when the end of a sentence is reached. If that were so, computers could be "taught" to read. Meaning is delivered by the interaction of words. It is the meaning delivered by words working together that must be retrieved so that the reader understands. This is accomplished according to generative-transformational grammar theory by means of a series of transformations.

Transformations are essentially rearrangements of phrases in a sentence that make its underlying meaning more explicit. Transformations are conducted according to the rules of syntax. These are the rules that every speaker of English has learned inductively despite the fact that all the rules cannot be specified. Some linguists believe that humans are born with a predisposition toward acquiring these rules. Meaning is gained from reading by recovering the deep structure of language using the rules of syntax. Authorities have not yet agreed on the exact nature of *deep structure,* but it is thought to be a basic grammatic form that serves as a point of reference for understanding.

In effect, a sentence is read at the surface level (the printed page). The reader understands the ideas communicated by the author by engaging in a series of transformations that take him to the deep structure. For example, all three of the sentences below have different surface structures, yet two have the same meaning. Therefore, those two sentences have the same deep structure. The third sentence has a different meaning, hence a different deep structure.

1. He drew a brown bear.
2. He drew a bear brown.
3. He drew a bear that was brown.

In order to gain meaning from the printed page the reader must be able to recover deep structure. In Chapter 3 we described the language acquisition process briefly. We pointed out that formal instruction in language typically does not occur, and yet children learn the rules of syntax. The question to be asked, then, is: Should reading instruction focus on syntax as a means of improving comprehension? Different authorities answer that question in different ways. Some writers, such as Hoskisson (1974, 1975), argue that children can learn to read much as they learn to talk—by being immersed in reading. Hoskisson's strategy, called *Assisted Reading,* is described as:

Assisted reading is the natural extension of what many parents already do—read to their children. Many children ask to know what the words are that they see on signs, in advertisements, and on television. Parents extend this curiosity or develop it by reading to their children and having the children repeat the words after them. Words, phrases, or sentences may be read by the parent and repeated by the child. Thus, the visual or graphic configurations are presented to the children in an informal but pleasant situation. The child can look for the significant differences that will eventually lead him to establish the graphic features he needs in order to become a fluent reader. He begins to learn to read by reading, much as he learned to talk by talking. (Hoskisson, 1975, 313)

While Hoskisson would not avoid discussions about word endings, for example, these would occur only as the child initiated them. The parent or teacher would not systematically teach certain inflections, specific sentence patterns, or the like in a formal manner.

Other authorities believe certain aspects of syntax should be taught consciously and systematically. For example, Deighton (1966) cites four separate ways that words can be related to each other:

1. Subject-predicate relation
2. Coordinate relation
3. Complement relation
4. Modifier relation

The complexities involved in sorting out a sentence so that words are correctly related to one another prompts Deighton to recommend that reading instruction include the study of how sentence structures deliver meaning. As a first step in this direction he suggests that it is helpful to note the direction of word flow in a sentence. The flow is not, as we might suppose, consistently from left to right—it is not always additive. While some sentences have a left to right flow of meaning—for example, "Tom hit the ball"—in a great many English sentences the flow is circular:—"Tom is the president." The verb in the second sentence, a form of *be,* is called a linking verb. The words following the verb refer to the word preceding the verb. Thus, the flow of thought is from left to right and back to the beginning, or circular. To comprehend the sentence the reader must hold meaning in abeyance.

Deighton states that all linking verbs—such as *look, remain, stay, sound,* and *get* and *keep*—in certain constructions deliver meaning by identification, characterization, or description. They attribute specific features to the subject of the sentence, and therefore transmit information in a circular pattern.

Children's reading comprehension can be improved, according to Deighton, by planning instructional activities that call attention to different sentence patterns. For example, children can be taught that the presence of a linking verb in a sentence signals the circular flow of meaning described earlier. The teacher can provide exercises in which linking verbs are circled. Later the object of the sentence can be underlined and an arrow drawn showing the flow of meaning. Such activities focus the children's attention on those aspects of syntax that are important to reading comprehension. Similar exercises can make young readers aware of other sentence patterns.

Lefevre (1972) also recommends that young readers be taught to search for sentence patterns as a way of improving reading comprehension. Using a programmed approach to instruction, Lefevre systematically leads the reader to identify the parts of a sentence and how they work together in delivering meaning. For example, at an early stage the reader is directed to focus on the N V N sentence pattern: noun part, verb part, completer. He is helped to focus on the correct arrangement of the parts as follows:

"Do these three words make a sensible sentence? / saw Robert I / Can you put the words in the right order?"

Over a period of time the reader analyzes and studies longer sentences which involve more complex patterns and relationships. Lefevre's position is that children need to be taught how to develop *sentence sense*. He states this can best be done by "systematic instruction in how to decode whole sentences so as to derive meaning from the relationships of the main sentence parts to the entire message" (Lefevre, 1972, 230).

Ives (1964) recommends that word form *(morphology)* be studied through careful attention to inflectional endings as a means to improving reading comprehension. He believes the importance of syntax can also be taught. To illustrate, the plural marker *s* on the word *dogs* presents the reader with an important clue to meaning; *ed* on the word *walked* likewise provides a clue to meaning. Ives believes the reader should be helped to focus on word clues that reveal quantity and tense in order to recover these often subtle clues to meaning. The word *run* carries different meanings in these two sentences:

1. The dogs *run* fast.
2. He scored a *run*.

Exercises that help the reader see how word meaning changes in various contexts would improve reading comprehension, according to Ives.

Many other teaching ideas and procedures are being developed by those interested in the application of linguistics to reading instruction to help children deal with syntactic clues to meaning. We expect continuing research in the area of linguistics to provide further direction for these efforts in the future.

Assessing Language Abilities

The classroom teacher has various formal and informal means at his disposal for assessing children's language abilities. Some formal tests, such as the *Illinois Test of Psycholinguistic Abilities,* are comprehensive and thorough, but hardly practical for the busy classroom teacher in view of the time and special training required to administer them. We will concentrate below on measures that are within easy reach of a teacher.

Measures of Semantic Abilities

It is quite common for the achievement batteries and reading survey tests used in schoolwide or districtwide testing programs to include a vocabulary subtest. The *Stanford Achievement Tests,* for example, gives the child a series of tasks in which a term is presented along with four alternatives. The child is asked to select the one alternative that is closest in meaning to the term given. The child demonstrates his knowledge of word meaning by matching synonyms. Other vocabulary tests sometimes call for the child to match words of opposite meaning, or antonyms. Typical vocabulary test items are:

Directions: Select the word below that has the same or nearly the same meaning.
illumination

1. lighting
2. furniture

3. discrimination
4. destination

Directions: Select the word below that has the opposite meaning.
obscure

1. thirsty
2. timely

3. ravenous
4. transparent

One serious limitation of the testing procedure just illustrated lies in the fact that words vary in meaning depending on their use in context. Consequently, even children who know the meaning of a word may have difficulty deciding which answer is most appropriate, since different synonyms may be appropriate in different contexts. In fact, the child who knows many meanings for the same word may be especially confused when alternative answers are close in meaning, as in this example:

---

machine

1. organization
2. automobile

3. panel
4. furnace

The most obvious answer is *automobile.* However, some children might realize that an organization, such as a political party, can be referred to as a machine, and some may be familiar with a furnace that could legitimately be thought of as a machine because of its stoker, steam valves, and other related apparatus.

You, as a teacher, will want to be cautious in interpreting the results of vocabulary tests that fail to embed vocabulary in appropriate contexts. You should also avoid making this kind of mistake in tests or exercises you develop for the class.

Vocabulary can be assessed through the use of pictures. In tests such as the *Peabody Picture Vocabulary Test* (PPVT) the child is asked to select a picture that best describes a word from among several alternatives. Such tests measure the child's experiential background and opportunity to learn, and consequently can contain substantial bias. Nevertheless, they do assess the child's familiarity with vocabulary he is likely to encounter in many reading programs. A teacher can counteract this cultural bias in commercially prepared tests or in the development of teacher-made vocabulary tests, by including pictures known to be appropriate for his students. Other pictures that are relevant to the materials the children will read in the instructional program can also be included.

The classroom teacher who needs information about the semantic abilities of his students will find any number of opportunities to observe children's performance on a daily basis. The child's use of words in attempting oral and written communication give a clear indication of his semantic ability. Misuse of words or the child's failure to understand a word's multiple meanings gives the teacher specific information useful in planning language development activities. Through observation the teacher can identify vocabulary that children understand in receiving information (that is, *receptive vocabulary*), but do not use in their own communication efforts (that is, *expressive vocabulary*).

Teacher-made tests can be developed to determine children's understanding of vocabulary from the basal reader; the content areas, such as science and social studies; classroom discussions; and other classroom activities. Tests can reveal the child's understanding of compound words, roots, word origins, prefix and suffix meanings, and multiple meanings. The importance of context should be reflected in tests you develop. Several examples are given on page 66 to illustrate how teacher-made vocabulary tests can be developed. The distinct advantage of such tests is that you can include whatever words are important for the instructional program in your classroom.

The cloze procedure described here on page 123 can be used to assess the child's semantic ability. A cloze passage can be prepared by deleting either every *nth* word or words of a certain type (for example, nouns, adjectives). The child's ability to supply the deleted words provides a direct and clear measure of his knowledge of words. Obviously the cloze procedure does not measure semantic ability alone, since the reader is heavily dependent on syntactic clues when supplying words that have been deleted. Despite this complication the teacher will be able to gain a picture of the size, as well as the maturity level, of a child's vocabulary.

Sample Teacher-made Vocabulary Test

COMPOUND WORDS

Combine words from List A and List B to form compound words that fit into the blanks below.

earth	body
pan	worm
some	where
every	cake

1. I put an _____ on my hook and dropped it into the lake.
2. Mary looked _____ for her lost book.
3. We can make a _____ for breakfast.
4. Did _____ borrow my pencil?

PREFIXES

Write the usual meaning of the prefixes underlined in the following sentences:

1. Dad had to *relight* the fire. *re* means _____.
2. A *multicolored* rainbow followed the storm. *multi* means _____.
3. Our new car is a subcompact. *sub* means _____.

ANTONYMS

Substitute a word for the underlined word that makes the meaning just opposite in the following sentences:

1. It will be *frigid* outside tomorrow.
2. We were *elated* at the way the football game ended.
3. This *enormous* box can be put near the door.

Measures of Syntactic Abilities

The cloze procedure provides valuable information regarding the child's understanding of syntax. His ability to supply deleted words gives an indication of his ability to see the relationship among words.

Asking the child to identify an incongruent sentence among three with different surface structures (when two have identical deep structures), as described earlier in this chapter, is also a useful measure of syntactic understanding. For example, which sentences below would the child identify as having the same meaning?

1. I like to eat fish.
2. Fish is something I like to eat.
3. Something I eat likes fish.

A variation of this approach requires the child to complete sentences that have words missing in such a way as to give them the same meaning:

1. _____ is something I like to _____.
2. I like to _____ _____.

Another way to measure syntactic ability is to present the child with a sentence in which the order of words has been scrambled. The child uses his knowledge of syntax to recreate a sentence with a meaningful message. For example, *"dog up the stairs. ran The"* is reordered as *"The dog ran up the stairs."*

Teachers can gain a sense of the child's knowledge of syntax by observing his use of language in oral and written communication. Children who consistently confuse word order may have a language deficiency that can interfere with reading comprehension. Children who have difficulty understanding oral communications may have similar problems.

Expanding and Refining Language Abilities

Efforts to expand and refine children's language abilities should acknowledge the fact that language is acquired initially without formal, carefully

(Holt, Rinehart and Winston photo by Russell Dian)

FIGURE 4.4 Group discussions

Group discussions about a story help involve children in better communication.

sequenced instruction. The child learns language inductively by being immersed in language. Classroom activities can promote language development most effectively by creating many and varied opportunities to use language. Activities that actually involve children and build on their personal interests usually result in greater enthusiasm and participation. The child who is motivated by an intrinsic desire to communicate will develop the necessary abilities to do so over a period of time. Naturally, the availability of skilled users of language to provide feedback to children about their efforts at using language is important. The teacher's role becomes one of creating a stimulating environment and assisting children as they experiment with and try out language.

Activities that Promote Language Use

Many teachers find dramatic play and role playing to be especially good ways of encouraging language production. Props are often helpful in creating the right conditions, but they aren't absolutely necessary. Two children can be asked to pretend that they are going fishing or on a hike. Their conversation can center around preparations for the coming event, collecting equipment, planning a schedule, and so forth. Younger children take to such play without self-consciousness; older children may need more help in getting started. This is where personal interests can be useful. A scene involving a topic several children enjoy automatically encourages involvement and participation. Two eleven-year-old boys might pretend to be scouts who are hoping to recruit a basketball player for their team, for example.

Puppets and a puppet theater help children overcome their stage fright and use language more freely. Since it is the puppet "talking," not the child, spontaneity is encouraged. Flannelboards and shadow theaters can also be used to add variety to language activities. Children enjoy retelling favorite stories using these devices and making up their own stories.

Language can also be expanded and refined through group discussion. Topics for these sessions can range from current events to sharing of hobbies and avocations. Children often profit from class interactions following the reading of a story, when these are not turned into testing sessions in which dissecting the story is the main goal. Free-wheeling discussions can lead off into numerous byways, as topics and subtopics generate interest and stimulate sharing of children's related experiences. Vocabulary grows naturally in this and other, similar activities not because it is the subject of study but because it occurs in a context where ideas are examined and meanings are exchanged.

On occasion it is appropriate to make language the object of deliberate study. Children enjoy playing with words in games such as password, charades, scrabble, and so forth. Crossword puzzles often provide an enjoyable word-centered activity. Linguistic word blocks that are spilled and arranged to form sentences focus attention on a number of language elements. Bulletin boards that introduce unusual words or point out oddities about language

FIGURE 4.5   Dramatizing a story

(Holt, Rinehart and Winston photo by Russell Dian)

Dramatizing a story read by the class, with children ad-libbing their lines, helps them to expand and refine their language.

encourage language study. Word origins can be investigated, and the evolution of words or expressions can be traced in an historical context.

The cloze procedure can be used as a way of encouraging children to study language. A discussion among a small group of children concerning what terms might fit into a blank and how the use of different words affects sentence meaning can be most revealing. A transparency can easily be made of a cloze passage so that an entire class can work on the same exercise at one time, discussing and considering how the language in the passage functions.

Putting the Spotlight on Language Used in One Selection

One of the oldest traditions associated with reading instruction is the practice of introducing "new" words before a group of children read a whole selection. The intent of this procedure is laudable—to guarantee that children will understand the language they encounter in the story and thereby maximize everyone's chances for successful reading. In practice the procedure often falls far short of its goal, for this approach to vocabulary is merely a cosmetic one. The pronunciation and meaning of the word are introduced. Often the word is not presented in a sentence context, and the obvious limitations of this have been cited earlier. Even when the words are presented in context, however, the procedure is inadequate. Words are not objects to be strung on a necklace. They have true meaning and are integrated by the learner only when they help label some object, idea, or concept. One does not start with a word and look for a meaning in the normal course of events. Meaning evolves, and words are found to label or express that meaning. Words for a reading selection should be met in the context of a discussion which focuses on the key concepts in a story. If courage and loyalty are the important elements, for example, discussion before and after reading the story should help children remember and draw on their own experiences relevant to these elements. It doesn't help much to write those words on the board and "introduce" them prior to reading. Such an approach treats words as the most important factor in reading. The words *are* important, but only as they *reveal meaning.*

As a side issue we should also point out that the practice of teaching new words prior to reading as a regular routine relieves the child of the need to apply word attack skills when he meets those words in the context of the story. A good approach is to introduce irregular, hard-to-decode words if they seem to jeopardize understanding. Otherwise, key concepts can be dealt with and important vocabulary can be extracted from an introductory discussion. When children use a word, or when the teacher can introduce it in the context of preliminary activities, the word becomes tied to personal experience and has meaning.

The story "Earthquake" describes a major quake which occurred in Alaska in the mid-1960's. This description of a teacher in the classroom indicates how vocabulary can be extracted from an introductory discussion:

Arrange the children in a circle or semicircle so that visual contact and discussion is facilitated. Begin by showing the group a picture of a large building, bridge, or other man-made structure that has been heavily damaged by an earthquake. Invite the children to describe what they see in the picture. Ask for speculation concerning how the damage shown in the picture may have occurred. Group their suggestions into categories, such as "natural events" and "man-made events." Invite descriptions of personal experiences with tornadoes, hurricanes, fires, explosions, earthquakes, floods, mud slides, tidal waves, and other catastrophes. Draw out examples of the powerful forces involved in these events (for example, moving heavy objects, destroying buildings and homes, redirecting rivers). Introduce *collapsed* in this context by writing it on the board in the phrase: "The bridge collapsed during the flood."

Ask the group to think about how people react during such events. Encourage expression of personal feelings of fear, alarm, panic. Introduce *terror, screamed, fright* in this context by using the words in sentences on the board.

Explain that today's story is about one of nature's most powerful forces—earthquakes. Determine whether any of the children have experienced an earthquake. Discuss the cause of earthquakes and their usual locations (in or near mountains). Go to a map of North America, and ask individual members of the group to point out places where earthquakes might be expected to occur in North America.

Point to Alaska on the map. Ask whether it is likely that earthquakes would occur there. Invite speculation. Call attention to the mountainous nature of Alaska's landscape. If possible, locate the more mountainous areas of Alaska on the map. Show a picture of snow-covered mountains. Introduce *glistening* and *craggy* in sentences on the board.

Ask what danger there is to life in an earthquake. How might people or animals be injured or killed? Suggest the possibility of drowning as a cause of death due to earthquakes. Describe a tidal wave. Give a concrete referent for the size of a tidal wave (40 to 80 feet) by comparing its height to something familiar to the children (a building, water tower, or other local landmark). In this context introduce the terms *swell, ebb, tidal wave* in sentences on the board.

SUMMARY

Efforts to help children understand what they read often focus on the products of comprehension and ignore the process. The teacher who has a conceptualization of comprehension that can be remembered stands a better chance of improving comprehension because he can pay attention to its basic components and thereby affect the process.

A model of comprehension is presented in this chapter. Two major components, background experience and language abilities, are discussed with regard to the role they play in gaining meaning from reading. Background experiences provide the reader with a repertoire on which to draw when searching for an author's meaning. Language abilities grow around background experiences when the learner has an opportunity to discuss his reactions and questions with someone who uses language effectively. Meaning is communicated by semantic as well as syntactic clues.

The teacher must first understand how background experiences and language abilities are important to reading comprehension. He must also have strategies and techniques for assessing the child's experiential and language base. Where deficiencies that interfere with understanding are found in these areas the teacher must create opportunities and provide instruction that helps the child bring adequate resources to the reading task in order to facilitate comprehension.

Terms for Self Study

assisted reading   function word
cloze procedure   transformation

Discussion Questions

1. What experiences that a child would ordinarily have in his first nine years of life would enable him to find meaning in the story of Cinderella?
2. How is it possible for a child to "read" and understand a word in story and not be able to pronounce that word?

Reading Comprehension: Cognitive and Affective Factors

Practically everyone has had the experience of reading a page of print while thinking something else. The words are processed and the eyes move across the lines and down the page, but suddenly there is realization that the author's message has not been received; comprehension has broken down. Sometimes the page is reread and the mind wanders again. Such experiences serve to point up the importance of thinking to reading comprehension. Chapter 5 is concerned with how thinking and feeling relate to getting meaning from the printed page. These questions may help you focus on some of the significant issues we will deal with:

How are thinking and comprehension related?
How are feelings important to comprehension?
Why is having a purpose for reading helpful in comprehending?
What is a guided reading lesson?
What kinds of questions can teachers ask students in order to promote understanding?

In Figure 4.1 we looked at two of the factors identified as major components of reading comprehension. Three additional major components of comprehension also shown in the figure will be discussed here: thinking abilities, affective factors, and purposes for reading.

Thinking Is a Basic Component of Comprehension

As you read this text you are involved in a thinking process. As you read this book we have asked you to see relationships, make comparisons, follow sequences of events, and engage in any number of similar mental operations, so it should hardly seem necessary to persuade you that reading involves thinking.

As a teacher of reading you will want to involve children in activities that help them think as they read. To do that you need some understanding of how thinking abilities develop, and what the teacher can do to assess and help develop children's thinking.

How Thinking Abilities Develop

From the time he is born, the child is constantly bombarded with stimuli. Events and information gathered by the senses and impressions are fed to the brain. A great deal of speculation and research has been done to explain how the child begins to deal with the flood of data his environment provides. It seems fairly certain that each individual event or piece of information cannot be handled as a unique and novel incident. Apparently the child, even as an infant, begins to develop some structure for ordering his perceptions. Mental categories develop, and stimuli are assigned to those established categories. New stimuli are encountered and categories grow to include these data. Eventually new categories are created as the type and number of stimuli require them, and as the child's growing understanding of his environment permits this. Through a process of generalization and discrimination the child brings some order to his world. The child's structure for dealing with the world orders his perceptions.

As the child grows and matures, his way of ordering his observations changes. More and broader experiences with objects and people explain this change, in part, but the child also grows in his ability to deal with abstractions. He is able to move from the here and now to the past and to the future. He can move from the concrete to the abstract and from the specific to the general. It appears that every child reaches these more advanced stages of thinking via the same route. That is, the child goes through the same stages of intellectual, or cognitive, development. According to the cognitive psychologist Piaget, these stages cannot be hurried. Information and events are interpreted or perceived by the child within his mental structure. When he is ready to evolve a new structure the same information or event will be perceived or understood differently. Teaching that does not take the child's level of development into account will be unsuccessful.

To illustrate, a child who is operating at Piaget's preoperational level— away from self-centeredness but not yet logical—is prone to see everything from his own viewpoint. His thinking is self-centered, or egocentric. The "Soap Box Derby" story introduced in Chapter 4 would be interpreted by such a child from a strictly personal perspective. It would be fruitless to argue with a preoperational-level child that his interpretation of the story is illogical or that it is only one of many possible interpretations. Later—because of interaction with objects, peers, and adults, and because of maturation—the child will be ready to compare his thoughts with others. But formal and systematic instruction will not cause this change before the child is ready to make it.

Certain conditions can facilitate cognitive growth. These include an environment that encourages exploration, manipulation of objects, and "play"; peers and adults that interact with the child; and curricular goals that are organized in a hierarchical manner, from logical step to larger logical step. The learner must be active in the process of interacting with the physical and social environment. The learner's interactions with the environment should provide an opportunity to encounter cognitive conflicts that in turn will facilitate growth at the time he is ready to expand or refine his conceptual framework.

Assessing Thinking Abilities

The most commonly used and best-known formal measure of thinking abilities is the intelligence test. Individually administered IQ tests, such as the *Stanford-Binet* and *Wechsler,* and group-administered IQ tests, such as the *Kuhlman-Anderson* and *Otis-Lennon,* are based on the principle that more advanced levels of thinking enable a person to perform more difficult and more abstract tasks. It was assessment of intelligence with such tests that first led Piaget to become interested in intellectual development.[1]

IQ tests measure a person's cognitive ability by comparing his performance on certain standard tasks to the performance of a number of other people. One's "mental age" is determined by the number of such tasks successfully completed. You are probably aware of the hazards associated with this procedure and the frequent misuses of the results of such tests:

1. IQ tests are nearly always biased in favor of some culture.
2. A premium is usually placed on producing one "correct" answer rather than many possible answers.
3. Tasks often reflect the opportunity to learn rather than the potential to learn.
4. A time-limit factor tends to discriminate against deliberate, contemplative thinking styles.
5. Such tests fail to allow for differences in answers that are related to the child's level of cognitive development.

Despite these and other limitations, intelligence tests can provide some index of a child's thinking abilities. This is particularly true if steps are taken to

---

[1]Piaget was intrigued by children's "incorrect" answers. This led him eventually to the conclusion that children's answers make sense to them because they respond from the perspectives of their stages of cognitive development.

minimize the limitations (for example, a test that is as culture-free as possible can be chosen, a timed and an untimed score can be obtained, and so forth). Teachers can also employ Piaget's strategy of studying the child's answer on IQ tests to determine what stage of development it represents.

In all likelihood, teachers can learn more about a child's thinking abilities by observing his behavior, noting his contributions to a conversation or discussion, and studying how he solves a problem or completes a task than from an IQ test. For example, Josette may not be able to classify objects using more than one attribute at a time. She can group a pile of large and small objects according to size or function but not according to size *and* function. The teacher notes Josette's inability as a factor to be considered in assigning tasks to her. Difficulty with classification on a physical task signals a lack of readiness to classify in a more abstract process, such as reading. Josette might be able to classify characters in a story according to one trait (for example, age). But she should not be asked to identify characters in a story according to age and disposition, if her cognitive development does not permit it. She would likely confuse characters who are kind and elderly with those who are kind and young or mean and elderly. A discussion would have to focus on one character trait at a time in order to fit Josette's level of understanding. Observation can reveal such information to the alert teacher.

Promoting and Developing Thinking Abilities

As information comes to a person it must be processed. Various experts have developed explanations concerning how the child develops a scheme for dealing with his environment. The application of a theory of learning to classroom instruction is not a simple matter. Yet the classroom teacher needs some understanding of how thinking abilities are applied in reading so that instructional goals can be established, appropriate activities can be developed, and assessment of student progress can be made.

It is common to describe the application of thinking to reading by means of comprehension skills. Lists of such skills are often detailed and lengthy. Typically they include a mixture of procedures for teaching comprehension, uses for comprehension, and psychological processess involved in comprehension (Simons, 1971). The result is often a conglomeration that confuses the teacher more than it helps him. Long lists of skills also tend to overwhelm anyone who takes seriously the job of teaching each item.

We believe the needs of teachers and children can best be met by seeing the thinking process in terms of four operations: *identifying, analyzing, evaluating,* and *applying.* There is an obvious interdependence among all thinking operations, but for purposes of discussion, and to help the teacher keep a clear conceptualization in mind, let's ignore that reality for the moment.

At the most basic level a reader must be able to *identify* the ideas on the printed page. To do this he must draw on immediate memories or perceptions. Apparently one's perceptions are very much dependent on the person's stage of cognitive development. At the next higher level of understanding the reader must *analyze* the message. This involves examining the parts, studying the organization, and seeing the relationships. At a third level the reader must *evaluate* the ideas gained from reading. This involves the use of standards in arriving at judgments. The reader determines the authenticity or quality of an idea or point of view. Finally the reader *applies* what he has read to solve a problem or answer whatever question(s) were raised prior to reading. Information may also be rejected or stored for use at some later time.

Each of these thinking processes builds on previous levels. A reader cannot analyze or evaluate information, for example, if it has not been identified correctly at the outset. The development and effective use of these thinking processes in the reading act are dependent, in part, on practice. The teacher's role is one of creating opportunities for children to engage in activities that call for various kinds of thinking. Interaction with peers and adults who employ various thinking processes is a necessary condition of such activities. This underscores the importance of having children engage in exchanges with others to see what interpretations and reactions other people have to what has been read. The kinds of questions teachers ask and encourage children to ask also seem to be important to the kind of thinking children will practice. We believe teachers who have some fundamental idea of comprehension and thinking—one that is simple enough so that the major parts can be remembered—tend to ask and encourage better questions and set classroom conditions that promote a higher level of thinking.

Applying Thinking Operations to Reading

The usual approach to the challenge of helping children think as they read is to grill them on what the chicken said to the fox or what the boy loaded into his wagon. Questions that require children to recognize and recall details constitute 78.3 percent of those asked in Grade 2, according to a study by Guszak (1968). Even in Grade 6, the teachers in Guszak's study primarily asked questions calling for the lowest levels of thought. Questions requiring inference or evaluation were usually framed as yes-no questions.

The rationale seems to be that we teach children to understand by making sure they "get it." If they didn't "get it" we go back, reread that part of the story, and point out their errors. Later we gnash our teeth because children believe "whatever they read," yet we fail to look in a mirror for the culprit.

Since the questions teachers ask and the tasks they assign play a large part in determining what thought processes children will apply to reading, it is crucial that these opportunities not be squandered. Classifications by Barrett (1972), Sanders (1966), Meehan (Harris and Smith, 1972), and others are useful as a means for analyzing and classifying questions and tasks to determine what level of thinking these questions and tasks require. Although such classifications are not empirically based, they do offer a logical description and organization of various thinking operations.

We believe the four thinking processes (identification, analysis, evaluation, and application) can be used effectively as a means for classifying questions and instructional tasks. Although less specific than the classifications of Barrett and others, you can easily keep the four categories in mind. The details of intricate classification schemes are more difficult to remember.

The four thinking operations are described below in a way that should help you decide where a question or task fits:

1. *Identification* requires the reader to recall or locate information stated by the author. The author's ideas are understood.
2. *Analysis* requires the reader to examine the parts according to a scheme or structure. Information not stated is reasoned from what is given.
3. *Evaluation* requires the reader to judge information against a standard to determine its value.
4. *Application* requires the reader to do something with the information.

It is not possible to equate the use of certain key words in questions (for example, when, how) with any given level of this scheme, since an author may say *when* explicitly or it may only be implied. For example, a teacher might ask: "When did the ducks begin to fly South?" The reader may be able to find an explicit statement in the story such as: "In early October the ducks started their long journey South." Or he may find: "As the leaves began to turn, the ducks headed South."

Try to classify the questions and tasks below for the "Soap Box Derby" story in Chapter 4 (page 48), and fit them into the four thinking operations listed above:

1. What color is Charlie's racer?
2. Why does the driver of the green racer need a wheelchair?
3. Who do you think deserved to win the race? Why?
4. How old was Charlie when his brother won the race?
5. Draw a picture of Charlie's racer.
6. Estimate Charlie's age.

Items 1 and 4 are level 1. The story states explicitly that Charlie's racer is red and that Charlie was five when his brother won the race. Items 2 and 6 are not answered explicitly, so they are level 2. Item 3 involves a judgment, so it is level 3. Finally, item 5 falls at level 4, since it involves extending the story and doing something with the information given. You might want to write a question or develop a task related to this story for each level of the classification scheme. Discuss your results with a classmate or with your instructor. Don't be discouraged if some of your ideas don't fit neatly into one category. The scheme is only a means to an end. By using it you can concentrate on developing questions and tasks that encourage children to use various thought processes as they read.

To further illustrate the use of this classification scheme, let's consider what questions and tasks might be appropriate for college students concerning the first four sections of this chapter.

At the lowest level (Identification) basic factual questions could be asked:

1. What factors are thought to cause the child's cognitive structure to change?
2. What technique can the classroom teacher use for assessing thinking abilities other than IQ tests?

The answers to both of these questions are given in the text and require only that the reader understand exactly what the authors wrote.

At the next highest level (Analysis) the reader must use reason to answer a question. Questions that require analysis might be:

1. How would the child's cognitive growth be affected by an absence of stimulation in the environment?
2. What inaccuracies in intelligence assessment could result from comparing the performance of children with distinctly different backgrounds on an IQ test?

These questions relate to ideas presented by the authors, but require the reader to go beyond what is stated explicitly to see relationships and make inferences.

At the third level (Evaluation) the reader is asked to apply criteria in arriving at judgments. For example:

1. Which of the hazards associated with the use of intelligence tests listed by the authors is most pertinent to this discussion on thinking and comprehension? Why do you think so?
2. Do you agree with the premise that teacher's questions affect the kind of thinking children engage in? Why, or why not?

Both of these questions require the reader to make a judgment and explain the standard used in arriving at that judgment.

The fourth level of question or task (Application) requires the reader to do something with the information. These tasks involve application:

1. List three things parents can do to help their children develop the thinking processes necessary for reading.
2. Write out questions which involve analysis that children could be asked to answer after reading a story.

The reader is asked to use the information gained from reading to solve some need or problem.

The four-step scheme can be used to classify questions you intend to ask in story discussions, written assignments, group activities, enrichment activities, workbook tasks, and so on. Depending on the age level you teach, the evident needs of the children, the type of material being read, and the objectives of the instructional program, you can adjust instructional activities to emphasize the application of thinking to reading.

The program should pay attention to all four thought processes regardless of grade level, but some developmental sequence should be planned. Logically, you would emphasize the more fundamental processes with younger children, but not ignore higher-order processes. Even beginning readers are ready and able to make inferences within the realm of their experiences and cognitive levels. Older children should concentrate more on higher-order thought processes, but not to the exclusion of identification. Depending on the topic and the child, individual differences suggest that certain thought processes may be more appropriate than others at any point in time. On the topic of whales, for example, eight-year-old Bruce may be able to analyze and evaluate a selection effectively, whereas twelve-year-old Terry may find identification of meaning a chore.

Normally the increasing complexity of the reading material children can handle as they become more fluent readers provides a natural developmental sequence for applying thinking processes in reading. In other words, Sandra will be able to engage in all levels of thinking to some degree in the Grade 2 reader when she is seven years old. By Grade 4 the selections have become more difficult so similar thought processes applied to stories in the fourth-grade reader continue to challenge and stretch Sandra's comprehension abilities.

Another Type of Thinking: Moral Reasoning

From the time he is first able to engage in reflective thought the child makes judgments about whether something is good or bad. At first the decisions are based on the determination that something is pleasant (exciting) or painful (fearful). He has no rules, nor has he internalized any concept of authority. Gradually, through interaction with his environment, the child begins to understand that society applies certain rules in a way that labels things good or bad. The rules are not understood by the child at first, however; they are perceived on a physical level as reward or punishment. At this stage authority is equated with the physical power of the person who explains the rules and assigns the labels. The child's sense of morality continues to develop as he matures, interacts with his environment, and has the opportunity to learn about higher levels of moral decision. According to Kohlberg, the child can reach the highest levels by passing through these stages:

Stage 0. Premoral Stage—Good is pleasant; bad is painful.
Stage 1. Preconventional Stage—Culture labels good and bad; authority enforces rules.
Stage 2. Relativist Stage—What is satisfying to self, and secondly to others, is right.
Stage 3. Interpersonal Concordance Stage—Good is what pleases or helps others.
Stage 4. Law and Order Stage—Right behavior is doing one's duty, maintaining the social order.
Stage 5. Legalistic Stage—What is best for the greatest number is good.
Stage 6. Universal Justice Stage—Right is a self-chosen ethical matter (Kohlberg, 1969).

The development of moral judgment is of special interest to some psychologists. The classroom teacher should also be concerned about the child's growing sense of right and wrong. In our discussion we need to see how reading comprehension is influenced by this aspect of thought. The child's reflections about what he reads are intimately tied to his sense of fairness, his notions of justice, and his idea of right and wrong. We indicated earlier that in the "Soap Box Derby" story, Charlie's acceptance of defeat in the race may not be understood by the immature child who judges the actions of literary characters along a pleasantness versus unpleasantness dimension. Better understanding of literature may or may not be sufficient reason to be concerned with how moral judgment is important; the fact is that principles for living a better life can be learned from literature. One of the noblest reasons for learning to read is to learn from collected human wisdom. Fine literature embodies and imparts those principles to the reader who is ready to internalize them.

Assessing Moral Development

One useful approach to determining the child's stage of moral development is to present him with a dilemma and ask for an explanation of what he thinks is right or what he would do in that situation. For example, in a study by Harris (1967) elementary school children were asked to respond to a taped dramatization in which Susan lends her bicycle to Mary, her sister. Later, Susan wants to use the bicycle herself so that she can go to the movies with her friends. Susan is faced with a dilemma. Should she repossess her bicycle to serve her own interests or honor the agreement made with Mary? Children in the study wrote a response indicating what they would do in Susan's situation.

This approach is one you can use with the children in your classroom. Situations of various types can be created and children can be asked to indicate their thoughts on solving a social problem. You will be able to make some determination of the child's sense of right or wrong from his solution to the problem. Children at similar stages of development will have similar concerns, and will likely offer the same general solution. For example, a child who operates at a self-centered level will reclaim the bicycle in the Harris study on the grounds that it's Susan's bicycle. A child with a more advanced social conscience will seek a solution that satisfies all parties (for example, "Susan can give Mary a ride on the handlebars.") or honors the commitment (for example, "Mary will go to the movies another time.").

A word of caution: The child's solution must not be viewed as inferior or incorrect if it does not show "maturity." From the child's perspective—in other words, according to his stage of cognitive development—his sense of justice *is* rational. Growth or progress in moral judgment evolves as the child grows uneasy with his way of handling conflicts, and not before.

Encouraging Growth in Moral Judgment

Biskin and Hoskisson (1974) have created a strategy for helping children advance to higher levels of moral judgment using the moral dilemmas posed by children's literature. Basing their work on the research of Kohlberg, Biskin and Hoskisson suggest that children can be exposed to moral arguments that are one stage above their levels of operation. This is a way of causing children to question their solutions to a dilemma. The researchers suggest that stories with a dilemma be read and discussed in class by a small group of children. For example, two characters in a story might solve a problem by deciding that it is all right to cheat on a test because others have cheated too. The teacher asks questions in a follow-up discussion that focus attention on the inconsistency of the characters' solution with a higher stage of moral judgment. The purpose is to expose children to a higher order of thought, so that movement to that level is encouraged. Ideally, all children would advance systematically to the highest level of moral thought. Practically, they are encouraged to move beyond the less-advanced levels where they might remain in the absence of such discussion and exposure to moral issues.

Other researchers reject Kohlberg's position that universal values exist, and concentrate instead on helping children recognize the values they currently hold (Casteel and Stahl, 1975). No systematic attempt is made to change children's values in a values clarification approach, such as the one described by Raths, Harmin, and Simon (1966). Their position is that no one has the right to impose their own values on another person.

Whatever theoretical position you might take on this issue, the opportunity of having children consider alternative solutions, interact, and discuss questions of right and wrong is an important part of the elementary school curriculum. Reading comprehension draws on the child's thinking processes relative to moral issues. The teacher can assist children in their development and application of moral judgment by raising questions of right and wrong, justice, and respect for the rights of others as children read and discuss literature.

To illustrate, these questions might be asked about the story, "Soap Box Derby":

1. Why did Charlie want to win the race? How do you feel about his reasons? Why?
2. How would you feel about losing the race if you were Charlie? Why?
3. Which is more important—winning or being a graceful loser? Why do you think so?

This important and complex aspect of the development of thought requires much more discussion, and you may want to pursue the ideas summarized here in any of the references cited earlier in the chapter or in Piaget (1956).

Creating a Classroom Atmosphere for Thinking

We have seen how different kinds of thinking are related to reading comprehension. Evidently one way of promoting children's thinking is through asking questions. But, the problem of promoting thinking is too complex to be resolved so easily. Because thinking is a mental function not subject to direct assessment, we are almost forced into a process of elimination to determine whether poor thinking or some other factor is causing a child's comprehension difficulties. If a child's language skill, background experience, and intelligence are adequate for a reading task, poor thinking may well be causing the problem. In addition to asking good questions, what other alternatives are open to the teacher?

One is simply to wait for the child to mature. Some thinking processes apparently are not hastened by instruction, as we have seen. In practical terms this means that the child should not be asked to comprehend material that requires thinking processes he does not yet possess. An accurate time sense is an example of a thought process that requires some time for development. Thus, most second-graders cannot study historical fiction with any true understanding of events occurring within fixed periods of time. The best alternative for the teacher may be to wait for the process of maturation to overcome this limitation.

A second alternative is to give direct instruction on the thinking processes. Authorities on children's thinking agree that instruction will not hasten maturity but it can maximize learning once the child is intellectually ready. Demonstrations on the constancy of matter, for example, can help a child who is ready to understand this concept. Experiments with liquids, clay, and beads can be conducted to illustrate that a quart of milk in a tall, thin beaker is exactly equal to a quart of milk in a short, squat beaker. Other concepts, such as cause and effect, can also be demonstrated for the purpose of maximizing growth.

A third alternative is for the teacher to read aloud and discuss with the class the thought processes implicit in a selection. A good lesson can often be learned by listening to others explain their thoughts on a topic—teacher and classmates alike.

Perhaps even more basic to the matter of promoting thought is organizing a classroom that really allows thinking to occur. Whether by design or by accident, many classrooms place an emphasis on following directions. Children are given little freedom to choose or pursue topics of personal interest. Little problem-solving or inquiry learning is permitted. Memorization and acquisition of knowledge for its own sake dulls children's natural curiosity and rewards them for *not* thinking.

The classroom should be an environment that stimulates exploration and discovery. The child should be an active agent in that environment, pursuing questions that have relevance and meaning to him personally. In such a setting thinking is encouraged and rewarded. Divergent thinking is given equal time, and the child's level of cognitive development is acknowledged in the classroom that is child-centered. (*See* Stephens (1974) for a detailed discussion of how to create classrooms that promote thinking.) Chapter 16 of this text gives suggestions for organizing a classroom that respects the child's individuality.

Affective Factors Are Important to Comprehension

We have presented the view in this chapter that children need guidance in learning how to respond to a printed message. So far we have focused on

(Holt, Rinehart and Winston photo by Russell Dian)

FIGURE 5.1   Classroom displays

Various displays in the classroom—bulletin boards, books, artwork, and others—stimulate exploration and discussion by children.

cognitive and moral responses to information. No one would argue that intellectual processes are unimportant to understanding, yet by virtue of neglect we often seem to believe that emotional responses are unimportant. Certainly much of what literature offers is as much emotional, or affective, as it is cognitive. The teacher needs strategies for helping children respond to affective factors in order to maximize comprehension.

One of the most encouraging trends in the elementary school curriculum concerns greater attention to the affective domain. Educators and parents are increasingly recognizing that the child's interests, motivations, attitudes, beliefs, and feelings are important factors that cannot be taken for granted or ignored in the educational process. While they are significant matters in their own right, we will consider affective variables here as they relate to reading comprehension.

Let's begin with the premise that reading comprehension is improved when a child reads about a topic that interests him. Whether this observation is true because interest in a topic normally grows from experience, and it is experience that actually explains greater understanding, or that a reader attends better to material that interests him is hard to determine. In any case, the fact remains that a child who is excited about rock collecting will better comprehend material on that topic than, let us say, on tea-leaf processing. Teachers often find that a child will persist in and gain much from reading material that is "too hard," when he is keenly interested in a subject. You will want to capitalize on this by creating numerous opportunities in the reading program for children to read about topics of their own choosing.

Children's attitudes and beliefs are frequently closely linked to their interests. Attitudes and beliefs are learned, and usually reflect background experience and they play a role in comprehension. Material that expresses a viewpoint similar to one held by the reader is comprehended best; whereas opposing views are easily misunderstood, disregarded, or even ignored. Education is not intended to indoctrinate but rather to help individuals arrive at conclusions consciously. The teacher's task is not one of imposing certain ideas but is one of helping the child recognize his own attitudes and beliefs and to be aware of the need to consider new evidence that may cause a change in attitudes and beliefs. The age and maturity of the class, the community setting, and the willingness of parents to support a teacher are important factors to be considered in deciding what issues to raise with students. The topics chosen are probably not as important as the act of helping children recognize the influence their personal attitudes and beliefs can have on their understanding of an author's message.

(Photo by Carl B. Smith)

FIGURE 5.2   Reading corner

Although he has trouble with classroom reading materials, this boy is fascinated by *Hot Rod*. The teacher capitalized on his interests in cars by including many books and magazines on the subject in the reading corner.

Assessing Affective Factors that Influence Comprehension

Chapter 11 of this text is devoted in large part to children's interests, assessment of these interests, and how to capitalize on them in a reading program. Interests must be assessed almost exclusively with informal devices. Questionnaires, conferences, and teacher observations are excellent ways of identifying topics that appeal to individual children.

Attitudes and beliefs can be assessed in exactly the same ways as interests. It is a relatively straightforward matter to determine what a child's attitude or belief is concerning Santa Claus, for example. You need only ask him how he feels. Feelings on a more complex topic can be discovered by means of a simple inventory. This survey form can be adjusted to gather information on many topics and for older or younger children:

Topic: Energy Conservation

	Strongly disagree	Disagree	Don't know	Agree	Strongly agree
1. People should be able to buy as much gasoline as they want.					
2. New houses should have a certain amount of insulation.					
3. Gasoline should have a 15¢ per gallon tax added to discourage people from buying it.					
4. The countries who produce oil are wrong to raise oil prices.					
5. Most people waste energy.					
6. Electric companies should be allowed to burn soft coal even though it's dirty.					

Developing the Affective Domain

Classroom activities can be planned to make children aware of their feelings. Once awareness has been gained, activities can be conducted to cause children to analyze and evaluate their feelings, compare them with the feelings of others in the class, and recognize the influence their feelings have on their interpretation of what they read. This strategy is offered as a way of helping children deal with their emotions consciously, not as a way of eliminating emotions or totally objectifying the world.

Emotions are a fact of life. Feelings develop early when infants find some things pleasant and others unpleasant. Most people grow up with the full range of emotions. Schools do not literally need to teach emotions, but it is probably a good idea for schools to help children understand these emotions to the end that *some* control over them can and should be gained by each individual. Obviously the school cannot accomplish this goal by itself, but neither can the home, church, or any other social organization. If the school fails to participate in the task of helping children master their emotions, one major source of input is eliminated.

Life would be very dull without emotions. Countless books have been written, movies made, and television shows produced about a stereotyped, supercontrolled individual who approaches life unemotionally. Invariably such a person experiences a catharsis that makes life more meaningful and more fun. The lesson such tales tell is that some spontaneity is important to life. But society expects individuals to have some control of their emotions.

Another common theme in popular entertainment features uncontrolled rage, hate, passion, or other emotion. Individuals who lack restraint menace the existence of others and are often institutionalized or isolated. Evidently some middle position is endorsed by society. People are expected to have feelings, but not in the extreme, and they certainly are not expected to express feelings violently. Since literature helps define the type of behavior society will tolerate, and ways that emotion can be expressed constructively, some attention to this aspect of literary content seems necessary. Even if this were not the case, full appreciation of good literature requires that emotions be understood as an important story element.

The teacher's fundamental technique for dealing with affective variables is again question-asking. Through questions the teacher helps the child come to grips with an emotion or an issue relative to an emotion (for example, "How did Wilbur feel when Charlotte died?" in a discussion of E. B. White's book, *Charlotte's Web*. "When someone is grieving over a death, how can someone else show concern?")

The classification introduced earlier for the cognitive domain can be used to plan questions that focus on the affective domain. At first children will need to deal with basic tasks, such as identifying the emotions in a story. Later they can analyze and compare emotions in a story to ones they have experienced themselves. Next they can be led to make judgments about the appropriateness of an emotion in a specific context. At the highest level, application, the child gains a better understanding of emotions as they apply to his life. He is able to bring principles learned from literature into actions of his own.

Referring again to the "Soap Box Derby" story in Chapter 4, discussion of the affective domain might take the following form:

1. *Identification.* How did Charlie feel before the race? How did he feel after the race?
2. *Analysis.* When have you felt as Charlie did after the race? How was your disappointment different than Charlie's? How does this story make you feel? Why?
3. *Evaluation.* Was it right for Charlie to feel glad about the other car winning?

Why? What feelings that Charlie had before the race were inappropriate in your opinion? Why?

4. *Application*. Why is it important to be able to accept disappointment? How can envy change a person?

Many teachers find that by reading a book aloud to their classes they create opportunities for a discussion of feelings and emotions. Certain books— *Charlotte's Web* or *The Yearling*, for instance—are touching stories that involve many emotions in a natural, unforced way. A heightened sense of feeling is often introduced by an effective oral reading.

Dramatizing a story is another good way of focusing on emotions. Good stage directing calls for a discussion of the emotions contained in a scene and how they should be portrayed by an actor. Pantomine and dance are also excellent techniques for expressing the feelings contained in a story.

Purposes for Reading

The mature reader varies his approach as his purpose for reading changes. This ability to adjust reading behavior according to different purposes takes on special importance when consideration is given to the wide variety of reasons for which people read. Consider the difference between reading a newspaper report of a football game and following a recipe for making fudge. The newspaper story may present a considerable amount of detail, but we usually read such material for the main ideas—the final score, who scored the touch-downs, the team's record, and so on. Occasions arise when main ideas are not enough and a more thorough reading is desirable of any kind of story. On the other hand, one normally reads a recipe for quite another purpose—to follow step-by-step directions for preparation. Nothing less than a careful word-by-word reading will enable us to achieve the purpose of correctly following a recipe.

Purposes for reading have been regarded as important for comprehension because they help the reader focus on the specific aspects of a selection. Common sense and research evidence have long supported this view (Beaucamp, 1925; Distad, 1927; Shores, 1960).

Since there are a host of purposes for reading, it is common for the teacher who wishes to help children become better readers to plan lessons where reading for a particular purpose is emphasized (for example, to identify a cause-effect relationship). On other occasions other purposes are established, and over time many purposes for reading are practiced. Many sets of instructional materials claim to "teach" children to read for lengthy lists of purposes. There is great variance among such lists and practically no explanation of how one purpose is different than another on the same list (for example, How is reading to draw conclusions different than reading to make generalizations?).

Recent research has questioned the practice of having children read for specific purposes (Goudey, 1970; Brady, 1974). Goudey and Brady (in separate investigations) used procedures which contrasted the reading comprehension of children who read with a specific purpose assigned prior to reading with the achievement of children who read only for the general purpose of understanding. The researchers found that specific purposes for reading actually seemed to interfere with comprehension. Certainly further research with children needs to be done before drawing final conclusions on this matter. One possible explanation for these findings, however, is consistent with the view of comprehension presented in this textbook. It seems reasonable to hypothesize that purposes for reading assigned by someone other than the reader himself may not aid comprehension because such purposes assume a state of readiness and a frame of reference that is inappropriate for the given reader. For example, a teacher might ask a group of children to read "Soap Box Derby" for the purpose of identifying Charlie's motive for entering the race. That purpose may help some children focus on a key issue and as a result better understand an important aspect of the story. The same purpose may be inappropriate for other children, however, when they lack experience with family traditions, or for egocentric children who perceive all human behavior as self-serving. While a purpose for reading may seem logical to an adult, the child's stage of cognitive development and experiential background may undermine that logic.

If we believe purposes for reading are important, as we do, but that the teacher can seldom determine these purposes successfully for children, what are we proposing should be done with respect to reading instruction? The answer is: Lead children to establish their own purposes prior to reading.

Suppose some beginning readers are going to read a story about a pet dog that gets into trouble by digging in a neighbor's yard. If asked without preparation to decide why they are reading the story, typical six-year-olds or even nine-year-olds would have little success establishing their purposes for reading. By involving children in a discussion concerning their pets or ones they know about—how pets can cause trouble, and what can be done to keep pets from being a nuisance—a teacher can help those youngsters generate some ideas of their own around the topic. They can then come up with questions such as, "What kind of trouble could Rex, a dog, cause in the story?" Or "How is Rex like my pet?" The teacher's task is one of leading children via a preliminary discussion into recalling and drawing on relevant personal experiences and concepts so that questions are raised which the story may answer for them. Obviously the kinds of issues and questions the teacher introduces during these preliminary activities is most influential in determing what purposes the children will finally have for reading the story. Not all children will or should develop the same questions, but a follow-up discussion after the story is read can incorporate a range of responses to the advantage of all in the group. Here again the issues and questions raised by the teacher in a follow-up discussion are critical in terms of stimulating the child's level of thought. This in turn affects the purposes the child might bring to a future reading task.

The teacher may seem to be a rather passive actor insofar as purposes for reading are concerned. But quite the contrary is true. The scope and nature of the introductory activities which are planned by the teacher promote the kinds of questions children will want to answer as they read. A stimulating debate on how dinosaurs became extinct stands a good chance of pulling every child into the discussion. Models of dinosaurs that appeal to several senses, pictures that create visual images, open-ended questions that create opportunities for speculation, and the like lead children quite naturally to a state of anticipation. They are anxious to learn what position the author takes on the topic or to see whether events in the story bear out their *predictions*. We use the word predictions because as children ask questions (set purposes) they can be helped to anticipate what they believe to be the answer to the questions. Reading to verify predicted answers makes reading an active search process that improves comprehension. And that is just the point of setting purposes for reading: to improve comprehension.

In Chapter 4 a detailed description was given (page 58) concerning how background might be built for the story, "The Airport." As the children tell of their experiences with jets, air terminals, handling of luggage, and so forth the teacher is attempting to build a state of readiness for reading the story. As George recalls a trip he took across country by airplane he begins to wonder whether the characters in the story have experiences similar to his. Are Ben and Matt frightened by the roar of the jet engines? Do they hit an air pocket, as he did, and drop like a roller coaster? What do they have to eat on the plane? These are questions the teacher cannot pose for George, since every child's experiences are different. Yet they are real and meaningful to George because of where he is in a developmental sense. The teacher can help George formulate these and other, more significant questions by planning introductory activities that trigger his memories and arouse his curiosity.

Initially it may be wise to have each child share aloud his purposes for reading or to write them on paper to reinforce the notion that one begins a selection with a specific purpose in mind. Later the procedure may be less formal—less artificial—as the child develops the habit of setting his purpose for reading. Certainly there are no rules that must be adhered to rigidly. The teacher can offer a purpose for reading to a child that he thinks is appropriate to see how well it is handled or to broaden the child's thinking. What should be avoided is the teacher routinely making the determination of what purposes a child will pursue as he reads.

The teacher must study a selection ahead of time to determine what purposes might successfully be pursued by youngsters in his class when they read a story. The teacher can then set the stage via appropriate introductory activities. Even then a child may occasionally be disappointed that his purpose for reading is not satisfied by the selection. That is a reality the mature reader must face also, and the fact that it occurs should in no way discourage us from having children take the lead in setting purposes for reading.

Obviously, purposes for reading must be established before a selection is read. Only through this procedure can the reader properly direct his attention during the reading. Afterward, the stated purpose can be used as a basis for discussion to determine whether the reader has achieved his goal.

Adjusting Reading Rate to Purpose

Just as the reader must adapt his reading to meet various purposes, he must also adjust his reading rate. The answer to a specific question concerning supporting detail will require the reader to skim for the right section and then read that section carefully for the correct answer. Following directions calls for slow, careful reading, as does reading an account of a scientific experiment. Recreational reading and newspaper reading often call for a rapid rate, but usually not as fast as skimming.

Generally the reader should read as fast as he can and still achieve his purpose. It is widely accepted and often demonstrated in practice that good readers tend to read faster than poor ones. In some respects rapid reading accounts for good comprehension, since thoughts and phrases are more easily gathered into wholes in this way. Slower readers sometimes miss the point of a sentence or paragraph because they concentrate so intensively on individual words that synthesis of thought becomes difficult.

The teacher has two primary tasks with regard to reading rate:

1. demonstration of the need to adjust reading speed according to purpose
2. encouragement of maximum speed for all reading.

(A more complete discussion of improving reading rate is given in Chapter 15.)

A Strategy for Getting It All Together: The Guided Reading Lesson

One message that should stand out clearly is that no simple or easy solutions are available for solving comprehension problems. You will need to work continually on many fronts with children in the classroom to promote and develop the ability to understand the printed page. Numerous factors alone or in combination can stand in the way of comprehension. In addition to the ideas already presented in this chapter, here is one general strategy for minimizing comprehension problems: the guided reading lesson.

In a guided reading lesson the teacher organizes and plans a number of activities that lead children through a selection. It involves a minimum of six steps, and provides a format that helps the teacher address the major factors affecting comprehension. It is no panacea and is not intended to become a ritual that takes on a worth of its own. It is merely a means to an end, and requires adaptation and variation.

The guided reading lesson involves these six steps:

1. building background
2. setting purposes for reading
3. independent reading
4. follow-up discussion

5. development of related skills
6. extending and applying ideas from a selection.

Building Background

The section of Chapter 4 on background experience demonstrated the importance of a reader having some familiarity with a topic before reading about it. Vocabulary, concepts, and, in large degree, interests, attitudes, beliefs, and feelings are based on background experience. The teacher's first task is to help the child recall background experiences he will draw on to understand a story and at the same time to create an interest in the topic by showing its relevance to the child's life. Learning theory suggests that these introductory activities be as concrete as possible and involve the child as an active participant for maximum effect.

Setting Purposes for Reading

Once the teacher is satisfied that adequate background has been built, the child should come to have some purposes for reading. If the introductory activities have been effective the child, even at an early age, should be able to identify purposes that logically grow from those activities. A discussion of volcanoes, for example, might lead him to ask how they come to exist. The story can be read to find the answer. Naturally the purposes for reading must be keyed to the content of a story, as well as to the abilities of the children. Imposing a purpose that is ill-suited to a story's content or inappropriate for the child does not improve comprehension or provide useful practice.

As the child sets about the task of reading he should have easy access to whatever purposes for reading have been agreed upon. He can write them down on a piece of paper or the teacher can put them on the chalkboard. This point of reference helps the child to remember why he is reading.

With younger children the teacher may at first need to play a larger role in setting purposes. Gradually more of this responsibility should shift to the child, since that is where it resides ultimately for the mature reader. This can happen only if the introductory discussion arouses interest and helps create an attitude of anticipation in the child.

Independent Reading

The teacher should be available to help when children read a selection independently, but the emphasis should be on children conquering difficulties themselves whenever possible. This does not mean the teacher must remain with the group, but it is not a good idea for him to be completely removed from the area. Most children, even beginners, can read silently and without page-by-page discussion, if materials of appropriate difficulty are selected and if the introductory activities have been satisfactory.

Follow-up Discussion

Whereas introductory activities lay the groundwork for comprehension, it is the follow-up discussion, we believe, where the teacher has his greatest opportunity to actually teach comprehension. Particularly through the kinds of questions he asks, the teacher directs the application of thinking operations. This is an excellent time to re-enter the story to study the topic being emphasized in a lesson. Questions must focus on various levels of cognition and yet not neglect the affective domain.

Schedules do not always permit the ideal, but whenever possible the discussion of a story should follow independent reading immediately. The story is fresh in the children's minds at this time, and confusion or misunderstanding can be cleared up while a problem is still vivid.

The discussion should not be a time for testing whether each child remembers every detail of the story. Instead, it should focus on the purposes established ahead of time and permit children to share their reactions to the story. It may be necessary to return to certain passages of the story for clarification. Different interpretations of incidents are natural and should be taken by the teacher as an opportunity for studying the author's wording or plan of organization.

The teacher's role during the follow-up discussion is that of a diagnostician. Evidence of misunderstanding can be obtained from children's com-

(Holt, Rinehart and Winston photo by Russell Dian)

FIGURE 5.3   Story discussion

Discussion of a story that has been read by all the children in the class often helps clarify its meaning and theme.

ments. These responses can provide the insight for planning additional instruction later on.

Written responses to questions can occasionally be asked for so that evidence of each child's understanding is available. Discussions sometimes limit the number of responses that can be heard, and the ideas of some quiet children may go unnoticed.

Skill Development

One of the most important aspects of teaching comprehension begins once a reading group has completed a selection and discussed it. When children don't understand what they have read, it is for cause, and the teacher must begin to deal with those causes. The ideas in this chapter should direct the teacher toward a sense of what might be done.

Skill instruction can often effectively be based on the story a group has just completed. By returning to a passage that caused some pupils difficulty the teacher can demonstrate the application of a principle. For example, comprehension may have faltered because a figurative statement—"Jack was up a tree."—was taken literally by the children. To overcome this problem several other figures of speech might be cited by the teacher and discussed by the group. A practice exercise could then be assigned on interpreting figurative phrases.

This example illustrates the important role of the teacher in actually providing instruction. Resource material, such as a teacher's manual, can be highly useful, but the teacher is still responsible for guiding a learning experience in the classroom. If sequence of ideas is the skill causing difficulty, a demonstration of following a sequence might be given by the teacher. Or he may guide the group in identifying a sequence of events. The actual teaching technique used will vary from teacher to teacher and from group to group. What must be avoided is the notion that children learn to overcome difficulties simply by being given a workbook assignment, or similar written activity, or that they will understand what they read by being encouraged to "think harder" or "concentrate."

Extending and Applying Ideas from a Story

Unless the story is to serve as an end in itself (which may happen on rare occasions), the interests generated, the topics explored, the related topics identified—all lead the child naturally to further reading, writing, speaking, and listening activities. Some stories are better in this regard for some children than for others. The diagnostic teacher should attempt to detect how each child reacts to a story, and the various possibilities it offers for extension, and then adjust his expectations for each child accordingly.

The teacher should also attempt to adjust to the learning style of each child as much as possible. The child who enjoys art activities can easily capitalize on this strength in extending a story through drawings or illustrations. The youngsters who read widely can read library books on a given topic. Naturally some variety ought to exist, and each child should try new experiences occasionally. Indeed, group activities should be pursued frequently.

The goal of enrichment activities is to broaden and deepen the child's understanding of a world of ideas and thus stimulate communication. Through dramatizing, role-playing, and other expressive acts the characters and ideas in a story become more real and useful to the child and the desire to communicate is kindled. Chapter 12 of this text, "Creativity," provides many suggestions for helping children extend and apply what they read.

Guided Reading Is Only One Component of a Total Reading Program

Not all reading should be in groups, nor should reading always be done with the teacher's guidance. Without question the child should have numerous opportunities to select materials of personal interest and read them independently. Every well-balanced reading program will include nonguided reading activities that place the child in control. Only by selecting and reading materials without introduction by the teacher will the child learn to become a self-reliant reader. This observation in no way negates the value of the guided reading lesson. Your task is not to choose between group or individual reading, and between guided or unguided reading, it is to find the proper balance for students, given their level of development and ability.

Comprehension Is Personal

The results of an achievement battery, reading survey test, or informal reading inventory often indicate a level of comprehension for a child, this is a fallacy we must address. Every person is actually a composite of *many* levels of comprehension, depending on the topic. The child who has been to the circus many times, toured the performers' quarters, fed the elephants, smelled the atmosphere of the animals' quarters, and talked with a clown has a vivid, rich personal field of reference to draw on as he reads a circus story.

Another youngster, who "reads equally well," may not have had such meaningful experiences with circuses, and his comprehension naturally suffers in consequence. Change the topic to soap-box racers and one child's strength becomes another child's weakness.

Obvious? Perhaps; but classroom practices belie that such a basic principle is really understood.

Too often children reading at the same "level" are expected to read and comprehend all stories pretty much equally. Moreover, it is typically the teacher's level of understanding and enthusiasm for a topic that determines how much all children should "understand." That is, unless children can answer those questions *the teacher* feels are important, their comprehension is often judged wanting.

Since differences in background dictate differences in understanding on almost any topic, such differences should be accepted and respected. Everyone can remember reading something a second time, months or years later, and finding meaning they missed before. What has changed? Certainly not the story. Obviously the reader has changed.

Yet we are often unwilling to accept this phenomenon among children. As a result we too often rework a story to be sure everyone "gets" it. Gets what? What the teacher got? The teacher is older, more experienced, a different person than the child. Why should the teacher set the arbitrary standard of minimum comprehension?

To avoid this trap we must regard comprehension as a personal matter and make provisions for "levels" of comprehension within each person.

Improving Comprehension

The concerns discussed here lead us to offer these guides for improving comprehension:

Build background before reading.

Create interests and develop concepts with real objects children can see and handle.

Develop vocabulary in the context of a discussion or activity.

Follow up reading experiences with discussions that explore the main as well as related issues.

Show how topics children read about are relevant to their lives, thoughts, and feelings.

Use a reading experience as a springboard to many exploratory activities.

Integrate reading with all curricular areas.

Expect different levels of comprehension, depending on the child's background and interests.

Encourage independent reading on topics of personal interest.

Form interest groups that facilitate interaction among children.

Provide for sharing of reading experiences through diverse means and varied media.

Establish a youth-tutoring-youth program.

Encourage children to set their own purposes for reading.

Expect children to think, especially along divergent lines.

Recognize opportunities to emphasize comprehension in all curricular areas.

Avoid expecting everyone to understand a story exactly as you, the teacher, understand it.

Use parents, local people, and the community as learning resources.

Encourage children to stimulate and learn from each other.

A classroom that follows these guidelines approaches reading comprehension as a part of a general concern for communication. The teacher is a facilitator, one who creates a stimulating environment.

The classroom is rich with displays, manipulative devices, learning centers, and unusual objects. Children interact with each other frequently as their interests carry them into topics that overlap. Much individual, independent learning occurs in such a classroom, but grouped instruction also takes place, as common needs and interests are identified by the teacher.

Skill instruction is provided, but not according to a rigid, arbitrary sequence recommended by a publishing company. The child's needs dictate when skills are introduced, a need the teacher consciously creates by the kind of environment he cultivates. Thorough and accurate records enable the teacher to monitor each child's progress and to individualize instruction accordingly.

Reading comprehension grows as the child's awareness of the world grows, because it is not torn from its roots in a total communication program. Comprehension is viewed as a thinking process in this classroom, not as the sum of the separate, isolated skills listed in a teacher's guide.

Nothing suggested here is inconsistent with using a basal reading series occasionally or even regularly. However, adjustments to the basal routine are necessary.

First and foremost, not all stories in a basal series will necessarily be read, and clearly the sequence of stories will be altered. Not all suggestions for skill activities will be followed. The preparation before reading will be expanded and made more concrete. Vocabulary will grow out of discussion where key concepts in the story are explained. Follow-up discussion will range far beyond the suggested questions, and will encourage children to think critically and creatively about topics and characters in the stories.

The stories will be viewed as springboards that launch the group into many related topics for further exploration—each perhaps following a different course.

Unlike the more mechanical aspects of reading, comprehension cannot be broken down, logically sequenced, and practiced until the child has mastered it. Comprehension must be viewed against a backdrop of the total child. Adjustments must be made to the background and interests of the individual. This makes instruction more complex—and more demanding—but ever so much more enjoyable for teacher and learner alike.

SUMMARY

Three important factors in reading comprehension are identified: thinking, affection, and purposes for reading. The teacher plays an active role in causing children to apply their thought processes to reading by the kinds of questions that are asked and the types of tasks that are assigned. Often neglected, the affective domain plays an important part in influencing what is understood by the children. Purposes for reading help the reader focus on information that is most relevant at a given time and consequently such purposes are most effective when established by the reader. Techniques and strategies for assessing student status with regard to these components are given in the chapter, as well as suggestions for strengthening the student's resources in these areas.

The guided reading lesson is described as a useful six-step play for helping children understand a story. The steps are:

1. build background
2. establish purposes for reading
3. read independently
4. discuss
5. develop skills
6. extend and apply ideas from the story.

Reading instruction must take into account the differences between children that make comprehension a personal matter involving not only what the author says but what the reader brings to the page. Efforts to improve comprehension will be most effective in a classroom environment where reading is viewed as one aspect of helping children explore a world of ideas.

Terms for Self Study

guided reading lesson	affective domain
cognition	moral judgment
identification	analysis
evaluation	application

Discussion Questions

1. How should a teacher respond to a child's interpretation of a story when it is clearly "wrong" from the teacher's perspective? What is the reason for your answer?
2. A visitor has complained to teacher Jackie Phillips that too much time is spent on follow-up activities that extend stories and not enough time is spent making sure the children really understand the stories. How should Jackie respond?

Assessing
Student Progress
and Needs

Have you ever considered the possibility that one day you might be retained in a teaching position or awarded a salary increase on the basis of how well your students learn to read? Not such a bad thought at first glance, is it? You intend to be a good teacher. Why not be rewarded according to how well you produce? But how will your "product" be judged? If you were a truck driver the number of boxes you haul might be a fair index of your ability. But how do we determine what children have learned? That is a complex matter. This chapter deals with assessment. Look for answers to these questions as you read:

How can student progress be determined?
What are the limitations of reading tests?
What kinds of reading tests are available?
What is an informal reading inventory?
How can children's needs be identified?

Imagine that one morning you wake up feeling ill. You call for an appointment with your physician, dress, and hurry down to the office. The nurse takes your temperature and seats you in an examination room. Dr. Whitcomb enters the room, notes your temperature, and explains that you have a severe case of malaria. How would you react? Probably with alarm and certainly with puzzlement. How can Dr. Whitcomb diagnose your problem, having done no more than read your temperature? You expect that you will be asked about your symptoms; the affected area will be examined; and tests on blood, urine, throat, and other parts of your body—as the ailment might require—will be run.

An interesting parallel can be drawn between the diagnosis a physician might perform on a patient and the assessment a teacher might make of a child's reading progress. Obviously, teaching and medicine are more different than they are alike, and any analogy comparing the two may be forced. Yet much like the physician, a teacher employs observation techniques. The doctor structures observations according to what training has taught him or her is important and useful. Some of the observations are more objective than others. Instruments help to read the blood count, for example, in a consistent, "scientific" way. A throat examination is more subjective. Is the throat abnormally red? Are the glands swollen? Experience and training are invaluable in arriving at a judgment on these matters, but it is a judgment nonetheless.

A teacher must also structure his observations of a child's reading performance. Some techniques he uses are less judgmental than others; some involve more scientific rigor than others. The physician's task is difficult and important, to say the least. But because the physician deals with physical matters, the observations can be more precise than the teacher's. The teacher is dealing with an extremely abstract matter—a mental operation. It is crucial that teachers understand the nature and limitations of the diagnostic means at their disposal.

Educators, parents, and even children tend to look for exact measurements in reading. The physician has a thermometer, blood tests, urine tests, and so forth. What similar quantified measure does the teacher have? The answer is none. Every reading measure—standardized or informal, published or homemade, extensive or brief—is nothing more than a means for gathering samples or observations of an abstract operation. These observations must then be interpreted in light of their limitations. But the situation is not hopeless. The teacher who has a mental map of the reading process and knowledge of the various means for assessing progress in acquiring reading competence is clearly better able to individualize instruction than someone who lacks these tools. Previous chapters have presented the mental map, or conceptualization, of reading. In this chapter student progress and needs are discussed.

Assessment Involves More than Testing

Like all specialities, education—particularly reading education—is bedeviled by a surplus of terms. Some terms have very precise meanings; others are vague and imprecise. At times a variety of labels are applied to the same concept. Often shades of meaning are signaled by words that later become synonyms. Perhaps more than any other area, assessment is complicated and confused by the vocabulary game.

To avoid this problem we must clarify some terms as they will be used here. *Assessment* refers to the far-ranging act of determining what a student can do and cannot do with respect to reading, understanding, and appreciating the printed message. *Diagnosis* is a term we use interchangeably with assessment; it usually refers to determining a student's understanding in a specific skill area (for example, we diagnose a child's needs with regard to his understanding of vowel sounds). The term *testing* is often misunderstood; testing and diagnosis are *not* synonymous. Diagnosis might well include the use of tests and testing procedures, since these refer to the practice of trying a person's ability to perform a task. Testing refers to more than paper-and-pencil tasks purchased from a publishing house, however. Let's pursue this matter briefly by separating tests into two categories: formal and informal.

Differences between Formal and Informal Measures

It is hardly adequate to identify *formal measures* of testing as those you remember taking in a whole class setting with a darken-in-the-box answer form, yet this description should cause you to recall a personal impression. Formal measures are those published tests that are given under strictly controlled conditions (for example, uniform directions to all, strict time limits). They are accompanied by information regarding their reliability and validity. (Reliability refers to the fact that the test will yield the same results every time it is given to the same subject; validity means that a test measures what it claims to measure.) Such measures have been "standardized" (a term often used synonymously with formalized), and often include tables of norms which indicate how a large sample of children scored on the tests previously, so that comparisons can be made.

Informal measures are different from formal measures in that no conditions are specified for their use, nor have they typically been studied for reliability and validity. From an assessment standpoint informal measures are valuable because they require the child to demonstrate what degree of mastery has been attained on a specific skill.

Informal measures include, but are not limited to, assessment devices the teacher makes himself. Examples would be teacher-made tests, worksheets, daily assignments, oral reading inventories, learning centers, reading games, and so forth. Many devices qualify as informal measures that are not teacher-made. The workbook available with most basal reader series is prepared by a publishing company, but the activities in it require a child to apply various reading skills. Workbook exercises can be used without specified time limits, as can literally dozens of other published devices that provide a teacher with informal assessment opportunities (for example, audiotapes with response forms, learning kits, games). It may seem strange to think of a game as a test, but looked at in this way games and other informal measures provide a steady flow of diagnostic information to the teacher.

We have said that assessment involves more than testing. But testing is one important part of assessment—perhaps the part that is most misunderstood. It is fashionable in some circles to reject tests and decry the value of testing. Critics cite the cultural bias built into many tests, describe the misuse of tests evidenced by some educators who seem not to understand them, and give examples of ambiguous or unclear items on tests. It is impossible to refute many of these criticism because, in fact, they are all too often true.

Tests and testing, especially formal measures, have attained an undeserved high status in the minds of some people—educators and parents alike. Such critics are often guilty of similar extremes when they dismiss tests, which are actually rather neutral. It is the way tests are used and interpreted that often merits criticism.

One of our purposes will be to describe how tests can be used in constructive ways, and to present alternatives to the easy misuse of published tests.

Assessment Is Central to Individualization of Instruction

Assessment is important to the teacher as a means of individualizing instruction, for it enables a teacher to identify a reading level where the child can work effectively on a daily basis, and each child's pattern of strengths and weaknesses.

Identifying the Child's Instructional Reading Level

As children gain competence in reading they are gradually able to handle selections of increasing difficulty. Common sense suggests that we do not confront the developing reader with materials that are so difficult that he cannot successfully decode and understand them. We would not ask even an advanced eight-year-old to regularly read Steinbeck or Baldwin, for example. At the other extreme, the developing reader must have exposure to materials that stretch him, or he will find it hard to get beyond the easy-to-read "big books" on the bottom shelf in the library. Somewhere in between these extremes is a "match" of child and material that challenges the child but doesn't overwhelm him.

The labels that reading specialists apply to *levels* of reading are worth knowing. The level that is "too hard" is called the *frustration* level; the level that is "just right" is the *instructional* level; and the level that is "easy" is called the *independent,* or *recreational,* level. Authorities do not agree on exactly how these levels should be specified in terms of actual reading performance. Opinions differ, for example, on how many word recognition errors on a given page indicate that a reader is operating at his instructional level. This complex and important issue is taken up later in this chapter under the subject of oral reading diagnosis. Different reading levels do exist, and it is extremely important that teachers make an effort to match each child with materials that he can handle successfully for daily instruction.

Without elaborating, it is important to note that every reader, young and old, will find the happy "match" of personal reading ability and difficulty of material occurring for him at different levels on different topics. High interest and rich personal background uniquely equip each individual to handle material in one area that is "harder" by some standard measure than they might handle in another area of little personal interest or experience. The discussion regarding the importance of identifying the child's instructional level needs to be read with this variable in mind.

The classroom teacher must plan and conduct assessment that helps him identify a general level of reading competence for each child. This determination is necessary in order to form groups of children that can profit from reading the same selections, as well as to assist each child in finding books he can read successfully on his own. Both formal and informal measures are helpful in identifying the child's instructional level.

Identifying Each Child's Pattern of Strengths and Weaknesses

Given the many variables that interact to enable a child to read, it is not surprising that no two children probably ever have exactly the same instructional needs at one time. Fortunately, children can adapt themselves to our organization and often profit from instruction that is less than optimum insofar as their own readiness is concerned. Yet all of the adjusting cannot be done by the child; it is our obligation as teachers to individualize instruction whenever we can. The diagnostic data available from formal and informal sources is basic to making such adjustments for individuals.

Without information that indicates who needs help with consonant clusters, for example, there is a strong tendency to give everyone in a group the same dose. Evidence indicating that Wanda, Charles, and Marlene have mastered br, cr, dr, and fr, but are confused about sc, sk, and tr helps the teacher plan appropriate instruction. The fact that Frank, Willie, and Lana perform tasks well that involve all of these sound-symbol associations encourages the teacher to give them other work, despite the fact that all six of these children normally read together in the same basal reader. It should be clear that assessment is most valuable when it helps the teacher set instructional goals.

Assessment Must Relate to Instructional Goals

Often we are asked by teachers to recommend a reading test. Sometimes it is possible to identify several reading tests the teacher might consider using if certain variables can be identified:

1. how old the children are
2. what materials the teacher is using for instruction
3. what other information is already available on the reading performance of the children.

Even more important than these variables in selecting a test is identification of the teacher's instructional goals. A test is worth little to a teacher if it does not provide information on where children are achieving in relation to the objectives the teacher has established. This is true whether the assessment is made before, during, or after instruction begins; or whether the test is a published one or is teacher-made.

Matching the objectives of a test and the objectives of instruction is very important. Testing is too expensive and too consuming of student and teacher time to be conducted for its own sake. Assessment of any kind, including formal testing, must provide a guide for instruction. A test that measures reading rate, for example, when there is no intention to provide instruction in this area is nonproductive. Even worse, it steals from the time and money that might be spent on assessing a skill that is of higher priority from an instructional standpoint.

You may feel that reading rate is important and merits assessment. If so, it should be identified as an instructional priority and included in the objectives of your program. But every reading skill cannot be included. If reading rate ranks high something else must be dropped from your goals and treated incidentally. Otherwise you run the risk of pursuing all skills at once and achieving none successfully because your energies are not focused on the skills your students need most. Goal-setting can be difficult when there is much that seems to need doing, but some decisions must be made early to give a program coherence and structure.

What test is best in a given situation hinges on the matter of objectives. What do you intend to teach? What does the test measure? Is there a match between the two? A test that measures performance in areas you intend for instruction should be used.

It is important to remember that individualization of instruction involves establishing different goals for different children. You will want to seriously limit the amount of testing you do of a whole class with the same measure. Your interest will be in finding measures that are useful with individuals or small groups, since you probably want to set instructional goals on this basis. Criterion-referenced tests are particularly helpful in this regard.

Criterion-referenced Tests Focus on the Individual

A *criterion-referenced test* assesses the performance of an individual against a predetermined standard of mastery. Only one skill or set of related subskills is included in a criterion-referenced test. For example, such a test could be developed to assess mastery of identifying root words. Twenty tasks could be designed that require a reader to underline the roots in a list of words. Successful performance on eighteen of the twenty tasks (90 percent) would indicate mastery of the skill.

On a criterion-referenced test the performance of an individual is not compared to the performance of others. When individuals are compared to each other someone has to be low (or last) and someone has to be high (or first).

Mastery of the skill gets lost in this comparison of people. Consider that in some situations everyone taking a test may do very poorly against a standard of skill mastery (for example, 90 percent correct). But when individuals are compared to each other, the top achievers seem to be successful. The fact that everyone taking the test has performed unsatisfactorily (if mastery of the skill is the ultimate goal) is obscured. Carried to its logical conclusion, thousands of children could graduate from our schools without having mastered crucial skills, while looking well-educated because they are consistently at the top by comparison with other children.

Tests that give meaning to performance by comparing individuals are called *norm-referenced tests.* These are not related in any direct way to mastery of skills. By their very nature, most norm-referenced tests survey many reading skills rather than assess mastery of any one skill. They are designed to create a range of scores; in fact, they require a range to rank individuals from high to low. Ideally no one will score perfectly on a norm-referenced test; the average performer will miss about one-half the items. These characteristics of norm-referenced tests limit their usefulness to the teacher who is looking for guidance in planning daily instruction. Norm-referenced tests are useful primarily for assessing the overall performance of a group (such as an entire classroom or school), and for classifying children into general achievement groups.

Criterion-referenced tests can assist the teacher in planning the specifics of an instructional program, since they indicate who has mastered a skill and who has not. To reinforce a point made earlier, assessment with criterion-referenced tests is likely to be tied to a teacher's instructional goals.

Recently, many criterion-referenced reading tests have flooded the market. Most new basal reading series include a set of criterion-referenced tests keyed to the skills program. The teacher who wants to use criterion-referenced tests will find his task mainly one of knowing how to use and interpret them. Two cautions should be raised here. First, some criterion-referenced tests attempt to measure distinct factors that may in fact not be separate, measureable skills. The unsuspecting teacher may thus become unduly concerned about minuscle factors which will result in an instructional program that is abstract, unintegrated, and unrelated to reading as a language-based process. Second, the hierarchial arrangement of reading skills assumed by most criterion-referenced tests is questionable. While it's obvious that some skills must precede others, the ideal sequencing of reading skills is unknown and probably nonexistent. The idea that one skill must be mastered before the next is begun, a notion criterion-referenced tests unavoidably reinforce, is inaccurate.

Despite these limitations criterion-referenced tests offer the teacher who is interested in individualizing instruction a valuable alternative to norm-referenced tests. We should point out that most informal measures are criterion-referenced in the sense that they are task-oriented and provide evidence of skill mastery.

Using a Classwide Screening Strategy

The tendency is strong to believe that what is good for one child is good for all. If a certain reading test is useful with Louis and Bill, for example, our natural inclination is to give it to everyone in a class. We should be cautious about such decisions, however, doing only as much formal testing as is absolutely necessary. Tests and time for testing are expensive, each in their own way. Money spent for tests obviously cannot be spent for books or other important resources. Time given to formal testing necessarily comes from instructional time. Children easily tire of tests and fail to perform at their best when testing gets overdone. The consequence is invalid results for many tests, when vaild results from one test would be preferable.

Since informal measures are routinely available for all members of a class, you need a procedure that optimizes the use of formal tests. We recommend that you follow a screening strategy that begins with the use of broad achievement measures on a whole class basis. With this approach the teacher can identify children whose level of performance and general needs are relatively clear. In many cases this requires no special testing because school districts often administer a general achievement battery each fall for administrative purposes (for example, reporting to the state department of public instruction, qualifying for federal funds, identifying curriculum priorities, and so forth).

Following this general assessment further measures of reading that become increasingly specific can be used with those children whose level of performance and needs are not yet so apparent. An inverted pyramid helps visualize the successive levels of approaches to screening (see Figure 6.1). At each level the assessment becomes more detailed and involves fewer children. Economy of time is especially important for the busy classroom teacher who cannot do an in-depth analysis of more than a few youngsters with formal tests.

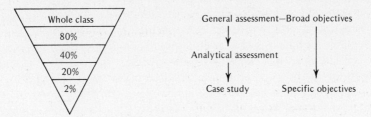

FIGURE 6.1

At each step in the screening procedure more intensive methods are applied to determine the needs of students.

The other advantage of this approach is that some basic achievement information, often needed for initial decisions regarding group placement, can be gathered for everyone in a class.

Formal Reading Tests

Because of their obvious popularity and frequent misuse, formal reading tests require some further discussion. Two general categories—standardized group tests and individual tests—will be presented.

Standardized Group Tests

To review, standardized group tests, or formal tests, are administered under specific conditions following directions given in an examiner's manual. Usually the time period allotted for completing such tests is also standardized. Often the performance of other children on the test is given as norms for the purpose of comparing achievement. Proper use of these instruments can add much to the teacher's understanding of each child's progress and individual needs.

Standardized group tests are helpful to the teacher because they provide information on every child in the class. They correspond to the first level of assessment in Figure 6.1. Achievement batteries—such as the *Iowa Test of Basic Skills, Metropolitan Achievement Tests, SRA Achievement Series,* and the *Stanford Achievement Test*—can be used as initial screening devices. These tests usually give an estimate of general reading levels and several subscores in such areas as vocabulary, deriving paragraph meaning, and study skills. These tests *do not* identify specific strengths and weaknesses in reading, however. It is often a good idea for a teacher to study the errors an individual youngster makes on such tests to obtain some specific information on his performance. Many errors of the same type can alert the teacher to a possible problem. Unfortunately, a teacher seldom has time to do such detailed study for every child in his class. When used with a good ability measure, achievement batteries can help the teacher decide whether a child is doing as well as might be expected in reading.

While the actual number of items a child must complete varies considerably from test to test, and even from section to section in the same test, achievement test batteries typically sample relatively few reading skills and in rather brief fashion. For example, of the sixty test items a third-grader must answer in the reading comprehension section of the *Iowa Test of Basic Skills,* only about five require the child to summarize. Even fewer items require the child to apply critical reading skills. Consequently, the results of such tests must be interpreted in view of this rather important limitation; achievement tests include only a limited number of items on the skills they assess, and even then they do not measure all reading skills. Several items typical of an achievement test are given on page 107.

The second level of screening in Figure 6.1 might be accomplished with reading tests such as the *Gates-MacGinitie Reading Tests; Burnett Reading Series: Survey Test; New Developmental Reading Tests;* or the *California Reading Test.* These instruments are also standardized group tests, but focus

Achievement Test Items

VOCABULARY

Directions: Choose one of the four words that has most nearly the same meaning as the word in heavy black type above them.

1. A short **tale**
   1. end
   2. book
   3. story
   4. period

2. They **seldom** agree
   1. often
   2. never
   3. occasionally
   4. frequently

specifically on reading. Administration of a reading test to youngsters who have unusual results on their achievement battery can provide additional evidence to confirm or challenge the earlier scores. In most cases reading survey tests are longer than the reading section of general achievement batteries and thus sample additional reading behavior. Because of their greater length, they usually measure more consistently.

Group diagnostic tests, such as the *Stanford Diagnostic Reading Test* and the *Silent Reading Diagnostic Tests,* provide another level of screening. With these tests a profile of scores is obtained for each child. Patterns of scores may indicate areas needing special attention or point the way to more detailed analysis with specific skills tests—such as the *McCullough Word Analysis Tests,* the *California Phonics Survey,* or the *Doren Diagnostic Reading Test of Word Recognition.* Because of the time and cost involved in administering, scoring, and interpreting such tests, and the availability of other evidence, not all youngsters need this degree of analysis. It is also important to remember that group tests of the type described here have general, rather broad objectives that often will not correspond exactly to the objectives of the classroom instructional program, thus limiting their usefulness in planning daily lessons.

Individual Reading Tests

A second category of formal measures is individual reading tests. These tests have extensive subtests to determine a child's difficulties in specific skill areas. From a standpoint of providing information that can be translated directly into an instructional program, individual diagnostic tests have real advantages over group tests. They also have one major disadvantage: They require a substantial amount of time to administer. The administration of individual diagnostic tests should be studied and practiced under the supervision of a trained reading specialist. Typically, classroom teachers lack such training, since few undergraduate programs offer sufficient depth in reading instruction to include the use of individual diagnostic reading tests. Some teachers who have returned to college for advanced work may be able to give individual tests.

Ideally, you will be able to refer children who need extensive diagnosis to a reading specialist, who has the time and training necessary to administer one of these tests: *The Durrell Analysis of Reading Difficulty, The Gates-McKillop Diagnostic Tests, Diagnostic Reading Scales,* or *The Woodcock Reading Mastery Tests.* This is not to suggest that classroom teachers should avoid intensive diagnosis, but informal sources of information are readily available on a daily basis and probably are more valuable for identifying needs in the long run.

We should explain that various oral reading tests are available to make individual diagnosis possible. These will be discussed later in Chapter 6 as informal measures.

Evaluating Formal Reading Tests

For a good many years standardized tests have been the tail that wags the dog in reading instruction. Assessment of student progress has too often been limited to an annual administration of an achievement test. Reading groups have often been formed solely on the basis of grade equivalents obtained from standardized tests. Some teachers have unfortunately regarded such tests as sacred measures of their own effectiveness.

Standardized tests have a definite place in a comprehensive evaluation program. They can provide gross measures of overall performance. School districts can use the results of formal tests to make judgments concerning the overall effectiveness of their reading programs. Teachers can use the results of standardized reading tests in conjunction with intelligence tests to determine whether an individual child is performing up to expectancy. Or children who are reading at approximately the same difficulty level can be identified (this is most often the level a child can attain with maximum concentration, not the level at which instruction should be provided) for purposes of grouping. It is important that standardized tests be kept in proper perspective.

In order to understand fully the limitations of standardized tests, how to use them, and how to interpret them, some special training in educational measurement is desirable. We cannot provide that here, but we can make you aware of several valuable sources of information about formal reading measures.

Buros Mental Measurements Yearbook

The *Seventh Mental Measurements Yearbook* (1972) edited by Oscar K. Buros is a comprehensive source of information on standardized tests. One section deals with tests; a second examines books on measurement. We are primarily concerned with the section on tests, where entries are classified by type. One major section is devoted to reading tests; subsections include oral reading, reading readiness, special fields, reading speed, study skills, and miscellaneous reading tests.

Each entry provides the following information about a reading test:

1. Title
2. Description of the groups for which the test is intended
3. Date of copyright
4. Part scores (subtests)
5. Whether test is a group or individual test
6. Whether test is machine scorable
7. Forms, parts, and levels of test
8. Reliability and validity
9. Cost
10. Time required for administration
11. Author
12. Publisher

A test references section—which lists all known references, published and unpublished, on the construction, validity, use, and limitations of the test—follows each entry. Critical reviews of each test are also included. Some of the reviews are written especially for the *Yearbook;* others are published elsewhere and are only excerpted in the *Yearbook.* In either case the views of experts concerning the value of each test are provided.

One can find reviews of achievement batteries, intelligence tests, and tests for certain content areas (for example, mathematics, social studies, and science). The entries on character and personality tests may be of special interest to elementary school teachers.

The purpose of the Buros *Yearbook* is to help those who use standardized tests to select the best of what is available and to interpret correctly the results obtained from the use of the tests. Unfortunately, many teachers fail to use the *Yearbook,* perhaps because they do not know of its existence or because they do not realize the importance of doing so. It is clear from the reviews in the Buros *Yearbook* that the results of some tests are of practically no value, so great are the limitations of these tests, yet they are used and believed in. Classroom teachers must assume responsibility for obtaining the information needed for making judgments about the standardized tests they use.

Buros Volume on Reading Tests

Buros has complied information and reviews on reading tests in *Reading Tests and Reviews* (1969). This volume aids in the task of checking on reading tests. Since information has been taken from the first six volumes of the *Yearbook,* the necessity for following the cross-references used in the original yearbooks is eliminated. A copy of this reference should be available in every school district.

Informal Sources of Information

While every classroom virtually teems with valuable information that can help a teacher identify individual needs, we will describe only eight in detail here. These will serve to illustrate rather than exhaust the possibilities for informal assessment. It is our view that the teacher should approach every classroom activity with assessment in mind. Presumably, lessons or activities are planned because they contribute to the achievement of some identifiable goal the teacher has consciously set and sought. Children's progress toward that goal can be measured in numerous ways. The worksheet, the written assignment, the discussion, the learning center, the reading game, the cross-word puzzle, and so on can all be informal measures, if they are regarded as such.

Informal sources of information are particularly useful in providing continuous assessment of a student's performance, thereby providing the information necessary for prescribing day-by-day corrective instruction. Whereas most group tests measure broad skill areas, informal measures that assess specific skills can be selected and used with certain children. Furthermore, attitudes, tastes, and interests—all of which are difficult to assess by formal means—can be tapped by various informal measures.

Eight categories of informal sources of information will be discussed:

1. workbooks and worksheets
2. conferences
3. checklists and inventories
4. cumulative records
5. oral reading inventories
6. teacher observation
7. cloze procedure
8. trial teaching.

Workbooks and Worksheets Provide Diagnostic Information

Although they are usually regarded as exercises for practice and not as assessment devices, workbooks and worksheets can be extremely effective means for daily evaluation. For example, following the introduction of a new skill the teacher can assign appropriate follow-up exercises in a workbook or provide worksheets on a topic. In addition to providing practice in using the newly learned skill, such a procedure enables the teacher to determine which children might be regrouped for additional instruction, and which need individual attention. Teacher-prepared worksheets can be especially effective, since the special needs of individuals within a class are considered as the instructor writes the exercise.

It should be remembered from the earlier discussion that workbook or worksheet exercises serve the diagnostic function described here only when they match the teacher's instructional goals. Unfortunately, paper-and-pencil tasks are often given to children for the purpose of keeping them occupied quietly in their seats while the teacher is busy with other children. No careful match is made between the needs of the child, the instructional goals, and the workbook task. When this match is absent, the exercise becomes busy work that does little to provide useful diagnostic information. You can avoid this unhappy situation by selecting or developing exercises that tie into your instructional program.

Teacher-student Conferences Provide Opportunities for Assessment

The teacher can use conferences with individual children to gather information that is useful in planning daily instructional activities. Even teachers who depend heavily on grouped instruction should attempt to meet periodically and on a regular basis with each child. Interaction of this sort permits the teacher to know the child personally and identify his needs as no other technique can. The conference is uniquely suited to assessing the child's attitude toward reading, his reading tastes and interests, and his strategy for gaining meaning from the printed page.

Conferences can be structured in various ways to serve different purposes. Activities can range from open-ended discussions of a book the child is reading

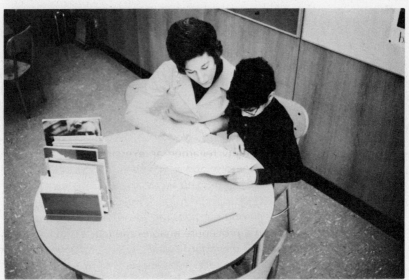

(Holt, Rinehart and Winston photo by Russell Dian)

FIGURE 6.2   Teacher-student conference

Regular teacher-student conferences on a one-to-one basis will give encouragement and information to both participants.

independently to in-depth analysis of oral reading performance. Other examples of possible conference activities include checking skill development, reviewing previously learned skills, clarifying misunderstanding, and reinforcing progress. The teacher who enters each conference with specific objectives in mind will be in a good position to decide what should be done to accomplish those objectives. While some activities may be strictly diagnostic, others may be instructional.

Not to be underestimated is the value of the child coming to have a pleasant association between reading and working individually with the teacher in a relaxed conference setting. This alone can be instrumental in building positive attitudes toward reading. The tutorial setting of a conference is also well suited to helping the child be successful with reading tasks in that complete adjustment to individual needs is possible even if it is only for a brief period of time. Insights gained from a concentrated ten-minute session every second or third week can assist the teacher in adjusting to a child's individual needs within those group or assigned independent activities conducted between conferences.

The frequency and length of conferences is an open-ended matter which depends on various factors. Some teachers prefer shorter, more frequent conferences; other believe longer conferences are better, even if they cannot be held as often. The teacher's use of groups, the materials selected for instruction, the age and ability of the children, and the experience of the teacher are all examples of factors that affect the scheduling and use of conferences. We suggest you start slowly and build up to a frequency that suits your style of teaching and the children's learning.

One useful strategy is to begin with conferences that are intended to explore personal interests and attitudes. A simple questionnaire can be used to help you ask pertinent questions (for example, "What hobbies do you have?"). Later, a series of conferences can focus on the reading children are doing for recreation. Questions can be general and largely open-ended (for example, "Why did you choose this book? What did you like about the book?"). Gradually you can add features to the conferences that supply needed information on skills growth. Comprehension questions can become more specific (for example, "Which character in the book would you want for a friend? Why?"). You can survey vocabulary and word recognition skills; the child can read a paragraph orally from a book.

Conferences are extremely helpful as a means of gathering important information. Unfortunately, much of the information can slip away if it is not recorded. While a narrative summary can always be written and dropped in a folder for each child following a conference, this is a time-consuming way to keep records. Teachers often employ another type of informal measure, the checklist or inventory, to record their findings and observations in a conference.

Checklists and Inventories Tie Directly to Instructional Objectives

Checklists and inventories are little more than lists of questions or skills that require a brief response or simple check to complete. They can be prepared for practically any aspect of reading instruction and may be completed by either teacher or child, depending on their purpose.

A sample inventory is given below to illustrate what can be done.

Interest Inventory Record

NAME _____

What games do you like to play best of all? _____
What other games do you like? _____
What do you like to make? _____
Do you have pets? _____
What things do you collect? _____
What are your hobbies? _____
Suppose you could have one wish which might come true, what would
    it be? _____
What is your favorite television program? _____
What other television programs do you watch? _____
What is the best book you ever read? _____
What other books have you liked? _____
Do you have any books of your own? About how many? _____
Does anyone read to you? How often? _____
Do you go to the library? _____
Do you read comic books? What is your favorite comic book? _____
What magazines or newspapers do you like best? _____
What kind of work do you want to do when you finish school? _____
What school subject do you like best? _____
What school subject do you like least? _____

This inventory is completed by the child and provides the teacher with information that may be valuable in planning instructional activities. Obviously books or stories can be found to capitalize on the interests revealed through this inventory. Children's attitudes, travel experiences, home background, and various other matters can be surveyed in this way.

Checklists can be developed that itemize the various elements in some area of reading instruction. This becomes, in effect, a statement of instructional goals. The child's progress toward mastery of each element can be noted on the checklist as a way of keeping records. The teacher can tell at a glance where work remains to be done or, by looking at a class summary sheet, who might be grouped together for a special lesson. A sample checklist is given below.

Common Prefixes

_____ knows the meaning of the following prefixes:
Child's name

Yes	No		Comments
		un	
		de	
		re	
		pre	
		non	
		tri	
		bi	
		post	
		ultra	

Checklists and inventories are valuable on a whole-class basis. Information gathered with these devices enables the teacher to adjust his program in a variety of ways in order to maximize individualized instruction. Examples of checklists and questionnaires, as well as other informal measures, will be presented throughout this text, and their use in special skill areas will be discussed.

The Cumulative Record Can Be Useful

The cumulative record is sometimes a source of useful information that has been compiled in previous years. The results of formal testing are normally recorded in the cumulative record. More important, the observations of the child's previous teachers are often reported, as well as pertinent information concerning health, attendance, and home background. The results of referral for special testing or training, if this occurs, are contained in most cumulative records.

You should be careful about letting the observations of a child's previous teacher prejudice your appraisal. With the proper precautions, the cumulative record file can provide much insight, possibly even showing where one teacher's personal perceptions of a child may have had adverse effects on his classroom performance. An in-depth study of one child often begins with the information contained in the cumulative folder.

Assessment with the Oral Reading Inventory

Both tradition and common sense suggest that a child's oral reading performance is an index of his reading ability. The reasoning seems to be that one who has difficulty reading aloud evidently has some problem that careful observation and analysis will reveal. There is some truth to this belief, but there is also much fiction.

Given appropriate training a teacher can learn much about a child's reading level, as well as his specific needs, by analyzing his oral reading performance. The procedure is far more complex than it appears at first glance, however. The time-honored custom of counting each "error" the child makes as he reads aloud in order to calculate his success is under widespread attack— and deservedly so. Before getting into the details of how oral reading performance should be interpreted, let's look at the nature and content of oral reading inventories. Discussion elsewhere in this book deals with oral reading that is not primarily for purposes of assessment.

Paragraphs Increase in Difficulty

Oral reading inventories are all very similar. They include a series of paragraphs that begin at a simple level and gradually increase in difficulty. Grade designations are usually assigned to each level. The child's task is to read a paragraph aloud and then recall what he read in his own words, answer specific questions about what he read, or do a combination of both. This occurs in a conference setting where distractions are kept to a minimum. The teacher's task is to make a written record on a second copy of the material of just what the child does as he reads and how well the child recalls the details afterward. With this technique the teacher tries to identify what level of material the child can handle successfully. Although criteria differ in terms of specifics, generally the instructional level is defined as that where comprehension and word recognition accuracy indicate the child is not overburdened. Powell (1968) recommends these specific criteria:

		Word recognition accuracy	Comprehension questions
Frustration reading level	Grades 1–2	84% or less	50% or less correct
	Grades 3–6	90% or less	50% or less correct
Instructional reading level	Grades 1–2	85–95%	60–70% correct
	Grades 3–6	91–94%	60–70% correct
Independent reading level	Grades 1–2	96% or above	80% or above correct
	Grades 3–6	95% or above	80% or above correct

The most obvious application of this procedure is in identifying what level of material children should read in the instructional program. Caution must be used in accepting the level indicated by this procedure, because the materials used for instruction may be graded differently than the oral reading inventory is. A 3.0 level on a commercially prepared inventory may not equal a 3.0 level in reading series P, Q, or R.

Skills Needs Can Also Be Identified

In addition to indicating something about the child's reading level, an oral reading inventory can be used to identify specific skill needs. The word recognition miscues[1] recorded by the teacher often follow a pattern. One child may consistently miss word endings, for example, or another child may skip words according to some discernable pattern (all words of three or more syllables in length).

The value of identifying patterns of miscues is that the teacher is alerted and begins to look for explanations for the behavior. Some oral reading problems are purely ones of oral fluency, and do not signal an underlying reading deficiency. The solution is one of improving the child's skills of oral interpretation. Other oral reading problems should alert the teacher to genuine instructional needs. When this is the case, appropriate corrective instruction is needed. A third explanation of oral reading miscues is that they may simply reflect the child's attempts to match his language with the language of the author. It is this possibility that makes oral reading diagnosis complex and potentially misleading to the teacher who does not understand the psycholinguistic aspects of reading.

It is not possible to explore the topic of oral reading miscues from a psycholinguistic viewpoint in sufficient detail here to do it justice. Some aspects of the relationship will be discussed in subsequent chapters and this will provide some additional insight. We will discuss here the implications of psycholinguistics for oral reading diagnosis as it fits into the issues being raised on assessment.

Oral Reading Miscues Reveal the Child's Reading Strategy

Reading is a process in which the reader scans printed symbols on a page for the purpose of retrieving meaning. The reader comes to this task with a lifetime of personal experiences to draw on and an intuitive understanding of how language operates. Drawing on his experiences and language, the reader uses cues from the page to understand the writer's message. As he scans, the reader predicts meaning. When he predicts well, he comprehends well. When his predictions are wrong, meaning breaks down and he must reread to pick up cues he needs to predict correctly.

The reading process viewed in this way is not a precise word-by-word

---

[1]A miscue is any oral response made by the child as he reads which differs from the expected response.

processing of the printed page. Quite the opposite. It is an imprecise searching process involving educated guesswork on the part of the reader. Every word is not processed. In fact, the better the reader is at predicting, the fewer cues he needs to read with understanding. His experience with the topic and his ability with language are more important than his skill at recognizing all of the individual words on the page.

The implications of this view of reading are many and far reaching; for the topic at hand, they are significant. As a child reads aloud the printed symbols trigger his speech. When the language of the reader differs from the language of the author the result is a miscue. Often the reader who is gaining meaning will correct himself, thus indicating he knows his attempt was incorrect. Other miscues may not be corrected, yet they do not alter the meaning of what is read and in that sense are not wrong. An oral reading diagnosis that simply counts errors without regard to their nature fails to reflect what is known about language and reading. In effect, not all miscues are equal, and any diagnosis that seeks to truly understand what the reader is doing well and what he is not doing well must involve some miscue analysis.

Deciding What Constitutes a Genuine Error

Some disagreement over what should be counted as an oral reading error is apparent in the directions for scoring the *Gray Oral Reading Test* and the *Gilmore Oral Reading Test*. Table 6.1 contrasts the categories of errors for these two tests. General agreement is found for five types of errors: Aid, omission, insertion, substitution, and repetition. Mispronunciation is an error according to either scheme; however, the *Gray* system differentiates between partial and gross mispronunciation. The *Gray* also calls an inversion a specific type of error; the *Gilmore* shows an inversion as a mispronunciation only. The *Gilmore* has special categories for disregarding punctuation and for hesitation.

TABLE 6.1   Comparison of Errors Recorded on *Gray* and *Gilmore* Tests

Errors recorded in the *Gray Oral Reading Test*	Errors recorded in the *Gilmore Oral Reading Test*
1. Aid	1. Word pronounced by examiner
2. Gross mispronunciation	2. Mispronunciation
3. Partial mispronunciation	3. Omission
4. Omission	4. Insertion
5. Insertion	5. Substitution
6. Substitution	6. Disregard of punctuation
7. Repetition	7. Repetition
8. Inversion	8. Hesitation

Disagreement over what constitutes an oral reading error is not limited to the *Gray* and *Gilmore* tests. Other oral reading tests—such as subtests of the *Durrell Analysis of Reading Difficulty* and the *Spache Diagnostic Reading*

Scales—contain other definitions of what constitutes an error. For example, the *Durrell* instructs the examiner to count as errors all words that are repeated. The *Spache* counts repetitions as errors only when two or more words are repeated. The *Durrell* counts any hesitation as an error; the *Spache* does not.

What causes this apparent confusion? When is an oral reading "error" really worth counting and when is it only a momentary stumble, a speech pattern, or some miscue related to the stress of reading orally? This question can best be answered in terms of the purpose of identifying miscues; namely, to provide a basis for improving reading performance. An oral reading miscue that interferes with the message or indicates an inability to attack an unknown word should be counted as a genuine error. Omitting *not* from a sentence changes the meaning of a message considerably and constitutes a serious error, especially if it is not corrected by the reader. Adding *and* to a sentence is unlikely to interfere with the message and can probably be ignored as an indicator of any serious reading problem.

Consider this situation: Juan is asked to read the sentence, "A bird hopped across the grass." Instead, he reads: "A robin hopped across the green grass." Even though Juan's version is different than the written one, he evidently understands what he is reading. In fact, one might argue that Juan's version is more vivid and descriptive than the written one, thus suggesting extraordinary comprehension.

Contrast Juan's reading with Karl's, who says: "A bird hopped across the run." A tabulation of errors would show:

Juan—2 errors
Karl—1 error.

Juan's miscues "make sense." Karl's indicate something serious; he does not correct a miscue that is grammatically incorrect, the substitution involves a word with a different meaning, and the words look different.

The *Reading Miscue Inventory* (Goodman and Burke, 1972) gives extensive directions for analyzing miscues. The *RMI* requires that nine specific questions be asked about every miscue:

1. Is a dialect variation involved in the Miscue?
2. Is a shift in intonation involved in the Miscue?
3. How much does the Miscue look like what was expected?
4. How much does the Miscue sound like what was expected?
5. Is the grammatical function of the Miscue the same as the grammatical function of the word in the text?
6. Is the Miscue corrected?
7. Does the Miscue occur in a structure which is grammatically acceptable?
8. Does the Miscue occur in a structure which is semantically acceptable?
9. Does the Miscue result in a change of meaning?

Goodman and Burke are interested in the nature of the child's responses in oral reading from a psycholinguistic perspective. Their view is based on the idea that all miscues are not of equal importance. In fact, some miscues may provide positive proof of a child's reading skill. For example, some substitutions may fit into the syntax of a sentence and not affect meaning (for example, Juan's substitution of robin for bird). Miscues of this type can indicate that the child is making heavy use of context and comprehending the message as he reads. Additional evidence to support this view is obtained when other substitutions that alter the meaning of a sentence, or fail to fit into the syntax of the sentence, are corrected by the child.

The classroom teacher can apply these general principles to interpreting oral reading miscues without engaging in an extensive analysis. At times the thorough analysis of reading samples may be justified for a few individuals.

A special word is needed concerning the assessment of oral reading miscues of children with regional or subcultural dialects. Some teachers unwittingly record and score as reading errors pronunciations that "sound wrong" to them. For example, *that* pronounced *dat* is sometimes scored as a mispronunciation. In view of our earlier recommendation concerning what to regard as a genuine reading error, pronunciations learned in a particular region of the country or in a particular cultural group should not be regarded as reading errors.

The translation of graphic symbols into their oral counterparts depends largely on the reader's background of experience and resulting language patterns. For example, Kasdon (1968) reports that black subjects in a study of oral reading consistently read *was* for *were* and sometimes pronounced *with* as *wif*. Latin Americans frequently substituted "b" for "p," as in *bet* for *pet,* and "v" for "b," as in *vrilliant* for *brilliant.* There can be no doubt that these subjects were reading, if reading is defined as gaining meaning from the printed page. Regarding these "mispronunciations" as *reading errors* is indefensible.

Oral Reading Inventories

Teachers can make their own oral reading inventories by taking paragraphs from materials they use for instruction, arranging them in order of difficulty, and developing questions or standards for judging comprehension. Such inventories are called *informal reading inventories* (IRI) and have the advantage of being truly representative of the material children will read daily. Many publishers now provide such an IRI for use with their basal series.

There are also a number of commercially prepared oral reading inventories that are similar in design and purpose. These include the *Gray Oral Reading Test,* the *Gilmore Oral Reading Test, Classroom Reading Inventory,* and the *Standard Reading Inventory.* These inventories provide instructions for administration and some information on interpretation. Some also provide norms—a feature of questionable value. The fact that two or three forms are usually included in oral reading inventories is laudable. This permits retesting and makes them useful for assessment of a child's progress over a period of time.

SCORING SYSTEMS FOR ORAL READING INVENTORIES

No two oral reading inventories have exactly the same system for recording miscues. Few oral reading tests are even in agreement on what should be recorded. Let us propose a scoring system that you can use with any IRI.

The *Gray* test requires that a line be drawn under any word not read by the child within ten seconds; the examiner then provides the word. The *Gilmore* requires that a check be made above a word not recognized by the child within five seconds and that two checks be made if the examiner then provides the word after five additional seconds. Is one system better than the other? Probably not. What is important is that a scoring system be simple. It must be memorized easily and used quickly. Elaborate marks cannot be made by a teacher as the child races along a line of print. Consequently, checks, circles, underlining, and similar marks are best. We recommend this following system:

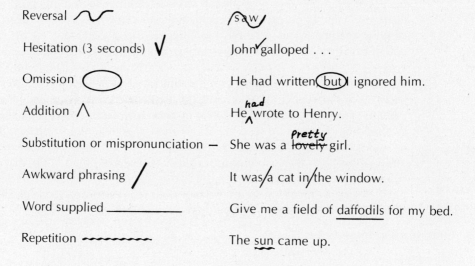

Reversal	/saw/
Hesitation (3 seconds)	John⌄galloped . . .
Omission	He had written (but) ignored him.
Addition	He ⌄had wrote to Henry.
Substitution or mispronunciation	She was a ~~lovely~~ pretty girl.
Awkward phrasing	It was/a cat in/the window.
Word supplied	Give me a field of <u>daffodils</u> for my bed.
Repetition	The <u>sun</u> came up.

Note what word-attack skills the child tries to use when faced with an unfamiliar word.

Use of this scoring system is demonstrated on p. 121. No serious reading difficulties are evident in this sample. In two instances (*quickly* and *jockey*) the reader did not attempt to pronounce a word. Other words with the same beginning consonants might be presented to this child to determine whether he is able to associate any sound with these symbols.

Oral reading can be an excellent source of information. Its greatest value is that the teacher can watch for certain behaviors as the need arises. Furthermore, the goals of the instructional program can easily influence what is observed. Goals can be adjusted as oral reading diagnosis reveals the instructional needs of children. This is true because the teacher is so actively involved in this kind of assessment.

Oral Reading Sample

The bay horse moved <u>quickly</u> to the inside of the track. Mud flew up from his hooves as he hit the soft, wet ground. ~~Several~~ *Some* other horses raced alongside the big bay, *horse* forcing him to run near the rail. Slowly the jockey moved his horse away from the soft ground (and) back to the firm *place* ~~part~~ of the racetrack.

As the/crowd cheered/the bay caught and passed the/leaders. Ahead, the finish line waited./Victory looked certain.

Teacher Observation

Teacher observation provides another means for gathering information on children's needs. We regard teacher observation as the single most important element in an evaluation program. In a single day the classroom teacher has countless opportunities to appraise the progress and needs of each learner. The teacher also has the opportunity to synthesize the diagnostic data gathered from all other sources and adjust his observations to fill in missing information. With the press of daily responsibilities, however, teacher observation often fails to provide the information desired.

This discrepancy between the potential and actual value of teacher observation can be overcome by three valuable techniques:

1. systematic observation
2. anecdotal records
3. samples of products.

Systematic Observation

The variety of activities occurring during a reading lesson, plus the number of children in a typical classroom, combine to form a complex set of interactions for the teacher to observe. It is essential that specific purposes for observation be outlined ahead of time. The teacher must decide on which child or children he will focus his attention and during which activities. These factors are determined by the need for information. For example, if test data, workbook performance, and daily work all point to specific instructional needs for a given child, the teacher may wish to confirm this information with his own observations. Through planning, systematic observations can be conducted. Haphazard observation on an incidental basis usually provides little useful information.

An example of systematic observation for a predetermined purpose may be helpful here. Suppose a teacher notices one of his students confusing the prefixes *pre* and *pro* in workbook assignment. By looking at an achievement test given in the fall, the teacher finds several vocabulary items answered incorrectly when *pre* is used, but several others of the same type are correct. He also recalls a tendency on the part of this student to occasionally substitute the wrong prefix during oral reading. In view of this information the teacher has a conference with the child to correct any misconceptions and thereafter pays special attention when the opportunity to observe this skill occurs. Evidence of continued confusion should lead to further instruction.

Anecdotal Records

Teacher observations can be further systematized by the use of rather simple anecdotal record-keeping. Pertinent observations concerning an individual child, gathered in either a systematic or incidental manner, are entered in a notebook or noted on file cards. During the press of daily duties a word or phrase can be noted on a slip of paper to aid in recall. Later, more explanation and detail can be written into a child's record. Patterns of behavior may emerge in such records, and careful documentation relieves the teacher of trying to recall all significant related incidents. Such records are often useful on a broader scale than simply for reading instruction. A sample anecdotal record appears below:

Sample Anecdotal Record

Ricky Owens
_____
NAME

September 2— Rickey brought a book from home to share with the class. He read orally with excellent expression and phrasing. Title: *Rasmus and the Vagabond.*

September 12— Especially interested in basal reader story, "Hide Rack," story of a dog. *Note:* Check to see if he has read *Big Red* by James Kjelgaard.

October 14— Workbook poorly done. Careless errors. *Note:* Watch Ricky to see if this reading group is too slow for him.

October 18— Moved Rickey to top group. Seems very pleased and anxious to succeed. His best friend George is in this group. This may be troublesome.

November 7— Absent today. Missed introduction to Dewey Decimal System. *Note:* Give Ricky individual help and a special worksheet to check his understanding.

November 21— Very emotional today. Disturbed his reading group during independent work. Check with principal to see if there are any known problems at home.

November 22— New brother born yesterday. Ricky is proud *and* more normal today.
December 4— Achievement test results indicate a deficiency in vocabulary. Use listening post and vocabulary-building record to begin corrective program.

Samples of Products

Samples of the child's work collected over a period of time can be especially valuable in evaluating a learner. Patterns of errors can be readily identified by this procedure, and progress can also be documented. Samples of work should be gathered in specific skill areas or spread across a broad range of skills, depending on the progress of an individual child. The simplest procedure for assembling a collection of products is to develop a folder for each child. Periodically a product from every member of the class can be filed; at other times a particularly revealing or timely product can be filed for individual children (*see* Figure 6.3 on page 124).

Information for individualizing instruction does not come from a single source, nor does it all arrive at one time. The instruments and techniques described in this section are used jointly and continuously to provide the information needed for properly individualizing instruction. As stated earlier, specific application of diagnostic procedures and techniques in specific skill areas will be made throughout the text.

The Cloze Procedure Is a Versatile Diagnostic Tool

A classroom teacher can gather useful and revealing information about a child's reading performance with the use of the *cloze procedure*. Cloze is a term derived from "closure," which refers to the human tendency to fill in or complete pictures, sentences, or other stimuli which are incomplete. For example, you are inclined to complete the following sentence by inserting the missing word: "A flock of ducks flew overhead as the sun sank slowly in the _____." Past experience and your psychological processes cause you to add "West" or some other synonym in the open slot. Similarly, pictures, such as the ones below, are "filled-in" and perceived as wholes by the mind:

You are aware that parts are missing, to be sure, but you perceive the whole nevertheless.

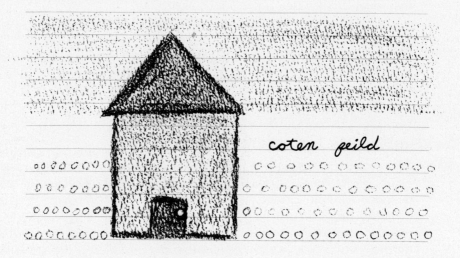

Reading

Martha   March 18

> Frederick Douglas
> fights for freedom
> is about Frederick Douglas
> born sometime in Febuary.
> He was born as a slave in the
> South.

coten peild

FIGURE 6.3   A child's daily work

This sample of a child's daily work reveals a good deal about the child's comprehension of a story. Children's illustrations are useful sources of diagnostic data.

This human tendency to bring closure has led to the use of the cloze procedure in identifying, measuring, and improving comprehension, and in assessing language competence. By determining how effectively a child can supply words that have been deleted from a passage, you gain a measure of how much difficulty he is having with the concepts and language it presents.

To illustrate, suppose you are interested in knowing which children in a class can be expected to profit from reading a book you have selected. You then follow these steps:

what a book,
what level.

1. Take a passage from the selection of at least 275 words that is not dependent on previous information from the story or book. (The beginning of a section or chapter is usually appropriate.)
2. Begin with the second sentence and delete every fifth word if you are working with upper-grade children, every tenth word if you are working with lower-grade children.
3. Type up the entire passage putting a blank in place of each deleted word. Be sure to make each blank the same length and leave enough space for children to write in their answers.

Your cloze passage is now ready to be completed by the students. Give each child a copy of the passage and ask him to write words that he thinks belong there in each of the blanks. Be sure to explain that you realize this is not easy, and it will be necessary for the child to guess occasionally. Encourage "educated guessing," based on what makes sense. Indicate that all blanks should be completed. Provide sufficient time for every child to finish the entire passage.

Next, compare the child's responses to the words that were deleted. Research with the cloze procedure suggests that you should rigidly adhere to the wording of the original passage in scoring the child's responses. The reason for being fairly strict about counting synonyms wrong is that the criteria developed for interpreting student performance are based on rigid scoring procedures. When you deviate by counting a synonym correct you introduce a subjective variable that influences the results. Since you are usually after a general sense of the child's reading ability when you use this procedure, and are not conducting a research investigation, your judgment concerning what to count as correct or incorrect is appropriate.

Students able to replace correctly 41 percent or more of the words deleted will normally be able to read the book without undue difficulty. Those who get less than 41 percent correct will probably find the book too hard to read. By studying the types of errors each child makes, you can gain further insight into their instructional needs. Many teachers obtain useful information by asking individuals to explain how they arrived at their answers. This can reveal much about the child's reading abilities.

A series of cloze procedures can be developed—one from each level of a basal series, for example—to determine where each child should be placed for daily instruction. You can experiment with this assessment procedure to determine what scoring criteria and procedures are most appropriate for the instructional program in your classroom.

Rankin and Culhane (1969) established these criteria for interpreting the results of children's performances on cloze passages:

Independent level—The student correctly replaces 61 percent or more of the deleted words.

Instructional level—The student correctly replaces 41 to 60 percent of the deleted words.

Frustrational level—The student correctly replaces 40 percent or less of the deleted words.

A sample cloze passage taken from this text is given below. Using these criteria you should be able to correctly replace *eleven* words:

An index is an alphabetical list of names, subjects, events, and so on, together with page numbers, and is usually placed at the end of a book. By consulting the index 1. _____ reader can locate exactly 2. _____ in a book the 3. _____ that he wants is 4. _____. Because of its utility 5. _____ index is one of 6. _____ most frequently used features 7. _____ many reference volumes. The 8. _____ of an almanac, for 9. _____, would be most unwieldly 10. _____ an index.

By the 11. _____ grades the increased use 12. _____ reading in the content 13. _____ will necessitate instruction on 14. _____ use of the index. 15. _____ must begin with the 16. _____ and move to the 17. _____ complex. At first, simply 18. _____ specific terms in the 19. _____ index and noting a 20. _____ page number is appropriate. 21. _____, using cross references, identifying 22. _____ that might provide information 23. _____ a topic, and employing 24. _____indexes for the same 25. _____ can be undertaken. The 26. _____ exercise illustrates an activity 27. _____ using the index.

WORDS DELETED:

1. a, 2. where, 3. information, 4. located, 5. the, 6. the, 7. of, 8. use, 9. example, 10. without, 11. intermediate, 12. of, 13. areas, 14. the, 15. Instruction, 16. simple, 17. more, 18. locating, 19. alphabetical, 20. specific, 21. Later, 22. entries, 23. on, 24. multiple, 25. book, 26. following, 27. on

---

Trial Teaching Yields Another Kind of Information

Trial teaching is a technique that can be helpful in gaining information about a child's needs and learning style. The label *trial teaching* is actually quite self-explanatory. The teacher identifies a skill or bit of information previous diagnosis has indicated the child needs to learn. A lesson is planned to achieve the desired goal and instruction is provided. By noting the child's responses, the teacher is able to see how prerequisite learning is applied and where confusion or misinformation creates a problem. The teacher can also note how the child goes about learning new information or skills. With insights gained from these observations the teacher can adjust subsequent instruction to draw on the child's strengths.

Typically, trial teaching is most effective in a one-to-one setting. The reading clinician often employs this technique in working with a reading disabled child, for example. Insights can be gained from watching a child tackle a learning task that no test of recall or application of skills will reveal. The conference setting is an ideal one for trial teaching.

Let's look at an example. Teacher Rhoda Howsam has noticed that Jackie has difficulty in reading maps. At their next reading conference Rhoda presents Jackie with information concerning how to interpret a road map. Symbols for a bridge, railroad, highway, and city are introduced. Jackie is asked to find an example of each on a map. Rhoda notices that Jackie confuses the symbols because she does not know how to interpret the map legend. Rhoda also discovers that unless the symbols are matched with pictures (symbol ⊨ with a picture of a bridge, for example), Jackie confuses them. As a result Rhoda learns that certain prerequisite information is not understood and that Jackie needs vivid visual stimuli to form the necessary perceptual images. Thereafter, Rhoda plans instruction for Jackie that allows for these factors. Thus trial teaching has provided information that is immediately applied in the instructional program.

SUMMARY

In order to individualize reading instruction the classroom teacher must have information about each child's reading performance. Assessment can be undertaken with formal and informal measures to identify the child's instructional reading level and individual pattern of strengths and weaknesses. To be useful in planning daily classroom activities, assessment must relate to the teacher's instructional goals. Informal measures are usually more helpful in this respect than formal ones.

Diagnostic information can be gathered from everyday activities, such as workbook assignments, conferences, and oral reading performance. The cloze procedure and trial teaching can also yield valuable information regarding student progress and needs.

Terms for Self Study

criterion-referenced test	informal measure
norm-referenced test	cloze procedure
instructional reading level	checklist
reading miscue	questionnaire
formal measure	anecdotal record

1. Why is individualization of reading instruction heavily dependent upon thorough and continued diagnosis?
2. Mr. Humbert is preparing for a parent-teacher conference. He wants to show Mr. and Mrs. Walker what progress their son, Mark, has made over the course of the school year. How would you suggest he proceed? Why?

part III

Initial Reading

The printed page is comprised of symbols that represent language. In order to read the child obviously needs to break the alphabet code. To accomplish this the child must apply what he or she knows about language to a system of written symbols. This part of the book contains chapters dealing with perception, visual memory, and decoding. Depending on the child, these skills may develop at different rates, at different ages, and in different ways. Subsequent growth in reading is built upon these initial reading skills.

7

Visual and Auditory Discrimination and Perception

"Ready or not, here I come!"

This cry from a children's game also applies to a child coming to school. It fits in two ways: whether or not the teacher is ready to meet him as an individual, he is still coming; whether or not he is ready for the "grade" that he is put in, he is still coming. These are the conditions of a compulsory educational system.

How often do teachers wonder where to start when faced with a class of beginning readers or when confronted with a class of older children, some of whom have not yet learned to read? Should the teacher check the student's vocabulary, give him two dozen words to memorize, teach him the ABC's, or give him a picture book to see if he can "read" pictures?

Since reading is an activity requiring a combination of skills, there must be some that are starter skills. What skills would you choose as *initial reading skills?* Try to establish an order of priority among the following by numbering items from one to eight. The child is able to:

---

look at a picture and tell the story of the picture.

pronounce instantaneously two dozen sight words.

identify a sentence.

identify and name the alphabet letters.

through pictures indicate the meaning of at least three hundred words used in
the school reading program
identify his own name and address in print.
hear and distinguish various word sounds.
associate concepts in first readers with his own experience.

Priorities—Concept and Skills

Though there is no "correct" order to the preceding list of beginning reading skills, there is enough to distinguish each so as to decide which has higher priority. Sometimes a child in class may confound any system of priorities. Nonetheless a list of priorities gives a sense of order and helps a teacher in observing and selecting instructional techniques. First of all the child needs to understand that reading is similar to having an idea in your head and describing it, as he would in telling the story of a picture he sees. He needs to understand that the marks on a page are letters of the alphabet and that together they form written words. He can hear differences in words, and he can learn words, just as he has learned his own name and address.

He should know that the printed page contains a story or a message using words and phrases similar to those he uses every day. He should know that he can decipher the message by learning to discriminate among the symbols on the page and associating them with the language sounds that he himself makes. He should know that he is to use his own experience to bring meaning to the words on the page. To get ready for reading a child needs these concepts and the skills necessary to make the concepts operational. A sense of storytelling, a small working vocabulary, the ability to discriminate among speech sounds, and the ability to discriminate among the letters of the alphabet are crucial skills in the initial stages of learning to read.

With those thoughts in mind a workable list of priorities can be constructed from the eight skills:

Priority	Skill
1. look at a picture and tell its story	
2. identify name and address in print	
3. associate concepts in first readers with experience	
4. pronounce two dozen sight words	
5. hear and distinguish word sounds	
6. identify and name alphabet letters	
7. identify a sentence	
8. indicate meaning of at least three hundred words used in school reading program by using pictures.	

But remember, there is no absolutely "correct" order. The list given here may or may not match the list that any reader of this text puts together.

This chapter focuses on initial word skills. The most obvious ones are related to auditory and visual discrimination. The question of reading readiness is also explored. The child needs perceptions; that is, meaningful images or impressions based upon what he sees and hears. (Refer back to Figure 2.2 for the place the perceptual image occupies in the reading process.) The role of maturation in the development of perception is treated, along with the specific visual and auditory symbols that enable humans to discriminate among the written and auditory symbols which enable humans to communicate through language. Means of evaluating and developing visual and auditory discrimination are also described.

Visual discrimination refers to the ability to note differences through vision, while *auditory discrimination* refers to the ability to note differences through hearing. *Perception* refers to the ability to construct an image or give meaning to what is seen or heard. The word discrimination should not be confused with acuity. Visual and auditory acuity denote the ability of the sense organs to receive impressions; that is, to see and to hear. Evidently, acuity is a prerequisite to discrimination.

Ready to Learn

At what stage in his development is a child ready to learn to read? This question may seem academic, since most children are introduced to reading in Grade 1. In many areas, however, reading education for all children of nursery-school age is being seriously considered. The federal government has attempted to overcome environmental deficits by early education programs for disadvantaged children, and more and more parents are teaching their children to read before they arrive in Grade 1. Thus the whole question of *reading readiness* is pertinent and significant to the educational process. Teachers and administrators must decide when instruction should begin, when and how each child is reading, and which methods to use for specific individuals in teaching them to read.

Background and Learning

Every human being brings some background experience to a new task. That background assists him in acquiring new knowledge and skill. Whether the learner is a graduate student or a six-year-old, the teacher makes certain assumptions before beginning instruction and adjusts the instruction according to what he discovers about the background of the learner. No one learns well unless he can bring enough knowledge and maturity to the task to grasp it and to see its significance (Ilg and Ames, 1965). In this sense there is a readiness factor in all learning. Through an assessment of background emphasis can be placed on the student and learning instead of on the teacher and teaching.

Too often a child's readiness for reading is measured in terms of physical-motor development and cognitive development. Tests of hearing, vision, motor coordination, vocabulary, and school-related concepts are administered by the teacher. But the child's interests, attitudes, and emotional behavior are ignored. It is important in the early stages of reading to determine what interests a child, what his attitudes toward school and books are, and what social-emotional responses he gives to typical events in school. It makes quite a difference in motivating a child to learn to read whether or not he has developed an interest in specific kinds of children's stories, has heard from relatives and friends that school and books are exciting, and has learned to listen and to share among members of a group. In order to personalize the initial stages of reading instruction the instructional plan must take these factors into account.

Even though many basal reader series include readiness tests for each grade level, most people think of readiness as belonging to kindergarten or the first grade. Typically, there is a readiness period in the kindergarten-first grade years. This has often been looked upon as a period of socialization for the youngster, a time to acquaint him with the behaviors that will help him succeed in daily school life. During this period an attempt is made to help him develop certain ordinary experiences and concepts that the child will be using in his early academic endeavors. Such an experience might be learning what a firefighter does and how the city is kept safe from fires. Concepts may include

FIGURE 7.1 A child's interests are important in his learning to read.

little versus *big, dark* versus *light,* and so on. The identification of certain basic shapes and forms, such as circles and squares, and the names of the numerals and the letters of the alphabet are usually included in the readiness program.

Some educators have questioned the need for the school to offer these kinds of experiences to all children (Ilg and Ames, 1965, p. 5). It is pointed out that watching television and traveling may well provide most of the early readiness experiences once offered in the school for many children. This is an assumption that the wise teacher will want to test, for children's environments, which dictate these experiences, vary considerably. Some children acquire a wide range of valuable perceptions through only a minimum of contact with them, while others require repeated contacts. Some children defy the group pattern because a parent reads to them or takes them to library programs. Nonetheless, it is necessary for the teacher to take time to diagnose the very beginnings of learning—just as he would do at some further point along the sequence of reading skills.

Interest in the Child

Educators sometimes become so concerned with statistical averages that they fail to look at the individual child. Ilg and Ames of the Gesell Institute of Child Development at Yale University have said: "Education sometimes seems to be interested in everything except the child" (1965, p. 5). This harsh indictment comes from their observation that a compulsory attendance age for first grade often brings with it instruction aimed at the "average child"—a statistical phenomenon and not a real entity. They point out that to be successful, the teacher must keep three factors in mind: first, the age and level of maturation of the child; second, the unique individuality of the child; and third, the specific environment of the child (Ilg and Ames, 1965, p. 6). The meshing and interrelating of these factors constitutes the person of the learner and the perceptions of the world that he brings to school. The need to accommodate the learning environment to that learner is all the more crucial at the early stages, for it is then that attitudes and patterns of behavior toward school and learning may be set for years to come.

Development of Perception

Since developmental factors, individual capabilities, and environmental influences all contribute to the child's ability to cope with any learning task, all three should be examined by the teacher who wants to lead the child forward and not just see that he marks time. Developmental aspects of growth are described in other texts such as Ilg and Ames (1965) and Piaget (1952). The developmental problem most often discussed in relation to reading is the capability of the child's eyes to accommodate to the printed page. There is a divergence of opinion as to the average best age at which to start a child on the visual discrimination tasks associated with reading. As reported in a review of the literature by Silbiger and Woolf (1965), there seems to be as much evidence that the eyes of a two- or three-year-old are able to focus and discriminate print as there is evidence that a child must be six or seven before his eyes are capable of the task of reading. In light of the research, then, it is visually feasible to have a two- or three-year-old read. This statement is not an endorsement. It simply indicates that if the child wants to learn to read, and the parent has the time and resources to guide him, there is little reason to fear eye problems at this early age.

Durkin (1966) conducted studies of children who read early to see what long-term effects such a skill produced. Durkin found that such children either led their peers in reading achievement after several years or at least were on a par with their age mates. Certainly no ill effects of early reading were reported.

Visual discrimination has an evident relation to reading. The eye must grasp word and sentence units as wholes while simultaneously using internal cues to perceive the sentences as meaningful utterances. Visual discrimination and decoding operations then lead to the threshold of meaning, to those basic initial reactions which we call perceptions in the Harris-Smith model.

Perception relies on accurate discrimination, but a learner perceives from many different vantage points. Perceptions reflect the socioeconomic, emotional, linguistic and motivational resources of a person. The teacher can use this diversity of perceptual response to show children that reading can be quite personal and yet have some general group meaning as well. When reading, children will use those perceptual cues they need in order to understand and interpret the printed page. It is the teacher's responsibility to see that the child has the visual discrimination skills necessary to focus on and select cues that enable him to receive the message of the author.

Although the connection is not as evident as with visual discriminations, auditory discrimination is also related to reading. Auditory skills must be refined so that not only whole words and whole utterances are perceived accurately but so that word parts or units of sound can be identified. The ability to grasp small units of sound and attach meaning to them is an important word-analysis skill and is therefore closely related to the development of reading skills.

Maturation and Perception

As the child grows and gains greater control of his body, he also develops more accurate and more meaningful perceptions. Most children develop a perception of themselves and objects in the world through physical exploration and curiosity (Piaget and Inhelder, 1956; Gibson, 1968). The child strives for distinctions that will bring order to his world of perceptions. Starting in infancy, for example, he distinguishes "objects" that give him food and cuddle him from those that do not do these things.

The environment usually aids perceptual development. The child is rewarded for recognizing that things are different. Verbal stimuli are used to encourage perceptual development. *Big* and *little, hard* and *soft,* and similar verbal stimuli are used in the environment to assist in the development of language perceptions. Even though the environment aids in this development, maturation seems to account for the child's continuing attempt to organize and stabilize his environment (Gibson, 1963).

Coordination and manipulation play a role in perceptual development, but precisely how important these factors are is not clear. Research does not demonstrate a strong relation between motor coordination skills and reading scores. Far more important for the classroom teacher is the need to concentrate on those skills that have an evident and direct relation to the process of reading—such as the auditory and visual discrimination skills already discussed.

Motor Development

Though the role of motor development in learning to read is not clear, it often assumes significant proportions in the eyes of the child. Observation in any kindergarten will convince you that a child's self-concept is considerably enhanced when his body accomplishes what older children can do. Marla's thumb is a case in point. Like most five-year-olds, she couldn't get her thumb to flex very quickly or easily and she worried because her thumbs were not straightening out as quickly as were those of her classmates. On the day that

FIGURE 7.2   Hand-eye coordination gives children a sense of accomplishment.

she noticed that her thumb was standing up straight, she paraded happily around the room showing this marvelous thumb to everyone. Marla felt better about herself. Her body was growing and working well. That's an important feeling for a young learner.

The teacher who plays catch with a child or works with balancing exercises and similar hand-eye coordination activities may be helping a child achieve a sense of well-being that extends beyond any known relation to competency in reading.

Perceptual Training

It would seem, therefore, that kindergarten and Grade 1 children generally are able to begin tasks associated with reading. Obviously a number of factors interact to determine readiness for reading:

awareness of language
physical ability to hear and see symbols
intellectual and emotional maturation
a vocabulary and body concepts for social exchange
a perception of the printed page as a means of communication.

These are typical tasks for beginning readiness:

1. picture interpretation
2. a speaking vocabulary that enables the child to be understood in class
3. left-to-right orientation
4. family and neighborhood experiences
5. desire to read
6. ability to attend to the task at hand
7. a sense of sequence
8. ability to follow directions
9. ability to discriminate visual forms (letters and words)
10. ability to discriminate similarities and differences in sounds (rhyme sounds and initial consonant sounds)
11. ability to see spatial relations and other visual-motor perceptions

The teacher provides training in these areas as his review of the children's skills indicates a need. Most of these skills are developed through a variety of social situations, the children hardly realizing that they are learning. The skills associated with visual and auditory discrimination and perception, however, are often given a more formal and direct treatment to insure their applicability for reading.

Visual discrimination, because of its obvious connection to reading, receives more emphasis in early reading programs than does auditory discrimination. Children come to school with considerable knowledge of the sound of language. Inductively, they have learned the sounds and the grammatical system. Most of that knowledge is not conscious, and so the teacher tries to improve the child's awareness of language by making him think about its sound system. Children usually have very little knowledge and skill in the graphic (visual) system of language. They need basic instruction to develop such knowledge; and they need frequent practice to acquire visual discrimination and perceptual response patterns that will enable them to read.

In an overly simplified view reading may be considered a series of word perceptions. To distinguish between words the reader needs letter, or grapheme (written symbol), cues. The purpose of distinguishing words is to relate them to language and communication. That goal must not be lost in exercises or isolated visual and auditory discrimination skills. Children must learn automatic responses to the sound and the sight of letters. The child's accuracy with these skills of auditory and visual perception seems especially important in the early stages. A nationwide study of first-grade readers found that the item most highly correlated with success in reading at the end of the first grade was the child's knowledge of the letters of the alphabet prior to instruction in school (Bond and Dykstra, 1967). To assist the child the teacher should show him how to perceive the sight and sound of letters in an accurate way.

These statements should not be interpreted to mean that a knowledge of the letters of the alphabet results in better reading performance on the part of the child. In reality, knowledge of the alphabet and early success in reading may both be manifestations of some language ability that we have not yet measured.

Visual Perception and Reading

When a reader looks at the printed page he must understand several things in order to comprehend what has been written. He must understand that the symbols on the page represent another person's message. He must know the conventions that are used in printing a message—that in English, writing starts on the left and moves to the right; that capital letters and periods are signals for beginning and ending an utterance; that the symbols represent the sound symbols used in speech.

Applying each of these understandings involves perceptual habits or skills. Moving the eyes from the left to the right across the page, identifying the punctuation and capitalization cues as indications of juncture and stress, and using the symbolic cues to recode them into speech patterns are all perceptual skills. All involve processes that take a visual stimulus and turn it into a meaning-bearing internal response. These perceptual skills do not develop automatically. They must be taught as part of the initial reading program, if the teacher determines the child did not bring them with him when he first came to school.

Auditory and Visual Integration

To start formal reading instruction the child must first perceive that the words he knows from speaking can be represented with visual symbols. Usually the teacher demonstrates how speech and print are integrated in the

reading process by pronouncing a familiar phrase: *The boy throws the ball.* —
and then writing it on the board. The teacher then uses the word *ball* as a
concrete example. He shows the class a ball and says: "This is the way the
word ball looks when I write it—*ball*. Now look in this book that I am holding
and see if you can find where the word *ball* is written on this page." Thus the
sound of the word is isolated; the isolated word is printed by itself; and the
printed form is viewed together with other words on a printed page. The
process of relating speech and print has begun.

Using name cards for the children in a class is another effective means of
introducing the idea that the sound of each name is different and is represented
by different visual symbols. The teacher can have each of the children examine
the name cards very carefully. "I am going to spread your name cards on the
table and see who can find his or her own card. Remember, every name is
different in its sound, and so it will be different in the way it is written." Some of
the children will already know what their names look like because they have
learned them at home. These children can select their name cards quickly and
then begin some other activity. The teacher assists those who have difficulty
finding their cards until some identifying features on the name cards help them
to find their own when they report to class on the following day. Care should
be taken by the teacher that the identifying feature is not a spot of dirt on the
card. Letter combinations, m-a-r in *Marla*, for example, should be stressed
instead.

Some teachers prefer to have children dictate sentences or stories which
are then written on a piece of paper or on the board as a means of demonstrating that speech sounds are represented by visual symbols. This technique,
known as the experience-story approach, was discussed in detail in Chapter 3
of this text. Whatever techniques are used, it is important to an accurate
perception of reading that children understand the relation between the spoken
word and printed symbols. In this way they will be able to decode the printed
page. If the language of a book is close to the language of the child, meaning
will be grasped easily.

A teaching technique sometimes used when children have difficulty in
integrating auditory and visual relationships is an expanded tracing technique.
The word or phrase to be learned is printed in large letters on rough paper. The
child traces over the letters as he slowly pronounces the word or phrase. This
technique was devised by Grace Fernald as a learning activity that involves
auditory (hearing), visual (seeing), vocal (saying), and kinesthetic (feeling)
integration—each reinforcing the other. The repetition of this process on key
words or phrases often succeeds when other approaches have failed.

Beginning Stages of Comprehension

From the beginning the teacher should emphasize that the printed page
carries a message; it is not simply a series of words. It is not enough to respond
to the spelling b-a-l-l with the sound /ball/. When *ball* is placed in conjunction
with other words, does the child have a visual perception of what is taking

place? *The ball bounced into the street.* "When you see the word *ball* in this sentence, Henrietta, do you have a picture in your mind of what the ball is doing? Can you see the ball bounce into the street?" Reminders of this sort by the teacher will assist children in their attempts to put various words together to form a continuous message.

Initially the teacher is primarily concerned with making sure that children have some image, some meaning that they ascribe to the words they see and hear. Evidently the teacher does not have to examine all the words that appear in the exercises to see whether all the children know them or not. It will usually be sufficient for the teacher to ask individuals: "What picture do you have in your mind when you see the word *busy?*" Such a reminder will encourage all the children to strive for meaning in the series of words they see.

Meaningful Units

Written words should be placed in phrases or sentences that are familiar to students. The sooner they use complete sentences, the more likely they will be able to perceive reading as a flow of ideas or as a communication, and not merely as a series of words that sometimes defies comprehension. *[Morning message]*

"I will write something on the board and you tell me what it says." For example, the teacher writes: *Good morning, children. The sun is warm today.* Provided they have already been introduced to each of these words, children will read what the teacher has written and be pleased that they got the message.

In practice exercises the children must see isolated words placed in phrases or in complete sentences.

Mother.
My mother.
My mother cooks.

Or the children themselves may be encouraged to provide meaningful units. They need not always restrict themselves to the words that have been developed for the entire group. As long as the words under study are put into a meaningful context, the children should be able to see the need to think with a series of words instead of just one word.

Rain.
It's raining cats and dogs.

Whenever possible, a concrete demonstration should be included in learning activities to help in the development of perception for reading.

Cool.
Check out that cool dude, man.

Once the child begins to read with a certain amount of fluency, he often relies on the known sound patterns to identify individual words and the message of the passage. There is often an automatic triggering of known sound

patterns by some of the written words that the reader sees. It is easier to observe this happening in children with certain dialect patterns than with children whose basic speech is similar to that of the text they are reading. For example, certain dialects often omit the "s" in the third person singular verb. *He says; he runs; he fights* turn into *he say; he run; he fight.* In reading aloud the teacher will hear children with those dialect patterns read: "Dan ain't (isn't) mean. But when he in trouble, he fight. Then he run to his moms and say . . .''

Teachers may feel compelled to correct a child whose dialect shows up in reading aloud, feeling that a reading error is being committed. But it is not a reading error; it is a language difference. It is clear that the child knows what is happening, even though he is reading a dialect version. Consequently, the teacher should *not* say: "You did not read those lines correctly." At an appropriate time, when children are mature enough to understand, the teacher may want to discuss different kinds of dialects and show that reading aloud is one way of learning how to pronounce the dialect that is used in most books. (For further discussion of dialect differences, *see* Chapter 3.)

The good reader quickly uses a combination of visual cues and relates them to speech, often triggering known sound patterns from ingrained speech habits (Gibson, 1968; Strang, 1968). He uses as many visual cues as he needs to set the images flowing and to trigger the language habits that were previously in existence. As the reader speeds up the process, he is in effect reducing the number of visual cues that he relies on. Initially, however, he may have to examine most words with great care to make sure that the gross and the internal cues are giving an accurate perception of the words and the images that are intended by the writer.

Diagnosing problems concerning the relation of reading to perception involves examining both auditory and visual *discrimination* abilities, as well as auditory and visual *perception* abilities. It is possible for a person to hear language and perceive it adequately—that is, give it valid meaning—yet not be trained to discriminate precisely among the minute sounds of the language. A person who looks at a series of words and does not gain an accurate perception of them may either have insufficient skill in discriminating among the visual cues available or may not have sufficient skill in discriminating among the sounds of words and within words. In either case the relation between sound and symbol is not adequately integrated, and the perception of the word is confused or reveals no meaning.

Teaching Auditory and Visual Discrimination

In actual teaching, auditory discrimination activities usually precede visual discrimination activities. In the next section on how to teach these skills, auditory skill instruction is described first, then visual discrimination.

Auditory Discrimination in the Classroom

According to Fries (1963), speech sounds are learned through a recognition of the contrasting features of words. A child learns the difference between the sound of *hat* and *bat* not because he is aware of their *at* similarities but because, through much practice, he has paid attention to the *h* and *b* contrasting sound features. Some linguists believe that the contrasting features in learning speech sounds operate also on a longer phrasal or an utterance basis (Lefevre, 1964). These linguists are saying, in effect, that the speaker has a built-in system for discriminating among sounds. If the teacher can make the learner conscious of those sounds and the relations among them as they appear in words, then the learner can move easily and securely into an analysis of printed words by using a sound-symbol pattern.

Correlation

A number of studies have been conducted over the years to analyze the relation between auditory discrimination skills and reading achievement. Duker (1962) reviewed thirty-two of these studies and concluded that there is a significant correlation between the two factors. It should be remembered, however, that a correlation between two factors does not necessarily prove that one causes the other. There may be a more general factor that accounts for both auditory discrimination skill and reading achievement. For example, Dykstra (1966) did not find a noteworthy correlation between auditory discrimination subtests in first-grade readiness tests and reading achievement at the end of the first grade. He did discover that boys *learn* auditory discrimination less readily than girls do, and that boys take longer to master the reading process.

A different kind of relation that adds insight to the value of auditory discrimination skill is that severely disabled readers almost always have a marked inability to discriminate sounds in words (Durrell, 1953). When children were subjected to specific training exercises in recognizing speech sounds there was a marked improvement in their ability to discriminate and to read better (Silvaroli, 1966).

As is the case with other language skills, a child's environment and his level of maturation affect his auditory discrimination. A social environment in which speech sounds are slurred or muffled obviously will not provide as much practice in discrimination as an environment which provides a model for clear enunciation (Deutsch, 1964). The developmental nature of the auditory discrimination process can be demonstrated from the fact that a decreasing number of children show problems in this area at each higher age level—27 percent with problems in Grade 1; 19 percent in Grade 2—according to a study by Wepman (1960). Similar findings were obtained in a longitudinal study by Thompson (1963), who recommended that:

1. first-grade entrants who show poor scores on an auditory discrimination test be given an extended readiness period in which exercises to develop this ability are presented
2. those who develop slowly in the ability also be introduced slowly to phonics instruction
3. those who score high on an auditory discrimination test be introduced to an accelerated program of word study.

Developing Auditory Cues

Since the child comes to school with a built-in sense of the contrasting features of speech sounds (Fries, 1963), he must be taught how to use that knowledge to help him with his reading, including word-analysis skills. He must learn to think of words as having sound components *(phonemes)* and be taught to pay attention to certain parts of words so that he can identify beginning sounds, ending sounds, and middle sounds. There are a variety of techniques and exercises that a teacher can use to teach auditory discrimination and a corresponding visual discrimination. Some of them include telling whether words rhyme, matching pictures with word sounds, identifying the similarities and differences in beginning and ending sounds in words, and identifying the limits of phrases and sentences by intonation patterns (the voice usually falls at the end of a sentence). Samples of these kinds of exercises are given below.

Auditory Discrimination Exercises

The following exercises are designed to develop the student's auditory discrimination.

A. Listening for rhyme words

This very simple exercise is a good one to use with prereaders.
1. The teacher pronounces two words.
2. If the words rhyme (mill-hill), the students say "yes." If the words do not rhyme (mish-mash), the students say "no."
   Examples: drum-hum, boom-bang, cap-mad, bake-cake, small-tall, fan-man, sit-hit, cold-gold.

B. Listening for the same word

This is a good exercise for prereaders, but it is a little more difficult than listening for rhyme words. The teacher says: "I am going to say several words. I will say one word twice. Listen carefully, and see if you can tell me which word you hear two times. Raise your hand as soon as you know what the word is."
Sample lists: ball, girl, fork, ball
                tree, fish, tree, boy
                girl, boy, run, boy, plan
                cat, pig, tree, cat

C. Listening for initial sounds

The teacher says: "I am going to say several words. Most of the words begin with the same sound that the word bat begins with. Raise your hand when you hear a word that does not begin with the same sound as bat. The words are: big, boy, sick, basket, camera, bomb."
   Either single consonants or consonant blends can be used in this exercise.

D. Listening for middle sounds

The teacher says: "I am going to say several words. Most of the words have the same middle sound as the word cat [pronounce very distinctly]. Raise your hand when you hear a word which does not have the same middle sound as cat. The words are: fat, get, man, ham, sit."
   In this exercise most of the middle sounds are vowels.

E. Listening for final sounds

The teacher says: "I am going to say several words. Most of the words end with the same sound as the word big [pronounce very distinctly]. Raise your hand when you hear a word which does not end with the same sound as big. The words are: bag, fig, mad, sag, help, leg, sick."

In these exercises make sure the children know the meanings of *beginning, middle,* and *end.*

Exercises in workbooks and in basal texts offer similar activities for the teacher's use in helping students develop auditory discrimination skills. All children need not do all of these exercises. The exercises should be applied selectively, based on specific and identified weaknesses in students' auditory discrimination. Equipment, such as a tape recorder, can be used to great advantage with these exercises because children can listen to sounds as often as they need to and can record their own attempts at reproducing sounds.

Evaluating Auditory Discrimination

As has been said, hearing, or auditory, acuity naturally plays a role in auditory discrimination. If a child has defective hearing, he may not be able to identify certain kinds of sounds. For example, some hearing loss reduces or eliminates the reception of high-frequency sounds. Those sounds associated with the consonants f, s, k, and similar sounds would go unnoticed or be effectively obscured with a certain kind of hearing handicap. An individual with this kind of hearing deficiency needs reading instruction that emphasizes visual techniques instead of a strong auditory-visual relation (Rosenberg, 1968). The teacher cannot diagnose a specialized hearing loss, such as the one just described, but many schools conduct hearing examinations using auditory screening devices called audiometers. If a hearing loss is indicated by the general school screening, the child should be referred to a physician for a more complete examination and correction. The teacher would then use the knowledge of the deficiency and the doctor's recommendations to modify instruction for the child.

In some instances the teacher may notice symptoms of a hearing deficiency in a child. If the child turns his head as if to listen with one ear or cups his ear or does not respond to fairly low-volume instructions these are clues to a possible hearing problem. In the light of these symptoms the teacher may want to conduct a rough screening test of his own. This can be done by having two or three children sit with their backs to the teacher, who then whispers their names or their birth dates or other key words. The children are to raise their hands when they hear the words that apply only to them. If such an exercise adds evidence to what the teacher has previously observed about hearing difficulties, the child with the problem should be referred to the school nurse for further testing. Again, instructional technique should be adjusted to enable the child to function as best he can with his disability. For example, he can be given a seat close to the teacher.

Tests of Auditory Discrimination

Assuming that the child has normal auditory acuity, the teacher needs to know how well he can distinguish sounds in words before asking him to make specific sound-symbol connections. Most first-grade readiness tests, such as the Metropolitan and the Lee-Clark, contain subsections devoted to exercises in auditory discrimination. As Dykstra (1968) has indicated, however, these short subtest scores are not reliable for an individual diagnosis. They can be looked upon only as very weak indications of the student's skill. The teacher can use the *Wepman Auditory Discrimination Test* as a separate instrument. This test poses a series of paired words *(meal-veal, ball-ball)* and the listener is asked to indicate whether they are exactly alike or whether they are different. The list of words includes comparisons and contrasts for all the consonant and vowel sounds in initial, middle and final positions. A guide indicates which sounds the student is missing and how many errors constitute a serious problem at a given age level. Armed with the information the test reveals, the teacher can set up a series of exercises to teach specific discriminations needed by the child. Or the teacher can proceed with other kinds of instruction if the test shows the child makes adequate discrimination in all sounds.

Teacher Test

The teacher can carry out a procedure similar to the Wepman test using his own list of words, such as the one shown below for a test of auditory discrimination. By providing students with a simple answer sheet such as this one, the teacher can test a whole group at one time.

Auditory Discrimination Answer Sheet

Mark + if the words are exactly the same; − if words are different.

1. ———	6. ———
2. ———	7. ———
3. ———	8. ———
4. ———	9. ———
5. ———	10. ———

When the teacher makes his own test he can check on the specific sounds he has taught or he can use it as a pretest for a group of sounds. The students do not *have* to respond in writing. A list of paired words can be administered to an individual or two who sit with their backs to the teacher. The students raise their hands when the words are different; and the teacher records their correct responses.

The suggestion that teachers construct their own auditory discrimination test needs a caution. Informally constructed tests are always subject to the vagaries of the test-making skill of the inventor of the test. The noise level in the room and the volume, pitch, and articulation of the teacher's voice obviously play a part in the reliability of such informal techniques.

Here are sample directions and words that can be used in an assessment of auditory discrimination (Shack, 1962):

General directions: Try a few samples in each category to make sure the child understands what he is to do. He may respond "yes" if items are the same, and "no" if they are different. Have the student face away from the examiner for testing. Be sure not to give any clue, by vocal emphasis or otherwise, to the correct answer. Record responses.

I. Auditory discrimination (Informal test)

A. Initial consonant discrimination
Are these words the same or different? Call one pair at a time.

tip	dip	feel	veal	hill	fill
red	red	boon	moon	leaf	reef
cheap	jeep	bum	dumb	den	ten
pin	bin	yes	yes	peach	beach
shin	chin	sip	ship	fall	fall
pal	pal	fix	fix	cheap	sheep
zip	sip	mold	cold	some	come
goat	coat	yard	lard	feel	feel
coast	toast	thin	fin	yawn	lawn

B. Final consonant discrimination
Are these words the same or different?

rack	rag	cup	come	swim	swim
leaf	leave	had	hat	tide	tight
moon	moon	good	good	rub	rum
pit	pill	then	them	seed	seat
razz	rash	sob	sop	wig	wing
rip	rib	ride	ripe	steam	steep
bus	buzz	clay	clay	take	tail
home	hope	Ruth	roof	bat	bad
run	run	much	mush	live	lip

C. Vowel discrimination

cop	cap	been	bun	hat	hun	beg	big
hit	hat	rod	rod	doll	doll	cut	cut
rub	rib	bug	bug	leg	leg	hit	hut
mat	mat	luck	lock	bit	bet	rip	rap
big	big	had	head	dock	duck	but	bat
odd	add	but	bet	lid	led	ball	ball
man	men	lap	lip	pen	pan	cup	cop

II. Evaluation

1. Disregard one error in each category. In kindergarten and first grade expect more than one error in each category. A few errors may occur by chance.
2. Study errors for patterns and clues. Finding error patterns is much more significant than counting the number of errors.
3. List the specific difficulties:
   Beginning position _____
   Ending position _____
   Middle position _____
   Consonant errors _____
   Vowel errors _____

After instruction has been given in specific discriminations the teacher should construct a test or an exercise that will evaluate the child's achievement. The criteria for the test are determined by the elements that have been taught. Success for the child should not be measured by his score on some general instruments, such as a standardized readiness test, but on his ability to discriminate the specific sounds that have been previously identified and taught in class. If the teacher has taught the sound discriminations between /p/ and /b/, /d/ and /t/, and /ch/ and /sh/ the test should focus on words that enable a child to show his skill in distinguishing these sounds. For example, /p/ and /b/ could be tested with word pairs such as *pear-bear, pail-pail, cop-cob, rob-rob,* and so on.

Visual Discrimination in the Classroom

Visual acuity—the ability to see the fine lines that make up letters—is only one factor in discrimination, but it is an important one, as Strang indicates:

> All but a few exceptional children learn to read by associating the sound of familiar letters and words with their corresponding written symbol. Consequently, both visual and auditory acuity are a basis to success in beginning reading.
>
> To see clearly, eyes must work well together, diverge and converge at will, and integrate two images into one. To achieve this, numerous experiences of integrating sensations are necessary. Normal vision is an important precondition of maximum reading comfort and efficiency; it is basic to perception. Probably far too many children have been handicapped in beginning reading because of undetected visual impairments, most frequently muscular imbalance and problems of convergence.[1]

Visual discrimination skill is evidently related to the development of perception as the child attempts to sort out and stabilize his environment. The

---

[1] Ruth Strang, *Reading Diagnosis and Remediation* (Newark, Del.: International Reading Association, 1968).

grosser visual discriminations of early childhood—for example, distinguishing between a happy face and an angry face—must give way to the fine distinctions of identifying letters of the alphabet in kindergarten and first grade so that the child can learn to read.

The teacher should note any indications of possible visual difficulty and refer potential problems to the school nurse or recommend that the child be taken to an eye doctor. Some symptoms of visual difficulty are:

cocking the head so as to read with only one eye
holding the side of one's head when looking at the book or board
rubbing the eyes during reading
red eyes, watery eyes
holding the book too close to the face
holding the book at arm's length
complaints of headaches
squinting, or other indications of strain
complaints of haziness or fading of printed symbols.

The goal of visual discrimination as related to reading is to enable the child to *identify accurately the written symbols* that an author has used to communicate a message. In order to do this the child must make use of both visual discrimination and visual perception. He has to hold in his mind simultaneously the whole word, its parts, and the sentence with its visual cues, punctuation, and capitalization. This means that the reader must pay attention to the wholeness of the word while distinguishing the internal parts that give it characteristic features. Until a child has developed a sense of the patterns of words and sentences, and until he has enough practice to give automatic responses to general configuration and internal-part cues, he reads rather slowly and laboriously. He has to take the time to see the whole word and then check rather systematically to verify that it is the word he wants to pronounce.

Because reading is a combination of responding to the whole word and to internal cues, both general-configuration memory techniques and letter-distinction techniques are used in teaching a beginner how to recognize words. It follows that both techniques should be part of initial instruction in word recognition.

Research on Visual Discrimination

Success in early reading greatly depends on the child's ability to discriminate among the letters of the alphabet and among basic word forms (Barrett, 1965; Bond and Dykstra, 1967). At least, recognition of letters of the alphabet and verbal forms is a better predictor of success in reading than the ability to discriminate nonverbal material, such as circles and triangles. This should not come as a great surprise, for the identification of letters of the alphabet encompasses the ability to identify grosser forms as well.

A number of research studies have helped to identify the kinds of visual discrimination skills that are possessed by good and poor readers. Vernon reviewed twenty-two studies relating to perception in reading and found that:

1. Good readers do not perceive every letter in every word, but focus on a few key words which they appear to perceive as a whole. They then infer the meaning of the whole phrase.
2. Most readers use the first half of the word as their cue rather than the second half of the word.
3. Deleting the lower half of words causes little difficulty in reading them, whereas deleting the upper half makes them almost illegible. For example, baby's crib/baby's crib for baby's crib.
4. Children of five years of age are sometimes unable to see the difference between a shape and its mirror image, even when this is pointed out.

Vernon concluded that:

> . . . acquisition of facility in well-integrated perceptual processes requires prolonged practice, much of it in tasks which are singularly difficult for young children. Even when the child has become thoroughly familiar with these processes and can perform them rapidly and easily, he is still at the stage of reading each word separately.[2]

The instructional consequences of these findings would appear to be a careful examination of visual discrimination skills and perception, and a careful programming of instruction for the child in the skills identified as weak.

Disabled readers—those who have had some instruction but have not made satisfactory progress—also give some insight into the need for visual discrimination in reading. Coleman (1953) found that a majority of the thirty-three subjects he examined were markedly retarded in perceptual development; that perceptual development lagged significantly behind the development of general intelligence in a majority of the subjects; and that retardation in perceptual development was cumulative with age. Once again the need for instruction in visual discrimination and visual perception tasks and their carry-over practice in reading was emphasized.

Environment may often play a part in the development of perception. Elkind (1965) endorses the Piagetian concept that training and maturation contribute significantly to perceptual development. In an environment in which there is little stimulation for making distinctions among various forms in infancy and early childhood, perceptual development may be retarded. For example, if the child does not see samples of circles (balls), squares (alphabet blocks), triangles (mobiles), and other objects that babies are often encouraged to play with, he may not develop the skill of discriminating among forms such as alphabet letters that are essential to reading. The same would hold true for auditory discrimination. A baby may be retarded as a result of lack of stimula-

---

[2]M. D. Vernon, *Backwardness in Reading: A Study of Its Nature and Origin* (London, England: Cambridge University Press, 1960), Chapter II.

tion. Environment may even account for the way a child learns easiest in school. If an auditory presentation alone makes it difficult for the child to learn, then a visual presentation or a combination visual-auditory presentation should be tried by the teacher.

Bateman (1967) found that an auditory-oriented program for first-grade children was substantially more effective than a visually-oriented program. With a sample of black males, Katz and Deutsch (1963) found just the opposite—that the visual presentation made for the greatest learning. The kind of language ability possessed by the two groups may be the factor that caused this difference. In any case, we should be cautioned against jumping on the bandwagon of any one approach.

Developing Visual Discrimination in the Classroom

When using a diagnostic approach to the teaching of visual discrimination, kindergarten and first-grade teachers should first find out which children can identify the letters of the alphabet, both upper and lower case. Children who can already identify letters as a result of instruction they have received at home need only as much practice with the letters as will make their responses automatic.

The research of Muehl and King (1966) indicates a definite advantage to teaching discrimination through the letters of the alphabet. For children who cannot identify the alphabet when they begin kindergarten, the forms of the letters can be shown in large type or in plastic. The children can develop discrimination skills and a knowledge of letter forms through tracing letters, flash-card exercises, and seeing and identifying letters in words and in signs. As their visual discrimination and perception ability matures, the size of type can gradually be decreased, as is the case with elementary school readers.

The principles for developing visual discrimination and automatic recognition can be used in teaching at all levels, from nursery school up. The student must see the distinctive differences in the form of the letters or words, and must practice them in isolation and in context. Automatic responses should then be developed through practice with phrases, flash cards, and tachistoscopic instruments. A simple tachistoscope (pronounced tuh kiss' tuh scope) can be made by placing a list of letters, words, or phrases into a cardboard pocket that has a hole cut in the center which will reveal one letter at a time (see Figure 7.3).

Showing the letter or word on a card, drawing it on the board, and having the children make the letter in the air or write it on a piece of paper are part of an effective sequence. Discrimination activities should include pointing out the distinctive features of the letter that is being demonstrated. Research has shown that the upper half of the letter is especially important in correct discrimination. One study illustrated that four-year-old children can learn to overcome confusion about letters like "c" and "o" and "u" and "n" (Gibson, Gibson, Pick, and Osser, 1962). It takes emphasis and patience to overcome such confusions, however, because children easily read pictures upside down and are not

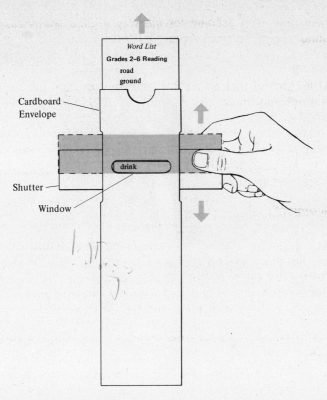

FIGURE 7.3   A cardboard tachistoscope

By moving the shutter up or down a word is revealed in the window for a brief second. The child responds, and the word list is moved so a new word can appear in the window.

bothered at first by seeing the symbols "n" and "u," thinking that they are the same symbol. Pointing out the difference in the top part of these and similar pairs of letters ("m" and "w") will assist children's ability to recognize the letters. Such a discussion should be followed up with a concrete experience, such as having two children bend over to touch their toes in a head-to-head position—they are the "m." Or having two children sit on the floor with their feet touching and raised in the air—they are the "w." (See Figure 7.4.) This exercise is a good example of combining motor activity with reading development.

Various types of worksheets are available to help children to develop letter identification and discrimination. Initially, an exercise that requires tracing the letter will force the youngster to look at and impress on his memory the exact lines of the letter through visuomotor means. Figure 7.5 presents a sample page of such a workbook.

A variation on tracing letters in a book can be achieved by having children work with plastic letters to get the feel of the letter—a kinesthetic reinforcement. Making letters out of clay, cutting them out of paper, drawing them in

(Photo by Suzanne Szasz)

FIGURE 7.4   Motor and letter learning

Learning the letters "m" and "w"

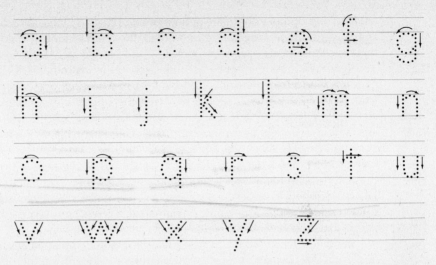

FIGURE 7.5   A workbook alphabet

Tracing the outlines of letters of the alphabet forces children to attend to specific differences and prepares children for writing the alphabet.

finger paints and in templates (a three-dimensional pattern) are also useful techniques.

Occasionally a child may not be able to discriminate between the letters of the alphabet. Because of developmental lag or lack of experience, he may have difficulty in making fine discriminations among some lower-case letters.

If the teacher observes that a student has a severe developmental lag, the teacher can refer to a text by Ilg and Ames (1965) which describes typical behaviors and products for different age levels. For example, at age six 58 percent of the boys and 66 percent of the girls in the Ilg and Ames study were able to print their first and last names. Ninety-three percent used capitals and small letters correctly, but only 22 percent used substitute letters (p. 276). A text of this kind might also be useful in helping a teacher prepare developmental exercises for a child who is significantly retarded in his visual discrimination ability.

Evaluating Visual Discrimination

Checking the visual acuity of students should be a function of specialized personnel. A visual screening test should be given annually until Grade 2. These early years are the ones in which visual changes seem most dramatic. After Grade 2 the test can be given every other year. The age of seven appears to be particularly crucial in this respect (Strang, 1968, p. 21). Screening should include a binocular reading test (using an instrument like the telebinocular) to observe the coordinated functioning of both eyes and the functioning of the eyes at far and near point. Some children's eyes function quite well at far point

(20 feet), but do not coordinate at near point (12 to 18 inches). Reading occurs at the near point. If irregularities are noted, the child's family should be told so that he can be taken to an eye doctor.

Readiness tests can serve as initial screening instruments for identifying children who need discrimination exercises.[3] Those who score high on the letter-discrimination tests should be given the opportunity to begin immediately to use letters in actual reading activities. Those who do not know the letters must be taught, and then examined again later to see if the teaching has accomplished its objective. Undoubtedly there will be some children who know some of the letters, but not all. They should be required to practice only those they fail to recognize. It should be a principle of teaching that the learner not be required to suffer "relearning" what he already knows. His attitude toward school and learning may be damaged by constantly having to cover the knowledge and skills he already has.

Readiness tests (and teacher observations) include other means for evaluating visual discrimination. Typical among these is identifying the one form out of four that is different (see Figure 7.6). When a child does not respond to direct teaching of the alphabet forms he may need exercises involving grosser forms—such as squares, circles, and triangles. Using cardboard or plastic pieces, he can learn to match forms, placing all the squares together and all the circles together, for example. Some simple children's jigsaw puzzles make pleasant exercises for working on visual discrimination, and also on visual perception. The child learns to bring closure to the picture; that is, to complete the total image of the picture by filling in its parts.

FIGURE 7.6   An aid in evaluating visual discrimination

Find the picture that is different. Similar forms are frequently used as tests of visual discrimination ability.

SUMMARY

Reading demands well-developed perceptual skills. These include not only visual skills but also auditory and general language skills. Since perception develops through a combination of factors having to do with maturation, individual ability, and environment, there is bound to be a range of perceptual

[3]For a more detailed analysis of reading readiness tests see R. Farr and N. Anastasiow. *Review of Reading Readiness Tests* (Newark, Del.: International Reading Association, 1969).

abilities in any given group of children. As with any other reading skill, perceptual abilities must be evaluated and taught at a variety of levels.

Because of television and the general affluences of modern society many typical readiness skills are being developed in the home and in nursery schools. This fact makes it possible for the schools to work sooner with some children on auditory and visual skills that are directly related to reading instruction. Care must be taken, however, to demonstrate that youngsters in the class do indeed have the other skills of language expression and the concepts that will carry them through their early experiences in school.

Research indicates that both auditory and visual discrimination skills are correlated to reading achievement, at least in the early stages, and that training in discrimination skills helps children to learn better how to use auditory and visual skills. It has been found that an accurate knowledge of the letters of the alphabet is one of the strongest predictors of success in reading at the end of the first grade. This finding suggests that six- and seven-year-old children are generally able to use letters in their early word-recognition activities.

Schools need to make periodic evaluations of hearing and vision in children to discover possible defects in acuity. Teachers should evaluate perceptual skills through criterion tests to assist pupils in making progress in learning to read. A caution was given in the chapter in regard to discussing isolated skills: No matter how many separate skills are identified, the ability to read seems to be greater than the sum of its parts.

Terms for Self-study

perception	correlation studies
readiness	audiometers
visual perception	binocular
auditory perception	closure
perceptual development	picture reading
auditory discrimination	visual discrimination

Discussion Questions

1. Regardless of the age of the child, how is "readiness" an important factor in reading?
2. How could one describe first-grade reading readiness in terms of competencies or skills?
3. What kinds of behaviors suggest a child has difficulty with visual perception tasks? With auditory perception tasks?
4. Suppose that after considerable practice opportunity a six-year-old child still cannot follow letters and words in a left-to-right progression. What should the classroom teacher do to help him?

8

Visual
Memory
of Words

A kindergarten teacher once claimed that she could teach the children in her class to read in a very simple way. She used highway signs. All around her room were a variety of actual road signs. Any visitor who wished to test the children would find that they all knew what each sign said.

Can you think of a way to teach kindergarten children to read these signs?

By the time children reach kindergarten age most of them are accustomed to using different shapes as marks of identification. From television and the labels on breakfast cereal boxes they soon learn that a certain kind of script means Coca Cola; that the name of their favorite toy company appears in a figure eight; that landing on a circle in their race-car game means they get another turn, while landing on a square means they must stop. Some will also know that the octagonal sign on the street corner means "Stop."

Because children already have some orientation for using different basic shapes as a means of identification, it does not take a special magic—unless

158

imagination is magic—to get kindergarten-age children to remember what six or eight road signs mean. After all, adults respond to the shape of a road sign before they read the message on the sign. They may not realize it, but they do not read "Stop" every time they approach a stop sign. The octagonal shape at the intersection means "Stop" to them!

While actually driving, the driver must read carefully what some road signs say. It makes a big difference, for example, whether the triangle indicates a curve to the left or a curve to the right. While the child, too, needs more than a response to the general shape of a sign to say that he knows how to read, these road signs can be an effective start to reading. The child can learn that these geometric forms represent an idea they can respond to.

As you read this chapter see if you can find the answers to these questions:

Do competent readers decode the words they meet or do they respond to the general shape of the words?

What is meant by a visual memory of words?

What words are likely prospects for learning through a visual memory approach?

How can difficulty in learning words through a visual memory approach be overcome?

Do you know several means for increasing the effectiveness of a child's visual memory?

Developing Automatic Responses

Most of the effort that goes into teaching children to read words is aimed at developing instantaneous, or automatic, responses to as many words as possible. The more words a person can respond to automatically, the easier it is for him to read a message quickly and with a minimum of effort. He can concentrate on analyzing and evaluating the message, instead of spending effort on deciphering words. It is not feasible to train most readers to respond instantly to all the words they will meet in their reading. That is why every reader continues to need and to use a wide variety of word-analysis skills. The more a person reads, the less frequently he will see a word that causes him to stop and analyze; because of frequent and on-going practice he will have an instant reaction to new words, the result of using a variety of cues.

A fluent reader responds instantly to a whole word, perhaps to an entire phrase. He goes through no evident analytic process as his eye sweeps across a line. He stops for analysis only when he does not have an automatic perception from the visual stimulus. Much like the kindergarten children who responded automatically to road signs, the competent reader is using visual memory of the shape of the word to assist him with an instant response. But unlike the kindergarten children, who would not be able to tell the precise difference between two square signs which contained different written directions, the competent reader is able to simultaneously use internal cues that enable him to distinguish *horse* from *house,* though the gross shapes of the words are identical. His repertoire of skills and response patterns enables him to respond instantly to either *horse* or *house,* making use of both the general shape, or *configuration,* of the word and other cues without being conscious of any analysis that is taking place. He also uses the context and syntactic cues to trigger responses. (Refer to Chapter 3 on language for a reminder of the role of syntax.)

Children learn early to respond instantly to shapes and forms. No matter how crude the art, most children at three or four years of age can instantly respond to the silhouette of a camel, an elephant, or an alligator. These are distinctive animal forms they have seen in pictures, in television cartoons, and in the drawings of their friends. But at an early age they do not respond automatically to a tiger versus a mountain lion versus a leopard versus an alley cat. These animals have very similar shapes. One has to read the spots and the stripes in order to tell one kind of cat from another. Once the child learns the internal cue system, however, he soon knows the difference between the tiger and the leopard.

With such examples the teacher can make the child aware that the goal of reading instruction is to get him to react instantly to words, but that the shape of the word is only one of many cues he will use.

Using a Variety of Word-recognition Techniques

Word recognition, as used here, means the ability to recognize the *sound* and the *meaning* of words in a printed message. Word recognition refers not only to the identification of words that a reader already knows by sight but also to the reader's ability to "unlock" words that are not familiar in their printed form. The teacher helps the child develop various techniques for unlocking and recognizing words independently. Such methods include *sight words* (those that are a part of the visual memory mechanism), *context clues,* phonic analysis, structural analysis, and linguistic analysis. No one learns all of these techniques at once, and so the school and the teacher must decide which skills to introduce first.

The first-grader about to begin formal reading instruction already has some familiarity with sounds, words, and communication. In his daily conversations he uses thousands of words in complex sentence patterns, and has little or no difficulty in listening to and understanding the talk of others. As long ago as 1940 Seashore and Eckerson estimated that the typical six-year-old had a listening vocabulary of approximately 25,000 words. Most of the words in the reading material prepared for the first-grade child, therefore, are almost entirely from the child's listening vocabulary. The words are usually unfamiliar only in written symbols, not in sound or in meaning. This is an assumption the teacher will want to evaluate with each group of children he teaches, for young children do not always have a clear idea of how to distinguish one word from another (Kingston *et al.,* 1972).

An initial task of beginning reading instruction is to have the child understand that the printed word is a symbol for the spoken word. Picture stories and experience charts can be utilized to demonstrate for the child what words in print mean. Simple experience stories are especially helpful in showing the child that symbol units stand for a flow of speech.

One of the first steps that most children take in learning to read is to identify words by remembering their total form or shape. Probably their own names are such words. Others might include *the, is, girl.* Thus, they can immediately "read," *The girl is Patricia.*

Out of curiosity and pride beginning readers strive to memorize more and more words so they can prove that they can read. This does not mean that the letters within the words should be ignored in the classroom. On the contrary, the children should see from their initial instruction that ability to discriminate among the letters of the alphabet will aid them in learning to recognize individual words. In describing the distinctive features or shapes of words, the teacher should demonstrate how letters of the alphabet contribute to these distinctive features. The name *Tony* has a tall *t* at the beginning, whereas the name *Marla* has a tall *m* at the beginning and a tall "l" near the end of the word (Muehl and King, 1966). The child's early training in discrimination seems to be useful in learning to identify words (McDowell and Youth, 1973).

Associative Learning

Visual memory techniques for learning whole words fit into the category of associative learning activities. Basically, the learner attempts to associate a written symbol with an image, or a perception, of an object or person. Common ways for making an association are associating pictures with their names, labeling objects in a room, and relating an individual's own word patterns to the way the words are printed—for example, through an experience chart.

Labeling

Labeling pictures constitutes a frequently used technique for teaching children to visually associate the printed word with the image of the object it stands for. Pictures with labels on the back can be purchased from publishers, or teachers and students can make their own file of matching words and pictures. The picture should be fairly simple in composition so that the child will easily and immediately recognize the content.

The teacher asks the child: "What is this picture?"

"A horse."

"That's right. And here I have written the word *horse*. It begins with a tall letter, *h*. Do you think you will remember what the word looks like the next time you see it? What other letters are there in the word *horse*?"

Reinforcement of this learning is provided by having the child later identify the word *horse* in a group of two or three other words; or he can match the picture with the word. The word and the matching picture should remain on display for at least one day so the children in the class can have ample opportunities to see the associated pair.

The matching procedure does not have to be limited to pictures and posters. Many objects in the classroom can be labeled. The door, wall, desks, closet, pencil cases, and bookshelf can serve as object lessons of the relationship between speech and print. All the teacher has to do is tell children why objects in the room have labels, and let their curiosity and powers of observation motivate them to retain the words for future reading use (*see* Figure 8.1).

Experience Stories

Through the experience-story approach the teacher leads the child to proceed from the known—his oral language—to the unknown—the graphic representation of that language. The teacher helps the child conceptualize that what he can say can be written, and what can be written he can read.

(Photo by Suzanne Szasz)

FIGURE 8.1   Labeling classroom objects

(Photo by Suzanne Szasz)

FIGURE 8.2   Animals often provide a warm, common experience which gives children an opportunity to develop vocabulary and experience stories.

Most early primary-grade pupils want to share their experiences. It is relatively easy, therefore, to elicit "stories" from an individual or from a small group. Experiences that occur during the school day can be discussed by the children and incorporated into charts. The teacher guides the discussion and motivates the children to follow the development of their story on the chart. One value of the *experience chart* is that it can be used to develop several sight words for the entire group.

Experience stories can be developed around anything that interests children. One class acquired a pet hamster. When the initial excitement had subsided, the teacher mentioned the possibility of having the class write a report for the local newspaper about their pet. Even if the newspaper did not print the story, the children could put it on the school bulletin board. Then everyone who came into their room could read about the pet hamster (*see* Figure 8.2).

The teacher led the children in a discussion, having them note significant items that should be included in the report—such as the name of the hamster, where she lived, and how they felt about her. The children then dictated sentences which the teacher wrote on the board. As each sentence was written, the teacher reread it immediately. Several children were also asked to reread the sentence. Since their reading was primarily a recall of what had been said, the teacher asked others in the group to make any corrections when a child failed to say the words exactly in the order in which they had originally been dictated. The students then determined which sentences best described the hamster. Here is the final product the class put on their experience chart:

Our Hamster

We have a hamster in our room.
Her name is Miss Lori Blackberry.
She lives in a cage.
She likes to roam around the room.
We like our hamster.

On the hamster's cage the teacher printed a label that said: "Miss Lori Blackberry." The label was a major clue for the children to use in identifying the words on their experience chart. After the chart was completed, the teacher reread the entire story for the class. Two children were assigned to illustrate the chart so everyone would know what Miss Lori Blackberry looked like. The teacher made a second chart with the same story on it. She cut the sentences from the story so that each was on a separate strip of paper. First as a group exercise, and then individually, the children were asked to put the sentences in order. The entire story was hanging up on the bulletin board, so they could match the separate sentence strips with their counterparts on the bulletin board. Matching their arrangement with the one on the board was a way of checking to see whether they had the sentences in the correct order.

Next, the teacher cut each sentence up into individual words. Sentence by sentence the children put the story back together again, checking with the model on the board to see if they had the words in the proper order. This time the matching process called upon their knowledge of the letters of the alphabet. First, however, the process relied primarily on the children's sense of form and shape to identify and remember the words in the story.

Because of its high motivational value the experience story offers many opportunities to have children engage in sentence- and word-matching activities.

Variations

Some classes make up a bulletin-board newspaper. Children in the first grade can prepare daily reports about the weather, holidays, birthdays, and personal items about children in the class at home or with a teaching assistant. Through experience chart techniques a wide sight vocabulary can be built, and all of it is based on the language the children themselves use.

The experience-story technique can be utilized effectively as a spontaneous writing activity. Broadly interpreted, writing an experience story can begin in kindergarten. For example, a child draws a picture on one side of an open notebook (8½ × 11 sheets). He then dictates a story about the picture to an aide or to the teacher, which is printed on the facing page of the notebook. Ample space should be left between lines of print to enable the child to trace over the letters or to copy them directly below the line on which they are written. No marks should be placed on the booklet to correct or grade the child's writing. Nothing should be done at this point that might inhibit or kill the child's desire to express himself in writing. The child will usually build his own story booklet so that he can "read" it to himself and to others. It can become a source of great pride for the child and provides excellent one-to-one contact.

One first-grader's notebook contained a drawing of a blue car accompanied by this story: "We have a new car. It is a 1976 Chevie." The child took his picture and story home to show his drawing to the family and to show that he could read the words accompaning the drawing. A short note from the teacher suggested to the parents that they could help the child by writing each word from the story on a separate slip of paper and using these as flash cards to help him recall the words. If he could not recall a word, the child was asked to match it with its counterpart on the experience chart.

Configuration

The major emphasis of making experience charts or labeling pictures and objects is to develop the realization that sounds and symbols are related. Along the way the child forms definite visual perceptions of what specific words look like. Often he gains these perceptions by remembering the *configuration,* or shape, of words. This does not mean that he does not use other cues, such as the first letter of the word. Initially, however, visual memory techniques are used to develop a few sight words; that is, words recognized instantly from visual memory, as opposed to any systematic decoding technique.

Many words have individuality in their general contour, or word form. The individual configuration is apparent only when the words appear in lower case letters, for example:

When they are printed with capital letters, the individuality of form is lost, except for length:

| STOP | | HELP | | APPLE | | GRANDFATHER | | GRASSHOPPER |

In teaching children to use configuration as a device for remembering words the teacher points to certain striking characteristics. The word is long or short, and it has some tall or high letters or some letters with tails that hang below the line. The name *Tony,* for example, begins with a tall letter and ends with a tail letter, and it is a short word. It looks like this: Tony

The utility of configuration as a word-recognition device is quite limited. The teacher should restrict its use to words that have rather evident or unique characteristics, such as *alligator,* or to words that have a high emotional value to the child, such as his own name or that of his pet. *Mother, father, thunder, laugh,* and *house* are examples of words that elicit strong feelings of happiness, sadness, fear, and security. Various cultures give an assigned emotional value to specific words (Ashton-Warner, 1963). As with their own names, children will want to learn such words quickly and will apply extra energy to retaining them through visual memory techniques (Braun, 1968). These short words should be learned in phrases and sentences. One technique is to place them on word cards and ask the children to match those words to the same words in sentences on the board or in a book (see Figure 8.3).

More than one word should be used to show children what configuration cues are. An effective practice is to use words they have already seen in some manner. Take the story about the hamster, Miss Lori Blackberry. Some cues that might be indicated are the length of *Blackberry,* the two tall letters in *hamster,* and the two *o*'s in *room.* The teacher might list five such words on the chalkboard. Then she and the children together could note the characteristics of each word—such as length, double letters, ascending *(b)* and descending letters *(y).* As the analysis proceeds, the teacher can box the word stop to show the class differences in word form.

Special Words for Visual Memory

Though it was recommended earlier in this chapter that visual memory techniques be used only on a few initial words in the child's reading vocabulary, some words are learned best and easiest through a visual memory technique. Many short words with a high frequency of use and often having an irregular spelling pattern are prime candidates for learning through visual memory technique. Examples such as *the, there, when, was,* and *would* are words which must quickly become sight words for the child. Many words which linguists call *function words* are also probably best learned by a visual memory approach (LeFevre, 1964). One way of teaching these words is to use them in context as captions for pictures—for example, Mary *and* Tom *are* running.

"Because they didn't stop to think,"
said Mr. Brown. "And the people who own
that factory over there are polluting
the water, too."

"Can we do anything about the pollution?"
Bob asked Mr. Brown.

"How can we make the water clean again?"
Ellen asked.

"There are some things we can do,"
said Mr. Brown. "I don't know if we can
ever make the lake really clean again,
but we can try."

Figure 8.3 Find a new word on the page.

The words listed below are samples of many of the high-frequency words that need to be learned early and without undue emphasis on decoding.

Eighty-five High-frequency Short Words

about	do	is	over	this
after	don't			those
all	down	many	please	though
along		may		to
also	each	might	second	
another	eight	most	seven	two
any	every	much	shall	
are		must	should	very
around	first	my	some	was
as	for	myself	such	were
	four			what
because	from	near	than	when
both		not	that	where
but	goes		the	which
by	have	of	their	while
	his	off	them	who
come	how	one	then	why
could		other	there	
	into	our	these	yes
didn't		out	they	you
			third	your

Extensive studies have been devoted to the cues children can and do use in order to recognize words. Some of these studies are listed in the bibliography of this book.

Word Meaning

To a degree, word meaning, or vocabulary, is taken for granted in many of the word-recognition exercises in beginning reading instruction. Yet vocabulary development is an integral part of the reading program. At first the child needs a constant expansion of vocabulary and must be shown how to use his background to learn new words and concepts. In the middle and upper school grades vocabulary must become more precise; and technical words in science, social studies, and mathematics must be learned in addition to a general vocabulary.

Evaluation

Several means can be used to check on a student's knowledge of the words being used and to encourage the development of a basic vocabulary. For example, ask the child to describe the picture in his mind when he hears a word such as *bargain*. Have someone in class use the word in a sentence. Encourage children to ask about a word when they do not have an image or perception in their minds, or when they find that they do not know how to use the word correctly in a sentence. Question children in the class about the meaning of special words that appear in an individual's experience chart.

Children can exchange their experience stories and help one another to read them. They can be made conscious of the need to explain to others some of the words they have used. The boy who dictated an experience story about his pet dog "leaping off the basement stairs and bumping into the steampipe" presents two possible vocabulary problems for other members of his first-grade class—*basement* and *steampipe*. Many of the other children in class may have no perception of these words. Both the teacher and pupils should be alert to such situations, and make use of them to expand the vocabulary of the entire group.

Other Teaching Techniques

These pages have described the teaching of words through matching pictures and objects, labeling, and making experience charts. Still other ways of building a sight vocabulary through visual memory approaches follow.

Standard Technique

The teacher writes a word on the chalkboard or on a card. Then he uses it in a sentence and asks a child to repeat the sentence. The teacher and child discuss ways to remember the word—by configuration, striking characteristics, picture clues, concrete demonstration. Through some practice exercise the child learns to recognize the word. In the early stages of learning the teacher usually introduces the written symbol and assures the child that he can proceed securely in matching a word sound with the written symbols for it.

Words may be introduced in isolation, as they are when associated with a picture or with an object, or they may be introduced in a complete statement, as they are in an experience story. Either way, at one point the word is isolated so that the child must respond to the word as a separate entity; at another point the word should be placed in context to see if the child can recognize it in actual reading. Both procedures are essential to learning to read. In context, the child has the opportunity to test himself on recognition accuracy. If the word that he calls does not seem to make sense in context, then the chances are he has not correctly identified the word.

The very nature of a sight word means that it is overlearned. It is practiced until the learner can respond automatically, without any conscious effort to recall or to associate the word with configuration or picture clues or other methods of analysis. To reach this overlearned stage the teacher must provide children with frequent practice activities, hopefully in high interest workbooks and books. Practice activities can take many forms as indicated in these sample drills.

Clap Your Hands

The child is told to clap once when the teacher displays the word card containing a word he names. For example, the teacher may say *three* and begin to flash the word cards. The child claps his hands when the word *three* appears on the card. If the child fails to identify several of the words in the series, the teacher must provide additional instruction on those words.

Word Hunt

The teacher writes a vertical row of words on the chalkboard and then writes the same words, but arranged differently, in a second row. Two children have a contest to find each word in their respective rows, as the teacher or an assistant reads one word after another. The rest of the students serve as judges and keep score as to who identified the words first.

Word Bingo

Each child has a card marked with squares. The words to be practiced have been written in the squares. The teacher says a word aloud. If the child has the word on his card, he places a marker on it, as in "Bingo."

Train Game

The children are divided into two groups, each group representing a train. Cards are flashed to the engine (first child), and then to the rest of the cars in order. Any child who does not know the word which is flashed is given the card to hold. The train with the lightest load (the fewest number of held cards) wins the train race.

Captions and Pictures

Pictures are displayed on the bulletin board. Appropriate titles using the sight words that are to be practiced are prepared on cardboard strips. The child must match the written caption with the correct picture. Sample titles would be "School Bus" or "Two Fishermen."

Picture Dictionary

When a child learns a new sight word he writes it in a notebook. He then either draws a picture of the word or finds one in an old magazine that he can paste next to the word.

Word Pairs

Words that are often confused by children are written on the chalkboard or on a worksheet in pairs:

when	where
house	horse
there	then

As the teacher says each word, the child draws a line under that word.

These are just a few of the practice activities that a teacher can develop to promote the visual memory of words. As mentioned earlier, words must be used in context immediately following any drill with isolated words. Numerous other activities can be found in books like *Reading Aids through the Grades* (Russell, 1951); *Spice* (Platts, Scholastic Publications, 1960); and *Decision Making for the Diagnostic Teacher* (Cooper *et al.*), the laboratory manual associated with this text.

Word-flashing Devices

Technology has made large strides in helping youngsters learn mechanical tasks. The visual memory approach to learning words is particularly suited to the use of mechanical devices to relieve the teacher of time-consuming responsibilities. For example, instruments which resemble film projectors enable the learner to respond to a symbol (or a word or phrase) flashed on a screen at a controlled speed. The general term for these machines is *tachistoscope*. A word list on a filmstrip is inserted into the machine and each word is flashed at a set speed; after the learner responds, the word is repeated on the screen so he can check the accuracy of his response.

Some of these devices are simply manually operated shutters. They add a semblance of technology to a drill that teachers often accomplished in the past by means of 3″ × 5″ flash cards. Other, computer type of machines tell the pupil whether his answer is right or wrong, and then provide him with a new problem to solve (a new word or phrase) in keeping with the kind of response that he made on the previous problem.

Some audiotape machines are also programmed to develop a sight vocabulary. Typically, the student looks at a sheet of paper or a card on which is written the word or word list he is to learn. The tape pronounces the word while the student looks at it on the card or on the worksheet. The student may be asked to write the word on paper or in the air as a means of reinforcing the image. While these machines do not provide a flashed image, they make it possible for a student to repeat an exercise as often as is necessary so that he can fix the image of the word in his memory while listening to the sound of the word. The Bell and Howell Language Master is an example of a specialized tape recorder than can be used for these purposes.

Most schools try such aids on a pilot basis before working them into the teaching system. Even though there are problems in training personnel to use machines, and in designing the curriculum and classrooms to take full advantage of technology, these mechanical aids to reading instruction can substantially increase the freedom of the teacher to act as a diagnostician instead of a drill master. Certainly machines provide no learning panacea. They are only one more factor making it feasible for diagnostic teaching to grow in the schools.

One weakness of most machine programs is that the word lists and other exercises that are used may not fit the needs of the children in the class. The teacher must examine these programs carefully and match them with the needs of his students. Otherwise students will be trapped in a stereotyped machine program under the guise of giving the teacher more time for diagnosing and treating specific needs.

Assessing Progress in Sight Words

As with any other skill, progress in learning sight words is measured in terms of the specific objectives the program has set as its goal. If the objective is to recognize the Stone and Bartschi (1963) basic word list, then test words must be selected from that list and administered to the children through a flash type of procedure so that success in instant recognition can be determined. If the objective is to have the child learn a number of words that he has proposed through experience stories, then each child should be tested with words selected from this kind of story or group of stories, if these were used.

In grades two, three, and higher the Stone and Bartschi word list (see Appendix D) may be an appropriate criterion, for at these points most children would have gained instant recognition of such high-frequency words. The development of a sight vocabulary continues throughout the grades. Though the student gains more independence in reading because he acquires a variety of word analysis skills, he needs reminders and assistance in systematically enlarging his sight vocabulary.

At the beginning of a new school year the teacher should check on his students' knowledge of visual memory techniques. A checklist, such as the one below, would enable the teacher to see which students need additional guidance.

Sight Vocabulary Checklist

1. Has the child been exposed to the following methods of spontaneously discriminating among words by similarities and differences?
   a. Unusual length (for example, *grandmother*).   yes——no——
   b. Configuration (for example, *fudge,*).   yes——no——
   c. Root words (for example, *play* in *played*).   yes——no——
   d. Compound words (for example, *mailbox*).   yes——no——

e. Initial letters or sounds (for example, *hat, bat, cat*).   yes——no——

f. Double letters (for example, *butter, took*).   yes——no——

2. Is the child capable of building a word bank of words that have been identified originally by some other method but through repeated encounters have become sight words?   yes——no——

3. What is the child's reading level on the Stone and Bartschi word list or some other appropriate list?

Since we are concerned at this point primarily with the skills needed to get the learner started in reading, we would not anticipate that long lists of words—such as those constructed by Stone and Bartischi (1963), Stone (1956), Fry (1957), and Dolch (1942)—would be used as criteria of success. A much more limited group of words should probably be the criterion for the initial weeks of reading instruction. A teacher's list of two dozen emotion-packed words, for example, or twenty words from the experience charts, or a 10 percent sample of randomly selected words from the basal reading word list are more appropriate criteria.

In addition to checking the child's skill in recognizing two dozen flashed words, the teacher should determine whether the child recognizes those words in context. Testing word recognition in context emphasizes for the student that the only purpose of word exercises is to enable him to read better. Meaning is stressed when words appear in context, and the child doesn't fool himself into saying that he is reading when he pronounces a single word in isolation.

If the teacher finds that a student does not respond with a high percentage of correct answers on the sight word criterion test, he can proceed with several alternatives. It is entirely possible that the student's poor performance has its cause in some vision problem. Such a possibility was discussed in Chapter 7. It may also be that the student learns slowly by means of sight only (the visual modality), in which case the teacher may find an auditory approach more successful. The child may have poor memory habits, and will have difficulty building a sight word vocabulary no matter what instructional techniques are used. He must first receive help in building habits of memory.

Building Memory Habits

Memory habits may have a great deal to do with the child's success in the initial stages of reading. Unless a child can compare word forms, noting essential likenesses and differences, he will have difficulty in using either phonic analysis or structural analysis effectively. The following suggestions for building memory habits may be of assistance to the child:

1. List a series of numbers on several cards.

175   78906

2389   098673

Show one card to the child for half a second and then ask him to repeat the numbers on the card. As soon as he is able to make several correct responses with four digits, move on to cards with five digits, and so on. The concentration and the use of left-to-right progression will be extremely helpful habits for use with words. A similar procedure is employed in the Wechsler Intelligence Scale for Children to build auditory memory. The examiner calls out numbers which the child tries to repeat.

2. Use a group of related objects, such as a pencil, a pen, an eraser, and a notebook. Children observe them carefully for a second and then hide their eyes. The teacher adds (or removes) a ruler or some other related item. The children then try to identify what has been added (or removed). Or the arrangement of the items may be changed and the children are asked to duplicate the original arrangement.

3. In order to test a child's skill at recognizing words in context, the teacher can give him a passage in which several criterion words are found, and then listen while he reads aloud. With a check sheet the teacher can identify the words that the child recognizes without hesitation and those that he does not recognize in this manner. If the test involves a group, the teacher can construct multiple-choice test items similar to these:

Indians _____ in Florida.

     like   live   give

The ball _____into the street.

    bounded   bubbled   robbed

Tony _____with Father.

     will   want   went

To fill in these items the child has to use meaning clues as well as word-form clues.

Limitations of Visual Memory Techniques

The goal of all reading instruction is to move the child from being a dependent reader to being an independent one. The cues used in sight-word recognition contain limitations. Confusion may arise when the beginning reader sees a new word with a configuration similar to one he already knows. *Blueberry* may be confused with *blackberry; grandfather* with *grandmother; book* with *look.*

When words of similar configuration are confronted by the child (*went* and *want*) he has no distinctive cues to help him identify the word, except its meaning in the sentence. In other words, the word must always be checked against the context of the words around it.

Some children will find it difficult to remember large numbers of words. Even for those who find it easy, visual memory techniques are inefficient in trying to develop a large reading vocabulary. It makes good sense to use the visual memory approach initially because it requires the child to read on the very first day of instruction. The techniques immediately show that there is a relation between words in speech and words in print. The child also needs word-analysis techniques that will give him a greater sense of independence in reading and will enable him to proceed at the pace that his skill in analysis permits. He needs to know not only that words in speech are represented by written symbols but that sound units within words have graphic counterparts. This relationship makes sound-symbol analysis for the native speaker a fruitful way of deciphering the printed page and of becoming an independent reader.

SUMMARY

Configuration and the striking characteristics of words provide cues for the recognition of whole words through visual memory. Such visual memory techniques aid the child in associating written symbols with words that are already in his listening and speaking vocabularies. Use of visual memory learning techniques for word recognition is known as the sight-word, or the whole-word, technique. In this approach a whole word is presented to the child, first by saying it and then by relating it to pictures or concrete experiences or by constructing experience charts. The child then establishes an association between the pronounciation of the word and its printed form. Through a variety of practice activities such words are overlearned and become sight words; that is, they are recognized instantly without analysis.

One goal of reading instruction is to create a vast reservoir of words the reader recognizes instantly. This enables the reader to concentrate on the message and not worry about the mechanics of analyzing words. Using context clues and his experience with syntax aids the identification process. The use of flash cards, tachistoscopic devices, and experience stories are some of the means used to establish the initial group of words to be learned by visual memory techniques. For purposes of practice, some words can be isolated. All the sight words need to be practiced in context, however, so the student knows from the beginning that words are used to communicate.

Some words, such as high-frequency short words and emotion-packed words, are probably learned best by the visual memory approach. The teacher should be cognizant of local environmental words that have high emotional value and use them as part of the sight-word group.

The assessment of sight words is directed to a small group of words that form the objective for the first few weeks of instruction. They should be tested both in a flash-word test and in context.

Though visual memory of words may be stressed during the first weeks of reading instruction, a child should be taught from the beginning that there are internal cues for distinguishing words with similar shapes (for example, *dog*, *dig*). Therefore he needs decoding skills as the basis for his independence in reading.

sight word
context clues
visual memory techniques
configuration
experience chart
phonics analysis

structural analysis
linguistic analysis
function words
tachistoscope
flash cards

1. If you encountered a child who could not read a beginning first-grade book in your third-grade class, what place would visual memory techniques have in your instructional plan?
2. In what sense is it helpful to think of language experience charts when considering visual memory techniques for word recognition?

9

Decoding
Word Symbols

Suppose your instructor printed the following symbols on the chalkboard:

ΔΗΚΩΔΙΝΓ ΘΙΣ ΜΕΣΕΓ ΙΖ ΛΙΗΚ ΛΕΡΝΙΝΓ ΤΥ ΡΗΔ.
ΡΙΗΤΙΝΓ ΙΖ Α ΚΩΔ ΦΟΡ ΣΙΙΗΧ.

Then suppose the instructor said: "What I have written on the board is a message in phonetic English, but I have used capital Greek letters instead of the ABC's to write it. How would you go about knowing what the message says?" Can you decode it?

Your Answer:

What skills must one know in order to decipher the message and get its meaning? A beginning reader is in a similar situation. Things an adult reader takes for granted have to be explained to the beginner:

that the symbols stand for a message

that there are ways of identifying the beginning and ending of individual utterances (punctuation and capitalization)

that there is a relation between the sound of speech and the symbols

that one has to know which sound or sounds each symbol stands for

that the pattern or arrangement of the symbols gives some hints as to how they will be pronounced; for example, the trigraph (three letters that stand for one sound) consonant-vowel-consonant, c-a-t, in English usually suggests a short sound for the vowel.

The decoding operation is not a simple process. It requires a great deal of background knowledge, in addition to the ability to translate individual visual symbols into speech sounds.

Now decipher the coded message using the symbols given below. The symbols are matched to letters of the English alphabet.

Code symbols   Α Β Γ Δ Ε Η Θ Ι Κ Λ Μ Ν Ο Π Ρ Σ Τ Υ Φ Χ Ψ Ω Z

Alphabet symbols   A B G D Ĕ Ē TH I K L M N Ŏ P R S T U PH CH PS Ō Z

As you can see, the code is not too different from the regular English alphabet, yet it looks quite confusing. Can you decode the message? Do you agree with the message?

This chapter will help you to answer the following questions:

How do modern reading authorities view the use of decoding techniques?

What is the difference between phonics and linguistics?

How does one teach sound-symbol relations analytically?

How does one teach sound-symbol relations synthetically?

What role does word meaning play in a decoding approach to word recognition?

A reader needs many means for identifying words if he is to become independent. A group of skills sometimes called decoding skills is one important means of identification. Everyone who has read children's mystery stories or has deciphered coded messages on the back of cereal boxes knows that decoding means translating visual symbols into ideas, usually into word sounds that represent ideas. For that reason, *phonics* is the term often used in relation to decoding when reading instruction is being discussed. Today's authorities will not question the value of using a sound-symbol relation in translating visual symbols back into the word sounds for which they stand.

There is more to the notion of decoding, however, than knowing that the letter "c" represents the sound at the beginning of the word cat or that "ph" usually represents the /f/ sound.

Decoding

The term decoding in the teaching of reading can be used in a very narrow sense to mean identifying the relation between the letters of the alphabet and certain sounds in words. Pronouncing a list of words or pronouncing nonsense words, such as *cac*, is decoding in this narrow sense. A broader definition of *decoding* includes making the sound-symbol relation, plus using many other cues that enable a reader to relate the printed page to communication through language. Inflection, dialect patterns, idioms, and punctuation are among the cues that place a passage in a broader language setting. In this view of decoding the reader translates the written code when he uses these cues to bring meaning to the printed page.

Both *phonic analysis* and *linguistic analysis*, which are discussed later in this chapter, may be included in the definition of decoding. Though professionals in the field of reading have not adopted a universally accepted definition for the term, we prefer a broad statement, and so use decoding to mean deciphering a printed utterance through a variety of phonics and language cues.

Since this chapter is concerned with initial reading skills, the decoding skills presented here are limited to those a child might acquire in the early stages of reading instruction. These would include understanding the letter-sound relations, some spelling patterns (phonic generalizations), and certain writing conventions (periods, commas, capital letters, and so on).

Written symbols cannot be used to communicate as fully as oral language. Gestures, inflections of the voice, and voice volume are three aspects of oral language that are not easily cued into written language. The wise teacher will encourage learners to try to pick up as many cues as possible in order to reveal such aspects of oral language. Action and emotion in words and incidents can be used to suggest how a passage would be spoken.

We recommended that instruction in symbol decoding be given along with instruction in visual memory techniques. Simultaneous instruction in these two areas will enable a child to read words and sentences from the very beginning, while learning other techniques with which to decipher unfamiliar words.

The Great Debate

At one time reading theoreticians fought over the question of whether to use a sight-word-only approach or a letter-phonics-only approach in initial reading. The issue today is whether decoding skills should be gradual and analytic (inductive), based upon a comparison of words the student already knows by sight, or whether they should be intensive and synthetic (deductive),

FIGURE 9.1

based upon a concentration of sound-symbol relations and spelling patterns. Synthetic refers to learning individual letter sounds and combining these into words. Which approach is better probably depends mostly on the teacher.

In a nationwide first-grade study (Bond and Dykstra, 1967) most of the twenty-seven research projects included (synthetic) phonics or linguistics materials as one alternative method. Comparison between methods showed generally that children taught by a synthetic phonics system achieved higher scores in word recognition and in deriving paragraph meaning at the end of the first grade than children taught by a gradual analytic phonics approach. A second-grade follow up (Dykstra, 1968) on those children showed similar advantages on word recognition tests for those who received early and intensive teaching of sound-symbol correspondence. They did not, as a general rule, however, demonstrate superiority in reading comprehension in the second grade.

In 1967 Chall's *Learning to Read: The Great Debate* focused critical attention on the teaching of reading. Following her review of research from 1912 to 1965, Chall concluded that a code-emphasis method, using intensive synthetic decoding, produces better results than a meaning-emphasis method using gradual analytic decoding. She cited correlational studies that showed a significant relationship between the child's ability to recognize letters and the sounds these represent and reading achievement. She noted that this knowledge appears to be more essential for success in the early stages of reading than other factors, such as intelligence and oral language ability. Chall pointed to the need for a systematic method of introducing decoding skills to the child rather than leaving the acquisition of those skills to chance, haphazard practice, or inductive learning.

The research evidence is not strong enough to convince every reading authority that intensive decoding is the way to begin instruction in reading. There have, however, been demonstrable changes along these lines in the early reading materials that are being published. New basal readers and the revised editions of traditional basal readers are introducing more phonics earlier and are sometimes providing supplementary phonics workbooks. The latter often give a synthetic, intensive presentation, working alongside the gradual analytic approach of the basal readers they support. At the same time the new basal readers are increasing their emphasis on language and language experience activities.

Teaching Initial Decoding Skills

From the previous discussion it should be clear that the relation of symbol to sound can be demonstrated for students either analytically or synthetically. Initially a teacher emphasizes one method or the other to keep the learning technique fairly simple, but both techniques should be used later in the development of word-analysis skills. Both initial approaches have proved effective in achieving their goals, as is attested by today's many mature readers who once learned decoding skills by these means.

Gradual, Analytic Method

The gradual, analytic method initially presents the student with a list of words that become part of his sight vocabulary through visual memory techniques. Subsequently he is taught to analyze these words by identifying certain common sounds that appear in them. For example, the sight words *milk, man,* and *mother* are shown to the child, who is asked if he sees anything about these three words that is the same. Having identified the letter "m," which is common to the words, he then "reads" them. The teacher cautions him to listen to the sound he hears at the beginning of each word. "Whenever we see this letter, 'm' in a word we will hear the sound that we hear at the beginning of *milk* and *man.* Can you think of some other words that begin the same as *milk* and *mother?*"

The proponents of the analytic method contend that it keeps decoding as part of the reading act, since the sounds are never isolated but are always taught within the context of the word and perhaps the sentence.

Synthetic Method

In contrast, the synthetic method advocates the teaching of letters and their sounds in an intensive manner before reading is begun. Sounds are then combined, or synthesized, into words. For example, the pupil has learned the sounds of the letters "c," "a," and "t." The teacher writes the word *cat* on the chalkboard. The child synthesizes these known sounds into a word. This could be done as follows: "What is the sound of the letter 'c'? That's correct, 'kuh.'" The same procedure eliciting the sounds of the rest of the letters in *cat* is then done. The three separate sounds are then combined (kuh-ăă-tuh) into the word *cat.*

Some commercial reading programs isolate letter sounds, and some identify the association of sound and symbol only in whole words. Some linguists, such as Fries (1963) and Hall (1960), deplore the total isolation of letter sounds because they say this total isolation tends to distort the sounds. Some children, however, fail to discriminate the sound within a word and may be able to learn it best in isolation, as experience with remedial reading cases has shown. The teacher therefore adjusts the procedure to fit the individual child's needs.

Since English spelling does not provide a one-to-one correspondence between distinctive word sounds (phonemes) and the letters of the alphabet (graphemes), a system for analyzing the spelling patterns that correspond to sounds in words must be carefully developed and systematically taught in class. It is not sufficient, for example, to condition children to respond with one sound to each letter of the alphabet. There are only twenty-six alphabet letters, but there are approximately forty-three distinctive sounds (phonemes) in the English language. Most instructional materials for teaching initial decoding skills use English spelling as it exists, but some use specially devised tools to set up a one-to-one correspondence between sound and symbol. The ITA (Initial Teaching Alphabet) and Words in Color charts are two devices that have been developed for helping the beginning reader simplify the decoding problem.

ITA

If English spelling (orthography) had one symbol for each of the forty-three to forty-seven phonemes (opinions vary on the number), the decoding problem in reading instruction would be relatively simple. A teacher could condition children to respond with a specific sound each time they saw a letter symbol. By blending sounds the words could be decoded or, more precisely, recoded from writing into sound. The Initial Teaching Alphabet (ITA) attempts to simplify the decoding problem by creating a symbol for each phoneme. The forty-five symbols that ITA uses, and some examples of the way the symbols look when they are put together in words, are shown in Figure 9.2.

Proponents of ITA claim it eliminates many of the failures usually associated with beginning reading. They point proudly to the creative writing that many first-grade children produce since ITA enables them to disregard traditional spelling hazards (Downing, 1967). Opponents of ITA claim that comparative research studies are inconclusive, and that the problems of ITA are great, especially when the research in favor of the use of ITA is not strong (Marsh, 1968). The problems most frequently referred to are those associated with the student's transfer from ITA to traditional spelling. A certain amount of unlearning has to take place to move the child from one system into another; and there is the possibility of spelling problems being created when children begin using the traditional alphabet. Research studies to date, however, do not indicate that spelling problems for children who first learn to read with ITA are greater than for the child who is started on the traditional alphabet.

Words in Color

The charts developed for the initial reading system called Words in Color give a realistic picture of the decoding problem faced by a reader of English.

girls and bois lern

tω reed with i|t|a

(From *The Story of ITA*. Copyright © 1965,
Initial Teaching Alphabet Publication, Inc.
Reprinted by permission of the publisher)

FIGURE 9.2   The Initial Teaching Alphabet

The sound-symbol correspondences shown demonstrate the similarity of ITA to the traditional alphabet.

The Words in Color system lists under each of the English phonemes the various ways that the phoneme is spelled in words. Each phoneme is represented on the charts by a bar of color. Initially students are taught to respond to each color bar with a distinct phoneme. When the teacher points to the red bar, for example, the student responds with the sound /a/. Even though the sound /a/ has several spellings in English, initially the student learns to respond only to the color symbol. He learns to respond to the colors rapidly and blend them into complete word sounds (/k/-/a/-/t/). The blending technique is then applied to the first letter symbol in each color bar—usually it is a single letter. The sounds /k-a-t/, therefore, have a one-to-one correspondence to cat. Because other spellings are superimposed on the color bar, the student realizes that eventually he must learn to respond with the same sound (phoneme) to each of those possible spellings for the sound represented by the color bar (see Figure 9.3).

ITA and Words in Color represent tries at a solution to the irregularities of the English spelling system. They also indicate the kinds of problems associated with finding a new means for overcoming such difficulties—tradition and lack

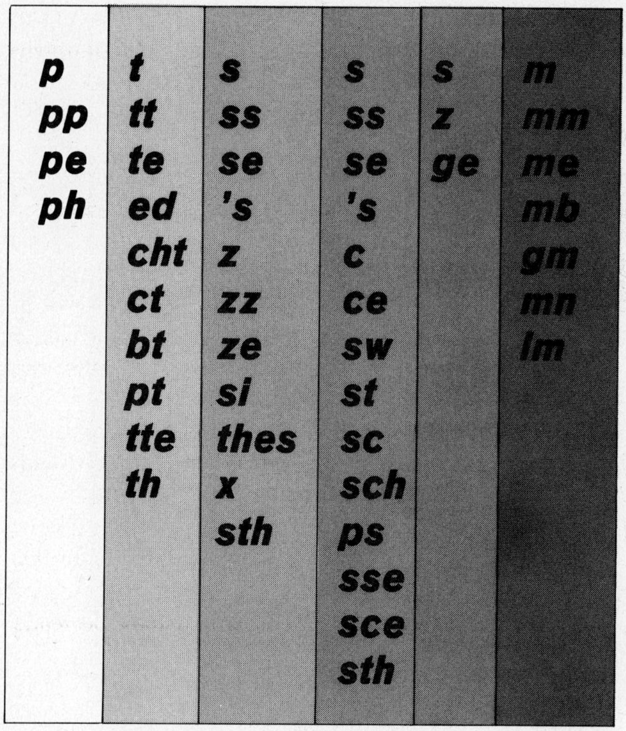

p	t	s	s	s	m
pp	tt	ss	ss	z	mm
pe	te	se	se	ge	me
ph	ed	's	's		mb
	cht	z	c		gm
	ct	zz	ce		mn
	bt	ze	sw		lm
	pt	si	st		
	tte	thes	sc		
	th	x	sch		
		sth	ps		
			sse		
			sce		
			sth		

FIGURE 9.3   Words in Color

The actual Words in Color system lists each English phoneme in a bar of a different color. Students respond to the color bars with a distinct phoneme during a practice session.

FIGURE 9.4

The C-V-C pattern can be easily demonstrated and practiced on the chalkboard.

of materials. Indeed, it becomes clear why most educators and publishers prefer to develop solutions within the framework of traditional spelling.

Phonics Techniques

Most methods for teaching initial decoding skills work within the regular English spelling system. They try to give the student some generalizations about this spelling system and its relation to word sounds. The student then sees that there is considerable regularity within the English spelling system which assists him in applying sound and symbol patterns as part of the decoding process.

To avoid confusion the teacher should ordinarily limit the first lesson on the sound-symbol relationship to words that have a fairly consistent one-to-one correspondence. Trigraphs—such as *man, bet, pit, pop,* and *cup*—in the consonant-vowel-consonant pattern often have a one-to-one correspondence between phoneme and grapheme and are therefore good examples to use in early lessons. After providing instruction on the sounds related to the symbols /t/, /p/, /c/, and /a/, and the sound of "a" in the consonant-vowel-consonant pattern, the teacher can present the words *at, cat, tap, cap,* and *pat* and expect students to pronounce the words. In these examples each letter represents a single sound (phoneme).

After establishing the phoneme-grapheme relation for several letters of the alphabet the teacher should begin to introduce the children to patterns in which the phonemes and graphemes occur. Initially the patterns should be simple ones. Many of the phonics and linguistic reading programs begin with the consonent-vowel-consonant pattern. These patterns usually include the short sound of the vowel: *bat, bet, bit, bop, but.* Phonics programs often teach these patterns through rules or generalizations which may be learned either deductively or inductively (*see* Figure 9.4).

Phonics Generalizations

Modern reading programs give the learner certain rules or generalizations to help in analyzing words. Several researchers have questioned the utility of some of these generalizations (Clymer, 1963; Emans, 1966; Bailey, 1967). Of the forty-five phonic generalizations examined in these studies, some seem to have high utility for the elementary school child while others appear to be quite useless. Clymer examined materials from the primary grades; Emans materials above the primary grades; and Bailey took samples from the six most popular basal readers of the 1960's for Grades 1 through 6. These researchers first asked whether the phonic generalization seemed to fit at least twenty words out of a 2,000-word sample. They then applied the generalization to see whether it gave the reader an accurate pronunciation of those twenty words.

If the generalization applied to only 30 to 50 percent of those words, the student would have at least that much assistance in deciphering the words. This does not mean that a student should memorize all of these rules; most of them should become operational through practice with words in context (Smith, 1966).

Emans wrote eighteen generalizations that had a high percentage of utility in the middle grades. They are reproduced in Table 9.1. But learning those generalizations is fruitless if they are used strictly without regard to meaning in context. If a child is taught to identify words only by means of a pronunciation guide, his daily lessons could degenerate into word-calling mechanics. There is a wide variety of spelling patterns, or graphemes, for the same sounds or phonemes in the English language. This variety encourages teachers to guide students in finding generalizations and applying them. Some words—about 8 percent according to Hay and Wingo (1960, p. 13) and Fries (1963)— defy phonic analysis. These must be learned by the whole word method through visual memory techniques and the syntactic clues in a sentence.

Linguistics

In the early forties the Yale-based linguist, Leonard Bloomfield, proposed that word recognition be taught according to sound patterns (1961). He argued that there is a direct correspondence between the sound of a word in the spoken language and the way it is written.

Bloomfield pointed out that linguists have devised frequency tables to identify the most often used vowel and consonant sounds. In his suggested exercises he starts with words and phonic elements that will be simple and useful for the beginning reader. These elements, he says, are the short vowel sounds, followed by the long vowel sounds. After the graphic symbols for these sounds have been mastered, the irregular sounds and symbols can be introduced.

By arranging regular words in consistent, sequential patterns, Bloomfield would teach the child to identify the phoneme-grapheme relation and to build on previously mastered knowledge of sounds. Bloomfield's method starts with words that have a one-to-one sound-to-letter relation. He first uses words that have the short sound of "*a*" and then proceeds with the short sound of *e, i, o,* and *u.* The student is taught a large number of three-letter words, all having the short sound of the vowel. Bloomfield's practice sentences take the *Dan can fan a man* pattern. He then presents his second pattern—the long sound of the vowel. Here, too, consonants remain in a single, uncomplicated form. Each

TABLE 9.1   Modifications of the Original Forty-five Generalizations

Generalization	Percentage of utility
1. The letters *io* usually represent a short *u* sound as in *nation*.	86
2. The letters *oo* usually have the long double *o* sound as in *food,* or the short double *o* sound as in *good.* They are more likely to have the double *o* sound as in *food*.	100
3. When a vowel is in the middle of a one-syllable word, the vowel is short except that it may be modified in words in which the vowel is followed by an *r*.	80
4. When the vowel is the middle letter of a one-syllable word, the vowel is short.	80
5. When the first vowel in a word is *a* and the second is *i*, the *a* is usually long and the *i* is silent.	83
6. When the first vowel in a word is *o* and the second is *a*, the *o* is usually long and the *a* is silent.	86
7. The vowel combination *ui* has a short *i* sound.	79
8. The two letters *ow* make the long *o* sound or the *ou* sound as in *out*.	100
9. When *y* is used as a vowel it most often has the sound of long *e*.	92
10. The letter *a* has the same sound (ô) when followed by *w* and *u*.	84
11. One vowel letter in an accented syllable has the short sound if it comes before the end of the syllable, and the long sound if it comes at the end of the syllable.	78
12. One vowel letter in an accented syllable has the short sound if it comes before the end of the syllable, and the long sound if it comes at the end of the syllable, except when it is followed by an *r*.	97
13. When *y* of *ey* is seen in the last syllable that is not accented, the short sound of *i* is heard.	97
14. A *-tion* at the end of a four-syllable word indicates a secondary accent on the first syllable, with a primary accent on the syllable preceding the *-tion*.	95
15. Taking into account original rules 5, 28, 29, 31, and 41,* one sees that if the first vowel sound in a word is followed by two consonants, the first syllable usually ends with the first of the two consonants.	96
16. Except in some words with a prefix, if the first vowel sound in a word is followed by a single consonant, that consonant begins the second syllable, and the vowel sound in the first syllable will be long; *or* if the consonant ends the first syllable, the vowel sound will be short.	84
17. A beginning syllable ending with a consonant and containing a short vowel sound is likely to be accented.	95
18. When a word has only one vowel letter, the vowel sound is likely to be short unless the vowel letter is followed by an *r*.	78

*5. The *r* gives the preceding vowel a sound that is neither long nor short. 28. When two of the same consonants are side by side only one is heard. 29. When a word ends in *ck* it has the same last sound as in *look*. 31. If *a, in, re, ex, de,* or *be* is the first syllable in a word it is usually unaccented. 41. When the first vowel element in a word is followed by *th, ch,* or *sh* these symbols are not broken when the word is divided into syllables and may go with either the first or second syllable.
Source: Robert Emans. "The Usefulness of Phonics Generalizations above the Primary Grades," *The Reading Teacher* (February 1967), pp. 419–425.

element is introduced in the order of its frequency of use in oral language.

Another linguist, Charles Fries (1963), advocates teaching reading according to spelling patterns. Like Bloomfield, he insists that the beginning reader should not be asked to identify irregular words before he has mastered regular patterns. Fries insists that the simplest spelling pattern be stated first—not only because it is simple but also because it represents the most frequently encountered spelling pattern in the English language. Fries identifies two major spelling patterns:

I. consonant-vowel-consonant; for example, *m-a-d*.
II. consonant-vowel-consonant-vowel; for example, *m-a-d-e*.

According to the Fries method the child should not be asked to identify words in Pattern II until he has mastered all the regular forms of Pattern I. No irregular words should be introduced until all the regular spelling patterns have been mastered. In Pattern I, for example, *b-a-d* can be distinguished from another word of the same shape by noting the difference or contrast in either the first, second, or third position; *p-a-d, b-e-d,* or *b-a-t* indicate the changes that can take place by altering one letter only. Table 9.2 gives comparative data on the decoding programs suggested by Bloomfield and Fries.

Fries's method of teaching word recognition rests on his theory that learners develop high-speed recognition responses to the written word by noting the different features of words (*mad* versus *made*). These high-speed responses are developed through much and frequent practice. The contrastive features are shown by differences in spelling; that is, the arrangement of the letters. It follows, therefore, that the alphabet is the basis for high-speed recognition responses to words.

Both Bloomfield and Fries insist that the phoneme-grapheme system is fairly regular and can therefore be more easily taught first through its regular forms. The words to be identified are set up according to scientific principles of regularity, simplicity, and frequency. More recently, linguist Ronald Wardbaugh suggests that reading selections for the beginner should reflect the natural language of speech and should not be artificially controlled except perhaps in skills practice exercises (Wardhaugh, 1975).

Multiskills Attitude

It is not physically or psychologically possible to develop all reading skills simultaneously and at once. No one expects competency after one week in school. But there is a psychological and instructional value in letting the child know that reading requires more than one skill, though these various skills will be developed over a period of years.

The teacher attempts to teach as many of the reading skills as are feasible. While children are learning that their own speech can be written down and read, they are also learning to recognize words through visual memory techniques and are being taught the rudiments of decoding. These three elements seem best interwoven in the initial teaching stages. The child wants to build a large storehouse of instant words, but he knows that for those words he does not recognize instantly he can use the letters of the alphabet and spelling patterns (generalizations) to assist him in identification. It is a reasonable

TABLE 9.2   Linguists' Methods of Teaching Reading

	Bloomfield	Fries
Basic principle	Alphabetic principle Phoneme-grapheme relation Phoneme orientation; that is, start with sound	Words are identified through visual or perceptual contrasts Develop recognition responses to graphemic contrasts Grapheme orientation; that is, start with spelling
	Sound-spelling Patterns	*Spelling patterns*

Reading readiness	Visual discrimination
	
	Left-to-right progression
	
	Auditory discrimination through rhymes
	
	Visual recognition of alphabet
	
	Auditory recognition of alphabet
		Oral language responses to familiar situations (pictures)
		
		Alphabet
		  Letter names
		  Visual recognition with 100 percent accuracy on upper and lower case

General procedure	Teach the children to respond to all the regular sound-spelling patterns; then teach them systematically to respond to the irregular sound-spelling patterns	Develop automatic recognition responses to words by identifying graphic contrasts within a pattern and graphic contrasts between patterns

		c-v-c	c-v-c-v	c-vv-c
Regular	*Irregular*	mad	made	maid
kid	knit	met	mete	meat
kin	knife	bit	bite	tied
kit	knee	hop	hope	boat
		cut	cute	dues

Overpractice the regular patterns. Once the base of regularity is formed, the deviations will not cause trouble

success story: "Reading makes sense, and I have a system for deciphering the words, which, in turn, will enable me to get the message."

Teaching Decoding Skills

For diagnostic purposes all teachers should be able to identify the more commonly used patterns or generalizations of words. You might try the brief phonic test that follows and then discuss the answers with others.

Teacher's Knowledge of Phonics

Circle the item that doesn't belong with the others. Give a brief reason for your choice.

1. pr, gl, tw, (sh,) spr _____ *(handwritten)* new sound
2. l, r, (o,) t, z _____ *(handwritten)* vowel
3. gh, ch, ph, th, (tr) _____
4. gnat, wrap, pneumatic, knee, (press) _____ *(handwritten)* his no silent beginning letter
5. a, e, m, i, y _____ *(handwritten)* m — no vowel
6. can, red, pill, (boat,) rug _____ *(handwritten)* og
7. sh, (sp,) ch, th, ph _____ *(handwritten)* ph
8. (ci,) ai, ea, oa, ee _____ *(handwritten)* ci
9. cot, road, doe, soul, beau _____ *(handwritten)* cot — short vowel
10. thin, thing, thick, (this,) path _____ *(handwritten)* th at end
11. pro, re, (ness,) in, ab _____ *(handwritten)* ness word ending
12. can, crust, (sup,) (cone,) cent _____
13. able, ly, ship, age, (mis) _____ *(handwritten)* suffix

A study by Emans (1967) identified eighteen phonic generalizations with a high percentage of utility. They were presented earlier in Table 9.1 and may assist the reader in making decisions about correct answers for the test just given.[1]

Phonics Generalizations

A teacher will recognize many of the generalizations even if he is not able to consciously formulate them. Certain generalizations should be memorized by teachers, especially those with a high usage potential. They can then be recalled to assist students who have difficulty.

Given below are generalizations that every teacher should know well in order to guide students through their initial decoding experiences.

1. *Short vowel rule:* When there is only one vowel in a word or syllable that vowel usually has a short sound, if the vowel stands at the beginning or in the middle of the word; for example, *at, but.*
2. *Long vowel rule 1:* When a two-vowel word or syllable has a silent e at the

[1]Answers to teacher's test:

1. sh	6. boat	10. this
2. o	7. sp	11. ness
3. tr	8. ci	12. cone
4. press	9. cot	13. mis
5. m		

end, the first vowel in the word usually has a long sound; for example, *made, side.*

3. *Long vowel rule 2:* When there is a double vowel in a word or syllable the first vowel usually has a long sound and the second vowel is silent; for example, *maid, beat.*

4. *Murmur rule:* When a vowel is followed by an *r* it has a modified sound that is neither characteristically long nor short; for example, *car, hurt.*

5. *Diphthong rule:* Certain double vowels have linked sounds that make use of both vowels; for example, the *ou* in *house, ow* in *now, oi* in *oil,* and *oy* in *boy* (C. Smith, 1967, p. 21).

Along with knowledge of the more common phonic generalizations, the teacher should have in mind a sequence for teaching phonics skills, and should be acquainted with materials and techniques for giving a child practice in decoding (phonics) skills. With that knowledge the teacher can observe and test students to determine what skills they have and how well they are learning the new ones being taught in class.

Sequence of Decoding Skills

Though it is appropriate to plan a sequence of decoding skills, we must constantly show the child where decoding skills fit into the reading program. The long-range goal is to provide the child with a word-solving strategy. He should try context clues first, then use the simplest decoding clues available until they unlock the word or until he needs to consult a dictionary or some other convenient resource.

Assuming that the child has the prerequisite background, auditory and visual discrimination skills, and vocabulary to make himself understood in school, and knows the names of the letters of the alphabet in order to talk about them in class, this sequence of decoding skills may be used:

1. Match rhyming words, such as *cat* and *mat.*

2. Identify the sound of beginning consonants and their letter symbols. Initially the consonants should be presented so that there is a sufficient contrast between one and the next. A teacher might start with *b, s, t, c, p, w, h,* and so on. These sounds and their symbols should be developed through whole words and not in isolation: "You can hear the sound of *b* at the beginning of the word *bat.*"

3. Identify the sounds of consonants at the end of words. Again, demonstrate with whole words: "You can hear the sound *b* at the end of the word *tab.*"

4. Identify short vowel sounds in trigraphs: *cap, bet, pit, cot, but.* One of the phonic generalizations and the consonant-vowel-consonant pattern apply to short sounds in trigraphs.

5. Identify consonant blends at the beginning of words; then at the end of words. *Br* in *bread; nd* in *sand.*

6. Identify long vowels in words that have a silent *e* or that fit the consonant-vowel-consonant-vowel pattern: *make, bite, rope, cute.*
7. Identify consonant digraphs at the beginning of words; at the end of words. *Ch* in *church, sh* in *show, ph* in *digraph.* (Consonant blends and digraphs are consonant clusters for which a reader learns an individual response to each set of consonants.)
8. Identify the long vowels in words that have a double vowel or that fit the consonant-vowel-vowel-consonant pattern: *maid, seat, boat.*

This sequence would normally be spread over the first year of instruction for the average child. For a longer list, and more technical information about phonic and linguistic skills, there are short texts devoted specifically to this subject (Lamb, 1968; Cordts, 1956; Heilman, 1967).

The sequence by itself indicates very little about strategy and instructional techniques. Various combinations could be made within the sequence to make the instruction clearer and more interesting. There is no reason, for example, why all of the consonants have to be learned before a vowel can be introduced. In order to start practice in decoding an entire word, the teacher would be wise to introduce a short vowel as soon as the child has learned enough consonants to pronounce a few words using those consonants and the vowel he has learned: *b, t,* and *s* plus short *a* give the child enough sounds and their symbols to analyze words such as *bat, sat, tab, at.* This assumes that the child also knows that the trigraph consonant-vowel-consonant pattern often indicates the short sound of the vowel.

Minimum Phonics Knowledge

For those who use the gradual analytic approach to teaching decoding skills, the sequence listed above has only a minimum value as far as instructional strategy is concerned. A teacher might use the sequence as a means of knowing which elements to test for and emphasize as opportunities arise in class. It could also serve as a general schema for diagnosing decoding problems and prescribing instruction to help a student who has failed to keep up with needed skills. If a child cannot blend the trigraph *cat,* he may need instruction in the effect of the consonant-vowel-consonant pattern on the sound of the vowel, or he may need instruction in identifying the sounds of consonants in the initial and final positions.

Teachers who use the gradual analytic approach—for example, in the language experience method—need many ready answers and instructional directions about decoding words. They need to be thoroughly acquainted with phonic generalizations and the sound-spelling patterns of English. Some of the basic information that a teacher needs follows:

The English alphabet is divided into consonants and vowels. The vowels are "a," "e," "i," "o," "u," and sometimes "w" and "y." The vowels are the most important sound elements in the language because they carry the open or unobstructed sound of the words, and they can be easily pronounced when they are isolated from words. The consonants act as interrupters and modifiers of the vowel sounds.

Vowel sounds are said to be long or short. They are long when they say their own name. The vowel "a," for example, is long in the word *made* and short in the word *mad*. Because of certain letter combinations the vowel may be modified so that it is different from the short sound or the long sound. The "a" in *car* is modified by the "r" which follows it. The vowels "o" and "i" in *boil* are also modified. Their separate sounds cannot be heard clearly. Only closely linked modified sounds can be heard. Phonic generalizations attempt to organize the sounds of the vowels and consonants into usable patterns. One way to get children to practice a generalization, once it has been introduced or discovered through class work, is to have them search the daily newspaper for words in headlines or in the stories and to mark those that fit the rule or rules they have just learned. Beginners will be restricted mostly to one-syllable words.

If a teacher wanted to construct an exercise based on the regular words that match phonics elements, which have been introduced in class, he might write a simple story like this one as an exercise:

A Cat and a Rat

Can a cat bat a rat?
A cat can bat a rat.
Bam! Bam! Bam!
Bad cat.
Sad rat.

A child could read the story aloud, applying the consonant-vowel-consonant sound pattern. The teacher should observe the child's attack of each word and supply guidance on individual sounds or upon the pattern, as needed. Questions can be asked to check on meaning: "What did the cat do?" With a story like this, however, the subject matter is exhausted with one or two questions.

Irregular words which do not follow a pattern-for example, *the, there,* and *is,*—are learned by visual memory techniques. They are developed as sight words and should be taught in context: Tony *is* a tiger.

Activities for Decoding Skills

Some ways to induce beginning readers to learn the decoding skills listed in the sequence given earlier are presented in the following paragraphs. The examples should help a teacher diagnose a child's need or help the teacher construct an appropriate training exercise. They will also allow the teacher to know what to look for in the materials available in the classroom.

Alphabet Sequence

Have children match plastic letters with those written on paper. Then scramble the plastic letters and have the children put them in alphabetical order.

Children can learn the lower case letters by tracing over a set of printed letters. Then they should write the letters in sequence (if they have been taught to write them while they are learning), or use cutout letters to place them in sequence.

Rhyme Sounds

First ask children to tell which word rhymes with "Joe." Then ask them to make up a two-line poem using the rhyme:

I know a boy named Joe
Who froze his little toe.

Later, when rhyming seems easy for the children, ask them to supply a rhyme word that has been left out of a two- or more-line poem:

There's a big black bunny
That looks very _____(funny).

Associating Sound and Symbol

At first, each letter of the alphabet should be given a regular sound value ("z" as in zipper). The exceptions and combinations can be developed after the regular values are learned by the children. Teach the letter sounds as they are heard in words. Do *not* try to isolate letter sounds; for example, saying "tuh" for "t." Rather say: "You can hear the sound of 't' at the beginning of the word *top*. I am writing 't' on the board. You write it in the air."

The examples in Table 9.3 indicate the regular sound values for consonants and vowels. The cue given should be concrete and familiar to children.

One way to develop a sense of beginning consonant sounds is to have the children cut pictures from magazines and newspapers to indicate things that begin with those sounds. They should find pictures of things other than those used as cue words.

TABLE 9.3   Regular Sound Values for Letters of the Alphabet

Consonants	(short)	Vowels	(long)
b-bed	mad	a	made
c-cat	pet	e	Pete
d-dog	bit	i	bite
f-fish	hop	o	hope
g-goat	cut	u	cute
h-hem		w	know
j-jump			now
k-kite	baby	y	cry
l-lip			
m-mud			
n-nose			
p-pop			
q-quart			
r-rob			
s-sun			
t-top			
v-vat			
w-wish			
x-x-ray			
y-young			
z-zip			

Vowel Generalizations

The teacher and pupils can make lists that demonstrate the patterns, or generalizations, that are being introduced. Children should be encouraged to make up as many words as they can think of to fit a given pattern.

	Pattern I	Pattern II
Teacher Chart:	mad	made
	pet	Pete
	bit	bite
	hop	hope
	cut	cute
Student Chart:	bad	
	cap	cape
	had	
	can	cane
	ham	

The newspaper continuously serves as a valuable source for word-identification work. When a pattern has been introduced in class, have children take one section of the paper and mark all headline words that fit this pattern. The children see that their efforts pay off in daily reading.

Blending Sounds

Blending sounds in order to achieve recognition of the word is a difficult and crucial skill. Sometimes it is helpful to play a tapping game with children as an introduction to the blending of letter sounds: "Tap after me." The teacher taps a pattern and the children tap in imitation:

```
I        I        I
II       II       II
III      III      III
I        III      III      II
```

Then transfer the finger tapping to vocal tapping: "Repeat after me."

```
s-s-s-at-at-at
s-s-s-s-at-at-at
s-s-at-at
s-at
sat
```

Use a similar technique to test blending, but work with nonsense words so that visual memory will not interfere with your check of children's skill in blending. For example: "Here are some nonsense words. They are not words at all, but I'd like to see if you can read them anyway."

fis	lort	faim
tope	kim	hin
bute	keat	vin
gud	muts	hife

Assessing Decoding Skills

The use of nonsense words is one way of checking on an individual's skill in decoding. It eliminates the possibility of the student using visual memory for correctly answering some of the test words.

The teacher of beginning reading should make up a check sheet with a sequence of skills on it that he has set up for a semester's program. Through a combination of tests and observations the teacher can note the skills that each student has, and therefore the point in the sequence where instruction should take place.

To assist in the collection of information about the student's performance several sample test exercises on decoding skills are provided below. All can be administered to groups and provide criteria by which the teacher can judge a student's competence with that specific decoding skill. Also available are formal, standardized group tests, such as the POWER system criterion tests (Winston Press, 1975).

Sample Test Items of Initial Consonants

Give a copy of the test to each child. The teacher pronounces the two words in each row, asking pupils to listen to the beginning sound of each word. Pupils are to find the letter that represents the sound and circle it on the answer sheet.

Look at row 1. The words are *wagon* and *window*. The pupils should circle the letter "w" on the pupil answer sheet.

1. wagon	window		4. tail	tent
2. girl	gate		5. carts	car
3. lion	leaf		6. met	map

Pupil Answer Sheet   Name _____
                      Grade _____ Date _____

1. r	w	l	m		4. d	h	f	t
2. c	j	p	g		5. g	n	r	c
3. r	w	l	f		6. n	h	m	w

Sample Test Items of Vowels, Vowel Digraphs, and Diphthongs

The teacher pronounces each pair of words. Pupils listen carefully and then circle on the answer sheet one of the four vowels or vowel combinations which represents the vowel sound heard in the word.

1. cake	tail		7. for	more
2. bad	cat		8. up	just
3. hot	top		9. play	day
4. fur	turn		10. wait	tail
5. tie	kite		11. sound	about
6. farm	barn		12. boy	toy

Pupil Answer Sheet   Name _____
                      Grade _____ Date _____

1. e	a	i	o		4. ar	er	or
2. u	o	i	a		5. e	o	i	u
3. e	u	i	o		6. ar	ur	ir

7. ir   or   ar
8. u   o   e   a
9. ay   ea   ew   oy

10. ea   ou   oi   ai
11. oi   aw   ew   ou
12. ay   ou   oy   aw

Test of Initial Consonant Clusters

Review, if necessary, the principle that consonant blends represent more than one sound, whereas consonant digraphs represent only one speech sound. The teacher pronounces the two words that begin with the same consonant sound. Ask pupils to circle the letters that make that sound.

1. cherry chicken
2. grass green
3. step stairs

4. truck train
5. crowd crow
6. flag floor

Pupil Answer Sheet   Name _____
                       Grade _____ Date _____

1. cl   ch   sh   th
2. cr   gr   ch   bl
3. sl   fr   cl   st

4. th   dr   tr   fr
5. cr   dr   ch   wr
6. ph   fr   gr   fl

Sample Test Items for Consonant Cluster and Digraph Phonograms

Have pupils look at the three phonograms that follow the first two letters. One of these phonograms added to the first two letters forms a word the children know. Direct pupils to circle the phonogram that forms the word, and then write the word in the blank.

1. bl   ame   ate   ay   _____
2. bl   urch   ock   im   _____
3. br   ud   ool   ing   _____
4. br   ick   ank   out   _____
5. cl   ab   ock   ine   _____
6. cl   ack   ace   ight   _____

Any word-analysis skill must be assessed in terms of the student's ability to derive the meaning of a complete sentence. Within the context of a sentence the student should be able to use decoding skills and gain an accurate concept of the meaning of the sentence. Once he has pronounced a given word, he should demonstrate what it means in context. The teacher can say: "Tell me in your own words what that sentence means. Tell me what that word that you figured out (sounded out) means."

SUMMARY

The whole-word approach to reading represents an attempt to overcome meaningless word pronouncing through a letter-by-letter phonics approach. Although authorities disagree about when to start decoding and how it should be taught, all believe that it *should* be taught and that it is an extremely important tool in analyzing words.

Some educators believe that decoding should be taught gradually and analytically from a meaningful context; that is, as the opportunities for using a skill arise while reading is going on. Others believe that an intensive and synthetic approach ought to be used in the beginning stages of reading. Research on commercial materials, though beleaguered by weaknesses in design, indicates that intensive synthetic materials produce superior results at the end of the first grade on word-recognition sections of standardized reading tests.

We recommend combining phonics analysis in context and in synthetic practice material. In order to teach children well teachers must themselves know what the generalizations and patterns that help in decoding English spelling are. They should likewise have in mind a sequence of decoding skills that will guide them in diagnosing the competencies of their students and in planning instruction that will make students more independent readers.

Terms for Self-study

analytic phonics	grapheme
synthetic phonics	consonant clusters
linguistics	diphthongs
phoneme	spelling patterns

Discussion Questions

1. In what ways could nonsense words *(cac)* be used in testing or teaching decoding skills?
2. Where do decoding skills fit in a broader strategy for solving unfamiliar words?
3. How could a teacher combine analytic phonics and synthetic phonics in daily teaching?

part IV

Primary Reading

alphabet
recognition
meaning

Once a child has learned to break the alphabet code, word recognition should become rapid and automatic in order to facilitate concentration on meaning. A variety of word recognition and word analysis skills are described in this part of the book. Special attention is also given to the importance of interest and success in reading. The application of standards to what is read, critical reading, is presented here as an activity which must begin early and receive continued attention throughout the elementary school years.

10

Word Recognition – A Strategy

Everyone who reads extensively is occasionally faced with a word he has not seen before or at least has not seen often enough to recognize instantly. For the adult it may be a new technical term, such as *multivariate analysis,* for the elementary school child it may be a word as common as *schoolbus.* Both the adult and the child foresee that they will meet the word again, and the next time they would prefer to respond automatically to it instead of having to analyze it. How does one go about analyzing a word and then fixing it in memory so that it becomes part of his reading vocabulary? How does one teach a child to do this?

All kinds of cues are available for the reader who knows how to use them. The more the reader knows about word cues and the techniques for identifying and getting the meaning of words, the more likely he will enjoy reading and have to spend less time on the mechanics of reading. The child who has been trained to sweep his eyes over an unknown word to see what kinds of cues he can use to analyze it will quickly solve the word *schoolbus.* Almost without thinking he knows that there are two parts *(syllables)* to the word, because there are two vowel positions, ''oo'' and ''u.'' He then looks for known words and finds two, *school* and *bus.* He has learned each of these words separately in previous reading. Blending the two words yields the compound word *schoolbus.*

What about *multivariate analysis?* How would the adult reader solve its pronunciation and meaning? This chapter provides a number of possible solutions to that problem as it considers these questions:

203

Why does word recognition receive so much attention in the teaching of reading?

What word-recognition skills does a competent reader use?

How do word analysis and automatic word recognition differ?

What is meant by context clues, structural analysis, and association skills?

In what order should word-recognition skills be taught?

What means does the classroom teacher have for assessing the word-recognition skills of his students?

In what ways are word-recognition skills and meaning skills related?

No area of reading education receives more attention in school than how readers analyze and recognize words. A system for teaching children to recognize words seems so central to learning to read that most of the controversies of recent years have focused on a variety of word-recognition techniques. As we stated early in this book, reading involves many skills other than word recognition, but the learner starts with words because they are the visual units that make up the message he must understand. Even though word-recognition skills are only one of the many skills a competent reader uses, they are thought of first when reading skills are discussed.

Word-recognition skills are a variety of decoding and perception skills that enable the reader to decipher, pronounce, and form a basic understanding of the words he sees on the printed page. In terms of the Harris-Smith model (Figure 2.2) word-recognition skills fall into the decoding and perceptual image categories. By looking again at the model one can see that a major interference in decoding and perception prevents concepts from being formed and so prevents the message from being identified. Facility in these skills, therefore, stands as a crucial launching point for the entire reading process. That accounts for the great concern teachers have for word-recognition techniques.

The competent reader employs a variety of skills in identifying or analyzing words. He either recognizes a word instantly or he applies analyses that will enable him to identify the writer's meaning. By definition, the competent reader rapidly, almost concurrently, employs all the techniques he needs to solve problem words—context clues, phonics, syllabication, sound-spelling patterns, structural analysis, association, and picture clues. During the years that he was learning these skills he developed his own routine or strategy for applying them. But the beginning reader needs assistance in developing a word-analysis strategy.

Most mature readers probably use context clues as the initial skill for word identification. If that does not give a clear identification, they apply other techniques, depending on the evident cues available in the word. Perhaps using the beginning and ending consonants along with context will reveal what the word is. If that fails, syllabicating the word, analyzing its meaningful parts, or trying to associate it with other words or objects may be devices used to bring forth the correct response. Though the competent reader may first use context, the beginning reader often cannot start comfortably with that skill because he must first learn what a printed word is and how it is formed.

A Strategy for Word Analyses

This chapter describes many different word skill practices. Over years of training a child learns to use these skills habitually. But he will probably need guidance in deciding how to employ the skills he uses. Isn't there some pattern that will help him, so that he does not apply them randomly? He wants to make sense out of the word-recognition skills he has, and the teacher can give him a strategy simply by asking the same set of questions each time a word problem is discussed in class. For example:

1. Do the words around the problem word give you an idea of what it is or what its meaning is? *(context clues)*
2. Do context clues and the sound of the first part of the word tell you what the word is? *(context clue plus initial sound)*
3. If the first two steps do not produce the word, does adding the final sound in the word reveal it? *(Context plus initial sound plus ending sound)*
4. If the first three steps do not produce the word, can you get it by looking for sound-spelling patterns, such as consonant-vowel-consonant, consonant-vowel-double consonant, consonant-double vowel-consonant or other word parts?
5. If the first four steps do not produce the word, ask someone, or look up the pronunciation in the dictionary.

Through this set of questions the teacher reminds the student to move systematically through his skills for word recognition—whatever those skills are at his stage of development. Initially he searches his repertoire in a conscious manner. Later, after much practice and repetition, the search is more automatic, less conscious. Through the five-step pattern the child learns to use as few clues as possible in solving word problems. He can stop after any one of the steps when the word is identified. It is conceivable in the following example that the unknown word could be identified after Step 1 or after Step 5, depending on the background and skills of the child:

The big brown fox $\underline{\quad 2 \quad\quad 4 \quad\quad 3\quad}$ over the lazy dog.

Step 1. Context: The fox does something over the dog.
plus Step 2. Initial sound. /j/j.
plus Step 3. Ending sound. /t/ed.
plus Step 4. Sound-spelling pattern. c-v-cc = short u plus /j/ plus /t/ed.
plus Step 5. Ask your classmates.

The system emphasizes the additive or combining features for solving unknown words.

Word Skill Categories

For the sake of remembering word skills it is convenient to arrange them in three groups: visual memory skills, analytic skills, and syntactic skills.

Visual memory skills are concerned with words already in the child's listening vocabulary that seem best learned by repetition and association. These include the short function words—such as *a, an, the, these,*—and words that have unusual length or other unusual features that lend themselves to a visual memory approach—such as *llama* or *corps* in Marine Corps.

Analytic skills include knowledge of phonics, spelling patterns, syllabication, structural analysis (for example, roots and affixes), and context clues. In this case more than a conditioned response is used to work out the pronunciation and meaning of the word. Though the process may be rapid and there may be a crossing over of some synthetic skills with the analytic, the reader categorizes the word and responds on the basis of analysis.

Syntactic skills include punctuation cues, and identification of the position and function of the word in the sentence structure. For example, a reader has certain internalized, anticipated responses to the kinds of words that are underlined in the following sentence: "Justus was *warned* against swimming in the *lagoon.*"   1
        2

Assuming the reader did not instantly recognize those underlined words, their positions and functions indicate a past participle verb for 1 and a word for a body of water in 2. The auxiliary verb *was* and the prepositional phrase *in the* create those expectations in the native speaker of the language. It is believed that most syntactic skills result primarily from internalized language habits and not from a teaching scheme. Syntactic cues are specialized instances of context clues. They give to the word associations and to the emerging meaning of a passage an added predictability based on language patterns.

Time for Word Skills

All of the techniques discussed in this chapter may be taught in the first grade, depending on the development of the child. They are, however, especially applicable to older children. Along with the previously discussed sight word skills and decoding skills at least the rudiments of these word-recognition techniques may be introduced in the first year: context clues, structural analysis, syllabication and syllable phonics, and association. Most reading curricula introduce a variety of word-recognition techniques in the first year and then expand, refine, and reinforce those techniques in succeeding years. A teacher, therefore, has a variety of means available with which to help a child so that he can find his own best way.

Association Techniques

Association techniques are means of relating an unknown word to another stimulus—visual, tactile, and/or auditory. This association between the word and a stimulus aids the reader in recognizing the word when he meets it in subsequent readings.

Good teachers often use association techniques to teach children word symbols. Reading tests use association techniques to evaluate reading vocabulary. Words denoting concrete objects *(truck)* and sensory impressions *(fire)* lend themselves well to associative learning techniques. The senses of touch, smell, hearing, sight, and taste can be exploited to impress a word on a reader's memory; for example, *garlic—The smell of garlic filled the gourmet restaurant.* Braun (1969) found that children more readily learn words that are associated with things in which they are interested. A popular book, *Teacher* (Ashton-Warner, 1963), reported similar success with words that were associated with deep emotion; for example, *mother, shark.*

The association process is often used cooperatively with another word-analysis technique. Where one technique ends and the other begins is difficult to determine, however.

Associations made by one person can differ greatly from those made by another because they are all tied up with experience and language. The connection that is formed is a highly individual one. The value inherent in this technique is the unique and personal image that the association process enables each individual to make. The teacher's task is to develop the child's observational powers so that he can utilize these personal examples and associate them with the written word.

Here are several examples of the personal images some individuals have associated with words in their reading lessons:

Sarah associates *whistle* with the noon factory whistle she hears every day during recess. *(hearing)*

Rhode remembers the word *chocolate* because she visited a candy factory and tasted samples of chocolate. *(taste)*

Tony's reading lesson contains the word *pony*. He recalls pictures of Indian ponies that his father showed him. *(sight)*

Obviously those associations work only if there is a word or phrase in the passage to trigger the image the child has. The teacher can foster and encourage the use of association as an aid to remembering words by providing materials and experiences in the classroom. One teacher presented new words through a filmstrip about a farmer. The picture of the barnyard was projected on the chalkboard. She then labeled the various objects in the picture (barn, tractor, silo, fence, and so on), writing the words on the chalkboard and pronouncing them. The children were able to associate the word with the pictured object from the filmstrip. When the teacher switched off the projector the words remained on the chalkboard, but the memory residue from the film would continue to help children identify the words. Their position on the chalkboard was related to the location of objects on the film, which can be shown again to reteach and reinforce the association.

Further development of associative processes can be encouraged through the use of matching games and exercises, which put the written word and the associated stimulus together:

1. The child can match words with pictures on a bulletin board or flannel-board. *(visual)*
2. The child can match colored squares of paper with the names of the colors. *(visual)*
3. Pieces of cloth—for example, velvet, corduroy, or wool—can be matched to their written symbols. *(visual and tactile)*

be careful
of color blind

The teacher's role is similar to that of a guide. While he is ready to point out the association that can be derived or used to remember the word, he is also ready to stand back and allow the child to bring his own interpretation and association to the written symbol.

Structural Analysis

Many basic words undergo changes in meaning and pronunciation because of prefixes, suffixes, inflections, and compounding. Making use of these word parts to arrive at the meaning or the pronunciation of words is called structural analysis. For example, the sentences above have a number of words containing structural parts—*means, subjected, under/go, mean*ing, *reader, pre/fix/es,* and so on. The utilization of this technique by the mature reader is a result of instruction and practice. Children must be taught to use it, too. The visual learner should find it particularly helpful, for the reader is searching primarily for visual cues to identify meaningful word parts. Auditory skills are also operating, especially with regard to inflectional endings (like *s* or *er*).

The teacher must lead children to analyze the word into meaningful units, and derive recognition and understanding of the word. This is not an easy task, for the cues that are a part of structural analysis are many and varied. Some of the cues children must learn are:

Root word. A word base that is not compounded or modified by a prefix, suffix, or inflectional ending, and that remains unchanged through such modification (for example, *bound*ed).

Compound word. Two or more root words that are combined to form one word. Sometimes the compound word keeps the meaning of the original two words (for example, *classroom*); but frequently the meaning of the compound is completely new (for example, *broadcast*).

Inflectional endings. Endings that change root words grammatically, such as case, gender, number, tense, person, mood, or voice (for example, *girls*).

Prefix. A unit of meaning attached to the beginning of a word, thereby changing that word's meaning (for example, *re*port).

Suffix. A unit of meaning attached to the end of a word, thereby changing that word's meaning (for example, *wonder*ful).

Contraction. A shortened form of two words that have been combined into one word. In this process one or more letters has been omitted. Such missing elements are indicated by the addition of an apostrophe (') (for example, *can't*). (Smith, N. B., 1963, p. 216)

Instruction in the recognition and use of structural analysis cues can begin as soon as words containing prefixes, suffixes, inflectional endings, compounds, or contractions begin to appear in the child's reading material. When that occurs, the child has a supply of sight words which the teacher can use as a basis for teaching structural analysis. In the early stages of instruction the teacher alerts the learner incidentally to structural components, waiting to introduce them formally until the child has mastered more basic skills.

Suppose these sentences appeared in the children's text: *They got on a bus. They go to school.* An exercise for introducing structural analysis might use the compound *schoolbus,* thus using two familiar parts to make up the new form. Identifying the two parts of the compound and labeling a picture of a schoolbus would be one way of introducing children to the concept that words change by combining and adding parts.

By using words from the child's supply of sight words the teacher develops an understanding of what a root word is. This understanding must be taught early because it is the basic word unit, the root word, which then is modified or changed. If the child can identify the root word in a modified word, he has mastered a basic concept in the use of structural analysis.

An explanation of the root word generally is not given to children until the reading text shows a root that has been modified by a prefix or an inflectional ending. For example, *David went walking down the street.* Suppose the reader had previously learned the word *walk,* but stumbled and was unsure of this new form, *walking.* The teacher could write *walking* on the chalkboard, covering the inflectional ending "ing" with his hand. "What word do you see here? That's correct—*walk. Walk* is a root word, or a base word, to which we can add parts. We have added "i-n-g.'" The teacher removes his hand and continues the root-plus-ending explanation.

A similar process is effective when leading the child to identify the root in other modified words—for example, *report, raincoat, wonderful.* Instruction should not stop with mere identification of the root word. Each of the various additions and changes that take place must be demonstrated, and the student needs opportunity to practice them. This demonstration is not accomplished in one short lesson. Different kinds of word changes are discussed at different places in the sequence of the reading skills program. A lesson on compounds and one on inflectional endings often will be taught in the first grade, while a unit on prefixes and suffixes may not be developed until the second or third grade.

Sequence

As with other kinds of reading skills, structural analysis should not be tied to a specific grade level but rather should be taught as the child develops and

FIGURE 10.1   As children grow, so do the number and flexibility of their word skills.

can assimilate (or needs) a new skill. Given below is a sequence of structural-analysis skills that may guide the teacher who is working in a nongraded or an individualized curriculum:

MEANING-STRUCTURE SEQUENCE

1. Basic words; for example, *boy, run*
2. Inflectional endings; for example, *s, es, ed, ing*
3. Compounds; for example, *sailboat, capgun*
4. Identify root words; for example, *loading, loaded, loader*
5. Introduce prefix; for example, *mismatch*
6. Introduce suffix; for example, *artful*
7. Effect of certain form words on the structure of the word that follows; for example, *a man, the men,* or *the man, these men.*

Compound Words

Early in his reading program the child meets words that are made up of two or more simple words. Such words are *compounds.* Identifying compounds is usually not difficult for the student. Generally, the compound words the child meets are composed of shorter words he already knows. However, the instructor should not conclude that just because the child knows the parts of the compound in isolation he will be able to transfer this knowledge and recognize the parts when they are compounded. To the child the compound is a new word regardless of the fact that it is made up of two or three words with which he is familiar. He has never met them in this form. His visual perception mechanism has not been prepared for the combined form. It is advisable at first to help the child see the separate word units in the compound word, if he cannot do it alone.

The following tasks will help to illustrate compounds to a child and make him adept at identifying them:

1. Auditory perception of the two or three words within a compound word may be developed by having children listen to the teacher say a new

compound word; for example, *schoolbus*. They must say what two words they hear. The compound may be written on the chalkboard, and each word identified visually.

2. The teacher writes the compound word on the chalkboard. With his hand he covers up one of the words. A child must identify the uncovered unit. The teacher then proceeds to cover the other word, and a child identifies that uncovered unit. This leads the children to see the two word units in a compound word.

3. As the teacher points to compound words on the chalkboard he tells the children that the words are made up of two separate words. They must find these two words. For example, "Search for the two words in *sailboat*."

4. The children can be given two columns of words. The column on the left contains the first part of the compound words; the one on the right the second part. The children must draw lines connecting the words in the two columns so that together they form one compound word:

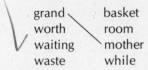

grand   basket
worth   room
waiting   mother
waste   while

Inflectional Endings

Inflectional endings occur frequently in all reading material. In fact, the addition of the simple endings *-s, -es, -ed,* and *-ing* to known words may often be the first use a child makes of structural analysis. Instruction in inflectional endings should be relatively simple. The child is asked about the meaning of the word, while his attention is called to the ending. The teacher can use the same technique whenever the child confronts words having these endings. "What happens to the meaning of the word *walk* when we add '-s,' '-ed,' or '*ing*'? Read the new word."

The child already knows and uses inflectional endings in speech. Relating speech sounds to the written symbol may be quite helpful in teaching the concept of inflectional endings. The goal of instruction is to lead the child to *read* the endings that he automatically uses when *speaking*.

Here are sample exercises and procedures for developing an understanding of inflectional endings:

1. The teacher can write an uninflected word on the chalkboard; for example, *hat*. He then explains: "I will add an ending to this word to show that there is more than one hat." After *-s* is added, the children or the teacher will pronounce the new word. This word is then used in a sentence: "Do you have two hats?"

2. The words *want* and *kick* can be written on the chalkboard. The children pronounce the words, after which the teacher adds the endings *-s, -ed,* and

-ing. The children frame the root word in each instance and then speak a sentence using the inflected form. want s, kick ing

3. For example: Written exercises similar to the items in 1. and 2. can be provided:

a. Circle the root in these words:

plays	playing	played
walked	walks	walking
planting	plants	planted

b. Draw one line under the root word and two lines under the part that has been added to it:

raining	played
throws	asking

c. Write the correct word in the blank:

John is _____ for his hat.

   looked
   looking
   looks

He _____ ball yesterday.

  plays
  playing
  played

As the child becomes familiar with inflectional endings, he can begin to make some generalizations concerning their spelling and therefore their pronunciation. These are primarily spelling concerns:

1. Very often, inflectional endings are added with no change needed in the root word (for example, *walking, matches, called, girls, going*).
2. If the root word ends in a final *e*, the *e* is usually dropped when adding an inflectional ending that begins with a vowel (for example, *hoping, taking, baked*).
3. When a root word ends in a single consonant following a single vowel the final consonant is usually doubled when an ending is added (for example, *running, dropped*).
4. When the word ends in *y* preceded by a consonant the *y* is usually changed to *i* before adding the ending (for example, *cried, ponies, cries*).
5. If the final *y* is preceded by a vowel, the ending is added with no change in the root word (for example, *buys, monkeys*).
6. If the word ends in *f*, the *f* is usually changed to *v* before adding an ending (for example, *calves, wolves*).

Prefixes and Suffixes

A technique similar to the one used to recognize words with inflectional endings is also used to identify words with affixes (prefixes and suffixes). The root word is first identified; then the affix is isolated.

Probably the best way to develop an understanding of prefixes and suffixes is to have the children draw a line around the affix and tell how it changed the meaning of the root word. Knowledge of the meanings of some of the more common prefixes and suffixes will aid the pupil in recognizing the derived word and attaching the proper meaning to it. Tables 10.1 and 10.2 list some of the most common prefixes and suffixes.

TABLE 10.1   Common Prefixes

Prefix	Meaning	Example
ab-	off from, away	absent
ad-	to, toward	admit
co-, con-, com-, col-, cor-	together, with	contest
de-	away, down, out of	depart
dis-	not, opposite	dislike
ex-	out of, formerly	extend
in-, im-, il-, ir-	in, not	immoral
pre-	before	precede
pro-	forward	proceed
re-	back, again	review
un-	not, opposite	unhappy

TABLE 10.2   Common Suffixes

Suffix	Meaning	Example
-able	capable of, worthy	lovable
-ance, -ence, -ancy, -ency	act or fact of doing, state, quality, condition	allowance
-er, -or	person or thing connected with, agent	teacher
-ful	full of, abounding in	helpful
-less	without, free from	helpless
-ly	like, characteristic of	kingly, queenly
-ment	state of, quality of	amazement
-tion, -sion, -xion	action, state, result	election, tension

Development of the meaning of prefixes and suffixes is not a simple task because some have more than one meaning. However, by first presenting those affixes that are fairly consistent in meaning, the problem will be diminished.

Here is the procedure one teacher used to present the prefix *un-*. She wrote the sentence—*His shoes were not tied.*—on the chalkboard. The children then read the sentence. She rewrote it, this time using the prefix *un-* in place of the word *not*—*His shoes were untied.* The explanation was given that the two sentences said the same thing because *un-* often means not. Further practice was used to reinforce the learning of this prefix by writing other root words on the chalkboard—such as *happy, kind, dress.* The prefix *un-* was added to each of these. The children read the new words and discussed their meaning when *un-* was added. The words were then used in sentences.

Children must know what a prefix and suffix are in order to use them in recognizing words accurately and efficiently. Using prefixes and suffixes to dismantle words and discover their meaning is an important skill (Dawson and Bamman, 1959).

Exercises such as the following will enable children to practice the analysis of words containing prefixes and suffixes:

1. When the child comes to a word such as *unlike* the teacher can draw a line under *like* and ask what that part of the word means if the child knows the word *like.* The child should then identify the prefix and combine it with the root of the word.
2. Have children make a list of common prefixes—for example, *mis-, im-,* and *ir*—along with the words in which these prefixes appear—for example, *mislike, impossible, irresponsible.* Do the same with suffixes.
3. Use the following written exercises:
   a. Add the suffixes in Column 1 to the words in Column 2. Write the new word.

Column 1	Column 2
-ness (state of being)	1. cold
	2. happy
	3. kind
-er (one who or more)	1. labor
	2. long
	3. wish

   b. Draw a line through the word in each row below that does *not* have a prefix or suffix:

1. dislike	will	react
2. knee	enclose	unlock
3. boundless	wonderful	book
4. recount	real	return

   c. Draw a line from the letters in the left column to the word in the right column which uses that that prefix or suffix:

-ly	wiser
-er	careless
con-	proceed
-less	connect
pro-	lovely

d. Underline the root word and write the prefix or suffix (or both) in the correct column.

	Prefix	Suffix
indirect	(in)	
regardless	(re)	(less)

e. Read the following sentences and supply the missing word:

A laborer is a man or woman who _____.
A farmer is a man who _____.
A helper is a person who _____.
What suffix is added to all of the above words? _____

f. Draw a line under the prefix in the words below and tell how it changes the meaning of the root word:

unhappy	dislike
displease	retake
unknown	mistreat

As often as possible these exercises should be carried out in conjunction with the reading of sentences and paragraphs. Without application in a meaningful context the practice activities may be sterile.

Contractions

Contractions appear frequently as a part of everyone's speech. A person rarely says: "I do not want that." Instead, he generally abbreviates, saying: "I don't want that." In fact, it may even sound like "Idonwannat." The contraction is a shorter way of saying two separate words. Since these words are generally contracted in everyday speech, reading and writing them in a shortened form is a logical step.

Explaining this logic to the child may help him with a sometimes troublesome analysis, for contractions may not always sound like either of the words they stand for—such as *don't* for *do not*.

The teacher can write the words *let us* on the chalkboard, after which the contraction *let's* can also be written. It is explained that *let's* is a shorter way of saying *let us*. The teacher will then say: "This mark [pointing to the apostrophe] shows that some letters have been left out. We call this mark an apostrophe. In *let's* the apostrophe tells us that one letter has been left out. What letter is it?"

As with other instruction in word-analysis skills, the instructional sequence should proceed from simple to complex. Words in which single letters are left out *(is not, isn't)* should be taught first. Later, the words in which two or more letters are missing *(he would, he'd)* should be presented.

The following exercises give the child practice with contractions and related spelling concerns:

1. Draw a line from the words in the first column to the correct contraction in the second column:

   does not   can't
   is not   doesn't
   cannot   isn't

2. Rewrite the sentences below substituting a contraction for the words in italics.

   He will go to the house. _____
   I *do not* want to go. _____
   You will have to do it. _____

3. Write the words that each contraction stands for.

   I'll _____   you've _____
   we've _____   can't _____
   we'll _____   it's _____

In all exercises involving structural analysis the reader should be encouraged to search for the largest possible unit that he can recognize and then figure out how the other part(s) of the word change the pronunciation and the meaning of the basic unit. The reader should not feel compelled to look first for the root and then the affixes of *reconstruction* when he instantly recognizes the entire first part, *reconstruct*, and knows that it means "to build again." Structural analysis is not a mental gymnastic but a tool to assist the reader in figuring out the pronunciation and the meaning of a word not recognized at first glance.

Syllabication

Syllabication and syllable phonics may be considered an extension of the phonics skills presented in the previous chapter. As a reading skill syllabication involves the separation of longer words into pronounceable units (syllables). As the syllables are recognized and pronounced, they are synthesized to yield the pronunciation of the entire unknown word. Accent in words is an intrinsic part of this skill.

Prior to instruction in syllabication the child must have mastered the basic vowel and consonant sounds. For that reason the teaching of syllabication usually comes relatively late in the sequence of word-recognition techniques.

To keep from being overreliant on syllabication for reading instruction, the teacher should recall that the concept was originally developed primarily for printers. Rules for syllabication, therefore, are more apt for writing (dividing words at the end of lines) than they are for reading instruction. Even so, there are certain aspects to syllabication that relate to reading and can aid the learner in his discrimination and pronunciation of words.

Instruction in syllabication is usually started with ear training, which is designed to help the child hear the syllables within words. An understanding of syllables can be given to children with the following procedure: "The word *sun* has one syllable, or part. The word *sunny* has two syllables. What do you think a syllable is?" The children's responses may include the notion that a vowel sound is needed for a syllable or that you can tell the number of syllables by the number of "beats" (rhythmic beats) in a word. In this way the teacher moves the children toward a definition of syllables.

Practice is necessary before children will recognize the number of syllables in words. Exercises such as these will provide such practice:

1. Have the children say their own names in unison, clapping their hands for each syllable as they say it. A chantlike effect will result: "Ted-dy, Sar-a, John, James, Rho-da, An-dre-a . . ."
2. The teacher can pronounce words having one or two syllables. The children are told to respond when they hear a word having two syllables. Responses can be by clapping, raising hands, and so on.

Eventually children should be led to the awareness that a word has as many syllables as it has sounded vowels. Very often, in fact, a vowel alone constitutes a syllable. However, a child must also recognize that a syllable may contain more than one vowel, but that those particular vowels are pronounced as one (for example, *boat*).

To develop an understanding of the vowel-syllable relation the teacher can provide children with a list of words. They must identify:

1. the number of vowels
2. the number of vowel sounds
3. the number of syllables.

For example:

	Vowels	Vowel sounds	Syllables
fact	1	1	1
summer	2	2	2
float	2	1	1

Accent

Knowledge and awareness of accent in words is helpful because accent affects vowel sounds. For example, "the vowel 'a' has the long sound when accented in *able*, but a different sound when unaccented in *apart*. The vowel principles apply to accented syllables, but they usually do not apply to unaccented syllables" (Smith, N. B., 1963, p. 235). The child should be aware of accent so that he can use it to apply the correct vowel sound to each syllable.

Another part of the syllabication technique is recognizing accents in words. In words of two or more syllables, one syllable is usually pronounced more forcibly than the rest.

To develop syllable accent the teacher can tell the children: "Listen carefully while I say this word—*básket*. Now listen to me say it again." This time he puts the accent on the second syllable—baskét. The children must identify which pronunciation is the correct one. They should also discuss why *básket* is the correct pronunciation. They may reply that *básket* just sounds right, while *baskét* sounds odd because the second part is too loud. The teacher can then explain accent by saying: "In words that have more than one syllable we usually say one syllable more forcibly, or loudly, than the others. This loudness, or stress, is called accent."

A feeling for accent can be developed further when children are instructed to tap or beat the accent with their fingers or with pencils as they pronounce lists of words. They will tap harder for the accented syllable.

One of the troublesome aspects of applying vowel-sound rules is that unaccented syllables generally have a muted sound known as the schwa. No matter what letter is used to spell it, the unaccented syllable sounds something like the short ŭ sound (as in *hut*). In acceptability, for example, both the "a" and the "i" are used in syllables with the schwa sound. Experience indicates, however, that pupils do not need to understand the effect of the unaccented syllable on the spelling of that syllable as it relates to its actual sound. The syntax of the sentence aids recognition of the word when reading. Accurate spelling requires different learning.

When the child has mastered auditory recognition of syllables and accent, he is ready for formal instruction in dividing written words into syllables. This will enable him to analyze unfamiliar many syllable, or polysyllabic, words in context.

The child's ability to divide written words into syllables is greatly facilitated if he knows some generalizations. The teaching of these principles should be done inductively; that is, the child should analyze many words that fit under one principle. Then, with teacher guidance, he will generalize the process, or principle, that can be applied when dividing these words into their component parts.

Syllabication Generalizations

Syllabication should be an aid where it can be used. The teacher must determine which guidelines are useful for reading.

These six generalizations may be helpful:

1. When two consonants fall between two vowels the division of syllables is usually between the two consonants (for example, *rab-bit, sis-ter*).

2. When a vowel is followed by a single consonant the consonant usually begins the second syllable (for example, *be-fore*).
3. When a word ends in *le,* and a consonant precedes the *le,* then that consonant goes with the *le* syllable (for example, *ta-ble*).
4. If the word contains a prefix, the division comes between the prefix and the root word (for example, re-*view*).
5. If the word has a suffix, the division comes between the suffix and the root word (for example, *like*-ly).
6. Consonant digraphs and blends are never divided (for example, *ro*ck-et).

The recognition of a word's pronunciation does not entirely stand or fall upon the child's being able to know exactly where the breaks between syllables occur. For example, knowing whether the division of syllables in the word *amble* comes before or after the *b* does not assure accurate pronunciation of that word. For that reason, and because those principles of syllabication do not apply to all words, they are recognized as being generalizations, not rules. They are helpful clues that the child usually can rely on to aid him in dividing a word into syllables, which can then be subjected to phonic or structural analysis so as to arrive at proper pronunciation or identification.

Correct division of a word into its syllables will, however, greatly facilitate the child's correct pronunciation of a word because of the effect that open and closed syllables have on the vowel sound. A syllable ending with a consonant is termed a *closed syllable*. The vowel sound in a closed syllable is short. If the syllable ends with a vowel, however, it is called an *open syllable*. The vowel sound in this case will be long; for example, *Bantu*. Therefore, correctly dividing a word into syllables yields clues for determining that word's pronunciation.

Context Strategy

Suppose a child is reading an article in the library and comes to a place where the page has been torn. A word has been obliterated from the selection. The illustration given below illustrates such a dilemma.

What will he do? Abandon the article? Probably not. More likely he will provide a word that will fit into the meaningful pattern of the sentence. Perhaps he will insert *patient* or *subject*. Either word is suitable in meaning to complete the text.[1]

Studying the setting of an unknown word for clues to help in identifying the word is what is meant by context clues. Use of context as an aid is not limited to a deleted word on a torn page. Context is also effective as an aid to word recognition when the word is available in print but unknown by the reader.

Utilization of context to aid in word recognition is a necessary and valuable technique, whether one is a beginning or a mature reader. Any unknown word must fit into the thought pattern of the sentence or paragraph.

[1]Article from *Science News,* vol. 96, no. 23 (1969), p. 147.

Use of context clues forces the reader to think while he reads. Context will always provide a check for the other word-recognition techniques used by the reader. Most reading authorities agree with Tinker and McCullough (1962), who cite context clues as being "one of the more important aids to word recognition" (p. 150).

BLAIBERG DIES

Borrowed time ends

The world's longest-surviving heart transplant... died at 7:40 p.m., Sunday, Aug. 17, at Groote Schuur Hospital in Capetown, South Africa. Chronic rejection was the cause of death. Rejection problems have led to a decline in the number of heart transplant operations (SN: 6/21, p. 598).

Dr. Philip Blaiberg, the dentist whose own heart's failure would have cut off his life at the age of 58, lived to be 60 —19 and a half months after Dr. Christiaan Barnard transplanted the heart of 24-year-old Clive Haupt, who died of a brain hemorrhage. Dr. Blaiberg received his new heart on Jan. 2, 1968. He had pneumonia as well as kidney and liver failure when he died.

As of Aug. 18, 143 heart transplants had been performed; 38 survive.   ◇

In the example of the article with the torn word the reader used context to decide on an appropriate word. A mature reader uses the same skill frequently to "guess" at the meaning of new words. Perhaps he learned to use context clues on his own. Some persons do. However, successful acquisition of a skill is questionable when left to chance. All children will benefit from direct, well-planned, and sequential instruction geared toward developing awareness and the use of contextual aids.

The teacher can promote the use of meaning clues in class. For example, during story time he can stop momentarily at an appropriate place and ask: "What word do you think will come next?" The children will provide words that they think make sense. The words they contribute can then be checked by inserting them into the actual sentence. The children can decide if their words fit.

"Perhaps the best way to develop contextual sensitivity and ability is to make the most of each functional opportunity while the children are reading" (Smith, N.B., 1963, p. 184). The teacher can give help in identifying an unfamiliar word using contextual clues whenever the opportunity arises.

Instruction should not rely on the teacher's beguiling encouragement—"Guess the word." Such guidance can become misguidance. Instead of leading the children to think, it may lead them to make wild guesses. Therefore, the teacher should ask: "What word do you think would make sense here?"

If the word doesn't snap into place with that question, then the child should be encouraged to use other decoding skills in systematic order until he finally gets a satisfactory match. Through repetition of a standard set of questions, the teacher helps the child use context and other cues in solving word problems.

This set of questions can serve as a guide to using the fewest number of cues possible:

1. Can you think of a word that makes sense in that spot?
2. Using context and the sound of the first part of the word, can you figure out what the word should be?
3. Using context, the first part of the word, and the sound of the last part of the word, can you figure out what the word should be?
4. Using context, and applicable sound-spelling patterns across the whole word, can you figure out what the word should be?
5. If the word is still unknown, go to a dictionary to look it up or ask someone.

Another suitable instructional technique is to take children's language experience stories and write them on the chalkboard with some words left out as in the following example:

We have a hamster in our _____.
Her _____ is Lori Blackberry.
She lives in a _____.
She likes to _____ the place.
We like our _____.

Cloze Method

The teacher does not have to rely on experience stories for material with which to construct context exercises. He can make use of paragraphs that he has written or that he has selected from books.

Mother planned a birthday _____ for Mary.
Mary invited all her _____ from school.
She planned _____ for her friends to play.
Her friends gave Mary _____.

Exercises like this incorporate a technique known as the *cloze method.* Based on the psychological studies of the gestalt idea of closure, which is the impulse to complete a structured whole by supplying a missing element, the reader provides closure of the sentence by filling in missing words. Practice to develop the child's ability to use contextual clues can be given with isolated sentences that require the addition of one word to complete the meaning. Pupils are asked to supply words that fit the blanks and thereby complete the sentence. When using the cloze method the teacher can ask: "What word do you think should go into the blank to finish the sentence?" The word or words that are volunteered by the children are checked by inserting them in the sentences. Several may be correct.

Often, in exercises using isolated sentences, the number of options that children can give will be larger. For example, take the sentence: "Dick _____ home after school." Any of the following words could conceivably be used: *came, ran, walked, went, skipped, called.* Now, if he wishes, the teacher can utilize other word-recognition techniques to narrow the choice to one word. He may say: "All of these words could be used, couldn't they? But now I want you to tell me what the word is if it begins with the letter *r.*"

Practice to strengthen contextual hints can also be provided by having pupils choose from a group of words that one which fits the meaning:

Jeff played _____. *(boy, bit, bat, ball, work)*

For beginning readers it may be helpful to supply several possible choices. Once they have the idea, though, the cloze method makes them more conscious of a variety of cues.

These and similar exercises should develop the child's ability to utilize context clues to aid in word identification. Frequently a teacher provides informal guidance in context clues when he tells the children to read the rest of the sentence and then come back to the unrecognized word.

The cloze technique can also be used to estimate the appropriateness of a book for a child. Bormuth (1962) deleted every fifth word in passages from elementary school texts and found that the accuracy with which children could supply the exact words in the blanks was significantly related to their scores on comprehension tests. He found the following equivalents, for example:

Percent of cloze (items passed)	Percent of comprehension (items passed)
50	95
40	80
30	65

The percentage points on the comprehension items are often used in making judgments about success in comprehension and sometimes in determining how difficult the book is for the student. A teacher can get comparable data from a cloze test. By deleting every fifth word from classroom books a teacher can test a child's capability to read them.

What should a teacher do if 50 percent of the cloze items are passed? If 30 percent of the cloze items are passed?

There are no simple answers to those questions, but an adjustment in the difficulty of the books seems appropriate where tested materials seem too easy or too difficult for instructing the child.

Types of Context Clues

As a child moves through the grades and masters reading skills he should be taught various types of context clues:

1. *Definition type*   The definition of an unknown word is provided by the sentence in which that word appears. "Jane and Susan live next door, so they are my *neighbors*."
2. *Experience type*   The child must rely upon his own experiential background to predict the unknown word. "The mouse *gnawed* a hole in the box with his sharp teeth."
3. *Comparison type*   Words in the sentence that contrast or compare with the unknown word give the clue. "You do not have to go around the mountains; go *through* them."
4. *Synonym type*   A synonym for the unknown word is included. "The *twins*, Tom and Don, moved next door."
5. *Familiar expression type*   A knowledge of everyday expressions is necessary for clues to be received from this type of context. "The tired old bunny thought the grass felt as soft as *cotton*."
6. *Summary type*   The unknown word provides a summary of the ideas that preceded it. "They marched all in line, just like a *parade*."[2]

Often the context alone will indicate the appropriate word, although sometimes context clues do not work. Therefore other word-analysis skills are needed to check the accuracy of the word chosen or to identify it in the first place.

The identification of an unfamiliar word through contextual clues is not a matter of chance. The reader must carefully consider the meaning implied in a sentence or paragraph as a whole, and in the light of this meaning deduce what the unrecognized word might be.

The context clue is widely used by mature readers. This does not imply that it is used to the exclusion of other word-recognition techniques. Instead, the context clue is most successful when it is used in conjunction with other techniques, and children should be directed to utilize it in this way.

Vocabulary Expansion

Most children are interested in words. They hear new ones and try them out. They have an intuition that words are power—an increased vocabulary is a sign of maturity. For that reason a teacher may find that he can have children

[2]Constance McCullough. "Recognition of Context Clues in Reading," *Elementary English Review*, vol. 22 (January 1945), pp. 1-5.

gain practice in word-recognition skills by capitalizing on their desire to expand the listening and speaking vocabularies they use.

By establishing a "word-for-today" routine the teacher can encourage groups or individuals to learn one new word each day. "Gertrude, it is your turn to provide a new word . . ."

"Astronomy—astronomy is the study of the stars."

"Now who can write it on the board for us? Can someone use it in a sentence?"

With such an approach the teacher leads students to look at a word and use all their word-analysis techniques to fix the word in their memories. "How many syllables are in the word? How is each syllable pronounced? What other word has a similar beginning?" (Astronaut) The vocabulary exercise helps children recognize the word for reading, and the motivation stems from the children's own internal drive for self-improvement and growth.

Some classes may enjoy keeping a vocabulary notebook. Or the notebook idea can be expanded to include a vocabulary bulletin board. The teacher can reserve bulletin board space for new words for a week. Every day the children display a new word they have discussed. The word, its definition, and a sentence using the word are then mounted on the board. At the end of the week the children can enter the words from the bulletin board into their notebooks so that they can review them and be inspired to keep vocabulary notebooks of their own. The bulletin board can be stripped at the end of the week for a fresh supply of words in the following week.

Continuous Development of Vocabulary

Vocabulary expansion and related word-analysis exercises are not limited to the early grades in school. In fact, they are more important in the upper grades as subject work becomes more complicated. From the primary grades

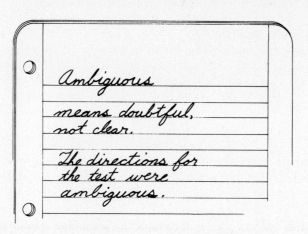

Ambiguous

means doubtful, not clear.

The directions for the test were ambiguous.

FIGURE 10.2   A vocabulary notebook

through the secondary school teachers and students should consider word power an important part of their lessons and their conceptual growth.

In the early years of school more emphasis is placed on building concepts though firsthand experiences than on gaining them through vicarious means. Teachers want to involve students as directly as possible so that words and concepts in stories and in class composition activities have a clearer and more vivid meaning. As trips to factories, museums, libraries, and zoos become slightly less important to children, teachers can begin to involve them more in projects, experiments, and exhibits—such as building scale models of towns, collecting seashells, and so on. A teacher who guided an experiment in the speed and direction of the wind added these words to his student's reading vocabulary:

direction	measure	intensity
pressure	anemometer	instrument

It is not always feasible for the teacher to provide the child with real experiences. Happily, much worthwhile experience and vocabulary can be gained vicariously. Secondhand experiences are obtained from films, pictures, maps, radio and television presentations, recordings, stories, and so on.

Providing children with experiences alone will not expand their vocabularies. A child can conceivably go to the zoo and not learn a single new word. There must be conversation; he must hear the new words. He must then be encouraged to use the words over and over until he integrates them and their meanings in his own vocabulary. The teacher's task is to present words visually for analysis and storage in the reading vocabulary bank.

One of the most effective means of enriching the child's vocabulary is to encourage him to read widely. In this way he meets many new words in different fields and also becomes familiar with their different meanings in a variety of contexts.

Vocabulary can be enriched by giving children experiences with *figurative language*. For example, they can study sentences using figurative patterns of speech to determine the meaning of the sentences:

His face fell.
Don't throw your money away on that.
He threw himself into his job.

Having the child find synonyms, antonyms, and homonyms for words he already knows provides another means of vocabulary enrichment:

Synonyms Words that have similar meanings (for example, *often, frequently*).
Antonyms Words that are opposite in meaning (for example, *warm, cool*).
Homonyms Words that are pronounced alike but are unlike in both spelling and meaning (for example, *wait, weight*).

Direct, structured instruction in these types of words is a necessary and meaningful development in the vocabulary building of the elementary school child. Exercises such as the following may be helpful in this way:

1. Underline the word in each row that has the opposite meaning:

   run   walk   race
   good   go   bad
   big   large   small

2. Which word in each row means the same as the first word? Which word means the opposite?

   merry   gay   was   sad   time
   soft   green   hard   sack   pliable

3. What words are pronounced the same in the following two sentences? Do they have the same meaning?

   Jack wore a blue tie.
   The wind blew.

The techniques described in this chapter are concerned primarily with words the reader already has in his listening or comprehending vocabulary. An often neglected means of getting children to learn and remember words for reading is to teach ones that are new to their vocabularies. At the same time the word is pronounced and defined, it should be spelled out and written on the board or on a piece of paper so it can be analyzed and discussed as a word to be recognized and read. The technique the child uses to commit this word to memory may be a single or a combination of word-recognition methods, but the motivation for learning is provided by the fact that he is noticeably expanding his vocabulary.

The average child has an interest in learning new words, and the teacher can use that interest to relate a general-meaning vocabulary to an analysis of a word for reading purposes. Once the child's interest is focused on a word, only the teacher's imagination limits the ways the word can be presented for visual analysis.

Appraising Word Skills

Word-analysis skills, like other skills, should be assessed shortly after they are taught. Since word-analysis skills are developed gradually over five, six, or more years; and since it is generally assumed that the skills build on one another, it is important to identify success or failure in a skill before trying to push the child on to some new area. The teacher has four general means for diagnosing reading: informal testing, observation, introspection, and formal testing. Depending on the situation, he will use one or all of these general means for appraisal. Table 10.3 indicates typical classroom activities and applies the four means for assessing word recognition to them.

TABLE 10.3   Means for Assessing Word-recognition Skills

Materials activities	Ways to Observe			Formal testing
	Informal testing	Observation	Introspection	
Oral reading				
Word lists				
Workbook exercises				

After teaching a specific word-analysis skill the teacher may ask individual children to read a word list aloud. As the child pronounces the words the teacher notes whether he is applying the skills that have just been taught. The teacher also looks at the child's practice exercises, whether on worksheets or on the chalkboard. If he observes several repeated errors, the teacher will want to schedule additional instructional time in the skill for that child.

As the child reads aloud from a book the teacher can note whether he analyzes words using recently taught skills and can also ask the child to explain what he is doing as he meets a new word that requires analysis. At times, the child's own description of his word-attack techniques will guide the teacher in planning instruction for the student. For example, a student reads *combine* for *consider,* saying he saw *com* and that *combine* made sense in context. The teacher must then show him how to look closely at the internal elements of the unknown word.

Workbooks and reading texts often contain tests to determine mastery of a given skill. Teacher-made tests and the tests provided by publishers for specific achievements in reading should be used as diagnostic instruments as much as possible. Their purpose is to isolate a specific skill, such as using initial consonants and final consonants as a clue to word identity. Since tests are constructed to examine specific tasks, the teacher should examine them to see whether or not the child can perform these tasks. The pattern or the regularity with which the child applies the skill, or fails to use it, is the point of the observation.

In the case of each of the word skills discussed in this chapter, the teacher wants to know two things:

1. Does the child know the generalization that will assist him in analyzing the words?
2. Can the child apply the generalization in a variety of situations—reading aloud, doing a workbook exercise, taking an achievement test?

Context Clues

Because of the nature of context clues, a simple word list does not provide an adequate testing device. A connected communication must be provided. Suppose that you want to determine whether or not a child understands that he has to think as he reads in order to use the context clue technique.

*read
p. 208
209*

Probably the most direct means for determining a child's ability to use context is to ask him what he does when he meets an unfamiliar word. He may respond that he *thinks* while he is reading and gets a good idea of the word from the context.

To appraise his ability to apply context clues the student needs some reading exercises that will try to answer these questions:

1. Can the child supply a reasonable substitute for the blank in the sentence?
   Henry dropped the egg, and it _____ all over the floor.
2. Can he use internal word cues, in addition to context, to help him find the correct word?
   The drowning man gr——p—d for the log.
3. Can the student infer meanings of words from the context?
   Being fired from his job was Henry's *Waterloo,* for it was a defeat from which he never recovered.

A series of evaluation questions can be asked about the other word-analysis skills discussed in this chapter. It is not absolutely necessary for the child to be able to articulate the generalization behind the skills, but it reassures the teacher if the child remembers the generalization. The important determination is whether or not the child can apply the skills and thus answer questions like those that follow:

Begin **Appraising Structural Analysis**

1. Can the child recognize root words in derived words? (for example, *information.*)
2. Can he recognize compound words? (for example, *cupcake.*)
3. Can he analyze and define words made up of familiar roots, prefixes, suffixes, and inflectional endings? (for example, *predated.*)
4. Can he add necessary prefixes, suffixes, and inflectional endings to words to give them the appropriate meaning and form needed in the sentence? ("Can't stand it!" *un +bear +able.*)

B **Appraising Syllabication**

5. Can the child identify the number of syllables he hears in a word?
6. Does he know that the number of sounded vowels in a word indicates the number of syllables?
7. Can he apply syllabication generalizations to words when dividing them into syllables?
8. Is he aware of the effect of accent in words of more than one syllable?
9. Can he apply common accent generalizations?

Appraising Association Skills

10. Can the child match the printed word with the visual, auditory, or tactile stimulus symbol used in instruction?
11. Does he recognize the word when he sees it subsequently?

Appraising Vocabulary Acquisition

12. Can the child write, say, or find the correct word when the definition is given?
13. Can he give the meaning of a new word?
14. Can he use new vocabulary words in writing sentences and in conversation?

Any evaluation of pupil performance in these skills should have the direct effect of indicating to the teacher which skills should be retaught in subsequent instruction. If the child has grasped the skill, the teacher can continue to present other skills in the sequential program. If evaluation indicates that the child is not able to utilize the skill in question, the teacher should then schedule further teaching and practice.

Words Have a Meaning

The various word-recognition techniques that have been presented in this and in preceding chapters are designed to help the student identify words. They are also aimed at giving the child methods of acquiring meaning from what he reads. The whole point of reading is getting a message from the printed page. No one reads merely to pronounce words. The reading teacher, therefore, must guard against giving too much emphasis to word identification and pronunciation without correlated emphasis on meaning. The teacher's responsibility is to demonstrate how to get meaning through a variety of word-perception skills. He creates an attitude about the basic importance of meaning, while building perception skills that enable the students to achieve meaning.

In beginning reading exercises most words are meaningful as soon as the child recognizes their sounds. Thus when the word is pronounced, it is also understood. This occurs naturally because the textbook writer uses words that are a part of the average child's listening and speaking vocabularies, and uses them in stories with a familiar setting. Evidence of the child's listening and speaking vocabularies is seen in his ability to participate actively in conversations with his teacher, parents, and classmates. Such participation calls for a grasp of words and their meanings. If a child can gain meaning from the words he hears and speaks, he should have little difficulty in transferring his knowledge of those words to print. As the reader advances into more difficult selections the vocabulary and concept load become heavier. Acquiring meaning, therefore, demands an increase in instructional time and in the student's energy.

To keep the acquisition of meaning a prime goal of reading, both instructional and practice reading materials must coincide with the background and performance skill of the child. Disregarding that prescription will not only provide the child with extremely frustrating and unhappy reading experiences but it will also result in his focusing attention on pronunciation rather than meaning.

The provision of graded reading materials will not, however, guarantee that the child is reading for meaning. The importance of reading for meaning can be illustrated to the child when word-analysis techniques are taught and practiced in context frequently and systematically. Combining recognition skills with meaning was suggested earlier as a reliable method of checking the word that has been analyzed.

The relationship between pronouncing (identifying) the word and understanding the word (meaning) can be shown during any reading lesson. For example, prior to reading, words that are new or that consistently cause difficulty for children can be pulled out of the reading selection for purposes of analysis. Following identification of the words, through the use of appropriate word-analysis techniques, the process can be reversed by replacing the words in context to show their function in developing the meaning of the passage. In addition to this procedure, exercises similar to those discussed earlier in this chapter in the section on context clues are appropriate for demonstrating the relation between word recognition and meaning.

Linguistics and Word Meaning

Linguistics is also concerned with words and their meanings, as was discussed earlier in this chapter under "Syntactic Skills." (A broader discussion of linguistics and meaning appears in Chapter 3.)

Linguists maintain that larger utterances—for example, phrases and sentences, of which isolated words are a part—provide keys to word meanings and also determine word use. The meaning of a given word depends on the other words with which it forms a sentence, as well as on the position it has in the sentence.

A word does not act independently of the other words in a sentence but joins and interacts with them. This interaction determines the exact meaning of a word. In one sentence a word may have one meaning, while in another sentence it has a different meaning. The range of possible meanings a word can have is reflected in the definitions found in a dictionary.

FIGURE 10.3 Words come to life in context

Take, for example, the word *nut*. Webster's New Collegiate Dictionary lists six distinct meanings for *nut:*

1. A dry fruit or seed having separate rind or shell and interior kernel or meat; also, the kernel or meat itself.
2. Something likened to a nut (sense 1) in the difficulty it presents.
3. A perforated block (usually of metal) with an internal, or female, screw thread used on a bolt or screw for tightening or holding something.
4. *Slang.* (a) The head
            (b) Fellow—used disparagingly
            (c) One whose thinking or conduct is eccentric
            (d) A crank
5. *Bot.* An indehiscent, polycarpellary, one-seeded fruit, with a woody pericarp, as an acorn, hazelnut, chestnut, etc.
6. *Music.* In stringed instruments, the ridge on the upper end of the finger board over which the strings pass.

A very real problem is now apparent. If someone hears the word *nut* in isolation, how will he know which meaning to apply to it? He cannot do so. Ascribing the appropriate meaning to the word *nut* is possible only when the word is used in a larger unit, such as a phrase or sentence. This concept is illustrated in the following sentences:

1. That math problem is a hard *nut* to crack.
2. She dropped her violin and broke the *nut.*
3. They went to the hardware store to buy some *nuts* and bolts.
4. You're a *nut,* you clown!
5. We're going to the woods to gather *nuts.*

When the word can be used for more than one sentence function it is even more apparent that the larger utterance vitally affects the meaning of the word. For example, here is a word used first to denote an object *(noun)* and then to show action *(verb)*:

1. He sat on a *chair.*
2. Harry will *chair* the class meeting.

Demonstrations of this type—that is, using words in a variety of ways in different sentences—can be understood by second-graders and even by many first-graders. As early as possible in school the teacher should make children aware of these variations in order to emphasize the need to use a variety of skills in understanding the printed page.

Wasn't the foregoing discussion simply another plea for the use of context clues in reading? In a sense it was. Linguists are not concerned with the cues a reader uses, however, but with the situations and rules that generate similarities and varieties that exist in the English language. If the insights of linguists can make reading specialists aware of how word meaning develops, perhaps teachers will discover clearer and more efficient ways of understanding, explaining, and illustrating techniques to children for identifying and comprehending the written word.

SUMMARY

Chapter 10 discussed word-recognition and word-analysis skills beyond the initial skills of visual memory (sight words) and sound-symbol decoding. A variety of word-perception skills are needed by a reader who wishes to cope with the printed page efficiently and competently. In addition to the visual memory and decoding skills discussed in previous chapters, a reader needs to be able to analyze words on the basis of syllables (sound structure); on the basis of meaningful structures, such as roots and affixes (meaning structure); and on the basis of context clues (thought and syntactic structure).

After visual memory and phonic techniques, syllabication and structural analysis techniques are usually taught. At first the child needs to understand the symbolic code and to decipher the parts and patterns that words exhibit. Once he has developed several semiautomatic techniques for analyzing and responding to words, the student can pay more attention to the running message that words carry in context, which in turn helps him understand individual words.

Linguists have recently reinforced a dictum from reading education—that word-recognition exercises should always end in a meaningful utterance in a sentence or paragraph. For words are hollow sounds and hollow shells when they stand alone. It is the whole utterance that gives them meaning.

Terms for Self-study

word recognition	syllable phonics
word analysis	phonics skills
visual memory skills	picture clues
syntactic skills	context clues
association skills	cloze method
structural analysis	figurative language
syllabication skills	analytic skills

Discussion Questions

1. Given the grade level at which you teach or will teach, what terminology would you use in helping children develop a word analysis strategy?
2. If you used a language-experience approach in teaching reading, how would you provide instruction for children in structural analysis, syllabication, and the other techniques mentioned in this chapter?
3. How could a teacher build and organize a repertoire of teaching activities related to word recognition?

11

Creating
Interest in
Reading

Most people who decide to pursue a teaching career have been fairly successful in their school experiences. They usually associate pleasure with school and wish to continue that happy relationship by becoming a teacher. Not too surprisingly, such people also are often avid readers. They probably found in their youth that learning to read was an interesting challenge they could meet successfully.

You probably fit this description to some degree. Given the choice, you would no doubt spend more time reading for pleasure than your busy schedule permits. Reading is enjoyable as well as functional for you.

Not all youngsters are so inclined. Reading is a last choice as a recreational activity for some children. As a teacher you must try to "turn on" these alienated and uninterested children. Your experience tells you that great joy can be found between the covers of a book. Your commitment as a teacher is to interest every child in reading. Enthusiasm is essential—but in and of itself inadequate for the job. This chapter provides help in finding answers to these questions:

What can the teacher do to encourage the habit of reading?
How can parents encourage their children to read?
Why do some teachers have a reading corner in their classrooms?

How can a child who refuses to read be encouraged to try a book?
Is it wise to teach the principles of literary analysis to elementary school
    children?
Should children be expected to read the classics?
Should book reports be required?

The teaching of reading in schools in the United States focuses primarily on the development of basic reading skills. The importance of a large sight vocabulary and effective word-recognition techniques is usually understood by teachers and emphasized by various instructional systems. Comprehension is central to the purpose of reading and thus receives a great deal of attention. Yet in teaching fundamentals of reading another requirement is too often overlooked or given only passing attention. This essential component is a genuine *interest in reading,* a lifelong commitment to acquiring information and enjoyment through the act of reading.

There is little point in teaching children to read if this skill is not used in later life. A recent Gallup Poll indicates that the average adult in the United States does not read as much as a single book in the course of a year. Few educators, however, would seriously suggest that we stop teaching reading because of this finding. Rather, such statistics demonstrate that greater emphasis must be placed on the use of reading in the daily lives of students. Hopefully students who learn the joy and value of habitual reading will carry a disposition to read into their adult years.

The first major section of this chapter discusses the home as the origin of interest in reading and describes what parents can do to encourage children to read. Next, the role of the school in developing reading interests is considered, with special attention being given to the importance of a classroom atmosphere that encourages reading. Some research on children's interests is reviewed, and implications for classroom instruction are presented. Several means available to the teacher for assessing children's interests are also described. The second major section of the chapter discusses techniques for helping children develop personal standards to guide their selection of books. Special attention is given to book reports and children's classics.

Creating an Interest in Reading

Interest in reading does not develop in a vacuum but is founded on personal interests. For example, the girl who enjoys collecting insects will probably enjoy a good book on this topic. A boy who loves and cares for a pet poodle will surely have a special interest in a book about grooming poodles for show. It may be much more difficult to create reading interest for a child who has few personal belongings, hobbies, or special interests. The first step in arousing interest in reading is to stimulate the child with life and the world around him. The home is a potent factor in this process; a factor that can predispose the child negatively or positively in his attitude toward reading.

The Home: Origin of Interest in Reading

Most children enter school with a broad variety of interests born of rich experiences during their earlier years. Typically, they have enjoyed a circus and are looking forward to additional trips to the zoo. Their backgrounds may include a vacation touring Disneyland or exploring the wonders of Mammoth Cave. The vocabulary and concepts gained from such experiences are fundamental to readiness, for learning to read. Perhaps even more important is the desire created by these experiences to read about other vacation spots. Growth in reading interests is almost spontaneous with children of this sort. Other children do not fit this description and require special efforts on the part of the teacher. Suggestions in this regard are provided throughout this text.

The parents of children with a wide variety of background experiences are frequently anxious for their youngsters to learn to read. Usually there are many books in their homes, books owned by the child and shared frequently with his parents. The parents themselves probably read occasionally. The child often sees a parent turn to the evening newspaper before dinner, read a book occasionally, and refer to the atlas when seeking information.

Reading is viewed as a desirable tool by the youngster from a background as rich as this one. Significant people in his life read; he associates enjoyment with books. An interest in reading is as natural to this child as watching television.

The recollections of one of our elderly well-read friends are helpful in describing the role of the home:

> My early days at home are a warm memory to me. I can remember well the winter evenings when the wind would tug at our roof and shutters while newly fallen snow drifted against the tool shed and animal shelters. My mother would wrap an afghan around her shoulders and invite me to squeeze with her into a big stuffed chair near the Ben Franklin stove. From that port we ventured off together on many journeys. We hunted with our young comrade in Prokofieff's tale of *Peter and the Wolf,* drifted over sleepy villages far below with *Peter Pan,* and scratched for our existence alongside *Robinson Crusoe.*
>
> Often, in the spring of the year, I would tag along with my father in the evening as he took our small herd of cows out to pasture. We shared the sight of geese heading north and bluebirds building their nests in our orchard. Later we might hunt in the *Audubon Handbook* for the name of a new bird we saw perched near the creek. Sometimes I sat on his lap listening to the late news broadcast wondering at how he could know so much about world events. He listened carefully when I ventured a comment and sometimes helped me look at another point of view.
>
> On Friday evenings we went to town for shopping and visiting. The county library stayed open until 8:00 P.M. and I worried every week that we would be too late to get in. Somehow we always made it in time. I was permitted to search for new treasures while my parents completed their errands.

Grandpa Knippling was the best storyteller who ever lived, it seemed to me in those days. He always claimed to be fresh out of new stories, but remembered one when I begged him. I even loved to hear the same stories again and again. Later in life I discovered in books tales like those my grandpa told. It was like visiting an old friend to read them, but not quite the same as hanging on every word, hoping Grandpa would not run out of chewing tobacco and have to stop in the middle of an old favorite.

Those early days had a great deal to do with my fondness for literature and reading.

The rich background enjoyed by this individual was a significant factor in building his interest in reading. Today the opportunities for extending a child's horizons are even greater.

The experiences that sensitize a child to his surroundings are certainly not limited to middle-class homes. (Indeed, in some middle-class homes parents are so involved with their own pursuits that their child is as deprived of enriching experiences as the child from a poverty-stricken home may be.) A trip to the Grand Canyon may be impossible for such children, but the opportunity to see and experience the wonder of a constantly expanding world can be theirs. A walk around the block or through the park with a parent who explains, discusses, and listens can serve the same purpose as a trip to a distant place. A parent with limited financial resources can take a child to the public library and share a book they select and borrow. Without a positive attitude toward reading, which such experiences provide, the child enters school with a severe handicap. Five or six years of influence in the home, the child's first and most powerful influence with regard to creating an interest in reading, have transpired before the youngster enters school.

The importance of early childhood experiences as a prerequisite to success in school has been underscored by programs such as Headstart. Children only three and four years of age are placed in an environment designed to provide the stimulation often lacking in their own homes. Teachers and trained parents read to these youngsters, listen to their ideas, teach them simple skills and concepts learned at home by more fortunate children, and generally enrich their backgrounds. Whether such programs are a satisfactory substitute for a varied and stimulating home environment is difficult to determine, but certainly they are a desirable alternative to no stimulation at all. The teacher who tells his class a story or gives the class a field trip experience is providing valuable experiences insofar as reading interests are concerned. While each child reacts individually to specific enrichment experiences, a variety of activities offers something to spark the interest of every child. One mechanically minded boy may be enthralled by a visit to the fire station, where shiny trucks with chromed engines wait. How eagerly he will listen to the story of *Engine No. 9* (Hurd, 1961). Later, his maturing reading skill can open many paths to enjoyment and information, paths that might not beckon to a youngster who regards reading and life in general as a dreary imposition. A little girl may be fascinated by a film about raising horses in Kentucky. Through discussions about horses and looking at picture books, as well as other techniques, the girl can develop an interest that leads to the writings of someone as good as Marguerite Henry. The joy of knowing literature of such quality might mean for this girl an understanding love for an animal.

What the Parent Can Do to Encourage Reading

Although this text is not written primarily for the lay public and therefore is not likely to be read by many parents, a program for building a powerful home environment for reading will be described for two reasons: First, many teachers are parents and are eager to know what steps they should take to help their children succeed in school. Second, and more important, teachers often have the opportunity to influence what goes on in the homes of their students. Many parents would gladly help their youngsters prepare for school if they only knew how. The teacher can be a supportive consultant in this regard.

Books are an individual matter, and the parent who wishes to encourage children to read should know something about books before beginning. Learning about books cannot be done overnight. Even before the child is born the parent can begin to explore what is available. A local bookstore or library is the logical place to start.

In deciding what kind of children's book to choose, the parent should keep several points in mind. First, the child can be read to long before he can talk. Nursery rhymes and other short rhythmic pieces will be enjoyed by the child who understands only the swing of the words and the beat of the language. Second, the parent should select children's books that he himself enjoys. The pleasure conveyed by the adult's voice and feeling is an important factor in determining the child's response.

The child's first books should be attractive ones that contain accurate and colorful pictures. Children usually prefer uncluttered drawings that stress familiar objects, such as animals and activities that they enjoy. Cloth books that can be handled by the child are an excellent investment, since small, uncoordinated hands are not likely to tear them. It is not possible or desirable to give a comprehensive list of recommended books for beginning readers, since personal taste should dictate the actual choices. However, the following titles may serve as point of departure:

Author	Title
Leslie Brooke	*Ring o' Roses*
Beatrix Potter	*The Tale of Peter Rabbit*
Ezra Jack Keats	*A Snowy Day*
Aileen Fisher	*In the Middle of the Night*
Róbert McCloskey	*Make Way for Ducklings*
Wanda Gág	*Millions of Cats*

A Parents' Guide to Children's Reading by Nancy Larrick (1975) is an excellent reference.

The parent should learn something about the child's interests by carefully observing his reaction to stories that are read aloud and by his choice of play activities. An appreciative response to a rhythmic poem, such as "There Was a Crooked Man," calls for more of the same. Naturally, a solid diet of this fare is undesirable, but the child's favorable reactions provide a clue for future selections. Similarly, his attachment to stuffed animals may suggest stories that contain such characters (*The Velveteen Rabbit,* for example).

As the young child becomes acquainted with picture books his taste in books and in other things will develop. His personal likes and dislikes will become evident. Opportunities for familiarity with a broad variety of books and topics are necessary to expand the child's horizons. The alert parent will not attempt to force classics or books on certain topics on the child if he shows a dislike for them. As a general rule, it is advisable to stop reading to a child when his attention or interest lags.

It is most important that books be available for the child to look at and

(Photo courtesy Fred Weiss)

FIGURE 11.1   Parents and children can share reading for pleasure and learning

An early interest in reading can lead to a lifetime appreciation of books, especially when parents and children share their pleasure.

"read" on his own. If possible, he should have personal copies of his favorite books. While he must be taught to treat books with care and respect, his fear of damaging books should not interfere with his desire to handle them. It seems better to risk a torn page than to keep books in perfect condition on a shelf inaccessible to the child.

Children who grow to school age in an atmosphere where books are a respected and familiar commodity usually have an early interest in reading. Most children even learn to read a few isolated words—such as *milk* or *stop*—before entering school. They often have the necessary attitude and readiness to conquer the demands of reading in first grade. With this background some youngsters, such as those described by Durkin (1966), go far beyond acquiring a few sight words to the point of actually reading second or third grade material before they enter school. The stimulating home environment facilitates early reading when the child is ready to do so. Most children will not and should not be expected to read before entering school. The home that provides an atmosphere of interest in reading and familiarity with books has done as much as the school can ask.

The Role of the School in Promoting Interest in Reading

Children enter school with a broad range of home backgrounds. These include the fortunate youngster who has his own books, parents who read to him, and a wealth of enriching experiences, as well as the child who has never seen anyone read a book for enjoyment. The classroom teacher has a responsibility for capturing and stimulating the interest of children in reading regardless of their home environments. In all instances, experiences similar to those provided in stimulating home environments are useful in school as well. Books can be shared, trips taken, discussions held, games played, poetry recited, and numerous other enrichment activities undertaken in the classroom.

The same experiences will not be appropriate for all children in a classroom. Differentiation of instruction to meet individual needs must begin immediately in the kindergarten and first grade. The child who lacks even fundamental knowledge about books, their use, and the wonder they can provide requires a program of experiences designed to build the background a more fortunate child has received at home. The youngster who owns a personal library and already reads a few isolated words may rebel at participating in some of the activities designed for a child without his background. The interest in reading the child has gained at home can easily be dampened by too much repetition of preschool activities he has already shared with his parents. He is ready for new experiences that take him from his present level and broaden his world.

Some experiences are worth repeating. Most children desire and enjoy the retelling of a favorite story or hearing a familiar book read time and time again. There is little danger of destroying interest in reading under these circumstances. In fact, good literature wears especially well. However, there is a real possibility that exposure to certain picture books, loved in the past but now regarded disdainfully as "baby books" by the mature child will turn him away from reading. The youngster without early reading experiences undoubtedly requires exposure to such material. Therefore, the solution lies in differentiated instruction. While some children are sharing a picture book such as *An ABC Book* by C.B. Falls with their teacher, those with a fuller background can independently read a book more suitable to their levels.

In one case recently called to our attention the importance of differentiated instruction was reinforced. A very mature first-grade boy read only two pages of a "linguistically" based primer: "Nan can fan Dan. Can Dan fan Nan? Dan can fan Nan," before indicating that he was bored with the book. A child less ready than he for more meaningful material might not find the nonsensical story so uninteresting. In fact, earlier in his life this same boy might have found the story about Dan and Nan engrossing. To keep all children interested in reading the teacher must strive to provide individualized experiences geared to their needs.

This is not to say that whole-class activities that benefit each member of the group are impossible. Listening to the teacher read *The Biggest Bear* by Lynd Ward (1952) is an experience all children in any primary-grade class could share with pleasure. Each child brings his background and reaps personal benefits from participating in this activity. However, activities related to a story must take into account the range of backgrounds represented in a group. For example, during a discussion the teacher cannot assume that every child has been to a zoo or museum and has actually seen a bear. A comment about *The Biggest Bear* that assumed such knowledge would only confuse some children. An adjustment must be made for the range of the children's backgrounds. The rich experiences of some youngsters may be used to increase the understanding of others. Johnny, who has seen and touched a bear, can share his experience with the class. Johnny benefits from the opportunity of sharing an experience, and others learn from his description and personal reactions.

A field trip is another example of a whole-class activity that can benefit each child by broadening his background. Suppose a class of second-graders visits a local construction site. Juan may never have seen large machines, such as a bulldozer and steam shovels, at work. The opportunity to watch and listen to their operation may arouse his interest in learning more about them and what they do. A book, carefully chosen by the teacher, or found by Juan with the teacher's guidance—*Mike Mulligan and His Steam Shovel* (Burton, 1939), for instance—might be the key to a new world for Juan. A girl in the same class may be very familiar with construction machinery, but be intrigued by the scientific principles that enable a steam shovel to lift heavy loads. Again, a book on simple machines may be found, or the opportunity provided for her to make models of such machines with an erector set. In each case, the broadening experience of taking a field trip is valuable for the child. The follow up to such a trip adds to its value from the standpoint of stimulating reading interests. Only an alert teacher can know the distinct needs of his students and adjust his teaching accordingly.

The Classroom Atmosphere Must Make Reading Attractive

Just as the parents' attitude toward reading is instrumental in molding the child's disposition toward reading, the teacher's attitude is also a significant factor. The child tends to imitate the attitude he perceives important adults displaying toward reading. The school environment, like the home environment, is a direct outgrowth of the adult's attitude. The parent who honors reading will buy and personally use books; the teacher must also procure, use, and respect books if his example is to be positive. The parent who wishes to encourage reading will make books available for the child, as will the interested teacher. Both the parent and teacher must take time to share books at first hand with children. A parent can respond one to one; the teacher usually must resort to sharing with a group. In short, the classroom environment must make it *easy* to read, and the classroom atmosphere must make it *important* to read.

The Availability of Books Is Crucial

It is a well-known fact that people tend to do what is convenient. The nearest market is usually the one we shop at; the closest gasoline station gets our business (provided we have the credit card they accept—and this is another convenience factor). The same is true of reading. People are more likely to read if it is convenient for them to do so. A book must be close at hand. This accounts in part for the popularity of paperback books which are displayed conveniently in nearly every drugstore and supermarket.

Burger, Cohen, and Bisgaler (1956) succeeded in tripling the amount of reading done voluntarily by a large sample of urban children. Their approach was simply one of making books available. Books were placed in classrooms, and during reading instruction periods children were encouraged to read books outside of school. A follow-up check noted that after a year the children were still reading voluntarily.

Bissett (1969) worked with a suburban sample of fifth-grade youngsters who were reading on the average only one-half a book a week, despite numerous advantages such as libraries, well-trained teachers, librarians, and reading specialists. When interesting books were added to the classrooms, the number of books voluntarily read by the children increased by 50 percent. A program of stimulating reading through recommendations by teachers and peers was then instituted, and the number of books read was tripled.

The habit of reading is founded in large part on simply that—reading. The availability of books is crucial in determining whether the habit will ever be acquired. (*See* Appendix A for a listing of book clubs for children.) An excellent means for making books available is by developing a reading corner in the classroom.

A Reading Corner Can Attract Children to Reading

The reading corner is a place in the classroom where books and other reading materials are conveniently and attractively displayed for children's use.

FIGURE 11.2   A classroom reading corner

A quiet corner of the classroom where children can spend free time with books is an inviting place in the schoolroom.

Ideally, the reading corner should be in a quiet and private location so that youngsters can enjoy reading without being interrupted by regular classroom activities. Classroom procedures should be instituted that encourage children to visit the reading corner freely whenever their time permits.

The selection of a suitable location for building a classroom reading corner involves finding a quiet, relatively isolated area. Often a corner of the room provides these requirements. Low room dividers, shelves, or even tables may be used to shape the physical environment of the reading corner, helping to establish an atmosphere of privacy for young readers. A good light source is an equally important consideration. The area may be made more inviting with plants, colorful book jackets hung on the walls, book displays, and child-sized chairs. Some teachers prefer a rug or mats, so that the children may sit on the floor as they read. Books on many levels of difficulty and covering a wide range of subjects should be made available. Children with free time or those pursuing special interests are then able to find books expressly to fit their needs.

Class projects and reference work will be aided by a well-planned reading corner. Children who have had a part in the planning will be eager to add their stories or poems to class collections which can be shared, enjoyed, and reread as part of the classroom library.

The children can adapt and employ a simplified cataloguing system for their books and stories. Children who finish a book can complete a card reporting the title and author, and adding a short annotation and recommendation for others. If books are brought from home, they may be catalogued also, perhaps including the owner's name.

Dioramas, posters, and attractive book displays should be a part of the reading corner. They can be changed frequently to reflect current units and incidental occurrences which have influenced class interests. The reading corner can contain filmstrips and a filmstrip previewer, a tape recorder and headphone set, a boxed reading laboratory, and literally dozens of other items. The creative teacher will think of many ways in which to make reading enjoyable, and will use the reading corner as a marketplace for enticing activities.

Ms. Dale, a second-grade teacher, found a likely place for her reading corner directly beneath the windows in the back of the classroom. With low dividers, she separated the area from the rest of the room. Because no bulletin board was available in the reading corner, she fastened brightly colored corrugated cardboard to the wall and developed the first display: "Look, New Books!"—a collection of book jackets. The school librarian helped her make a general selection of books geared for the interests and reading levels of second-graders at the beginning of the school year.

Ms. Dale decided that later on more specific selections could be included, and that the children in her classroom could add and request books for their class library. She also planned to use the public library as a resource, especially for supplementary and enrichment materials for classroom units.

One child brought a rug from home for the corner and Ms. Dale added two small rocking chairs and a table. The children placed plants on the window ledge, and began to take responsibility for the display board. Soon books were being brought from home to be shared in the free reading time. A shoe box covered with adhesive-backed paper became their card catalogue. The children took turns being librarian.

Ms. Dale made a "look it up" game for the corner, as the year progressed. Since some of her second-graders were beginning to use encyclopedias in conjunction with a social studies unit developed around "Our Country," she supplemented this activity with a question box. Cards drawn from the box by the children contained one question which directed them to a specific volume and page in the encyclopedia—for example, "What man became our sixteenth president after losing a race for senator?" Look under L, page 1435.

The children who found the answer wrote it on a separate piece of paper to be checked by Ms. Dale. Later, this activity was changed to reflect the growing independence of the children—only the volume was given.

All through the year the reading nook was a source of pleasure, information, and a storehouse for creative writing. Ms. Dale's children learned to use it efficiently and with enjoyment.

Reading Should be Made Important

Too often reading for recreation is permitted in the classroom only after all other work is finished. This unfortunate policy discourages recreational reading by making it the last thing to be done—almost a last resort. The policy is shortsighted, since other work is often hurriedly and poorly completed when this requirement is in force.

There must be regular and lengthy opportunities to read for enjoyment *in the classroom*. It seems incongruous to urge children to read, or to make books readily available, and then not treat recreational reading as an activity worthy of valuable class time. As we said earlier, an excellent grasp of reading skills is nearly worthless unless they are *used* by the reader. It seems appropriate that some class instructional time also be devoted to recreational reading (a better label might be *practice reading*). The daily, sustained silent reading (SSR) activity described by McCracken and McCracken (1972) is an excellent means for providing needed practice reading.

The authors recommend that at least once a week children be given the equivalent of a full reading period for recreational reading (not necessarily at one sitting). A logical time for providing some of this allotted time is immediately after the class has returned from the school library. Most elementary schools with a library arrange a schedule that reserves the facilities for each classroom for about a half-hour once a week. Book selections are made by the children when they are in the library, and some skill instruction may be provided by the teacher or librarian. When they return to the classroom, the children's interest in a book just selected should be at its highest. What better time to provide twenty or thirty minutes for free reading? This brief period of time permits the child to get a good start on his new book and thus increases the probability that it will be read in its entirety.

Recreational reading is an excellent independent activity for children not working directly under the supervision of the teacher during the reading period. Several times a week each reading group can be given a fifteen- or twenty-minute respite from workbooks and other written exercises to enjoy the use of their growing skills through recreational reading.

Another activity that emphasizes the importance of reading is oral reading by the teacher. At opportune moments during the day the teacher can share a poem with the class or continue a story. The enjoyment in a book evidenced by an enthusiastic teacher and the personal satisfaction gained by each child when a selection is shared orally emphasizes the contribution reading can make to one's well-being.

What Is Known about Children's Interests

Huus (1963) summarized the research on children's perferences as:

Interests of children vary according to age and grade level.
Few differences between the interests of boys and girls are apparent before age nine.
Notable difference in the interest of boys and girls appear between ages ten and thirteen.
Girls read more than boys, but boys have a wider interest range and read a greater variety.

Girls show an earlier interest in adult fiction of a romantic type than do boys.
Boys chiefly like adventure and girls like fiction, but mystery stories appeal to
    both.
Boys seldom show preference for "girls" books, but girls will read "boys"
    books to a greater degree.

Sebesta (1968) suggests that the reading interests of children are greatly influenced by the reactions of adults to "perceived" interests. For example, parents and teachers think Marie enjoys mystery stories, so they encourage and reinforce this perceived interest with discussions and books on the topic. Marie, who may or may not be especially interested in mysteries, responds to the expectations of those around her—not unlike the subjects who responded to teacher expectations in *Pygmalion in the Classroom* (Rosenthal and Jacobson, 1968). It is clear that differences in interests for the sexes are in part a product of fulfilling society's expectations.

The unfortunate aspect of this self-fulfilling prophecy is that children may read avidly on only those topics that teachers think interest them. Sebesta (1968, p. 21) states: "Interest studies generally describe preferences of the majority, while the child himself is a minority." The implications of this statement for teaching are important. While it is helpful to know that intermediate-grade girls in general enjoy horse stories, a fifth-grade teacher cannot assume that Jessie or Heather have either an interest in or the background for enjoying *Born to Trot* (Henry, 1950). Generalizations about children's interests are simply that—generalizations. Each child is an individual who may or may not fit the usual pattern. Weintraub (1969) concluded from an extensive review of the literature on reading interests that no single category of books will supply all children of the same age with what they want to read. He suggests that each teacher identify the unique reading interests of children in his classroom, and then try to supply the materials required.

Are we to conclude then that research findings on children's interests are not useful in the classroom? Not at all. A librarian or classroom teacher should build a book collection with an awareness of general interests. Research says that primary-school-age youngsters are more likely than sixth-grade boys to be interested in fairy tales. A school library should have fairy tales on the shelves, and a first-grade teacher should display fairy tales in the classroom collection. But both the librarian and classroom teacher should obtain many other types of books for youngsters who do not fit the pattern. More will be said later about the importance of broadening reading interests by making a variety of books available. Since individual youngsters may not have reading interests that coincide with those identified by research, some means for assessing children's interests are needed.

Assessing Interests

The best way of assessing a youngster's interests is to learn more about him as an individual. We know well the interests of our best friends and close relatives. Almost unconsciously we decide that Aunt Mary would enjoy seeing the latest play by Arthur Miller, but that Uncle Alex would prefer to see the Yankees play the Orioles. Or we may realize that our roommate will not appreciate hearing the latest folk-rock record album. An understanding of another's interests is based on familiarity with his likes and dislikes, our knowledge of his disposition and personality. Much the same is true of a teacher's ability to identify students' interests.

The pupil-teacher interview is an excellent way to get acquainted and a good source of information on interests. It is a technique that should be employed as often as possible. Unfortunately, the time to conduct such discussions is severely limited by a busy school schedule. One round of interviews would hardly be completed before another round would be required, for children's interests simply change too rapidly, especially in the primary grades, to depend entirely on this technique. Additional means for gathering information on interests must be used.

An informal questionnaire developed by the teacher can gather much of the information obtained in an interview fairly easily. An example of such a questionnaire, which provides highly useful information is provided below. The teacher can easily keep current on student activities with such data for each youngster. Providing the right book at the right time is accomplished more readily by having up-to-date information about interests. For example, Jerry may report on an interest questionnaire that his hobby of collecting insects has taken a slightly different direction and now focuses more specifically on bees. The alert teacher makes direct application of information about Jerry's leisure-time activity to recommend an appropriate book.

"Like to Do" Checklist

Name_____   Date_____

Age_____   Class in School_____

Directions: This is a list of things that some boys and girls like to do in their spare time. If you never do the thing shown, leave the line blank. If you like to do it, put one check on the line; if you like to do it very much, put two checks. If you put a check on the line, and a question is asked about it, please answer the question in the space provided.

Watching TV_____	Repairing things_____
Writing letters_____	Drawing and painting_____
Sewing or knitting_____	Driving a car_____
Dancing_____	Cooking_____
Hunting_____	Fishing_____
Loafing_____	Teasing_____
Singing_____	Playing a musical instrument_____
Playing cards_____	Playing chess_____
Playing other games_____	What other games?_____
Collecting things_____	What do you collect?_____

Making things with tools_____	What do you like to make?_____
Experimenting in science_____	What kind of experiments?_____
Going to the movies_____	What kind do you like best?_____
Going for a walk_____	Where?_____
Talking_____	What do you like to talk about?_____
Listening to the radio_____	What programs do you like best?_____

Another type of information the teacher will find useful in assessing interests concerns the child's background of experiences. This information can also be obtained by a questionnaire completed by either the child or his parents. Much the same information may also be obtained by asking the child to prepare an autobiography. Or the teacher can get valuable information about the child's background from the cumulative record folder. Regardless of how the information is obtained, the teacher can use this knowedge to recommend books that he believes the child will enjoy. For example, a boy who has just moved into a community can be introduced to *Roosevelt Grady* (Shotwell, 1963), a story about a family that has just moved. Or a youngster who has lost a parent might profit from reading *Rascal* (North, 1963), a story about a child who faced and overcame a similar tragedy. Crosby's (1963) *Reading Ladders for Human Relations* is a valuable resource for teachers who are seeking books with special themes.

Through daily observation the alert teacher can obtain continuous information about a child's interests. The daily reading period offers an excellent opportunity for using the child's reactions to stories, characters, and topics. A story about a dog may elicit an enthusiastic reaction from Bill. The teacher should note his response, and take the appropriate steps to introduce *Big Red* (Kjelgaard, 1945); *Silver Chief, Dog of the North* (O'Brien, 1933); or similar books. The teacher can also note special interests in other subjects, particularly social studies. For example, *Johnny Tremain* (Forbes, 1944) or *Caddie Woodlawn* (Brink, 1936) are excellent books that relate directly to United States history.

Children often reveal much about themselves and their interests during informal "show and tell" or group discussions. The teacher who watches for such information can do much to individualize the assistance he provides in selecting books. Aids for selecting children's books are listed in Appendix C.

Expanding Children's Interests

It has been said by Dora V. Smith that when a child enters school his reading interests are the teacher's opportunity; when he leaves school they are the teacher's responsibility (Smith, 1964). The teacher has the responsibility for broadening and deepening the child's reading interests and making him more fully aware of what books are available. The surest method of achieving this goal is by creating a classroom environment that arouses the child's interest.

When the question "How will Mafatu survive?" appears on a bulletin board in the reading corner the curiosity of an intermediate-grade child is sure to be stimulated. An illustration of Mafatu fighting a wild boar to defend his dog further stimulates interest. The final touch is to place a copy of the book *Call It Courage* (Sperry, 1940), on display with the recommendations of several classmates attached. Another excellent technique for advertising a book is to read an exciting passage aloud to the class and display other books by the same author in the reading corner. By carefully "setting the bait" a creative teacher can tempt many youngsters into trying a book.

Many teachers have found it helpful to keep some record of each child's recreational reading choices. With guidance, older children can easily do this for themselves. Younger children may copy the title of a book or simply sign their names on a sheet attached to the book. Another approach is to fasten slips of paper imprinted with the name of the author and title to the book. When a child has finished reading he can simply remove one of the slips and place it in his record folder. In any event, a record of the books each child has read enables the teacher to tell at a glance what kind of reading is being done. A steady diet of one type of book may prompt the teacher to instigate a "sales campaign" on another category for a child.

A chart like the one in Table 11.1 is often helpful in tabulating the reading choices of children. Concentration of titles in one section of the circle may signal a need for a greater variety in book selection.

Occasionally a child will read only books of one type. Such a youngster was Daniel, who refused to read anything except nonfiction science books, usually on rocks and minerals. When urged to try good fiction he responded, "I want to learn something when I read." How should a teacher react to this attitude: Daniel's motive for reading was certainly beyond reproach, even if it was a bit limited. An older child of junior or senior high-school age might be shown what can be learned about human nature from a well-written novel. Daniel might have been persuaded by this approach, too; but a different tack was taken by his teacher. Using the highly effective technique of *gradually broadening* Daniel's current reading interests, he was led to try other subjects. The teacher first suggested nonfiction science books similar to those Daniel usually selected, but the subject matter was on plants rather than rocks and minerals. Next, a biography of a well-known botanist was recommended. After reading several biographies about scientists Daniel was ready to read some historical fiction that enabled him "to learn something" in a fictional setting. Eventually he began to read other fiction stories, and soon had a well-balanced reading diet.

Daniel's case is interesting for several reasons. First, we see how interests can be broadened gradually by finding topics related to the child's main interests. Second, the question of how much reading of one type should be

Table 11.1

Name _____

Age _____

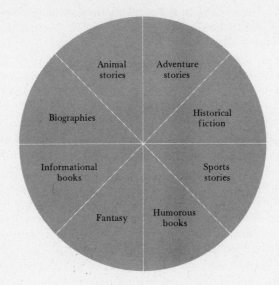

Directions: Write the title of your book in the space below and place the identification number in the proper category above.

Date	Identification number	Book title	Author
1.			
2.			
3.			
4.			
5.			

permitted is implicit in Daniel's case. What if he had steadfastly refused to budge from reading about rocks and minerals? We believe that reading, even of a singular nature, is preferable to no reading at all. There is always the chance that an habitual reader will change his interests, but far less chance that a "nonreader" will pick up the habit of reading.

Another point to remember is that some of our most "unbalanced" citizens—insofar as interests are concerned—have been major contributors to society through their intense dedication to one pursuit. Einstein is an obvious example, but others can easily be cited. Anne Roe (1961) discovered that the vast majority of eminent scientists she studied were regarded by others as unbalanced and not well rounded in their youth. This is not to say that a balanced reading fare is unnecessary for most children. But we must keep in mind that there are youngsters who rebel at external demands placed upon their reading. If well-planned guidance is ineffective in broadening the child's interests, it is advisable to stop short of badgering him to read more widely. He may be another Einstein or just a very persistent child; in either case, we should be pleased that he reads at all.

But what about the child who will *not* read? For example, Mark reads very poorly and flatly refuses to take a book out of the library. Teachers frequently ask how they can get a boy like Mark to read. There is no simple answer. One sure-fire way to fail with Mark is to threaten or coerce him into reading. Nothing is gained, since Mark will never read outside the classroom if he is literally forced to do so in school.

Often, refusal to read is simply the child's way of avoiding highly frustrating experience. Nobody seeks out an activity in which he constantly fails. The first step, then, is to help a child like Mark succeed in reading. This usually means finding a book that the child can read without difficulty. Perhaps this means going as far back as a preprimer to locate a book. It would be better if we could find an easy library book, since the preprimer-primer route is often partially responsible for Mark's lack of interest. After all, the failure to read probably started with these or similar materials.

Level of interest is a second factor to be considered in selecting a book for the child who refuses to read. Many easy-to-read books are now available on a variety of topics. Spache's *Good Books for Poor Readers* (1974) lists hundreds of them. Mark may be fascinated by submarines. The Harr-Wagner Deep Sea Adventure Series has a book titled *Submarine Rescue* which is written at a low level of difficulty and may meet Mark's need.

It is also important to remember that Mark may need help even with easy books. A friend or teacher's aide may have the time to read through the book with him. The teacher or Mark's parents may even be able to help him read it.

The key with most reluctant readers is helping them find success in reading. Until the pattern of failure is broken, interest in reading is unlikely. Quandt (1974) describes a practical plan you may find useful for helping children overcome negative concepts of themselves as readers.

The Elementary School Literature Program

We have seen how the home and school environments are related to children's interests in reading, and have considered various ways of stimulating and assessing such interests. Most teachers would agree that without an interest in reading, such skill instruction is largely futile. Wanting to read and having the skills needed to read and comprehend are not enough; one additional element is missing—taste in reading.

Literature is the vehicle that carries young and old alike through doorways they may never personally encounter. It has the capacity to give sheer enjoyment, to provide new perspectives and vicarious experiences. Literature can develop one's insight into human behavior and transmit the accumulated wisdom of humankind. Good literature provides beauty and inspiration for the reader. Because literature has much to offer it is essential that taste be encouraged, so that young readers will select the best that is available.

Reading interests determine what will be read—for example, fairy tales or sports stories. Reading taste determines the quality of what is read—for example, *Sport* magazine or *All American* by John Tunis. Taste in reading grows from the opportunity to read materials of varying degrees of quality. Without adequate guidance children's choices of books may be based on superficial and fleeting elements that have little connection with good literature. But the teacher is not a censor deciding what a child will or will not read. Only the child's parents have the right to provide such supervision—and the child himself. Neither should the teacher sit in judgment of what is and what is not good literature. It is his responsibility to help the youngster develop his own standards (Huck, 1976).

Literature Instruction Can Be Initiated Early

Perhaps because of the difficulties involved in defining exactly what constitutes a total literature program at the elementary school level, no research has been done on the extent of such programs. We know that the senior high school curriculum usually provides for the study of literature in English classes. Some junior high schools have formal literature study also. However, several factors operate to limit the amount of time devoted to literature at the elementary school level. First, most elementary schools in this country are without libraries. Without adequate materials the literature program is often limited to basal readers, not always a good source of literature of quality. Second, the emphasis on teaching basic reading, writing, and computational skills in elementary schools is so great that little time remains for other pursuits. It is our firm conviction that literature instruction cannot be separated from effective teaching of reading. The basics of literary analysis and evaluation can be introduced early in the primary grades regardless of the instructional system employed.

Given a scheme for analysis and a basis for making judgments, the primary-grade youngster can begin to evaluate basic elements in literature. Indeed, he *must* be taught these skills or become a nondiscriminating consumer of trivial writings that do little more than take up his leisure time.

The Teacher Can Encourage the Development of Personal Reading Standards

Our purpose in helping a child develop a taste for good literature is not to make a snob of him but to enable him to sort the meaningful from the empty, the rich from the bland. Whatever reading one does should be put in proper perspective. This is possible only through accurate analysis and evaluation of literature.

We all read material that is not great literature. It would be folly to suggest that we hold up for the elementary school child the unrealistic ideal of reading only great literature. Yet, by studying the elements that comprise good literature we provide the child with means for making his own assessments. This definition is helpful in setting the goal: Good literature and "imaginative use of language produces both intellectual and emotional responses. It will cause the reader to perceive characters, conflicts, elements in a setting, and universal problems of mankind; it will help the reader to experience the delight of beauty, wonder, and humor; or the despair of sorrow, injustice, and ugliness" (Huck, 1976, p. 4). Good literature helps the reader to better understand himself, those around him, and his surroundings.

If he has judged a book as one written without real purpose, the child can still devote as much time to its consumption as he wishes; he does so by choice, however, not out of ignorance. In many ways such reading corresponds to the interest some adults have in a James Bond. Ian Fleming hardly regarded his supersleuth as a Hamlet, yet millions have enjoyed *From Russia with Love* and *Thunderball* in books and movies. An adult who finds Fleming's characters more real and more significant than Steinbeck's Jody in the *Red Pony* apparently lacks sufficient skills to evaluate critically what he reads. We believe that the classroom teacher has a responsibility for guiding the child in the development of skills necessary for making evaluative judgments.

The Teacher's Role in Evaluating Books

The teacher has two primary roles with regard to evaluating books. First, he must generally appraise a book and decide for which child the book is suited. In this process he uses the traditional criteria for literary assessment that will be described in this section. Second, he is responsible for teaching skills of literary analysis so that the child grows in his ability to apply personal standards of taste independently.

Criteria for Evaluating Children's Books

Authorities in the field of children's literature classify books into a variety of categories; for example, fiction, picture books, biographies, and informational books. There is by no means complete agreement among experts on which classification scheme is best. It is important to note that regardless of the scheme used, different criteria are required for evaluating different types of books. It is beyond the scope of this text to present criteria for all types of books. For purposes of illustration we will discuss the evaluation of books of fiction as an example. The reader is referred to *Children's Literature in the Elementary School* by Charlotte Huck (1976) and *Children and Books* by May Hill Arbuthnot and Zena Sutherland (1972) for a more complete discussion of evaluating all types of children's books.

FIGURE 11.3   Evaluating books for children

Various criteria can be applied to evaluating different kinds of books for children.

Even within the category of fiction, a number of criteria are required to evaluate the various forms. Historical fiction, for example, cannot be judged according to the same standards as fairy tales or mystery stories. Evidently the first task of the teacher and the child is to identify the kind of book being evaluated in order to apply appropriate standards. Again, the reader is referred to Huck and to Arbuthnot and Sutherland for a discussion of the various types of children's books.

We suggest consideration of these factors in evaluating books of fiction: theme, plot, setting, and characterization.

1. The theme of a book is the *idea* of the story; the author's reason for writing is revealed through the theme. Some themes may amount to little more than presenting a moral; others focus on the meaning of friendship or courage. For children, the theme will have meaning only as it relates to their experiences. Cervantes' *Don Quixote,* which reveals that high ideals are the only goals in life worth pursuing, has little meaning and therefore little appeal to children in the primary grades. Yet the idea or theme of *Don Quixote* is a powerful one, and is most appropriate for older children.

    A theme must be judged on at least two counts: its worth for presentation to children, and the age level for which it is most appropriate.

2. The plot is the *plan* of the story. We can identify it by asking what happens in the story. What is the thread of events that carries the action forward? Good plots grow out of good themes. Actions in a plot normally progress in an interrelated fashion, leading to a climax.

For purposes of evaluation it is important to consider the credibility of the plot. It must not depend on coincidence or contrivance but must grow logically and naturally out of previous events in the story.

The plot of *Black Stallion* (Farley, 1941), for example, concerns a teenage boy who is marooned on a deserted island with a wild Arabian stallion. The boy tames the horse, is finally rescued, and returns to New York City with his horse. A special match race is arranged by a New York newspaper between the year's two greatest horses. The wild stallion is entered as a mystery horse and wins the race.

Some stories, such as Mark Twain's *Tom Sawyer,* succeed with practically no plot. In this instance a series of incidents is related in loose fashion. But most books require a strong plot to be successful.

3. The characters in a story must be *believable*. The author's ability to create individuals who possess strengths and weaknesses, who act in a manner that is consistent with their natures determines the success of characterization in his stories. Children can identify with believable characters. A story is carried by and come alives through these characters.

In additon to determining the authenticity of characters, we should also assess their depth. To be true-to-life, characters must be complex. Some facets of character will become apparent only after getting to know these people in the story very well. Seldom will a person be all good or all bad. These principles also apply to animal characters, such as Charlotte, the spider in *Charlotte's Web* (White, 1952), and humorous characters, such as Homer in *Homer Price* (McCloskey, 1943).

Effective characterization is also dependent on growth and development. As events occur, realistic characters often change in the course of a story. To be believable, change will be gradual rather than instantaneous. Mafatu, for example, in *Call It Courage* (Sperry, 1940) grew in bravery as he proved to himself that he was capable of assuming the responsibilities of a man.

4. The *background* against which a story is told is called the setting. The time and place of the story comprise the physical setting; the religious, moral, social, and psychological conditions comprise the emotional or spiritual setting (Georgiou, 1969). All aspects of the setting should affect a story in an authentic way or not at all. *The Yearling* (Rawlings, 1944), for example, is set in the scrubland of Florida. Physically, the isolation of Jody from other youngsters his own age is an important factor in creating the boy's longing for a pet. The poverty of his family is instrumental in making the destruction of a new corn crop by his pet deer a genuine catastrophe. The time of the story is insignificant, for the events and characters have almost no relation to the outside world.

Some stories, such as *Mountain Born* by Elizabeth Yates (1943), have a physical setting of an almost incidental nature. The story revolves around a shepherd and his flock; it can be generalized to almost any setting, given these few necessary elements.

Two additional factors may be considered by the teacher and perhaps by older students: *style* and *format.* When selecting books for a school or classroom library, these matters are of some importance since a variety of selections should be available for children to read.

Style is the author's particular way of expressing his ideas—his selection and arrangement of words. Just as different people speak in a unique manner, writing styles also vary. Older children, perhaps in Grades 5 and 6, may enjoy contrasting the descriptive style of Mark Twain with the terse presentation of Armstrong Sperry. Huck (1976) suggests oral reading as an effective means for studying an author's style. While a child may not be able to identify the specific aspects of style that appeals to him, he often prefers reading one author to another because of style.

Format concerns all physical aspects of the book itself, including size, shape, typography, quality of paper, durability, illustration, and length. Today's books for children are especially attractive in appearance. The teacher will want to evaluate matters of format primarily to decide on the appropriateness of a book for a particular child. A reluctant reader may require a book that looks "easy," with numerous illustrations and ample white space on a page. A more able student may insist on books that have more of an adult book appearance.

Since children often choose a book by its cover, if left to their own means, the teacher must also devote some attention to overcoming this tendency. Obviously the value of an attractive format must be balanced against the other factors mentioned. A good book in terms of theme, plot, setting, and characterization may lack a striking appearance. In this case children need to discover that it is necessary to look inside to judge the book's value. A striking-looking book full of sterotyped characters and dull action cannot be saved by an attractive cover or glossy illustrations.

These criteria can be used by children in both the primary and intermediate grades. The kind of analysis and the depth of understanding will vary from grade to grade and among children in the same grade. Most younger children cannot be expected to discuss how the setting of a story influences the lives of the characters and thereby the plot. However, many older children in Grade 6, for example, could handle this relation—*Tom Sawyer,* set in the middle of a large city, would greatly change the events if not the actual personality of the main character. Speculation concerning the effect this totally different setting would have on Mark Twain's classic is both plausible and instructional for most sixth-grade children.

Yet, even the first-grade child can be expected to tell what happened in a story (plot). He can also identify who is in the story (characters) and report where the story took place. Some evaluation is also possible. "Could this story happen?" "Could you ever take a trip such as the one the boy in the book took?" "How did you feel toward the man in the story? Why?"

A planned program of literary criticism is an essential facet of the total reading program. An early start at identifying and evaluating the various aspects of a story is necessary for developing active, knowledgeable readers who evaluate literature rationally. One possible approach to organizing a program of literary criticism is described in the next section.

Developing Children's Book Evaluation Skills

The purpose of helping children analyze and evaluate books is to increase their appreciation, deepen their understanding, and relate literature to their lives. By providing a system for studying the elements of a story the teacher leads the child toward gaining as much as possible from reading. If the analysis of a story detracts from the child's enjoyment, the program of literary criticism has gone wrong. Analysis just for the sake of pseudointellectual discussion has no place in the elementary school—or any other school for that matter.

Developed with the proper perspective, literary criticism permits the child to compare and contrast one selection with others by the same author, with other similar works, or with literature in general. The criteria suggested here or those developed by others are helpful in considering specific aspects of literature in an objective fashion. For example, the development of a character can be studied for authenticity and consistency.

Some aspects of literary criticism are reserved to each individual reader. Children should be encouraged to develop their own standards for assessing literature. The opportunity to explore books with the teacher and other students is instrumental in helping an individual arrive at personal criteria. The object of literature instruction is to encourage the *development* of standards, not to make children's standards uniform.

The Place of Children's Classics in the Literature Program

Certain children's books become classics because they have withstood the test of time; generation after generation of youngsters have enjoyed some of the same books. *Alice in Wonderland* is an example of a children's classic, as is *Heidi*.

Teachers often feel compelled to require children to read these classics.

TABLE 11.2

Sequential and Cumulative Literary Analysis Skills

Grade level	Skill
1	Name characters, identify setting, retell story, identify conflict, tell solution
2	Identify beginning, middle, and ending of plot
3	Describe characters, identify climax
4	Discuss characterization, note cause and effect
5	Discuss mood through choice of words
6	Discuss style through sentence patterns and approach

Others remember being bored by some so-called classics and are determined not to make the same mistake their teachers made. What is the place of classics in the elementary school literature program?

The fact that some books remain popular with children over long periods of time is a significant recommendation for them. Teachers should be familiar with such books and stand ready to suggest *The Jungle Book, Peter Pan,* or other classics to a youngster who is searching for something to read. But not all youngsters will enjoy these books. This reaction is understandable and should be acceptable to the teacher, who should not attempt to force a child to read *any* book, including a classic. Instead, the teacher must work very hard at enticing this student to select quality books.

The magnificence and enduring quality of *Treasure Island, Robinson Crusoe, Swiss Family Robinson, Tom Sawyer, Huckleberry Finn, Hans Brinker, or the Silver Skates,* and *The Secret Garden* guarantee that most youngsters will probably enjoy some if not all of these books. The teacher should read several such books aloud in order to be sure that all youngsters have some exposure to them, for the enjoyment these books provide should be experienced by all youngsters. Familiarity with children's classics is also important from the standpoint of giving children a means for assessing other books. In a sense, children's classics can serve as a measuring device. For example, other books can be compared to *Charlotte's Web* for effective character development. Or the plot of *Treasure Island* can be taken as a measure of excellence that is useful for assessing other literature. The greatest danger in this approach is that dull, uninteresting books will be called classics and held up as exemplars. Unfortunately, "Award Books," chosen by adult judges, are sometimes misused in this way. If children's classics are judged strictly on the basis of children's reactions over a long period of time, the danger is minimized.

Sharing of Books Can Encourage Exploration

Like children's classics, considerable difference of opinion surrounds the matter of book reporting. Properly handled, book reports can play a significant part in the literature program. Since a major goal of the reading program is to develop critical readers, the opportunity to analyze and evaluate books must be provided. Book reports that focus on this goal can be productive of growth in critical reading skills.

Unfortunately, in their desire to interest children in reading, teachers occasionally conduct contests to see who can read the most books. They often require book reports as evidence of children's accomplishments. Under these circumstances book reports, as well as reading books, can get badly skewed. No book report should ever be prepared simply to prove that a child has read a book. Contests involving the number of books read are ill conceived. The means and ends have become confused in cases where either of these activities occur.

The purpose of reviewing, analyzing, and evaluating a book is to increase one's appreciation and understanding of its contents. A book report should contain the reader's appraisal of a book according to some previously chosen guidelines. The goal is to maximize learning, not to satisfy an external requirement. Book reports should be written to provide some evidence of the child's response to a book. The teacher should regard them as a means for evaluating the child's reading growth. A child's reading tastes and interests are reflected in the type of books he selects and how he reviews them. His understanding and appreciation are also evident in his report on a book.

In actual practice book reports often contain little that is analytic and nothing that is evaluative. Typically, book reports are either written or oral summaries of the plot. The characters and the setting are mentioned if a teacher insists. The results of this approach are often not happy. Teachers decry the inability of youngsters to think; youngsters moan about the necessity for rewriting every book they read. If anything, *less* reading and *less* study of literature probably result from this procedure. Therefore, several suggestions for improving book reports are in order.

First, teachers should encourage children to report on books through a variety of means. They can be permitted and even encouraged to use various art projects for reporting on books. For example, dioramas, maps, murals, models, table displays, bulletin boards, and posters can take a book as a source. Or puppet shows, flannelboard presentations, mock radio broadcasts, and interviews with stand-ins for actual authors can be created. Book reports should be regarded as a means for encouraging children to *respond* to books. The more enjoyable they are for the reader and for an audience, the better the chance that these reports will encourage and reinforce reading.

Second, some skills of literary criticism should be taught. Skill teaching can be initiated in a group setting after children have heard the teacher read a story aloud. The teacher can encourage critical thinking and direct the children's attention to specific elements of the story. Characters can be evaluated for consistency. The plot can be studied for conflict. Later, children can be asked to study many of these same factors in a story they are reading independently. The technique of comparing books can also be introduced and encouraged by the teacher.

Third, a report on every book that a child reads should not be required. Some books should simply be recorded by author and title in the child's record. The child should have the option of choosing not to report on a book.

Fourth, a standardized book report form should not be used unless the youngsters have helped design it. Even then, only a few specifics—such as author, title, characters, and setting—should be included on the form. Other information should be reported voluntarily, for children's responses to books should be as individualized as possible.

Fifth, whenever possible book reports should be used to arouse other children's interest in a book. Reports can be displayed in the reading corner or on a bulletin board. One interesting approach is to have several oral reports

(HRW photo by Russell Dian)

FIGURE 11.4   Children respond to books when they are encouraged to do so

A shared reading experience can lead to better understanding and greater pleasure for each classmate.

given simultaneously. The teacher can announce what books are being reported on and then permit each child to attend the session that interests him the most.

Book reports are primarily a means for encouraging children to respond to books. But they are only a means to this end, and must not be regarded as an end in themselves. It is especially important that children be encouraged to respond to literature, because both interest and taste in reading are predicated on the personal involvement of the reader.

SUMMARY

Chapter 11 has made a case for the belief that lifelong reading habits are as important to a good reader as the ability to decode word symbols or comprehend an author's message. An interest in reading determines whether basic reading skills will be used with any frequency by an individual.

The home is the origin of interest in reading. Parents who value reading in their lives, and take the time to provide stimulating experiences for their children, facilitate their children's reading progress in school and promote healthy attitudes toward reading.

The school must build on whatever disposition toward reading the child brings to school. For some, interest need only be maintained and broadened. For others, a remedial program is necessary to build the attitudes and interests that were not created at home. The classroom atmosphere must make reading important and books accessible. A reading corner is recommended as providing these features.

Research abounds on the identification of children's reading interests. While some general sense of direction is provided by such evidence, the classroom teacher must still assess each child's interest individually. Both providing appropriate reading materials and encouraging broadened reading interests are the responsibility of the teacher.

The elementary school literature program is designed to help children learn to establish personal standards for guiding their selection of reading materials. Analysis of literature is helpful to the extent that it permits children to make rational judgments about reading selections. Book reports should also be regarded as a means to the end of selective reading, and not as an end in themselves. Children's classics should be available to children, but should not be assigned as required reading.

.Terms for Self-study

interest inventory
reading corner
children's classics

Discussion Questions

1. "If I had one wish," said Cleo Harper, a Grade 1 teacher, "it would be that all six-year-olds came from homes with books." Why do you think Cleo made that statement? What would your wish be for entering six-year-olds? Why?
2. How does censorship practiced by the teacher interfere with a child's development of reading taste?

12

Critical
Reading [1]

The day will come when you ask a child to pretend he is a critic of a story he has read, and he will say: "I can't criticize it. I like it too much."

Many people mistakenly believe that critical reading and thinking involve ripping and tearing and destroying. But that is a far cry from what is meant here. Reading critically doesn't mean a negative reaction to the story. It means reacting to it and judging it. Judgment can also be favorable.

Dispelling a false notion about the meaning of critical reading constitutes one instructional task for a teacher, though a fairly minor one. The teacher's major task is to conceptualize clearly what critical reading is so that he can describe it and lead his students to use critical reading skills. That task may not be simple. If you had to answer the following questions right now, what would your concept of critical and creative reading be?

How does critical reading differ from literal comprehension?
What kinds of questions would you ask a student in order to reveal whether or not he is reading critically?
Are certain students incapable of critical reading?
Are there valid ways of teaching a child to read critically?

---

[1]The authors are indebted to Dr. Nancy Roser, University of Texas, who wrote major portions of this chapter.

Critical reading was given considerable attention during the 1960's, but there was no agreement as to its precise definition. Some writers have defined critical reading broadly, even including literal comprehension; others have preferred a more narrow approach (King, Ellinger, and Wolf, 1967). All this discussion and concern, however, has resulted in very little attention being paid to developing critical readers in elementary classrooms.

The reading-communication model in Figure 2.2 shows where critical reading fits into the total reading process. Literal comprehension, then, is the ability to identify the main idea in a passage or selection, to recall fact and recount detail. Critical reading begins with analysis and includes evaluation. The focal point of reading critically rests on evaluation; that is, the application of criteria to a written passage.

Critical and creative reading lie along a continuum of skill development and are artifically separated in this chapter and the next so as to explain them more clearly. Chapter 12 defines critical reading, shows how to teach it through improved question patterns and through classroom exercises that focus on the way language is used to influence opinions, and discusses the need to select criteria for making judgments. Techniques for evaluating critical reading skills are also presented.

Who Needs to Be Critical

Even though the terminology and skills involved in reading critically may be somewhat elusive, the development of critical readers has come to be an undeniably important goal of the school curriculum. The rapidly increasing volume of printed material to be read, assimilated, and evaluated, plus the constant propaganda that pounds our senses, makes the ability to read critically a workaday tool and weapon. We use the term propaganda to mean one-sided advocacy of a particular idea or belief. From morning newspaper editorials to the commercials we watch on evening television, each day forces us to read and react critically to the obvious and the obscure.

For example, readers will recognize the different approaches to a school tax hike taken by the chamber of commerce and the local teachers' association; they will note inconsistencies between the headline and text in a movie magazine; they will question the advertisement that promises a bright future for the user of a certain toothpaste or cleansing cream. It is imperative that intelligent citizens read with care and that teachers are alert to daily opportunities to point out critical reading skills. The teacher must work toward situations that give pupils a chance to consider purposes for reading other than simple recall. Students must learn to analyze, to draw inferences, and to make judgments on the basis of some criterion.

What Is Critical Reading?

Robinson (1964) states that critical reading is the ability to apply relevant criteria in evaluating a selection. It is the judgment of the "veracity, validity, and worth of what is read, based on criteria or standards developed through previous experience" (p. 3).

Russell (1956) suggests four conditions essential for critical reading:

1. a knowledge of the field in which the reading is being done
2. an attitude of questioning and suspended judgment
3. some application of the methods of logical analysis or scientific inquiry
4. taking action in light of the analysis or reasoning.

Neither teachers nor their students will meet all these conditions at all times. Neither adults nor children can possibly be armed with background knowledge in every field in which they must read. Today's world is too big and human knowledge is too vast. It is necessary, therefore, to equip students with an attitude of general awareness so that they can detect unsupported statements, sweeping generalizations, and conclusions that have been drawn haphazardly. An attitude of suspended judgment may not always be possible. Earlier biases and prejudices affect one's ability to read critically at a later period, as do such factors as age, sex, home background, and sociopolitical attitudes.

As part of his training a student should be taught to recognize his biases and deal with them as a factor of the way he reacts to the printed or spoken word.

The teacher should foster an attitude of inquiry when he teaches the techniques of critical reading. Against such a background children will develop high standards for judging what they read.

Neglect of Critical Reading in the Classroom

A study of teaching time and emphasis in U.S. schools (Austin and Morrison, 1963) has indicated that more than half of the teachers questioned devoted "little or no time" to critical reading in the first and second grades. About one-third of the third- and fourth-grade teachers allotted "little or no" instructional time for teaching these skills.

Research has indicated that even primary-grade children can and do read critically. McCullough (1957) compared the abilities of first-, second-, and fourth-grade children to answer questions on detail, the main idea, and the sequence of a written piece with their abilities to answer questions in seeing relations, drawing conclusions, and passing judgments. She found that the students experienced no special difficulty with higher-level comprehension tasks at any grade level. Similarly, a study by Covington (1967) indicated that children with below average intelligence who were reading two years below their grade levels could read critically when materials were adjusted to their restricted proficiency.

It is likely that many students function at a constant level when it comes to determining author intent, detecting tone, differentiating fact from opinion, and so on. Consequently they attack every printed selection in the same way, and they are satisfied with a literal comprehension of the main idea and pertinent details. It appears that critical reading skills can and should be developed gradually from the early grades. Perhaps with a better understanding of what is involved in the critical reading process, teachers would devote more teaching time to critical reading in the elementary grades.

Steps toward Critical Reading

LITERAL COMPREHENSION

Before higher-level mental processes can function a student needs an understanding of the facts and ideas as the author presents them. An assessment of the student's ability to identify the main idea of the content and to recount important details is a check on literal comprehension. Basic comprehension skills were treated in Chapter 5. The reading-thinking skills closely related to critical reading move from a base of literal comprehension.

One task of the critical reader is to interpret the writer's message accurately, a process sometimes described as "reading between the lines."

Two levels of interpretation are presented in this chapter: analytical interpretation and inferential interpretation. These skills are discussed in the light of the complex reading selections found especially in the upper grades. As reading material becomes more complex, the skills of analysis and inference involve broader concepts and more abstract relations.

ANALYSIS

In the Harris-Smith reading communication-model (Figure 2.2), analysis follows literal comprehension as has been noted. It involves an attempt on the part of the reader to understand the logical unity of presentation from the printed material. At this point the reader begins to manipulate the author's ideas mentally in order to perceive relationships and visualize the structure of the selection. The reader asks· "What is the author's main thesis?" "How are the main points supported by detail?" "How do major points within the selection relate?" "Has significant information been overlooked?" The process involves the reader in forming a mental outline, weighing points for their relation and strength.

Children who can underline key words and phrases in a selection, who can strike out irrelevant sentences in a presentation, or who can select appropriate titles for stories are involved in analysis. Skill in analytical interpretation requires practice guided by the teacher and practical illustrations.

INFERENCE

Inference is an attempt on the part of the reader to understand what the author has left unsaid or what he attempts to say without words. An interpolating process, it involves deductive leaps from what is literally stated to what is actually intended: "This is what the author has said, but what does he actually mean?" An example of this type of reading is found in Marc Anthony's funeral oration in Shakespeare's *Julius Caesar*. Marc Anthony continually repeats the phrase: "But Brutus is an honorable man," while he implies the opposite—an effective strategy.

Inferential interpretations depend on a reader's background and intuition. The reader must put several clues together in order to predict possible occurrences or behaviors. He must become adept at using context as a sounding board against which inferences can be tested. And he may need more information about the author: Is the author a satirist? Does he try to manipulate his reader? The reader is involved in bridging the gaps in an author's presentation; he gathers clues as a springboard and then makes the inferential leap. This level of inference is different from those described in Chapter 5 on basic comprehension.

EVALUATION

How valuable are the ideas in what an author writes? The reader is called upon to make judgments as to the worth of the message. Evaluation depends not only upon literal comprehension and interpretation skills but also upon the reader's ability to appraise the truthfulness, validity, and accuracy of the material. The reader attempts to determine the accuracy of presentation, the author's professional competence, and the relevancy of his thoughts.

Students who are asked to make judgments while reading at times need the aid of *external criteria,* or other references and sources. A pupil with no previous experience with a subject should suspend judgment until he can establish a frame of reference through the use of valid outside sources. *Internal standards* may be all that are required by the student with a strong basis of experience in the area. His task is simplified. Difficulty may occur when a pupil's internal criteria, the product of his culture, are strongly in conflict with the prevailing outside sources. Because of an emotional reaction the reader may not be able to suspend judgment until a good deal of evidence is presented on a subject. For example, a Quaker reading a plea to expand the offensive power of the military is influenced by his beliefs to reject this argument regardless of its logic or rhetoric.

It is the teacher's responsibility to aid the student in clarifying the assumptions he brings to the reading task, in analyzing and ascertaining the assumptions of the author, and in broadening the informational background out of which more unbiased standards of judgment may come (DeBoer, 1967).

Judging the worth of a poem or prose selection is another aspect of evaluation that has come to be labeled as critical reading. We usually call this literary appreciation because it is treated in courses on literary criticism. It is actually a kind of critical reading, using criteria arising from the literary form and from the nature of the experience being described.

The Art of Questioning

When a teacher asks questions to determine a child's grasp of content, he not only gives the student a type of problem but also leads him to ask questions of his own and to set his own purposes for reading.

What questions might be asked about the following selection from a children's book? Formulate three questions a teacher might ask a second-grade child concerning this story:

> Susan and Billy watched Billy's new airplane sail through the air.
> "Look at it go, Susan!" Billy called. "It's as fast as lightning."
> "Let me fly the airplane," begged Susan.
> "No, you're too little," answered her brother.
> "Please?" Susan asked again.
> Billy handed the airplane to his sister. "Be careful," he warned. Susan raced across the yard. Gaining speed, she threw the plan into the air. It made a sudden turn and dropped to the ground in a nosedive. One of the bright red wings lay beside the plane.

Proposed questions:

1.
2.
3.

If a teacher asks questions such as: "What did Billy say when Susan asked to fly his plane?" Or "What color was Billy's airplane?" he asks for literal recall or a restatement of fact. If he asks questions such as: "How do you think Billy feels toward his sister now?" Or "What do you expect Billy to do now? What makes you think so?" he goes beyond literal comprehension to interpretation.

Tapping critical judgment would require questions such as: "Would it have been better had Billy never shared his toy?" Or "Could a toy plane fly as fast as lightning?" Questioning can also lead the child to see the application of the story in his own life: "Have you ever had to share with younger brothers and sisters?" "How did you feel about it?"

Critical thinking does not happen automatically. Using questions can lead pupils to become better readers by giving them an inquiring attitude. If the teacher's questions require only immediate recall, then reading for detail is reinforced and critical reading skills are neglected.

Wardeberg (1969) lists three qualities for constructing critical questions:

1. relating new ideas to the child's experiential background and personal involvement
2. developing critical thinking and the correct assessment of statements
3. integrating the structure of disciplines so that future learnings and past experiences can be encompassed in the structure.

A teacher's questions that lead to critical reading can be loosely categorized into three general areas—questions demanding literal recall; interpretation (analysis and inference); and critical judgment, or evaluation.

Questions for Literal Recall

Questions that ask children to recount or retell without necessarily involving them in any higher-level thinking demand *literal recall*. As discussed earlier these types of questions are most valuable when they serve as checks to determine whether concepts are grasped firmly. Such questions are the easiest to formulate and the easiest to answer. Often they are looked upon as the first step in a series of questions—necessary, but not nearly as deep as children need to have for a rich experience in reading. They are often questions of (1.) *detail* ("Who planted the flowers in the garden?"); (2.) *sequence* ("What happened after the rain?"); and (3.) main idea ("What was the story about?").

Questions for Analysis

Questions for analysis require the reader to extend what is actually stated in a written piece. He must use both subtle and obvious author cues to move beyond the literal presentation. This is a gap-filling process. Interpretations can be checked against what is actually stated:

In what season of the year might this story have taken place? What makes you think so?
Why do you suppose these Plains Indians made their homes from buffalo hides rather than from bark or logs?
Why was Mother eager for the rain to stop?
How did the author really feel about animals? How could you tell?
What is the organizational plan of the chapter?

The answers to these questions would not be stated directly, but rather would depend upon reader analysis.

Questions for Evaluation

Children are usually hesitant to question the printed word. They may view the author as an authority figure. Teachers who adhere to one textbook as the ultimate source of knowledge reinforce such an attitude; so do teachers who attempt to avoid controversial issues and debate in their classrooms (Heilman, 1967). A realistic attitude can be fostered through questions that ask children to distinguish fact from opinion, to recognize assumptions, and to judge author competence, for example.

Questions that demand critical judgment from the reader while using internal or external criteria force critical reading. "Was Billy's reaction the best one under the circumstances? Why, or why not?" "How does this author know so much about Smokey the Bear?"

The Teacher as a Critical Reader

A mature reader should be prepared to detect devices designed to influence a less perceptive reader. What kinds of questions might arise from this passage:

You know that I was born and raised in Austria. Do you know that there are no remedial reading cases in Austrian schools? Do you know that there are no remedial cases in Germany, in France, in Italy, in Norway, in Spain—practically anywhere in the world except in the United States? Do you know that there was no such thing as remedial reading in this country either until about thirty years ago? Do you know that the teaching of reading never was a problem anywhere in the world until the United States switched to the present method around about 1925? This sounds incredible, but it is true.[2]

A competent reader might ask: "How is a remedial reader being defined by this author?" "Does the author refer to remedial cases or classes designed to handle such readers?" (Refer to sentence four in the passage.) "What is the cause against which the author is building his case—his purpose for writing?" "What is his professional field of interest, his specialization?" "Where are the supporting facts for his assumptions?"

Although a reader may have no immediate knowledge with which to substantiate or refute this author's statements, the reader could detect some sweeping generalizations and a rather hastily drawn conclusion. Note the last statement: "This sounds incredible, but it is true." The author appears to have foreseen disbelief on the part of his readers and uses rhetoric to validate the argument. The mature reader knows that something is not necessarily true just because someone says it is. Children can only be led to a similar type of intelligent inquiry by teachers who are critical readers themselves and who ask questions which encourage evaluation (Meehan, 1970).

Classroom Exercises in Critical Reading

Truth versus Fantasy

In the primary grades one of the first critical reading skills the teacher attempts to develop in students is the ability to distinguish truth from fantasy. He is careful neither to discount fantasy nor to dismiss a story as unworthy because it is untrue. The teacher realizes that tales of fantasy can spark children's imaginations and elicit creative thought. Even first-grade children, however, can learn to distinguish the difference. They become aware of fantasy signals such as "once-upon-a-time" beginnings and of stories incorporating such traditional fantasy motifs as the beautiful princess, the aged king, the triumph of the younger brother or sister, and reliance upon magic powers and objects.

To initiate awareness the teacher may wish to start with isolated statements and have children respond with a "yes" or "no" depending upon previously established criteria as to the truth or falsity of the statements:

The moon is made of green cheese.
A dog can fly.

[2]This selection was taken from *Why Johnny Can't Read* by Rudolf Flesch (New York: Harper & Row, Publishers, 1955), a book which stirred much controversy in the late 1950's because of its indictment of United States schools for the lack of attention they gave to phonics.

Apples grow on cherry trees.
A kitten is smaller than me.
A boy can run.

By indicating agreement or disagreement the children grow aware of printed statements that are not true. Later, they can discuss the fantasy elements within stories with a "could this have happened?" approach.

Could the prince really have climbed up on Rapunzel's hair? Why, or why not?
Could a boy be as small as Tom Thumb?
Could the cabbage leaves actually have grown as large as a barn? How do you
    know?

Very young children can also detect the difference between fantasy events and those that are plausible or might have happened. Children can be directed to listen to two accounts of an event, one of which is more true to life than the other. Discussion as to which really could have happened can then be encouraged.

> The puppy shivered from the cold. No one seemed to notice him on the sidewalk as last-minute shoppers hurried home with arms full of Christmas packages. He huddled against a tall building to avoid being stepped on.

> Oliver Puppy shivered from the cold. "O dear," he sighed, "don't any of those people want a puppy to take home? I do *so* want a people." Just then he had an idea. "I'll ask one of them to belong to *me*!"

Children enjoy changing a factual presentation to one of fantasy by incorporating talking animals or magic events or other fantasy elements. As children get older it becomes easier for them to draw specific incidents from works of fiction that make the story depart from realism. They can also work successfully with tall tales and the writing of humorists to differentiate truth from fantasy when fantasy is presented as truth.

Connotative Power of Words

Awareness of the power of words is a crucial factor in reading critically. Words can comfort, coax, convince, and deceive. A first step toward intelligent and profitable reading results from the reader's ability to scrutinize a passage to determine what reaction the author is attempting to elicit through the use of words that appeal to the emotions, arouse sentiment, evoke sensory images, or incite to action. A competent reader can differentiate between the dictionary definition of a word—its denotation—and the images and implications the word suggests—its connotation.

Consider, for example, your reaction to the word *child*. Apart from the rather stark denotative definition, "offspring," the connotative implication calls to mind either the sum total of your experiences with children or isolated singular responses—perhaps your childhood memories, the children you teach, the dimpled baby across the street, or the freckled Little Leaguer in your family. Your reaction to the word may be positive and pleasant. On the other hand, words such as *death, disease, poverty,* and *hell* usually evoke an opposite reaction. These are often called *loaded* words because, whether you react positively or negatively, the author has intended to trigger a stereotyped response within you. Not all words have connotative power, but those that do can wield a tremendous influence on our lives. Becoming aware of the techniques of connotative language makes for more critical readers of printed words.

The advertiser is aware of connotations as he markets his product, appealing to the vanity, desires, and weaknesses of the public. Editorials that take a decisive stand on a controversial issue are rich with loaded words, which may either flatter the reader, by appealing to his highest virtues, or awaken fear and distrust for an issue that is new or different. Appeals from worthwhile charities make full use of connotative language for good causes. Election times provide an abundance of campaign material which carry loaded words that seek to win public approval for a cause or a candidate. In descriptive writing words that appeal to the senses, evoke mental images, and provide literary effectiveness and vividness are used extensively.

Primary Activities

Children who can recognize evocative language are better equipped to make rational judgments about what they are reading and to read critically. Exercises in the primary grades can be used to deal with identification of words with strong imagery. A teacher guides the children to spot such imagery through specific direction:

> Find the words that make you able to almost feel the kitten: *(fuzzy, warm, rough, wet tongue)*.

> Find words that give clues to how Mrs. Hill's farm may have smelled: *(fresh-cut hay, newly painted fence)*.

Similarly, children can find examples of words that appeal to sight, sound, and taste. Many words appeal to more than a single sense. Children with limited experiences develop fewer connotations. Those that develop first center around sensory impressions.

The teacher should look for opportunities to build upon a child's storehouse of personal connotations: "Tell me what comes to mind when I say a word." "Describe what you see or think about." (Use words very close to the child such as *home, mother, love,* and so on.)

Intermediate Activities

It is not the teacher's purpose to develop his students' analytical reading to the point where they scrupulously examine each word in a selection for an expected connotation. Literary works are sometimes better appreciated as a gestalt—the impact of the sum of the parts. Newspapers, ads, and political speeches provide excellent opportunities for working with connotative language in the intermediate grades.

For example, have children underline the loaded words in a political speech such as this one:

> Long have I been a citizen of our beloved community. I have watched my children grow here. But now I am deeply disturbed. Never have I witnessed a more tragic upheaval than our city has suffered under my opponent Major Davis. Taxes have skyrocketed, yet children lie awake at night too hungry to sleep. Our once fair city streets are littered and gutted. Graft and corruption have encamped at City Hall. But, my friends, there is hope. Beckoning us is a bright new horizon, involving us all as free Americans who want desperately to stop decay and begin anew. With a dependable team we can aim toward a better tomorrow. Continuing down the same path can lead only to certain civic death. The judgment is yours.

Lead children to note generalities, words with fuzzy meanings, and the ways in which words can be used to skirt issues and to embellish empty statements.

Discuss connotative words in advertising.

Find words an advertisement includes in order to appeal to the senses:

> "Hair that shines like the sun . . . soft and perfect all the time." *(shampoo)*
> "With all the sassy flavor, tender garlic, and mild sweet peppers . . . oozing with twenty-three herbs and spices." *(salad dressing)*
> "Seeks out and eliminates cooking odor, musty odors, all kinds of household odors—leaves a fresh clean scent, but never a telltale odor of its own." *(air freshener)*

Discuss some words that advertisers avoid. See if you can determine why some words are chosen rather than others. (For example, "scent" rather than "smell.")

Try to determine why a particular brand name was selected for a product. (Joy, Thrill, Halo.)

Find titles of books that have connotative power.

Think of words that have recently gained second connotation. ("Protest," "bohemian.") Which of these words have a general connotation (eliciting similar responses in the total populace) as opposed to a personal connotation?

Write advertisements or editorials incorporating as many loaded words and words with strong imagery as possible.

Facts versus Opinion

Often it becomes the reader's purpose to distinguish statements of fact from statements of opinion. Factual statements are objective and can be verified;

that is, measured in some objective fashion. The truth of the statement: "Johnny is seven feet tall" can be determined by any number of observers using a metric instrument. "Johnny is extremely tall" is not verifiable but rests on one's interpretation of the words *tall* or *extremely,* which may or may not coincide with another's viewpoint.

Consider the difference in presentation of facts and opinion in this example:

1. The temperature and rainfall in the equatorial zone make living there an unpleasant experience.
2. Alabama was admitted to the Union in 1819.

Perhaps proof of these statements does not lie within our personal realm of experience. It is not difficult to ascertain, however, that the truth or falsity of the second statement may be readily checked with a reliable encyclopedia. The first statement depends upon personal background, tastes, and temperament. Certainly some native of the area may consider it to be wrong.

Altick (1969) clarified the difference between fact and opinion by stating the condition for factual presentation: "Where there is no commonly accepted measure of truth, there can be no objective fact; everything that is judged by the individual on the basis of personal standard is subjective."

This is not to suggest that we cannot air an opinion unless facts are obtainable. Opinions are an important part of life. We depend upon the commentaries of experts and their opinions, which are based upon facts. We expect a senator to interpret economic developments, for example. We expect an editor to editorialize. The mature reader attempts to maintain critical awareness of the issues so that these can be weighed in relation to the opinions of others.

At times, however, facts are a necessity. We demand facts about daily occurrences in straight news reporting, for instance. We demand this same kind of factual presentation from textbooks.

Distinguishing fact from opinion is not always simple—especially when one's experience and background in a subject is weak. Then the reader must make use of outside criteria. When an author is giving an opinion, he often sends out opinion signals. Children can be made aware of these, just as they can be made aware of fantasy signals. Opinion signals include: "it seems to me," "although not necessarily proven," "in my opinion," "as I (we) see it," and so on. These indicate that the author's expert or inexpert opinion follows.

Children in primary grades can work with fact and opinion at a simple level. If the teacher makes sure that children have internalized criteria for assessing truth of *one* statement, he can teach them to watch for an obvious signal in another.

A dog is an animal.
I think dogs should be kept outdoors.

At an intermediate level isolated statements of fact and opinion may give way to materials taken directly from the content area. Truths may be rewritten as opinions, and vice-versa. The teacher should help children to understand the importance of factual presentations in texts. For example, speculate as to how social studies books would reflect different views if written by strong-minded Republicans, Democrats, segregationists, English people, and so on. The teacher can offer statements such as the following and ask students to indicate which are facts (verifiable) and which are opinion:

Asia is the largest continent.
Asia is the most beautiful continent.
Thurgood Marshall became the first black to be appointed to the Supreme Court on June 13, 1967.
Thurgood Marshall deserved the honor of becoming a Supreme Court Justice.

Judging Author Competence

Teaching children to evaluate the printed word critically can be extended to guarded acceptance of the author's right to speak as an authority on a topic. Again, judgment of this right need not be delayed until the intermediate grades.

Two third-grade boys in a summer corrective reading class were involved in an animated discussion concerning the amount of gear needed by a deep-sea diver:

> "But I read it in a book!" Paul protested, when his argument was disputed.
> "Yes, but books say different things sometimes," David retorted.
> "But Jacques Cousteau wrote my book!"

The point was won, both boys resting their cases on their assessment of the competency of this hero.

A mature reader notes both the source of a publication and the author's background. Knowing something about an author's professional training and bias makes a reader more or less open to agree to the author's viewpoint.

Children in primary grades can be asked:

Is this author writing about something or someone he really knows?
How can we find out? (Lead students to the jacket flaps of books, to reviews, to the school librarian.)
Where might we look to check some of these facts? (Encyclopedias and other references.)

Resources

Children in intermediate grades can use such references as *Who's Who in America* and *American Men of Science* for biographical data. They can learn to check the card catalogue in the library and the *Reader's Guide to Periodical*

Literature in order to determine the scope of an author's work. Children in the middle grades will enjoy writing to publishers to obtain information about an author. They may want to know how much an author has studied in his field or they may ask about the depth and breadth of an author's reportage.

Children in the intermediate grades can use sources such as the *Junior Book of Authors*[3] or sections of the *Horn Book* or *Elementary English*. The school librarian may be an additional resource for reference books. How children learn about standard references is discussed here in Chapter 15.

Practical examples of evaluating author background, education, reputation, and professional position can be profitable for middle-graders. For example, when you read two blurbs about authors of science books you find that the first is head of a science department, director of research studies at a university, and has worked as consultant on several science textbooks. The second is highly interested in science, has read extensively, and is primarily a children's author. Ask the children:

> Which of the two might have more background for writing a book on leaf identification? What is the standard for selecting one author over the other?

> Can you determine whether publishing house publicity writers and the copy on book jackets have any reason to distort author expertness in a field? This may result in evaluating the source of the author's expertise.

[3]Edited by S. J. Kunitz and Howard Haycraft and published by Wilson and Company in 1951.

(HRW photo by Russell Dian)

FIGURE 12.1   Learning the author's purpose

Through discussion and questions children can learn about an author's reasons for writing.

Determining Author Purpose

Determining the intent of the author enables the reader to evaluate his message better. Does the author hope to inform, amuse, convince, or arouse? Does he wish to state facts, deprecate, or dispel doubt? The purpose of an author's work often determines where it is published. If he wants to increase the knowledge in a certain field substantially by reporting his research results he may choose a scholarly journal with limited readership. If he wants to appeal to a wide audience he might choose the *Reader's Digest*. Similarly, the *Congressional Record* probably carries a more direct account of a Senate bill you are following than the editorial page of your newspaper. The purpose for which each piece is printed is different.

Children can learn to become aware of how author purpose may slant a presentation. For example, Robert Lawson's delightful book *Ben and Me* is a fictionalized account of the scientific achievements of Benjamin Franklin as "told" by a mouse who takes full credit for Franklin's discoveries. It can be compared with the D'Aulaires' book *Benjamin Franklin,* a biography of this famous inventor. Author bias is obvious in this contrast. Children can be taught to discern differences in presentation because of differences in purpose.

Stories can be assessed for author purpose. A simple classification scheme such as "fun" or "information" may be a good starting point for beginning such work. Newspapers and varied news accounts make the point for intermediate-grade students. They may also engage in such activities as:

Reading selected paragraphs with readily determined purposes. For example, one paragraph may inform the children about the new school cafeteria— size, cost, seating capacity, and hours it is open. Another may urge students to take care of the cafeteria, reinforcing the rules while appealing to school spirit.

Writing articles with different purposes. Using the same subject matter, have children write a piece with a specific purpose in mind that is different from other children's pieces. The purpose can be to amuse, to inform, to frighten, and so on. Compare the different articles.

Collect different accounts of the same event which occur in several newspapers, or those which are presented in straight news style as opposed to feature presentations. Determine the slant of the articles, the author purpose, and the way author purpose can be determined in the article.

Propaganda Techniques

In 1937 the Institute of Propaganda Analysis reported seven techniques whereby unwary readers could fall victim to propaganda. Since then, more than in any other area of critical reading, identifying propaganda has been emphasized by teachers. The original 1937 list of techniques has been expanded, interpreted, and repeatedly redefined by its users. Basically, it consisted of:

The new cafeteria
will be open from
11:30-1:30 for lunch.
It will close at 3:30.

1. bad names
2. glad names
3. transfer
4. testimonial
5. plain folks
6. stacking the cards
7. band wagon.

Bad names is a method by which readers are encouraged to make a negative judgment about someone or something without examining the evidence cautiously. The writer intends to provoke an emotional reaction through the use of words with unpleasant connotations. Avoidance behavior is sought by name-calling: "Relieve irritating iching"; "The situation is a rotten-smelling mess."

Glad names is a method that is also dependent on the connotative appeal of words. In this case the propagandist appeals to our senses, our noblest ambitions, our feelings of love and of loyalty. "Lovers of justice," "seekers of truth and honor," "dedicated to democracy," and "delicate demure beauty" are examples of the ways glad names are used to arouse a pleasant response and insure acceptance or approval before the reader scrutinizes the evidence.

Transfer is the utilization of long-standing feelings of admiration for something in an attempt to precipitate the same reaction toward a different product or issue. Politicians cite their church affiliations, hoping for the transfer process. Beauty queens smile beside many different products, and the public desires to emulate the beauty who is selling the product.

Testimonial involves an authority or some well-known person who endorses or rejects some product, service, charity, or issue. The propagandist attempts to play upon the name and fame of the individual in order to convince the public to react in the same way this famous person does. Testimonial is similar to transfer; for example: "Janie Jansen, famous screen star, uses Tress, the shampoo for beautiful women."

FIGURE 12.2   Advertisements in newspapers are a form of propaganda

Newpapers contain advertisements which often serve as models for propaganda techniques.

Plain folks is the title given to the attempt—often by public speakers such as politicians, ministers, and business people—to gain favor and win confidence by imitating the speech patterns, dress, and interests of those whom they seek to impress.

Stacking the cards is a method of withholding some element of truth. Omission of truth or slanted judgment may make truth appear to be falsehood and vice-versa; for example: "You know that Roosevelt was betraying us because he made secret deals with Communist boss Stalin."

Band wagon is a follow-the-crowd approach. All are urged to join with the masses and to team with a winner; for example: "More doctors use _____," "the number-one selling brand."

Because there are so many categories of propaganda techniques it is particularly important for the teacher to help children become aware of the technique itself rather than to become expert in classifying them. A ready source for initial classroom work with propaganda is advertising. Ads are easily obtainable and highly interesting to intermediate-grade pupils. Newspapers and magazines are rich sources of advertisements.

Ability to recognize propaganda is not a sure indicator of the ability to resist it in its varied forms (Nardelli, 1957). Therefore the teacher should strive to give as many concrete examples and applications to actual experiences as possible.

Evaluating Critical Reading

The child who becomes a critical reader can, in retrospect, judge the veracity, worth, and validity of what he reads. He judges the author's work; he can distinguish fact from fantasy, can determine author purpose and competency, can note instances of evocative language, and can incorporate outside resources in order to check facts. He becomes aware of propaganda and the effect it can play in his life. He can successfully analyze arguments, grouping the points made and evaluating the conclusions. The critical reader makes use of his skill daily in newspaper reading, incidental reading experiences, and in reading for pleasure. He is likely to become a more intelligent voter, citizen, and consumer as a result of this skill.

By using the ideas and exercises described in this chapter a teacher can develop his own tests for critical reading. One of the surest ways to evaluate children's performance in this area is to ask a series of key questions. For each category of critical thinking that has been emphasized, select a question that channels the child's response. For example: "Is this passage an opinion or a fact? Give your evidence." Whether the response is in writing or through discussion, the teacher has an opportunity to determine the child's skill in

	Always	Usually	Seldom	Never
Can the student do the following: Recognize the significance of the content. Find the main idea of a paragraph. Find the main idea of larger selections. Develop independent purposes for reading. Identify the author's purpose. Develop standards to determine the accuracy and relevancy of information. Draw conclusions from the author's interpretation of controversial issues. Evaluate concepts gained by contrasting and comparing them with facts and opinions from several other sources. Suspend judgment until sufficient data is gathered. Recognize the inference implied by the author. Distinguish between fact and fiction.				

FIGURE 12.3   Checklist of Skills in Critical Reading

making that kind of judgment. If the child cannot do it, the teacher has a very clear objective for teaching him. By using a checklist similar to that in Figure 12.3 a teacher can record observations about the critical skills he has chosen or that the school has chosen for emphasis.

SUMMARY

Critical and creative reading are viewed as separate operations in the reading process, although there is actually considerable overlap. Critical reading is concerned primarily with the reading-thinking skills that enable a reader to apply criteria to a selection and make judgments about it. Thus, the thinking operations of analysis and evaluation relate primarily to critical reading.

A key factor in producing critical readers is the use of questions that lead students to go beyond recall and restatement. Students should learn to classify information or events and apply criteria to them. The teacher who is able to move the discussion systematically toward evaluation is most likely to develop critical readers.

Terms for Self-study

analysis
inference
evaluation

connotation
propaganda techniques

Discussion Questions

1. Why is it important for a teacher to distinguish between literal and critical reading?
2. Besides asking questions, what other means does a teacher have for teaching critical reading?
3. In what ways would teaching critical reading differ between the primary and intermediate grades?
4. How can the Harris-Smith reading model from Chapter 2 help teach critical reading?

part V

Higher Competencies in Reading

Reading is used to accomplish many purposes. The comprehensive reading program cannot ignore the importance of helping a child learn to use reading as a means for extending ideas, solving problems, or answering questions. In this part of the book creative responses to reading are discussed; the special demands of reading in the content areas are described; and the skills needed in locating and using information found in books are presented. These reading-thinking skills enable an individual to study independently and to enjoy literature—indispensible competencies in a world of communication.

13

Creative Reading[1]

In a seventh year classroom small groups of youngsters presented the following sequence:

1. Three girls and two boys dressed in bizarre costumes executed a gyrating modern dance.
2. A trio on trombone, guitar, and drums played a jazz number.
3. Four individuals displayed artwork.
4. Two girls recited poetry.

The teacher told some visitors: "These demonstrations are all part of a creative reading exercise."

But no one was reading!

What is creative reading?
Where does dramatic reading fit?
Does the creative emphasis shift between primary and intermediate grades?
How do you get children involved in creative reading?

[1]The authors wish to thank Dr. Nancy Roser for her contributions to this chapter.

Creative Reading

"Creative" is a term that evokes illusions of sparkle, mist, or dynamite explosions. Since most people want to be creative and want to encourage creativity, the term is used endlessly to describe what teachers and children ought to be doing in the classroom. Yet, the very personal nature of an individual's creativity suggests that we cannot measure a "creative" product or an output once it has been presented to us. Must we assume that any original activity or product merits the label creative? Must a discussion of creativity stop with a label because we don't have low to high criteria for creativity? Just how does one determine originality in the first place? Evidently we could easily get entangled in the vague meanings of "creative." But in this text we want to go beyond a general attitude that teachers and students ought to be creative—something you know already.

Why then do we use the term *creative reading?* This term calls forth many positive feelings in teachers and those who train teachers. As a starting point, positive feelings are not a bad place to begin. We can use that affective momentum to develop an operational definition of creative reading. Without such a definition we cannot know what we are trying to achieve nor whether our students have been successful.

What Is It?

Creative reading could be defined as many activities, but for the purposes of this text we want to relate it to the thinking operations listed in the Harris-Smith model of the reading process (see Figure 2.2). In Chapter 12 we related critical reading to the operations of analysis and judgment—not exclusively, but primarily. Creative reading, in a sense, builds on analysis and judgment and occurs when the reader tries to extend a passage beyond the limits provided by the author. This is an attempt to initiate fresh ideas or feelings or products. The extension can be traced directly to reading, and the reader can describe the relationship between the selection and the extension.

With those ideas in mind there is some sense in the teacher saying that the youngsters in her classroom were engaging in creative reading when they were performing a dance, reciting a poem, or presenting a drawing. Hypothetically, we assume that children can trace the relationship between their reading and the feelings expressed through these artistic and dramatic efforts.

That is not to say that extension activity must be artistic or a representation of feelings in order to fit our definition of creative reading. Quite the contrary! Most creative reading, as it is defined here, will probably fall in the cognitive area. A typical extension activity for a schoolbound learner is his attempt to incorporate what he has read into some framework of knowledge or experience. He tries to organize or to synthesize knowledge so as to retain it. By rearranging or filling in the gaps in a conceptual scheme the reader is using the reading selection to expand his view of the world; this is a cognitive activity.

Or the reader may predict what will happen next in a story, though the writer has stopped the narrative—another cognitive activity.

Creative reading is defined here as a unique expression stimulated by the reading material—whether this expression is thought, composition, dramatics, or art work. The objective is to transform the reading material into something usable for the individual.

Creative reading represents a kind of application and response to the material, such as giving reactions to what has been read. Upon reading about Alice falling down the rabbit hole in Wonderland one child says, "Oh, how scary!" Another draws a picture of Alice using an umbrella in the manner of Mary Poppins about to drift into the land of make-believe. Both responses flow from what is read and in that sense can be viewed as part of the continuous process of reading.

Torrance (1969) has summed up the necessity for creative reading:

> Until the ideas on the printed page become a real part of the reader—influencing his thoughts and actions, aiding his assessment of ideas and the way they are expressed, changing and reinforcing his point of view—until this material becomes a functioning part of his thinking and acting, the reading program has been only partially successful. It is not enough to read and react critically to the author's ideas. The ideas which pass the critical test of the reader's scrutiny must become a part of the reader's thinking and actions. For example, it is not enough to read and critically judge democratic ideals. These ideals must become an active ingredient of the reader's behavior.

Creative reading begins when new arrangements, applications, and relationships are drawn. In a sense the child actually enters into a form of co-authorship, so engrossed in the material does he become when encouraged by a teacher who also reads creatively. Thoughts and feelings spring up, ready to be channeled into a multitude of creative directions. This is *extension,* the final phase on the reading continuum.

Inherent in synthesis and extension is the building of a single logical reaction with many inputs. The reader employs a common foundation, the experience, upon which he can fashion a unique superstructure. In that way reflective thinking, as well as the ability to react in the light of one's own experiences, constitutes creative reading. It is valuable to emphasize that the desire to communicate through a creative product is a logical follow-up to any creative act. Indeed, the communication may itself be integral to the creative act, as in a child's spontaneous comment: "That poem makes me feel like a warm turtle dove."

Classroom Activities for Creative Reading

The satisfaction gained from extension makes for feelings of worth and a sense of individuality for each child. Teacher alertness to the many opportunities for creative expression will aid youngsters to develop not only the *experience* of reading but also to *expand* and *express* thoughts and feelings in a variety of modes. Those three "E's" should be remembered when setting the stage for creative expression. First, the child must be open to experience and then be drawn to reflect upon the situation and its consequences. Finally, he is encouraged to express his reactions in concrete images.

Sparking creative expression involves "expectation and anticipation" as the reading task is approached, and then "doing something" with the story. In order to facilitate discussion we group classroom creative activities into four categories:

1. oral activities
2. written activities
3. arts and crafts
4. dramatics.

Oral Creative Reading Activities

Reading aloud is one of teachers' favorite means of giving students a chance to express feelings and to show that they have good vocal command of a kind of reading. In all of the activities listed here the intent is to create an atmosphere in which the child can demonstrate his feelings and thoughts as he reads a particular passage. Nonetheless the teacher must remember that reading aloud tends to be a highly emotional experience for some youngsters. Each of us has experienced stage fright to some degree at one time or another. The prospect of standing before a group as a performer is intimidating to many children, particularly those who have difficulty with reading. It is important that an atmosphere of support and acceptance be created for oral reading activities. A healthy attitude toward self-improvement is necessary, but not to the extent that mistakes are feared.

The importance of preparation for oral reading by the child should be considered. The child must feel a certain sense of freedom as he approaches any oral reading as an activity in creative reading.

Oral Reading by the Teacher

We make the blanket recommendation that every teacher read orally to his students each day of the school year. While this goal may be difficult to achieve during some extremely busy periods—such as parent-teacher conference time, or when the annual music festival is being prepared—the value and importance of daily oral reading by the teacher is undiminished.

Oral reading by the teacher contributes in many ways to an effective reading program. First, it forms an integral part of the total literature appreciation program. Huck (1976) states that some children's literature is best discovered by a child in the company of an adult.

Oral reading by the teacher need not be limited to classics. In fact, a wide selection of books should be presented to children to broaden their reading interests and build their backgrounds in unfamiliar areas. The teacher can actually stimulate children's reading by the type and breadth of reading he shares with them. Children frequently read silently a book their teacher has shared, or find another book by the same author after the teacher has read a book aloud.

Oral reading by the teacher may stimulate a child's language development. The child's vocabulary is expanded and enriched through hearing how authors use words. Through encountering words in various contexts the child gains a broader understanding of their meaning. Moreover, the polished language found in many published stories provides a good model for the child to emulate in both his oral and written communications. Hearing a story in a group is an excellent stimulus to children's language development. Group discussions can center on characters and events met through this approach, and the children can try to use language with the vocal expressions indicated by the teacher.

With some thought and planning the teacher can select a book and prepare the class to listen for any number of specific purposes. For example, a story involving special attention to a sequence of events might be read to provide practice in this listening skill. Or the use of descriptive phrases might be given special emphasis with a story containing many such passages. General ability in attending to the spoken word is encouraged in children by any oral reading; however, leassons prepared with special attention to fostering specific listening skills are more likely to yield good results.

Oral reading by the teacher can also be an effective tool for building rapport with a group of children. The act of sharing a pleasant experience each day is bound to bring teacher and students closer together. Furthermore, the teacher can express his personal likes and dislikes in a very human way while sharing a story read aloud. The understanding that a teacher is a human being often comes hard to children; sharing a story provides some insight for youngsters in this area.

Oral reading can be used as a means for settling a group down or breaking the routine of a school day. Many teachers find that immediately after a physical education period or after lunch is a good time to read aloud. After an intensive period of concentration on mathematics or reading, a few minutes of relaxation while listening to the teacher read aloud will make the transition to another subject pleasant for the children.

Not to be overlooked is the bibliotherapeutic value of teacher oral reading. Books with a special theme can be selected to suit the needs of a group or the events of the day. *Ladycake Farm* (Hunt, 1952), a story of racial prejudice, may provide the opportunity for some youngsters to face their personal biases individually. Or group discussions can be stimulated where an exchange of ideas encourages reflection and self-analysis.

The skill of many teachers at oral reading can serve as an excellent model for their students. The effectiveness of proper phrasing, clear articulation and enunciation, and dramatic interpretation are very apparent to children when demonstrated by their teacher. Special attention can be called to these factors and the students helped to concentrate on each element in turn while the teacher reads orally.

Since not all teachers are effective oral readers, and because of the need for a variety of models, records and tapes of others reading aloud may be used. Leonard Bernstein reading *Peter and the Wolf* can be a valuable listening experience for students. Boys especially will benefit from the opportunity to hear male voices reading aloud.

CHORAL READING

The enjoyment of poetry is heightened by sharing it when read aloud. A teacher can take advantage of the rhythm of a poet's words by having young children provide accompaniment with rhythm instruments or improvisation (sand blocks, dowel sticks, honey-locust seed pods, coconut shells, or bottles). Children begin choral *speaking* almost naturally as they chime in on the chorus or a repeated line of a favorite teacher-read poem. From this simple beginning the rudiments for choral reading are formed.

Older children can find natural divisions in favorite poems for high and low voices, as well as locate parts that seem to require a solo voice or a sound effect. Thus, the way is paved for enjoying poetry together. Children hesitant to read aloud alone can join in. In this way they not only gain a sense of belonging but also derive a thorough experience with tone and voice melody. Care should be taken to avoid sacrificing the satisfactions derived from choral reading for the sake of arriving at perfect rhythms and harmony. The importance of choral reading is in interpreting the mood of the poem and in gaining pleasure from group participation.

Supplying Different Endings

An assumption that is too often made in many classrooms is that a story is completed when the final sentence is read. Much like a musical sentence, the plot is then resolved and the pupils must accept this resolution. But this need not be the case. Here is an opportunity for doing something new with a story. Reopen it; provide new solutions; let the children speculate on it, each according to his creative urges. Instead of accepting the happily-ever-after ending, why not conjecture what might happen to the "Gingerbread Man?" A whole new series of adventures can be built on the story's structure—a repetitive sequence—with the children becoming oral authors.

Modifying a crucial incident within the story may also lead to spinning off new endings. The teacher who encourages divergent thinking of this sort is helping children to respond creatively. They move out from the story, expanding it to consider new aspects. "The Valentine Box," a story by Maude Hart Lovelace, deals with the efforts of a lonely girl, new at school, to aid a classmate in recovering valentines blown from her hand by the winter wind.

Children involved in divergent thinking could speculate about a change in decision on the new girl's part. How would the story have changed if she had decided not to risk tardiness or the loss of her own valentines in order to help someone else? Several children can be given the opportunity to finish the story in different ways.

Creative story ending can be begun even with prereaders who are listening to a story. One first-grade teacher noticed a frown on the face of one boy in the story circle as *Peter Rabbit* ended.

"What are you thinking, Danny?" the teacher asked.

"Well, he shouldn't have left home in the first place!" Danny shouted defiantly.

Here is a chance to find out how Danny would reconstruct the story and make up new consequences. A lively discussion is certain to follow in a case like this, and the result can be a new twist to an old tale.

Dramatic Oral Interpretation

Oral interpretation helps children become sympathetic to the characters they portray. Reading parts can put life into a story, aid children in understanding the characters' motives, and offer a more direct experience with the story itself. Prior class discussion about the kind of person a particular character is can lend a sense of reality to the character's life, and may result in differing oral interpretations by students who view the character from a variety of vantage points. Abraham Lincoln and one of his famous speeches, such as the "Gettysburg Address," are favorites for dramatic interpretation in the classroom.

Written Creative Reading Activities

Students can vitalize stories by talking about creating new endings. They may also communicate such endings in writing. Especially since writing enables children to make direct visual comparisons, the notion is fostered that stories need not be static but can involve fresh, dynamic thinking.

PARALLEL STORIES

Parallel stories grow from the original plot but may follow a minor character into full development or fan out from a touched-upon but passed-over event in the story. They can develop from such discussions as "If I were Sarah," or from questions that draw forth speculation as to what must have happened before the event. Expanding a character provides opportunities for children to manipulate events and to assign characteristics, feelings, thoughts, and even environmental stimuli to enrich their reactions to the story. Children are often deeply drawn into discussions of two versions of a story prepared by their classmates. Sharing a story on parallel planes adds richness to the reading experience. Other opportunities for building parallel stories include:

Pretend to be a character who witnesses the action from a perspective different from the author's. Write this new interpretation.

Describe the conjectured personality traits of a character if he could be met face-to-face today in your classroom.

Pretend to be a certain character and keep a diary of his thoughts and feelings.

Compose a letter that one character in the story may have written to another, describing some event and his reactions to it.

Writing Plays

Children can turn stories of all kinds into plays, whether these are dialogue-based or straight narratives. The impetus for writing plays stems largely from the desire to participate actively in a story that lends itself to action. Aesop's *Fables* are a good start for novice playwrights in the classroom. The action is simple; the characters are few; the dialogues are simple and straightforward. Fairy tales, legends, and the favorite stories of the students themselves are also easily dramatized.

Poems and Songs

Writing poetry and songs as follow-up activities is possible when a child is caught up in a story or event. When these are not assigned, but arise from spontaneous appreciation of a shared reading experience, the enjoyment is heightened.

A first-grade class finished a story about a snowstorm. Later that afternoon big snowflakes began to hit against the classroom window. The children were excited to see the story coming to life. The teacher sensed this excitement. The teacher followed the repetitive rhythm of one child's chant—"It's snow, it's snow, it's snow"—on the piano, the first line resulting finally in a "many-composer" melody.

It has been said that every child is a poet. Indeed, poetry arises spontaneously from children who are deeply excited by an experience and intent upon communicating it. To encourage the writing of poetry, a teacher should read poems to his class—lots of them and of all kinds—and should enjoy sharing his pleasure in poetry openly. He should be alert to the poetry in the language of children, taking it down when he hears it. The children's poems need not rhyme, but should reflect and express their innermost thoughts.

Try poetry as a class project. The teacher can find descriptions in stories that lend themselves to poetry. And he should recognize that children's poems are sometimes lacking in elements considered valuable in adult writing. Children's poetry may be considered crude by some standards, yet children who write poetry as a reaction to what they have read gain confidence in their ability to communicate.

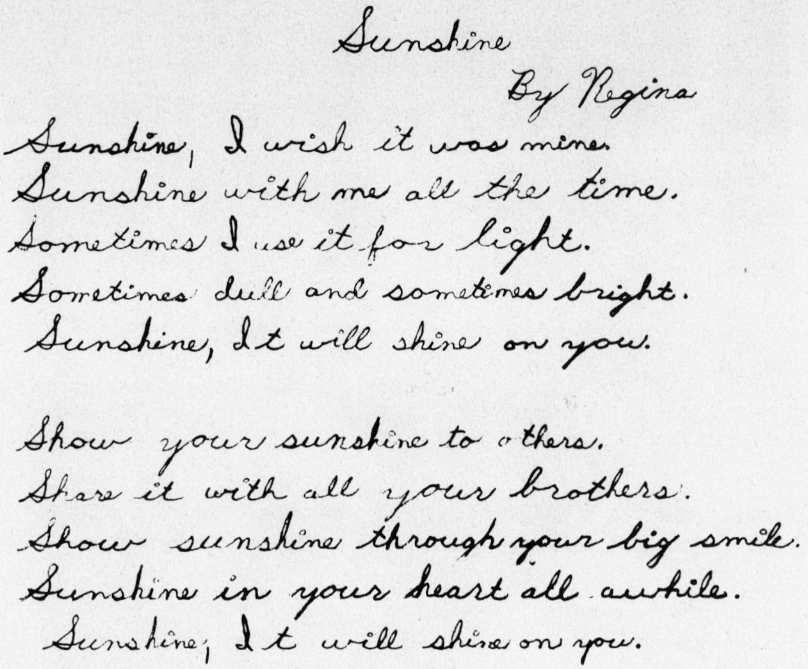

Sunshine
By Regina

Sunshine, I wish it was mine.
Sunshine with me all the time.
Sometimes I use it for light.
Sometimes dull and sometimes bright.
Sunshine, It will shine on you.

Show your sunshine to others.
Share it with all your brothers.
Show sunshine through your big smile.
Sunshine in your heart all awhile.
Sunshine, It will shine on you.

FIGURE 13.1   Children enjoy writing poems

Letter-writing

As mentioned earlier, letter-writing can be imaginary as, for example, a letter Jane and Michael Banks might have sent to Mary Poppins after her abrupt departure. Children also profit from writing letters to authors, expressing appreciation for a story they have read and perhaps suggesting alternate solutions or asking pertinent questions. Many authors respond to their small critics. Increased interest in reading and an immeasurable sense of self-worth will result from such communications among children.

Arts and Crafts

From children's illustrations of stories the teacher can learn much about what appealed to the child, what he remembered and considered crucial in the story. More important, the child is offered an opportunity to express himself in yet another way. Fingerpaints can be effectively used to illustrate stories and poems of mood and mystery, or those that draw on these elements for special effect. With splashes of blue and swirls of white young artists can create wind and rain. *Plink Plink Goes the Water in My Sink* by Ethel Kessler and Leonard

(Courtesy of VISTA)

FIGURE 13.2   Painting helps children express their feelings

Kessler[2] lends itself to this type of expression. Encourage children to sweep their fingers and swirl their fists in the paint to create movement, excitement, and texture.

The titles of *The Beach before Breakfast* by Maxine W. Kumin and *Hide and Seek Fog* by Alvin Tresselt suggest the creative moods they elicit. Watercolors can be used effectively as background wash for illustrations of either of these books.

Crayon resist—a method whereby foreground figures are drawn in crayon

[2]Published by Doubleday & Company, New York, 1954.

before watercolors are applied to the entire picture, with the crayoned part resisting the paint—is effective for depicting such graphic descriptions as:

> But out of doors the fog twisted about the cottages like slow motion smoke.
> It dulled the rusty scraping of the beach grass.
> It muffled the chattery talk of the low tide waves.
> And it hung, wet and dripping, from the bathing suits and towels on the closeline.[3]

Three-dimensional models are tangible interpretations of a shared story experience. Models can be sculpted from paper, clay, toothpicks, or odds and ends. Children involved in a unit of stories dealing with pioneers can fashion an entire village as a class project or work on individual dioramas—miniature three-dimensional scenes. Wire- or pipe-cleaner figures may represent characters in the stories.

Dramatics

When children respond to a story they move wholeheartedly toward a re-enactment of the tale. "With wonderful abandon they throw themselves into the various parts and relive the events of the story or book" (Torrance, 1969). Through children's imagination the author's words are brought to life. Panto-miming, role-playing, play-acting, puppetry, and shadow plays are all methods for creative interpretations.

Pantomime

Playing out a story through pantomime is one of the simplest forms of creative dramatics. Variations on the pantomiming technique include acting the story while selected readers describe the events, or free interpretation of favorite story parts. When pantomiming instruct the children to use only gestures and movements to convey their characters:

Skip through the woods as Little Red Riding Hood.
Run home from the ball as Cinderella.
Be the crotchety grandfather or carefree Peter in *Peter and the Wolf*.
Huff and puff with the Big Bad Wolf.
As one of the seven dwarfs, discover the intrusion of Snow White.

Role-playing

Role-playing involves assuming a character's traits and playing out imagined discussions or climactic scenes. Students from a third-grade class read stories of Christopher Columbus from boyhood to old age with interest. Decid-

[3]Maxine W. Kumin. *The Beach before Breakfast* (New York: G. P. Putnam's Sons, 1964).

(HRW photo by Russell Dian)

FIGURE 13.3   Music helps convey a dramatic mood

ing to act out his life, they constructed his ships from tables and chairs, designated the chalkboard as Spain, and set sail. Similarly, other schoolchildren, after following a moon flight through newspaper and television coverage, enacted the roles of the astronauts.

Play-acting

Play-acting differs from role-playing in that parts are assigned and usually "learned" in one fashion or another. Often such plays are written, produced, and directed by students.

Puppetry

Simple puppets are a joy for almost all children. They especially help the shy child to project his feelings and to extend his verbal experiences. Activities with puppets spark language expression, broaden understanding, deepen feelings and emotions, and develop sympathy and relationship with the characters of the story. Puppets can be made from paper bags, sticks, or with papier mâché heads and cloth bodies; they may be as elaborate as time, energy, and skill permit. They serve the function of allowing children to play out stories in a projected role.

Shadow Plays

Performing a story behind a suspended sheet with a strong light directly behind the players calls attention to bodily movements and gestures. These are shadow plays, which are an effective way to implement pantomime.

Dancing

Creative dance and rhythms are techniques whereby entire stories may be enacted or the emotion of a small portion of a story can be demonstrated with movement. Forms of creative interpretation include:

Move like the saggy, baggy elephant. Bend and sway, slowly, slowly.
Be a tiny seed under the ground. Feel the warm sun on your back. Stretch to reach the sun. Grow. Grow.
Be the Indian, Hiawatha. Greet the morning sun. Move to the beat of Indian tom-toms. Dance a joyful dance.

Books Alive

Book reports can kill enthusiasm for reading the book if the report identifies only the people and what they did. The listener or the reader of a report must be tantalized. Then the book comes alive. To make this happen, the reporter

FIGURE 13.4   Puppets fascinate most children

should briefly explain why he enjoyed the book. The report may jump with action as the reporter recounts a particular scene; or it offers insight because a character makes the reporter see himself differently. In any case, the report primarily reveals the personal excitement of the reader. This excitement leaps out to other children who may want to read the book. The story outline may remain untold or be quite sketchy. It is considerably more important for the book to come alive than for its outline to be given with monotonous routine.

Evaluating Performance in Creative Reading

Creative reading activities need not meet established standards or levels of perfection, except those set by the child himself or those mutually agreed on between child and teacher. That each child should experience creative expression in a time set aside for creative reading activity is an important goal.

Guiding questions for this activity which might be asked by the teacher include:

Did the creative activity achieve the purpose set for it?

Was the activity original; that is, was it a unique expression for the experience and age of the learner?

Have I as the teacher led and encouraged children toward an expression that is original for each child?

SUMMARY

Critical and creative reading were viewed in this chapter as separate operations in the reading process, although in reality the two cannot be sharply separated. Critical reading is concerned primarily with the reading-thinking skills that enable a reader to apply criteria to a selection and make judgments about it. Thus the skills of analysis and evaluation relate closely to critical reading.

Creative reading is concerned primarily with integrating the reading experience into the knowledge and feelings of the reader, and producing a response unique to each individual. The thinking skills of synthesis and extension are closely related to our definition of creative reading. In this definition there is a demonstration of a reasonable or an emotional flow from the selection to the way the reader uses the selection.

One of the major reasons for encouraging creative reading is that it fosters divergent thinking about what has been read, whether the results are expressed orally, in writing, through motion, or through a fine-art form. The teacher's attitude of encouraging, exploring, and valuing the extension and application of what is read is a critical factor in the development of creative reading in the child.

Terms for Self-study

extension   role-playing
choral reading   shadow plays
pantomime   synthesis

Discussion Questions

1. What would be some key elements in fostering creative reading in the classroom?
2. What goal statements, or objectives, could be used to give teachers a sense of direction for developing creative reading?
3. How would a teacher determine whether a response to reading was an original one?

14

Teaching
Reading for
Life

When Tony was four years old he brought home a pail of pond water in which there were some tadpoles. He was told to watch them to see what would happen. He watched the tadpoles develop through a number of stages, and two of them survived as frogs. The day Tony got up and found what had happened to his tadpoles, he commented: "Tadpoles make the nicest frogs."

What happened to Tony may provide some clues about reading in content fields. In a way Tony went through the kind of thinking a scientist engages in when he looks at nature and tries to make some conclusions about what he has observed. The pattern of observing nature, of making some inferences about the observations, of classifying the observations, and of arriving at conclusions may provide some important clues as to how to read content subjects. If the scientist's thinking is reflected in his writing, comprehending what is written could be aided by knowing about the scientist's typical thinking patterns.

Reading for real life plays an important part in most children's lives. They want to succeed in science, social studies, and math courses in school; and they want to enjoy reading magazines and newspapers at home. That's reading for life. It is different from reading in a basal reader. That is not a surprising statement, but it needs to be repeated because teachers do not often teach children how to handle expository writing, which is different from fiction and has a different purpose from the basal reader.

To determine what content reading is and how to teach it, think about these questions as you read this chapter:

What is the difference between reading content material and reading basal
    reader stories?
Is there a visual difference in content material?
What are the general skills needed to read content material efficiently?
What special reading skills are used to read specific kinds of content, such as
    science and math?
Are there instructional guidelines for teaching content reading?

Content reading is receiving considerable attention these days. Professional organizations are discussing the topic; publishers are producing reading
series that contain an increasing volume of expository material, and teachers
are listening to speeches about it at state conventions. The term *content
reading* sounds like someone's double talk. After all, if you do not read content
when you read, what are you doing?

Content reading is a term used for expository writing concerned with
giving information and the evaluation of that information. The term does not
usually refer to the reading of a short story or a novel; that is, a selection which
provides a vicarious experience or an emotional involvement in imaginative
living.

One reason for isolating content reading in a text on teaching reading is
that children need particular practice in reading content material. They have
been systematically introduced to the short story, for they spend most of their
first six years in school learning to read short stories. Teachers and pupils spend
much time building a short story vocabulary, analyzing plots, describing
characters, interpreting actions, and applying the morals stated in these stories
to their own living.

A Problem of Vocabulary and Concepts

When it comes to information subjects, such as social studies, most
instructional emphasis goes into recalling specific information and gaining
concepts. Students have to read in order to get these facts and these concepts,
but since this activity is not called learning to read, many teachers seem to feel
that no overt transfer of reading pedagogy is necessary. Even though the
content subject has a new vocabulary, often no effort is made to get children to
analyze the vocabulary and develop automatic recognition habits, as is always
done in "reading" lessons. Even though content is organized differently, the
writing is not analyzed in class as those hundreds of plots in readers are. The
attitude that creates a wall between learning to read and reading in content
subjects reflects a failure to understand what reading is. It is a tool, or a process,
whereby a learner communicates with an author.

Once the initial mechanics of learning the code of writing English are conquered, reading becomes a combination of reading and thinking—an inseparable union when an individual is reacting to a printed message. He has to read some content; he cannot simply read writing. The natural and relevant place for reading-thinking to take place is in conjunction with literature, science, math, and social studies. The question, then, is how does the teacher put the learner and the content author together so that the printed page communicates something. Communication involves, among other things, a common vocabulary between writer and reader, a common interest, and the ability of the the receiver of the message to follow the thinking of the writer of the message. Since individual writers have different thinking patterns, and since different content areas have different thinking patterns, the teacher has the responsibility of aiding students in identifying some of those patterns in order to open channels of communication.

Comparison of Material

Consider some samples of writing from various subject areas.

There is a story in one of the basal readers that is called "A Kitty for Kathy." It is a typical primary-grade story with characters and a situation or problem that the characters try to resolve. After students have read the story they are asked: "Who are the characters?" "What are they trying to do?" "How do they do it?" "Did they succeed in what they wanted to do?" Those are typical questions, because they indicate the organizational pattern of short-story writing.

"A Kitty for Kathy" is representative of that pattern. Kathy finds a kitty on her way home from the playground and asks her mother if she may keep it. Mother tells her that they cannot keep the cat because they are going to grandmother's house for a week. They cannot take the cat with them, nor can they leave it home alone. Kathy asks if she can keep the cat provided she finds someone to take care of it while they are away. Her mother consents to this plan. After a period of sitting on the door stoop Kathy has an inspiration. She goes next door and asks Mrs. Henrietta if she will babysit for her. Mrs. Henrietta says that she will be happy to do this for Kathy anytime. Then Kathy explains that it is a cat Mrs. Henrietta is to sit with. Mrs. Henrietta, being a nice neighbor, accepts the kittysitting job for the week, and the problem is solved. This pattern is typical of the short stories in their basal readers that children continue to analyze for four, five, and six years.

The child has to read other types of material as well. In expository writing a character, a plot, a problem to be solved, or some interaction between characters may not appear in the piece that is being read. What does the child do? What kinds of questions does he ask when he approaches the material and tries to comprehend it? The structure of this selection is different from the short stories he has previously read. It is not sufficient to tell the child that he will have to discuss the topic, and that he is to read the next several pages. It is not enough to tell him that he must answer several fact questions such as: "What is a tadpole?" "Where do tadpoles live?" "How do tadpoles develop?" The child must recall many facts and details from the writing, but he also needs suggestions on how to analyze the author's purpose and his thinking pattern.

Through a series of analyses of science, social studies, and mathematics texts students can see that there are different structural patterns, or different organizational patterns, in different kinds of texts. Science writing usually has an organizational pattern unlike that in social studies, for example. If students were alerted to these patterns they would have a way of organizing themselves so as to increase their comprehension.

To understand a selection a reader must get the main idea, know the important details, and see the interrelation of the parts. To analyze scientific data, classify them, and find some conclusion or resulting law, a reader must begin with literal comprehension. Beyond that he has to know what the various parts of the selection are, what relationships exist among the parts, and how those relationships lead to the conclusion. Even though that learning is very important, one wonders how often it occurs in schools where memorizing of content is stressed.

Readability of Content Texts

A child faces many problems when he comes to the task of reading science content. The teacher's guide for one book states that it was written for the lower track of junior and senior high-school groups, but no specific grade or readability level is given. Evidently it is meant to be read at some reading level below Grade 7. According to the Dale-Chall readability formula, it has a 7.8 reading level.[1] Thus, it would appear that some of the people for whom the book is intended will have considerable difficulty with it.

Another selection taken from a popular elementary-school science text is designed for Grade 5 according to the publisher. In the teacher's guide the authors say they were deliberately conscious of writing on a simple level so the book can be used by children whose reading skills are average or below. Using the Dale-Chall readability formula on that text produces a grade readability of 9.1 (Smith, Carl, 1969a).

Why should the readability formula indicate a much more difficult level than that the publishers and authors estimate? One reason is that the selections contain many difficult words; that is, words which do not appear on the list of easy words in the readability formula. The larger the number of difficult words, the higher the readability level will be. The list of easy words is composed of those that appear most frequently in basal readers. Through basal readers children are trained to read easy words. Then, for example, they are asked to read *heredity, Austrian, monk monastery, differed, traits, crosspollinated,*

[1]Readability formulas include the number of difficult words and the length of sentences combined with a mathematical formula to produce the grade equivalent of the material.

resulting, and *offspring* in an article about Mendel discovering the laws of heredity. All of these words appear in one paragraph of the text and are considered difficult words because they are not commonly used. In the next paragraph are the words *generation, pure-bred, produced, tallness, dominant, shortness, recessive, depressed.* One out of every eight words in the article is not regularly used in basal readers or in language arts texts. Therefore children are not expected to be able to respond to them automatically. They have to stop and analyze such words—provided they have sufficient word-analysis skills.

Consider a word like *hybrid* in the sentence: "He prided himself in having both hybrid corn and hybrid chickens." What does *hybrid* mean? A child can analyze all day and not know what *hybrid* means unless he is from a farm region. Even then he may not know precisely, but only know that *hybrid* is a word associated with a kind of corn. He has to have some way of relating words to his experience and some way of identifying words.

In the article on Mendel we have used as an example every eighth word has been systematically blocked out. It is still fairly easy to read the article because some of the deleted words are *a, the,* and *in,* and the omission of such words is usually rather simple to figure out. But if you block out *monastery, hybrid, crosspollination,* and *pure-bred,* as the child does when vocabulary is a problem, what happens to comprehension?

Mendel First Discovered the Facts about Heredity

_____ 1860, an Austrian monk named Gregor Mendel _____ to raise peas in the monastery garden. _____ found that they differed somewhat and was _____ as to why this was so. He _____ records of the traits of leaves, stems, _____ , and seeds. He noted also the shape _____ color of the seeds. He crosspollinated _____ by hand and kept careful records of_____ resulting offspring. If the offspring were _____ result of crossing different kinds of peas, _____ called them *hybrids.*

He crossed tall peas with short peas _____ found that the offspring were all tall. _____ when he crossed this generation of offspring _____ each other, he found that three fourths _____ tall and one fourth was short. When _____ crossed some of the tall peas with _____ tall ones, the offspring were all tall. _____ again, when he crossed tall and tall, _____ of the offspring were tall and some _____ short. So, he reasoned that some of _____ peas were *purebreds* which always produced because _____ and that all the short ones were _____ because they always produced short peas. But _____ of the tall plants must be hybrids _____ have the short trait hidden in them. _____ called these tall plants *pure tall* if _____ always produced tall offspring, and *hybrid tall* _____ they sometimes produced short offspring along with _____ tall ones. He also said that tallness _____ a *dominant trait*. And shortness was a _____ *trait*, because it was often hidden by _____ dominant.[2]

The paragraph below indicates a young reader's difficulties in reading. What comprehension questions can he answer? Can you determine what goes in the blanks?

The Digestive System

After you _____ the food, it passes down the _____ into your _____ . Juices from the lining of your _____ mix with the food. The juices soften the food, and _____ in the juices break up _____ into even smaller ones.

Most food is not completely _____ in the _____ . When the food is _____ and soft enough, a _____ at the end of the _____ opens, a little at a time. The partly _____ food flows into a long, _____ narrow _____ called the small _____ .[3]

This paragraph from the fifth-grade text that was rated 9.1 on the Dale-Chall formula presents even further reading difficulty. The first paragraph contains *esophagus, stomach lining, soften, chemicals,* and *particles*—all words not found in the easy word list. Other difficult words in the paragraph are *completely, digested, moist, valve, coiled, tubes, liver, pancreas, intestine, glands, molecules, bloodstream, capillaries, gristle,* and *stringy fibers.* One out of six of the words in the selection is not in the easy word list. If you eliminate one-sixth of the words in a passage comprehension must suffer. Many words that are essential to comprehension cannot be identified by the reader. It is evident, therefore, that vocabulary and word recognition play key roles in reading content selections.

Content teachers need to know ways to teach vocabulary just as a reading teacher would. They have to build background so the child has concepts to

[2]Davis, Ira C., *et al. Science 3, Discovery, and Progress* (New York: Holt, Rinehart and Winston, Inc., 1965), p. 438.
[3]Schneider, Herman, and Nina Schneider. *Science in Our World,* Book 5 (Boston: D.C. Heath and Company, 1968), p. 185.

work with; and they have to present vocabulary in terms of concept development, as well as in terms of word recognition.

In addition to difficult vocabulary in content material, there are diagrams, charts, and tables that often accompany the text and that must be comprehended. Usually it is important to relate the text to the diagrams. How does a child learn to do that?

Using Illustrations

Here is the opening paragraph from a story entitled "From Tadpoles to Frogs,"[4] taken from a second-grade book:

> When I first put my tadpoles into the bowl they were funny little things, I had never seen anything like them before. They stayed under water all the time.

For those who can find tapoles in ponds and creeks near their homes, this paragraph is no problem. But a student living in a large urban center might not know what a tadpole is. Children in Cleveland and New York City may never have seen a live pig, much less a tadpole. We know an eighteen-year-old boy from Brooklyn, New York, who took a train to go to school in the Midwest. When he arrived on campus he told his counselor that on the trip he had seen his first live pig and his first live cow. It is not unrealistic to say, therefore, that many second-grade children do not know what a tadpole is.

That is the reason why teachers have to build concepts and relate a text to the illustrations. Look at the sample page from the "Tadpole" story (Figure 14.1). The science text gives a diagram, a picture, or an illustration. A child

[4]Stratemeyer, C. G., and H. L. Smith, Jr. *Frog Fun* (Evanston, Ill.: Harper & Row, 1963).

The tadpoles are growing.
Oh how fast they grow.
They are turning into frogs.

Tell me, little frog,
what happened to your tail?

From *Sounds Around the Clock,*
a Sounds of Language Series, Bill Martin, Jr., ed.
© copyright 1970. Reprinted by special
permission of Holt, Rinehart and Winston, Inc.

FIGURE 14.1   Illustrations from *Frog Fun*

reads: "I'd never seen anything like them before. They stayed under water all the time." Without illustrations, what image would the second-grade reader have? What has he seen on television that stays under water and that he has never seen before?

The illustration demonstrates the growth of a tadpole. The teacher must explain: "Look at the pictures and go back to the text." This seems quite elementary, but for the child who has not had the experience, the teacher must show how to relate illustrations to the text. This is especially true when the illustrations are quite different from the illustrations of people in the basal readers.

The "Tadpole" story is from a Grade 2 science reader. In a Grade 4 science text the subject may be the operation of a refracting telescope. The conceptual problem is now compounded. Not only does the student not understand what a refracting telescope is but the teacher must study diligently at night to relate an illustration of the telescope to the text that describes it. Relating the drawing to the text is a reading skill that is needed often with science, math, and social studies tests.

Children must be shown how to move systematically through a diagram by locating the point where the text explanation and the diagram correspond. Reading the illustrations will help children to visualize, conceptualize, and understand.

Reading Skills for Content Reading

The primary goal of content reading is to teach the child how to comprehend the totality of the selection. He must comprehend what the science writer had in mind when he made an observation about nature. In a sense the reader wants to know how the scientist thinks when he writes. That is an excellent "handle" to give children: Read like a scientist; read like a mathematician; read like a social scientist. By trying to identify the structure of the content discipline, and typical patterns for presenting that information, the reader is prepared to comprehend.

If reading the expository material in content subjects needs a different approach, what are the skills required for efficient reading? Evidently most of the same skills that are used in reading narrative will also be used in reading content selections. *Word analysis and word meaning skills and skills leading to a literal comprehension of the selection will be employed in all types of reading.* In addition to those elements, however, content reading requires other skills related to using materials and skills of analysis and evaluation.

The general skills that enable a person to achieve literal comprehension include a basic reading vocabulary; the use of context to help determine the meaning of words; and the use of phonics, structural analysis, the dictionary, and illustrations as aids in deciphering words. The reader should ask himself these basic questions: "What is the main idea?" "What are the major parts of the selection?" "What are the important or supporting details to the main idea?" But in answering those questions the reader often finds himself faced with some of the problems that have already been identified as problems in content reading. *The vocabulary, format, references, point of view, and organization deviate from what he is familiar with.* He needs to employ a number of procedural skills that will assist him in locating information, examining it efficiently, and adjusting his reading rate so that he can achieve his purpose for reading the selection. The common study skills—such as summarizing, outlining, using references, and organizing time—play a role in comprehending content subjects. Study skills are treated here in a succeeding chapter. How to teach the other skills for content reading is discussed in this chapter.

As a reader grasps the basic meaning of a selection he can analyze and evaluate it. *Involved in the task of analysis are classifying, categorizing, and identifying the principles of organization. Evaluating requires the reader to formulate some criteria for judging the relevancy, utility, and validity of the information.* He has to make decisions about the content. If nothing more, he has to decide whether to remember it or not, and whether or not to make it a part of his concept of the subject area. If his evaluation indicates that the selection yields little or no valuable information, he will decide not to store what he has read.

Teaching Skills for Reading in Content Subjects

Knowing that content subjects require general reading skills, skills for using the specialized material, and analytic and evaluative reading skills does not make them automatically usable. Figure 14.2 indicates the variety and levels of skills incorporated in reading content material. Each of the areas will be discussed here in relation to teaching children how to read content material.

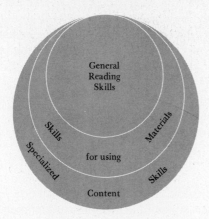

FIGURE 14.2   Skills for reading content selections

Reading content subjects requires general reading skills, as well as other locational and thinking skills indicated by the format of the material and the presentation of the ideas.

General Reading Skills

It is true that most children have the general reading skills to read content material, but they often do not realize that is the case. The teacher should demonstrate how general reading skills can be transferred or applied to science, math, and social studies. He should tell his students that reading content material should be considered a continuation of learning how to read. In one sense, reading of content material can begin as the child acquires the basic reading skill of word analysis and the recognition of a simple vocabulary.

Because developing concepts and a specialized vocabulary are integral to reading, specialized content instruction for reading in the content areas can be said to be always occurring. An eclipse of the moon is discussed in class in anticipation of the event. When this happens, students read about it in newspapers and magazines. With more attention paid to the purposes for which the student reads, learning content reading skills can be more naturally and easily achieved. Instruction for content reading begins before the child can "read," continues as he goes through the process of learning to "decode," and progresses throughout his encounters with reading materials and other classroom activities.

Recalling Basic Information

The focal point for the application of general reading skills is to assimilate the meaning of the passage. This is often called literal comprehension. In order to assimilate meaning the reader must first have an understanding of the concepts contained in the passage and be able to identify the words used. He must also be able to follow the writing style and the organization of the writing—all of which sounds fairly simple until it is applied to reality. Earlier, a passage from a Grade 5 science text on the digestive system was used as an example. The completed passage follows (you may wish to match your answers with the original):

The Digestive System

After you swallow the food, it passes down the esophagus into your stomach. Juices from the lining of your stomach mix with the food. The juices soften the food, and the chemicals in the juices break up particles into even smaller ones.

Most food is not completely digested in the stomach. When the food is moist and soft enough, a valve at the end of the stomach opens, a little at a time. The partly digested food flows into a long, coiled, narrow tube called the small intestine.[5]

[5]Schneider and Schneider. *Op. cit.,* p. 185.

The concept-development problems, definition problems, and word-identification problems in this selection are considerable.

Concept attainment is, in itself, a complex task. What is meant by a *system,* for example—a system for processing food? Vocabulary development (definition) is not necessarily a complete concept development. The meaning to be used in a particular context may not require recognition of the total complex of characteristics and relations making up the "true" concept symbolized by a particular word. In the classroom this is particularly true. Children's concepts develop over time and rely on their ability to perceive and understand the various components of a concept. The problem for the teacher is to identify the special words and the aspects of the total concept necessary for understanding the particular material being read in class. Those aspects can then be related to the knowledge the children already have to help them obtain adequate meanings from a text. For example, consider this sentence: "Landforms are closely and intricately related to man's use and occupation of the land." Special words to be defined and studied for recognition are *landforms* and *occupation.* The teacher may find it advisable to discuss *intricately* as well, not because of its special connotation but because it may not be part of the children's reading vocabulary. Depending on the age and education of the children, the teacher then works to establish and clarify the concept. Perhaps there are local examples or experiences which show that river valley land (landform) is used for cattle grazing or mining coal (occupation). By relating the words to the child's experience the teacher enables him to understand the sentence and probably the paragraphs that follow.

Developing Vocabulary and Concepts

A major problem with vocabulary and concept development is that the vocabulary assumes different technical meanings in different content. For example, *satellite* is a body orbiting around another body, a country whose government and control comes from another country, and a man-made object revolving around the earth. This variety of meaning makes it difficult to preview material and select at a glance the words that need concept development. Questioning students about the material should also provide information concerning their grasp of the meaning of a single word. Questioning should be carefully planned by the teacher, since reiteration of a statement in a book by the student is no indication of understanding. The question should elicit explanatory, definitional, or application responses. Restating or defining is relevant to certain concepts; for example: "What does *satellite* mean in that passage?"

The ambiguity of words is clearly illustrated in "story" problems in arithmetic. Children need to learn to translate words such as *is, more, less, times, greater* as computational signals and as indicators of relations between quantities. Direct and explicit instruction often assists in the acquisition of this skill. Another means of instruction is to use "headlines." A mathematical equation is

$2 \times 3 = 6$

FIGURE 14.3   What is the story that goes with this headline?

presented as a "headline" ($2 \times 3 = 6$ or $2 + 3 = ?$). The students are asked to tell a story that could be represented by the equation headline. That procedure reverses the translation process. Once the relation between story and equation is understood, the translation difficulty, or the reading problem, decreases.

Students need experiences equal to their grasp of concepts, as well as experiences that expand the level of their understanding. By planning instruction to draw on past experiences and concrete examples, vocabulary and concepts will usually develop routinely.

Vocabulary and concept development is critical across all grade levels. For some words a simple explanation in context will suffice; for others a special experience or set of experiences of varying degrees of "concreteness" is required. Picture dictionaries, flash cards, and word lists can be useful tools. If dictionaries and word lists are made, then occasional activities—even games—using the lists should be included in the curriculum. For a child to refer to the dictionary or word list upon re-encountering a word whose meaning is forgotten is essential for several reasons: Meanings of words are usually forgotten until repeated encounters strengthen recall; to establish the habit of relearning and to diminish a reluctance to use the dictionary.

Words

Word meaning in content subjects, then, can be developed by using such activities as:

1. First-hand experiences
   a. Real situations involving contact with names, concepts, principles
   b. Dramatization of a real situation
   c. Construction of examples or models representing the concept
2. Relating to personal experiences or acquired concepts
3. Exhibits
4. Films, filmstrips
5. Pictures
6. Context clues
7. Dictionary
8. Word lists
9. Flash cards.

Concepts

Concept development can be promoted by guiding a student's analysis of ideas. This analysis should include:

1. Comparing and contrasting instances and noninstances of the concept
2. Extracting relevant criteria belonging to the set of ideas
3. Identifying the relation of the concept to others and to the problem being considered
4. Using the concept in the immediate and in extended situations.

Literal comprehension of expository material also demands the ability to cope with the structure of the content and the style of the author. To aid learning, the most plausible approach for the elementary-school teacher is to consider each reading activity as a relatively separate task and to make sure that the skills required for that task are available to the student. Comparisons are not possible without adequate familiarity with the characteristics of different types of materials. In general, the teacher is the decision-maker who determines how explicit the instruction is to be with respect to attention to concept or vocabulary development and to structure and style of the reading material.

Skills for Using Materials

The second general category of skills for reading in real life contains all of the procedural skills one needs to handle efficiently the material one reads. Three sets of skills are found in this category:

1. locational skills—those procedures for using books and other materials efficiently
2. study skills—those procedures that organize and direct efficient and effective learning from printed material
3. reading-rate adjustments.

Each of these sets requires a knowledge of the skills, a demonstration of when to apply an appropriate procedure, and the actual implementation of the skills.

Chapter 15 discusses these matters in detail. They will be treated here only as they affect content materials.

Knowledge about procedures can be gotten through an explanation, but knowing when to apply and actually use the skills will remain in a semi-learned state unless a real need to use the skills is provided. Map-reading, note-taking, or scanning material will not become real skills for the reader who has few occasions to perform those skills in order to achieve a goal. Having a variety of materials available will be of little use if the reader can answer all questions with one or two books and without using maps, charts, notes, and so on. Activities must be designed to include a variety of skills with a variety of materials. Efficient use of a skill, such as notetaking, requires practice and refinement. Refinement will not occur if the student can achieve a goal without using the skill or by using it poorly.

LOCATION SKILLS

Locational skills are the *skills one needs to find information*. There is a body of knowledge to be learned. The reader needs to know the kinds of information obtainable from different types of books and reference guides. They include these items:

1. textbooks
2. dictionaries
3. encyclopedias
4. almanacs
5. trade books

The reader also needs skills in locating and using:

6. bibliographic references (authors, *Who's Who,* and so on)
7. table of contents
8. indexes of books, encyclopedias, and periodicals
9. card catalogue
10. bibliographies
11. glossaries.

In order to use these resources, the following skills are needed:

1. alphabetizing
2. use of multiple classification
3. use of pronunciation keys
4. use of titles and major and minor headings.

In a developmental sense the first content activities in the primary grades may begin with locational skills using:

1. picture dictionaries for practice with alphabetical knowledge and skill
2. table of contents with all books consulted
3. glossaries
4. indexes in all books consulted
5. headings, titles
6. pictures and simple graphs and maps.

Picture dictionaries can be made for primary science and social studies and, if needed, for basic arithmetic concepts. A table of contents can be used to find the specific location of a topic, or to preview the contents of a section. In the primary grades the use of glossaries, some indexes, headings, pictures, graphs, and maps can be developed as part of the basal reading instruction, as well as for the content curriculum. Index use and graph and map reading will need teacher guidance.

In the upper grades, as more reference material is required, formal instruction should cover the details. Exercises that clearly call for the use and practice of those details are essential. The desired skill should be called for frequently.

The skill should also be demonstrated through use with a specific article. Most students need assistance in accomplishing a transfer of learning from practice during the reading period to actually using the skill on science or math. For example, it is usually necessary for a reader to formulate the main idea of what he is reading. As a matter of habit, then, the teacher can ask for the main idea of a science selection, just as he would for a narrative: "You read the selection about Mendel and heredity. What is its main idea?"

Practice in specific locational skills can follow the same pattern: "Where in the book can I tell if there is a major section on heredity?" *(Table of contents)* "Let's look." "Where would I look for a definition of *heredity* as used by the author of this book?" *(Glossary)* "Let's see what it says."

The student's trained reaction to a new word, to scanning for an answer, to finding information on a chart, and so on depends on the patterns encouraged and developed by the teacher. No special tools are needed. Practice can be given with textbooks, since a table of contents, index, glossary, headings, pictures, graphs, charts, and maps are built into many texts. By employing these resources as one uses the text students discover the usefulness of skills for obtaining information quickly. Special exercises in using reference materials should be devised by the teacher to lend weight and reinforcement to skills introduced functionally. These exercises should be brief (able to be completed in fifteen minutes or less). They could include such problems as:

1. Pick a topic in early American history. What books does our library have on this topic? List their names and authors.
2. After you have selected a book to read, check the card catalogue under the author's name and list what the card tells you about the book. List other books written by the same author.
3. After you have selected a book to read try to find some information about the author. Check the encyclopedia, the bibliographies of authors, and the book itself.
4. Select a restricted topic and, using an index of three or four books, find the pages on which you find information about this topic.

Short problems such as these can be checked individually by the teacher. As each child indicates an ability to use a reference skill, he can go on to explore a topic of interest. Children can then use the skill as situations arise. The more frequently the need arises, the more important the skill becomes.

Subject teachers cannot assume that all students have knowledge of or ability to use all the skills effectively. By reviewing the skills needed to obtain information, those who have them can use them when they are called for, and those who do not can be identified for special instruction.

STUDY SKILLS

Study skills are those that enable a person to gather information and to organize it in such a way that recall, analysis, interpretation, and evaluation are facilitated. Some of these skills are the ability to:

1. arrange a proper setting in which to read, think, write, study
2. select the appropraite strategy to attain the purposes of study
3. take notes that can be used efficiently for review, recall, or writing
4. outline
5. summarize.

These are discussed in Chapter 15 on study skills, as is the question of adjusting reading rate to the purpose for reading.

READING RATE

Just as there is no "normal" speed for walking to school, there is no predetermined rate at which children should read science or math selections. It is valuable, however, for a reader to change reading rate depending on the purpose and content of reading. A student should read faster in trying to detect the main idea of a social studies passage than in trying to savor each incident in a mystery. The description of a chemical process usually demands slower reading than an article on the sports page. But many children will not make these adjustments if they are not informed about them and if they are not reminded regularly.

FIGURE 14.4   Reading speed follows from the purpose for reading

Children need to consciously adjust their reading rate
for specific purposes.

A reader can adjust his rate to suit different purposes when he is able to:

1. skim a page for major ideas
2. scan a page to locate a specific detail
3. organize his thoughts as a result of looking at the title and subheads
4. move across the print at a regular and determined pace.

Analytical and Evaluative Skills for Content Reading

In addition to general reading skills and skills for using content materials, there are special concerns related to the analysis of concepts and organization of the selection prior to evaluating it; that is, determining its veracity, relevancy, and utility.

Ordinarily a content teacher in a departmentalized staff organization will expect a reader to spend a good deal of effort in the areas of analysis and evaluation. The problem is, how does the teacher instruct and test for those higher-level reading skills? Since content material usually contains a heavy concept load, less easily identifiable organization or theme, and more inaccessible criteria for evaluation and use, a restatement and evaluation of the material is quite difficult. The instructional conclusions are:

1. The student needs special assistance in gaining the basic concepts—vocabulary identification and associations for concept development.
2. The student must be given demonstrations and practice in analyzing, expressing the organizational unity, and evaluating selections from content books.

In a certain sense this is equivalent to asking the reader to think like a scientist, to think like a geographer, to think like an historian. It might be more accurate to say, "to think like a science writer."

Given that kind of orientation, the reader or the teacher can first pose comprehension questions that draw forth a literal meaning. For example, ask about:

1. the main idea of a paragraph, section, or chapter
2. factual support for the main idea
3. sequence of ideas, events, acts
4. organization of the presentation
5. author's purpose, point of view, and style.

Studies with adult readers have shown that asking the same types of questions consistently (factual, recall, main idea) tends to produce greater facility in retention of that type of material. If instruction tends to be biased toward one type of thinking activity, that skill will be strengthened with little effect on the level of ability in the other skills (Meehan, 1970).

At the beginning stages one skill may be emphasized—such as that of identifying the main idea. Recalling details, then, will be overlooked, if it is always underplayed in payoff situations in class assignments. The same will be true of the identification and recall of main ideas if detail is always rewarded. The development of each of the comprehension areas mentioned above should be made methodically and regularly in view of the content area goal. Students need to receive reinforcement and concrete satisfaction for each type of answer.

(Office of Economic Opportunity photo by Paul Conklin)

FIGURE 14.5   In order to learn to think like a botanist students can use the care of plants to supplement their reading

A second group of comprehension competencies include these typical activities of analysis and evaluation:

1. Relate past knowledge and/or events to present knowledge and/or events.
2. Distinguish similarities and differences, fact from fancy and/or opinion and/or generalizations.
3. Make predictions about the outcome of events.
4. Draw conclusions or inferences.
5. Organize the material obtained to suit the purposes for reading.
6. Judge the relevancy, adequacy, authenticity, and utility of the information.

None of these abilities are mutually exclusive; and they presuppose the ability to isolate factors, discriminate among factors according to a variety of criteria, and apply new information through a set of criteria. In that way the reader prepares himself to make judgments.

To develop these higher competencies the reader has to be aware of the bases for analysis and evaluation. It is important that the criteria for making an analysis or evaluation be as clear as possible. For example: size, color, and weight may be criteria for analyzing and categorizing objects to determine similarities and differences; utility in an urban school may be a criterion for evaluating or judging a technique. Decisions for instruction have to be made according to the reader's abilities, the purposes of reading, and the necessary prerequisites for reading. Instruction should be tied to specific content and activity. No one should presuppose that transfer of reading skills will occur until the method of transferring the skill has been adequately demonstrated in one subject. This does not mean that the student will not recognize similarities between skills for reading narrative and reading content. But similarities will not be recognized without teacher demonstration. Research indicates that the process of thinking is modified by the organization of the material. Reading instruction in the content area, then, should take the form that will produce the objectives of that area. Once the reading and thinking processes of the subject discipline have been acquired, general reading skills will be more readily applied, with modifications to types of material.

Instructional procedures must look at both long-range goals—those that should be attained over the years—and at short-term goals—those to be attained within a particular unit of study. The short-term units must use a variety of activities, including consistent question patterns for the different reading and thinking skills. The reader should refer to the chapters on basic comprehension and on critical and creative reading for guidelines on question patterns in order to develop higher reading competencies.

Diagnostic Teaching in Content Subjects

The development of reading skills should be coordinated with the purposes and nature of the content material. The teachers of reading and the teachers of content areas should not operate separately as we have said. If they are two different teachers, they must work together to facilitate the student's progress. Reading skills are not independent of the purposes for which the material is being read, nor are the purposes for reading independent of reading skills. A basic consideration for instruction in reading content material is the coordination of the purposes of content and the reading skills.

This coordination of content with reading skills requires the identification of several factors:

1. The structure of the content material
   a. What concepts does the author assume the reader knows?
   b. What concepts, generalizations, or processes does the author develop?
   c. What style of presentation is used?
   d. What is the order of presentation?
   e. What assumptions does the author make about background knowledge of the subject?
2. The purposes for which the material is to be read
   a. What should the reader be able to do when he has read the material?
   b. What concepts should he have (before reading)?
   c. What concepts should he develop?
   d. What is the reader expected to do with the material?

3. The skills of the reader
   a. Can the student read the material and grasp the meaning of the vocabulary, the concepts presented, and intent of the author?
   b. What concepts and reading and thinking skills should the reader have in order to read effectively and efficiently?
4. The conditions under which the material will be read
   a. Is the length of time adequate for achieving the purposes for reading?
   b. Are distractions minimized?
   c. What is the time lag between reading and implementation of the information gained?

Instructional decisions rest on a set of teaching principles, which may be stated as:

1. The teacher has knowledge of the structure of the particular subject, as well as specific concepts and generalizations to be promoted in that subject.
2. The teacher must grasp the concepts, their dimensions, or levels of abstraction and be able to break them down into components for learning.
3. The teacher must propose appropriate learning activities which are suggested by the objective for that selection.
4. The teacher needs to tie a set of varied experiences to the concepts being developed.
5. Reading should be used as a medium of learning when it is the most effective method of achieving the teaching purpose.
6. The material used should be appropriate for the teacher. The teacher needs to know the:
   a. reading ability as reflected by tests and observation.
   b. nature and extent of the student's specialized vocabulary.
   c. rate of the pupil's reading in different materials.
   d. nature and extent of each pupil's reading experience.
   e. interests, personal characteristics, and social adjustment factors which affect reading.
7. Competence comes with practice and application in a variety of situations.

The first problem of a teacher who must cope with content reading is to identify the purposes of instruction in the content area. Next he must identify the reading and thinking skills required to achieve those purposes. Finally, he must isolate the skills that require development. That information provides a basis upon which to direct both the reading and the content instruction. If the skills are such that direct instruction and practice skills are needed for successful application to content purposes, then the teacher should work with those skills in isolation. Other skills can be taught simultaneously with work in the content area. The development of a child's thinking skills for a content subject should be integrated with the books he reads. Because so many trade, or general, books for young readers have been published recently, such coordination can be accomplished more easily than before. Browsing tables in the classroom can set conditions for exposure to trade books and provide an opportunity for students to become aware of a variety of books and materials. These activities help develop thinking skills:

1. questioning the truth or fantasy of a situation
2. deciding if action is plausible in stories not labeled fairy stories
3. leading children to judge competence of the author
4. judging the fairness and justice of others
5. judging the characters as real or lifelike
6. appraising titles
7. judging pictures
8. judging likenesses and differences in books dealing with children of other lands
9. setting up various types of comparisons of sources of information: biographies of the same person, books versus filmstrips, books versus television
10. evaluating oral or written reports
11. detecting propaganda
12. being alert to figurative language
13. being alert to words that arouse emotion
14. selecting pictures according to preferences
15. listening to the teacher retell a story with incorrect information
16. looking at bulletin board displays of pictures with incorrect and correct titles and judging which are correct
17. writing summaries of poems and making selections of correct and incorrect ones for a critique
18. completing teacher-made exercises designed to develop selected thinking skills
19. selecting relevant and irrelevant facts in a story
20. interpreting character traits
21. differentiating fact and fiction
22. drawing conclusions and inferences from stories.

The primary-grade teacher has an opportunity to develop through many activities the skills the child will need in reading to learn. On a day when a youngster brings a caterpillar to school the teacher can ask: "Will someone read about the caterpillar and report to us on how he grows and develops? Where will you look for information? What kinds of things will help us understand the life of a caterpillar?" Whenever possible, the use of locational and study skills may be introduced and illustrated. Deliberately planned activities that demand the use of a particular skill are essential for learning. Singling them out for new learning gives them an importance that many children might miss if they are treated only incidentally. The art of directing questions and activities toward concepts, reading, and thinking skills must be included in the instructional repertoire of the primary-grade teacher (Meehan, 1970).

Skills for Specific Content Subjects

Even if a student has a repertoire of all the skills discussed in the previous sections he would still have to be aware of the unique qualities of the disciplines of science, math, and social studies in order to move through their content with ease and competency. A number of suggestions have already been given on how to cue the student into content material so that he knows how its structure differs from another subject. There are additional aids, which are much more specific than the general admonition "to read as a scientist does." The items that follow list some of these specific cues for reading math, science, and several kinds of social studies.

The classroom teacher can use cues in a variety of ways. For example, the major headings under which cues are given may be models for asking questions about content: "What is the special vocabulary?" "What can you learn from the graphs or charts?" Or the teacher can take one cue at a time and demonstrate to students how they can use each cue for a clearer understanding of what they are reading. Below are sample selections on which you can try to apply some cues. Naturally, not all cues will apply to every written article. Children can be taught to look for these cues as aids in reading specific content subjects:

Math Cues

1. Vocabulary cues
   Essential key words or phrases help to determine operations or sets to be utilized:
   Addition: total, sum, add, add to, in all, altogether, plus
   Subtraction: difference, left over, minus, subtract, minus
   Multiplication: total, times, how many times, product
   Division: how many times more, divided by, how many would
2. Typographical cues (locational cues)
   a. Question mark (gives clue to the location of the question to be answered)
   b. Charts and graphs (give essential information for problem on page; often located in another area of the page)
   c. Illustrations (may act as road signs or directionals for the problem)
   d. Signs (percent, decimal point, operational signs indicate categories and math operations)
3. Kinds of readings—read for:
   a. skimming for the purpose and overall comprehension
   b. question asked
   c. key words or phrases
   d. operation(s) to be utilized
   e. key numbers (also eliminate extra numbers)
   f. write equation

g. reread problems to justify equations; redo if necessary
h. solve problem
4. Special considerations
   a. The same term is not always used to indicate the same operation (for example: and, added to, and plus are interchangeable)
   b. The same term can indicate different operations (for example: altogether could indicate either addition or multiplication)
   c. Several technical terms have different meanings in general conversation (for example: square, mean, product, and so on)
   d. Mathematics involves the understanding of the many terms that remind the student of absolutely nothing and must be learned by memorization (for example: multiplier, divisor, radius, diameter, circumference)
5. Organizational guides
   There is no specific order, but certain sections appear in most math problems:
   a. a situation is given
   b. a numerical question is asked
   c. an equation must be formulated from information given.

Trial Math Selection

Read the match problem given below. How many math cues can be used to help read the problem more clearly and so arrive at solutions?

CIRCUMFERENCE OF A CIRCLE

The circumference of the circle is 6¼. We often speak of the circumference of a circle as the "length" of the circle, or the "distance around" the circle.

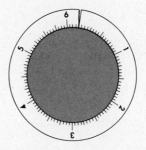

Since we cannot wrap our rulers around a circle, as shown above, we will look for other ways to find the circumference of a circle. Try this experiment:

1. Draw on cardboard a circle with a diameter of 3 centimeters. Cut out the circle carefully.

2. Draw a line 30 centimeters long on a piece of paper.
3. Mark a starting point on the circle. Use a pin and roll the circle along the line, marking the place where the starting point touches the line again.

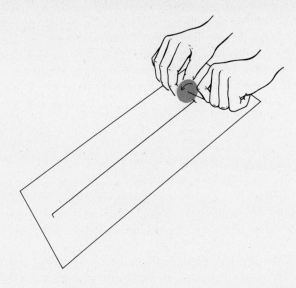

4. To find the circumference of the circle measure (to the nearest $\frac{1}{10}$ centimeter) the segment along which you rolled the circle.
5. Use this method to find the circumferences of circles with diameters of 4, 5, 6, 7, 8, and 9 centimeters. Copy the table and record your results in the circumference column.

Special factor		Diameter (cm)		Circumference
a	×	3	=	
b	×	4	=	
c	×	5	=	
d	×	6	=	
e	×	7	=	
f	×	8	=	
g	×	9	=	

Exercise:

After you have found the circumference of the circles with the diameters given, divide to find the "special factor" for each equation in the table. (Give the factor to the nearest hundredth.)[6]

[6]Keedy, M. L., et al. Exploring Elementary Mathematics, 5 (New York: Holt, Rinehart and Winston, 1970), p. 252.

Science Cues

1. Vocabulary cues
   a. There are certain words and realted concepts that all pupils should know in order to read almost any science material above the primary level:
      i. Things "in common," "characteristics," "various," "classified," "similarities." An understanding of these terms is quite helpful in comprehending the data that follow the terms.
      ii. Common Latin, Greek, or other derivations:
         hydro
         electro
         photo
         un
         bi
   b. Every new science lesson requires the teaching of terms pertinent to that selection.
2. Typographical cues (locational skills)
   a. In most science textbooks there are good subtitles and chapter headings to use.
   b. Often there are good summaries at the end of chapters.
   c. Typographical cues are especially important in the first survey reading.
3. Kinds of readings—read for:
   a. Surveying the material.
      i. Attention to pictures.
      ii. How many main parts? Use the subheadings.
      iii. Read the first paragraph and the summary, if given.
      iv. Formulate questions for reading from the survey.
   b. Answering the questions.
      i. Appreciation of facts and objective data.
      ii. Critical reading—what are the criteria?
   c. Reviewing the material read.
      i. The discussion and evaluation of the reading is probably the most important part of the lesson.
      ii. Pupils should be urged to report exactly what they have read; precision.

      "Most kinds of bats are useful to mankind because they eat harmful insects."
      "Some scientists believe there is life on Mars."

4. Special Considerations
   a. Ability to read symbols. AuH_2O = goldwater.
   b. Ability to follow diagrams; for example: a student must understand the idea of completeness, as in an electrical circuit or a chemical equation.
5. Organizational Guides
   Various organizational approaches typical of science selections are:

a. Generalizations are given first, then the examples and data; deductive.
   i. All mammals have hair, bear young alive, and so on.
   ii. The different kinds of mammals are listed.
b. Examples and supporting data.
   i. Information on different mammals—their size, speed, and so on.
   ii. In other selections—phenomena about light, heat, and so on.
c. Classification of data.
   i. Different classes of mammals, stars, and so on.
   ii. Differences and similarities among the classes.
d. Often the data is given first, then the science writer builds up to classifying and generalizing; inductive.

Geography Cues

1. Vocabulary cues
   a. Extend concept of a previously known word (for example: *range, mountain range*).
   b. Homonyms (for example: *plain, plane*).
   c. Refer to glossary.
   d. Develop vocabulary in context (for example: Bananas are a *tropical* fruit).
   e. Use illustrations to create perception of vocabulary.
2. Typographical cues
   a. Chapter headings, main headings, and subheadings are given.
   b. The format of the book includes illustrations, glossary, appendix, and index.
   c. The book is generally set up with two columns to make reading easier because of the shorter line of type and to facilitate scanning.
3. Kinds of readings
   a. Survey for overview.
   b. Read to answer specific questions.
   c. Skim to find specific answers and make generalizations (for example: "What are the natural resources of Manitoba? How does this affect the industries of Manitoba?")
   d. Detailed reading of charts, graphs, maps, and so on.
4. Specialized considerations
   a. Statistical reading: This type is developed through repeated use of statistics (for example: present statistical data and provide an exercise for using the data, such as comparing the area in square miles of several given countries).
   b. Symbolic language of maps (for example: a child's use of the map legend; *see* illustration page 324).
   c. Recognize that a map is a ground plan drawn to scale.
   d. Interpret different kinds of maps (for example: population, political, rainfall, topographical).

Political Map

✵ **Capital**

• **Other City or Town**

▲ MOUNTAIN

River

A map legend

e. Reading graphs (for example: The reader learns to interpret data of various types of graphs—circle, line, bar, and pictorial).
f. Authenticating facts (for example: The reader must verify the date of statistical information, such as the population of a given area).
g. The reader cuts across the author's organization and makes his own groupings of factual material for a given purpose.

5. Organizational guides
   The material in a geography book is generally organized in one of two ways:
   a. A specific area is given and all geographical aspects are examined (For example: The New England states would be thoroughly discussed as to topography, climate, population, industries, and so on).
   b. A geographical aspect is considered as it is found throughout the world.

Biography Cues

1. Vocabulary cues
   a. Pronunciation skills.
      i. Multisyllabic words (for example: *as-tro-labe*).
      ii. Foreign words (for example: *apartheid*).
   b. Meaning skills.
      i. Technical words (for example: *latitude*).
      ii. Abstract words (for example: *democratic*).
      iii. Concepts; abstractions (for example: *tolerance*).
      iv. General terms (for example: *elevator:* grain or passenger).
      v. Mathematical terms (for example: *ratio*).
2. Typographical guides
   a. Headings and subheadings provide clues to location of responses to questions.
   b. Use the parts of the book as reference tools.
   c. Relate text and graphic content such as maps, graphs, and cartoons to corresponding text material.

3. Kinds of readings—read for:
   a. Main idea and supporting details.
   b. Use of key words, concepts, and literal facts.
   c. Read critically:
      i. Appraisals.
      ii. Conclusions and inferences.
      iii. Propaganda.
      iv. Current events.
   d. Organize ideas to recognize relations and sequence of events; identify central issues.
   e. Graphic skills (maps, graphs, charts, diagrams, and pictures).
   f. Related reference skills (table of contents, index, cross-references, footnotes).
   g. Related materials (periodicals and mass media, such as radio, television, lectures, and field trips).
4. Organizational guides
   General organization of the content:
   a. Material in the social studies area is usually organized by the initial statement of a selection (for example: the current voter age limit), a practice (for example: selection of the President by an electoral college), an event (for example: passage of the Eighteenth Amendment), or a method (for example: representative democracy).
   b. Often a point of view is presented, usually subtly (for example: private enterprise is best for the country); in some cases, overtly (for example: dictatorships are bad).
   c. A relation often presented is one of conditions surrounding an effect: condition-effect relation.
   d. Chronological order often meets the organizational needs of social studies material.

"Go-go" Reading

Not all content reading is performed with textbooks. After a child is finished with school most of his reading will be content reading that may not include the contextual aids he has found in textbooks. Road signs, labels on bottles, newspapers, and magazines all demand content reading. Magazine and billboard advertisements require reactions that involve many of the same skills that have been proposed for textbook reading, and perhaps additional ones.

Tank trucks roll across the country bearing the red label *inflammable;* others, *flammable.* What is the difference between these two words? The reader of these signs had better protect himself by being able to read such signs.

Reading-on-the-go, or "go-go" reading, requires quick reactions. The reader must apply criteria in order to make immediate judgments. It is easy enough to decide not to drink a liquid when it has *Poison!* stamped across it.

FIGURE 14.6   Being able to read can be a life-saving skill

But the parent with a sick five-year-old child must bring other criteria to bear on his reading of the label: "Take one teaspoon four times a day. For children under six consult a physician before administering this medicine."

Though "go-go" reading does not occupy much classroom time, examples from the world of signs, television, the newspaper, and magazines afford excellent teaching examples of what reading-thinking skills must be used when examining content selections. Children will usually respond vigorously to exercises in examining popular commercials: "The computer confirms that Regi cigarettes give you whiter, brighter teeth"; "Senator Fogbound comes from the Midwest and knows the problems farmers face"; "Sandpaper tissue is so soft—buy the tissue with more of what you're looking for."

Each of these statements makes assumptions; some of them are quite misleading. In the first ad the reader must ask: "What do computers do?" They do not *confirm* anything. They simply report data. In the second statement the reader should ask: "What does coming from the Midwest teach you about farming?" A person could live his entire life in Indianapolis and not know how to milk a cow or disk a field. And in the third statement the reader should ask: "More than what?" There are other avenues to explore with these statements, but such brief comments indicate ways in which to show youngsters how to apply content reading skills to the "go-go" world around him. Short examples like these provide direct and pertinent demonstrations of some of the analytic and evaluative reading skills that are integral features of content reading.

CAREER EDUCATION

Many elementary and middle schools encourage youngsters to learn about careers through demonstrations, field trips, and through reading. Various alternatives gradually unfold especially through reading. Youngsters gain concepts about jobs and the work world by reading about them, and see that many occupations use written directions for workers to follow. They see quite early, for example, that they must be able to relate a diagram to associated written explanations. When catalytic converters were installed on automobiles to reduce air pollution, the manufacturers sent complex instructions for maintaining and adjusting those converters to garage mechanics. If a mechanic could not read proficiently, he could not take care of these devices to make sure they continued preventing pollution. It would be very helpful to show children a sample of such instructions as one instance of real-life, on-the-job reading.

Reading is a continuing and growing factor in the:

1. review of job skills and concepts
2. selection of an occupation (one cannot actually experience many careers except through reading about them)
3. training for a specific career
4. updating skills to advance in a chosen profession.

Both career information and the incentive to read become linked as real-life activities. Reading increases in value as the child understands that it is a tool for his adult life, as well as a way to experience pleasure.

Appraising Content Reading Skills

Chapter 12 discussed a means of asking graded questions in order to appraise the child's application of certain reading-thinking skills. The same method can be used in teaching the content material discussed in this chapter.

If the teacher expects a child to think like a scientist while reading science material, then the teacher should have some knowledge of the structure of that discipline. The teacher should know that what is called the discovery method in education is akin to the scientific method; that is, there is observation of data, classification of the data, and a prediction of conclusion that follows from the relationships observed.

Story problems in math involve a description requiring numerical solution. The specific problem question has to be identified, and elements in the situation have to be categorized in order to establish problem-solving operations which lead to computation.

Social studies is most often concerned with observing effects and trying to determine the conditions surrounding and preceding those effects. Time and space relations and people and government relations are conditions that surround important events which affect the lives of everyone concerned.

Part of the teacher's preparation for an appraisal of content reading skills is to make sure that the background of students warrant such an appraisal. In this case the examiner expects to find some skills and he is prepared to correct and develop those skills that need changing or adding to. He might use a checklist similar to the one given below to appraise his performance and the capability of the school system in carrying out a program to teach content reading skills.

These practices are often recommended for teaching special reading skills in various content areas. A teacher should check off the items that apply to his teaching and make an appraisal of what has to be done to prepare his classroom to teach these skills.

Checklist for Teacher Awareness of Content Reading

1. Text material used is suited in difficulty to the reading levels of students.
2. Students are encouraged through assignments to read widely in related materials.
3. At the beginning of the year adequate time is taken to introduce the text and to discuss how it may be read effectively.
4. The teacher is aware of the special vocabulary and concepts introduced in the various units.
5. Adequate attention is given to vocabulary and concept development.
6. Provisions are made for checking on the extent to which important vocabulary and concepts are learned, and reteaching is done where needed.
7. The teacher knows the special reading skills involved in the subject.
8. The teacher teaches the special reading skills in the subject.
9. Students are taught to use appropriate reference materials.
10. Adequate reference materials are available.
11. Plenty of related informational books and other materials are available for students who read *below-grade* level.
12. Plenty of related informational books and other materials are available for students who read *above-grade* level.
13. The teacher helps the poor reader to develop adequate reading skills.
14. Students are grouped within the classroom for differentiated instruction.
15. The teacher knows the reading level of the textbook(s) being used.
16. The teacher knows the reading ability of the students from standardized tests, other evaluative materials, and/or cumulative records.

Assuming that the teacher has enough knowledge of the structure of the subject discipline, the next step is to get a broad picture of the skills children have for reading content selections with comprehension. As was recommended for several other kinds of reading skills, careful observation of children during content reading may provide a picture of what the strengths and weaknesses are. The broad categories in the checklist could guide the teacher in a general appraisal. A teacher could also construct a checklist with a different set of skills, if specific skills were identified for individual achievement by the end of the term or the end of the school year. The kinds of observations indicated on the checklist are essential in order to differentiate instruction.

In any fourth- or fifth-grade classroom the range of content reading skills is likely to be quite wide. Some children will have learned to respond to cues on their own. That they use the skills well, or at least know what to look for, will necessitate only a minimum amount of instruction for maintaining and improving what they already know. Others may not be consciously aware of cues. Students who have difficulty in using special skills may need additional practice with supplementary materials.

Teach and Test for Specific Criteria

In assessing content reading skills it would be easy to slip into the practice of testing the child with a single selection and trying to estimate his use of all skills on the basis of a single response. Because so many factors are involved in demonstrating skills for reading content material, the teacher's assessment and the child's progress are more likely to benefit from several tests on specific criteria. For example, children should perform an exercise in which the teacher can observe their use of headings to determine the main parts of the article; or they should read a selection and then draw a map of what they have read to test visualization and following directions. In reverse, children could be asked to describe what a region or a city is like by looking at a map.

The major headings for which a teacher should test a child are *vocabulary, using heads, using charts, typographical cues,* and *organizational guides.* The test should include seeing if the child gets the facts straight, identifies the organizational pattern or principle of the selection, states the conclusion or prediction, applies criteria to evaluate the information and the selection, and uses the information to relate it to the life he knows.

On the basis of criterion tests of vocabulary, chart reading, organizational analysis, evaluation of information and procedure, and use of conclusions to make predictions or to integrate information the teacher can form instructional groups, place some children with study kits, and give some demonstrations to the entire class. This is part of a continuing process of making children aware of the power they have over printed information once they develop a few key reading skills.

SUMMARY

There is a difference between content selections and narratives, especially the short stories typically found in basal readers. Vocabularly differs with respect to the technical terms found in science, math, and social studies, but also because those disciplines have an organizational structure that often influences the way information about the subject is presented in an elementary school test. Thus, it seems important that teachers and children learn something about the way in which expository selections are written within specific subject areas.

There are various kinds of cues that a reader can use to assist in reading content material effectively. These cues relate to vocabulary, typography, expository writing patterns, and, in a sense, learning to read like the scientist or the mathematician who wrote the selection.

To teach content reading skills the teacher and students together should

Checklist of Reading and Study Skills for Content Subjects

	Bert Back	Tony Curt	Helena Rubin	Lyndon Bird
Word-meaning Skills				
1. Understanding of technical terms				
2. Use of dictionary				
3. Use of the glossary				
4. Use of new terms in speaking and writing				
5. Understanding of prefixes, suffixes, and roots				
6. Understanding of figurative language				
7. Understanding of personal and general connotations of words				
8. Understanding of technical vocabulary related only to this subject				
Comprehension Skills				
1. Recognition and understanding of main ideas				
2. Recognition of relevant details				
3. Recognition of relationships among main ideas				
4. Organization of ideas in sequence				
5. Understanding of time and distance concepts				
6. Following directions				
7. Reading maps, tables, and graphs				
8. Distinguishing between facts and opinions				
9. Judging and criticizing what is read				
10. Reading widely to seek additional evidence				
11. Drawing inferences				
12. Listening attentively and critically				
Study Skills				
1. Familiar with many sources of information				
2. Using an index and encyclopedia efficiently				
3. Constructing a two-step outline				
4. Organizing and summarizing information				
5. Adjusting rate of reading to suit purpose and content				
6. Skimming with a purpose				

Use appropriate rating symbol.

+: Strong

−: lacking

?: unknown

make a task analysis of the kinds of skills that are needed by individuals in the class, then construct criterion exercises where they are needed. Content reading is a part of the idea of developmental reading. Content reading includes reading signs, ads, tables, editorials, and news reports. The skills that are needed for reading a content subject text must also be adjusted to reading on the go. Verifying information, reading directions, knowing a vocabulary is just as important in our daily lives as it is in the more formal textbook area.

Finally, an appraisal of content reading skills should start with the teacher's appraisal of his knowledge of the structure of a discipline. In this way he can teach children to "read like a scientist," continue through an analysis of the capability of the school to teach content skills, and end with specific criterion tests—those to be used as a prelude to grouping and individualizing instruction in the skills of reading content selections.

Terms for Self-study

organizational pattern
readability formula
analysis
evaluation
expository writing

translation
locational skills
typographical cues
criterion tests

Discussion Questions

1. How could a teacher determine if the readability of the class text was too difficult for students?
2. What are several ways of demonstrating to children the differences between reading a story and reading subject-oriented content?
3. What means does a content teacher have for adjusting to the various reading abilities of students?

15

Library
and Study
Skills

Try to remember the last time you prepared a term paper for one of your college courses. Think for a moment about the skills you used to locate resources. Knowledge of the library and familiarity with various reference volumes determined in large part how efficiently you were able to go about completing your task. In addition, you used a set of specialized skills in gathering and recording the pertinent information from each resource consulted. You organized and reorganized your ideas so that they might follow logically and be properly documented. You were using library and study skills for the purpose of solving a problem.

Children also need specialized skills that enable them to gather and use information on a specific topic. This chapter discusses library and study skills and describes how the classroom teacher can provide children with appropriate instruction.

As you read this chapter look for answers to these questions:

What reference volumes should be introduced first?
What is a good strategy for teaching children to outline and take notes?
How can the classroom teacher teach library usage skills?
What can be done to increase reading rate?
Why is it important to teach the parts of a book?
How can needs be assessed with regard to library and study skills?

Reading is a skill needed for countless daily tasks. In a world as complex as ours it is not enough to simply read what is placed before us. We must also know where to look for a specific piece of needed information and how to use that resource once it has been located. Reading that helps us meet personal needs for information is dependent upon a specialized set of skills called *library and study skills*. These enable the reader to apply and use basic reading skills according to widely varied and constantly changing demands; in a real sense they make basic reading skills functional and give credence to the notion that we learn to *read* so that we may read to *learn*.

Suppose Bonnie and Pete decide they want to landscape their yard. The information they need about plants, their arrangement, transplanting, fertilizers, and so forth is available in a variety of places, including books. These do-it-yourselfers may be excellent readers and still not be able to take advantage of the many book resources available on landscaping if they lack basic library and study skills. This instance illustrates how important it is to be able to use reading as a tool. Bonnie and Pete need, first of all, to have some awareness of what kinds of reference books exist. Next, they need to know how to locate those books. They must also have specialized interpretive skills in order to understand diagrams, tables, and other graphic means used for presenting information. Finally, they must know how to organize the information they gather in order to remember and use it.

This chapter addresses each of these topics. Interpretive skills are treated more extensively elsewhere in the book (Chapters 4 and 5). We will first consider the role of the teacher in demonstrating library and study skills. Next, specific library and study skills will be presented. Then the techniques and instruments for assessing children's progress will be discussed.

General Guidelines for Teaching Study Skills

As with any reading skill, the development of library and study skills is a long-term undertaking that has its beginnings in the primary grades. Eventual mastery of complex skills, such as using an encyclopedia and writing an outline, are built on numerous prerequisites—for example, alphabetizing and finding a specified page in a book. The instructional program must be designed with reference to some overall scope and sequence of skills. The introduction and systematic practice of skills should be planned to avoid a haphazard approach to teaching. No one can teach all these skills alone. Planning is required on a school or district-wide basis. Most basal reading programs provide some guidance in teaching study skills, and many publishers have units available which show the sequential development of specific skills, such as dictionary usage or outlining.

The classroom teacher is responsible for demonstrating the actual use of reference materials and skills. Especially in the area of library and study skills, trial and error learning on a strictly incidental basis is most inefficient. Too often children are expected to grow in their ability to use an index by completing workbook pages or discovering for themselves how an index is organized. Exploration and discovery learning should not be ruled out. Indeed, it can be quite valuable to have children browse through a dictionary (or other reference volume) to note what information it contains. Even in this case some follow-up instruction is called for which will lead children to understand when and how the various parts of a dictionary are useful.

The teacher is just as responsible for planning and conducting lessons on library and study skills as he is for similar activities on word recognition and comprehension. Many teachers use an inquiry approach to the curriculum, thus giving children an opportunity to employ study skills in a problem-solving context. One teacher created the opportunity to teach and have children practice study skills by setting up this problem:

> Suppose a disaster such as a nuclear attack makes it necessary for you and your neighbors to relocate in the Colville River Basin of Alaska north of the Artic Circle. You are allowed to take only 100 pounds of equipment and supplies per person. What would you take? How would you prepare to survive during your first year?

Surrounded by catalogues, almanacs, encyclopedias, filmstrips, and so on the child is challenged in an interesting way to apply known skills and to learn new ones. Reading skills are integrated into a unit that focuses on solving a problem.

The present emphasis on career education opens up numerous opportunities for children to apply library and study skills in meaningful activities that are relevant to their interests. The girl who thinks she wants to be a veterinarian will discover the need for skill in reading charts, tables, and diagrams; for using the card catalogue and *Reader's Guide to Periodical Literature;* and for dozens of related skills as she learns about her planned career.

You can provide an opportunity for children to practice skills through activities that are built on general personal interests. The ten-year-old who is especially interested in motorcycles will enthusiastically pursue the topic by reading material that requires the use of various specialized study skills; the task of using these same skills to read about Brazil would simply turn him off. Skills are learned and practiced more willingly when personal interests are incorporated into the activity.

The teacher can also occasionally take advantage of classroom incidents to demonstrate or reinforce library and study skills. Suppose a seven-year-old girl finds a frog on her way to school. The teacher might show the class how to use the subject index of a library card catalogue to locate a book on frogs. As was stated earlier, all skill instruction cannot be incidental, but the interest generated by real-life events can be a powerful ally for the alert teacher.

Children should be provided with the opportunity to apply library and study skills in the content fields. They must be helped in transferring the use of their skills to social studies, mathematics, science, and the language arts. For example, the dictionary is especially helpful when children encounter specialized vocabulary in their history books. They should be encouraged to look up words that present special difficulties.

As with other reading skills, proficiency with library and study skills develops at varying rates among children. As much as possible, the teacher must determine individual needs and plan activities that build on each child's current level of understanding. For example, not all nine-year-old youngsters have exactly the same awareness of how to use an index. Some may be totally ignorant of this skill, while others demonstrate a good understanding. The teacher must differentiate instruction on library and study skills just as he would on other, more basic reading skills.

Reference Skills: Where Is Information Found?

Very early in their school careers children should learn that many books are not intended to be read from cover to cover. There are, in fact, over 5,500 standard reference titles that cover a broad range of topics. No child—indeed, no teacher—can possibly know so many resources. But beginning in Grade 1 children should become familiar with several standard reference tools. In each succeeding year their ability to use these references should increase, just as their awareness of additional references should expand.

The dictionary, for example, is a tool children can begin to use as soon as reading instruction starts. At this early date they can begin to learn the functions of a dictionary and how to look up the information it contains. Various publishers produce picture dictionaries—such as *My Little Pictionary* (Scott Foresman, 1964), *The Cat in the Hat Beginner Book Dictionary* (Random House, 1964), and the *Storybook Dictionary* (Golden Press, 1966)—that introduce the child to this reference. Picture dictionaries should be included in every first grade book collection.

The organization and purpose of picture dictionaries is fairly simple. A picture is used to "define" each entry. The child knows what object is represented by a word from the picture that accompanies the printed symbol; *dog* is "defined" by a picture of a dog, *tree* by a picture of a tree, and so forth. Figure 15.1 shows a sample page from a picture dictionary. In some dictionary editions guide words appear at the top of each page and the entries are alphabetized. Children can learn their first lessons about the dictionary from these simplified editions.

Another approach to introducing dictionary concepts is to have the child develop his own picture dictionary. As he learns to recognize certain words he can make appropriate entries in the dictionary. A "shoebox" of words and corresponding pictures on 3 × 5 inch cards can be developed, or a looseleaf notebook can be used. (The form of the dictionary can vary; it is the understanding that comes from building this resource that is important.) When the words included in his dictionary are ones the student chooses—ones that are personally meaningful—they have a powerful motivating effect for learning. Sylvia Ashton-Warner describes her use of this technique in *Teacher* (1963).

asparagus

Asparagus is a
green vegetable.

A

astronaut

The astronaut guides
his space ship.

automobile

Our automobile has safety
belts in it.

FIGURE 15.1   A picture dictionary page

Reprinted with permission from Rovers,
Rosemary, *The New Picture Dictionary,*
rev. 1973 (Cincinnati, Ohio: Cebco/Pflaum
Division of Standard Publishing, 1965).

In addition to teaching children how a dictionary is developed, a self-made picture dictionary can be used by youngsters as a practice list of words they recognize at sight, or to check the spelling of a word for an experience story. A growing dictionary of *Words We Know* stands as proof of the progress a class is making in learning to read new words.

As children grow in reading ability new dimensions can be added to their personal dictionaries. For example, entry words can be used in sentences; simple diacritical marks (symbols that indicate pronunciation) can be used for long and short vowels; definitions for words can be written; and multiple meanings for some words can be included. By studying other's dictionaries children may discover additional features they would like to add to their own volumes. Eventually a more sophisticated commercial dictionary will be appropriate. *The New Elementary Dictionary* (American Book Company, 1965) is an example of a simplified dictionary that children can use when a picture dictionary has been outgrown. *The Golden Dictionary* (Golden Press, 1944) combines some of the better features of a picture and a standard dictionary, thus making it especially useful as a transition vehicle.

Evidently children cannot learn all there is to know about the dictionary in Grades 1 and 2. What they learn in the primary grades is mainly a direct result of personal need. No formal instructional program on the use of the dictionary is usually undertaken until grade 4. Prior to that time instruction is more informal, with the teacher presenting skills as they are required by the children.

Formal instruction on dictionary skills need be delayed only until the child has the reading techniques and abilities required for advanced dictionary use.

In the intermediate grades most children are ready to begin formal instruction on the use of a dictionary. Various publishers have units available on dictionary usage. It is not possible to explore here all that goes into such units. By way of illustration a list of usual topics, not necessarily in the order given, might include:

Using the Dictionary

I. How to find words
    A. guide words
    B. finding the entry
    C. different words with the same spelling
    D. different spellings of the same word
    E. words that sound alike
    F. prefixes and suffixes

II. The main entry
    A. the entry word
    B. pronunciation
        1. accent marks
        2. diacritical marks
    C. Parts-of-speech label
        1. determiners
        2. modifiers
        3. intensifiers
    D. the definition
    E. examples
    F. definition by example
    G. illustrations
    H. labels
    J. inflected forms
        1. plurals of nouns
        2. comparative and superlative forms of adjectives
        3. principal parts of verbs
    K. idioms
    L. run-on entries
    M. usage notes

III. Pronunciation
    A. accent marks
    B. symbols for sounds
        1. vowels
        2. consonants
        3. foreign sounds

IV. Abbreviations used in definitions

V. Special sections
  A. persons and places
  B. weights and measures
  C. geologic timetable
  D. foreign monetary units
  E. Presidents of the United States
  F. states of the United States
  G. provinces of Canada
  H. countries of the United Nations

The term *formal study* indicates that planned instructional activities are conducted with reference to some overall scope and sequence of skills. This is in contrast to *informal,* or incidental, instruction. As much as possible, instruction should include application of skills to actual everyday problems. For example, in making a current events report to the class a group of children should be asked to use their dictionary skills to check the pronunciation of certain words using the diacritical marking system contained in the dictionary. This procedure would be particularly effective following a lesson in which the diacritical marking system has been introduced or reviewed. A detailed discussion of dictionary instruction is contained in Palovic and Goodman (1968).

In addition to the dictionary, primary-grade children should be introduced to the scope and use of an encyclopedia. Because of the reading difficulty of published encyclopedias for primary-grade children, the teacher may find it worthwhile to develop his own. Some authorities suggest that the primary-grade teacher create a picture file arranged in alphabetical order according to index words such as *animal, city, farm, transportation, weather,* and the like. Materials, especially pictures, relevant to each of the topics are then placed for future reference in the appropriate file. The children should be held largely responsible for finding useful items, classifying them, and filing them in the collection. Eventually, cross-references and other embellishments can be added, as the need for them becomes apparent.

The value of such a simplified encyclopedia is that through its development children begin to understand what an encyclopedia contains. They learn how this resource is organized, and how one analyzes a topic for entries of potential value. By asking: "What shall we look under to see what our resource file contains about animals on the farm?" the teacher initiates instruction at a fundamental level on a highly important aspect of encyclopedia usage.

As with the dictionary, in the intermediate grades children's reading skills and general knowledge are sufficiently advanced to make systematic instruction on using the encyclopedia profitable. Instruction should be based on a solid foundation of established skills learned in the primary grades and should proceed according to a sequential plan of skill development. A need to use the encyclopedia should be created in order to keep interest high and to give learning a goal. The teacher should demonstrate new skills and then provide for their immediate application in worthwhile projects. Exercises, such as the one that follows, provide an opportunity for the child to practice new skills. They also yield diagnostic information for the teacher.

Using the Encyclopedia

Directions: Below is pictured a set of encyclopedias. By looking at the letters on the spine of each book it is possible to decide which one contains information we might need.

Indicate in Column B which volume you would use to locate information about the topic in Column A:

Column A	Column B
1. Brazil	_____
2. baseball	_____
3. measles	_____
4. horses	_____
5. Colorado	_____
6. tropical fish	_____
7. beetle	_____
8. guitar	_____
9. knighthood	_____
10. Yellowstone Park	_____

The classroom teacher also has the responsibility for introducing children to other reference works—such as almanacs; atlases; *Who's Who;* index volumes, such as the *Reader's Guide to Periodical Literature;* newspaper and picture files; the telephone book; and special dictionaries. These and other reference tools will eventually be discovered by children as they mature and pursue varied interests. The teacher cannot possibly anticipate every resource that will be used, but he must introduce the major references mentioned here and arrange for their use by his students. Once these are found, the next concern is helping children learn how to use them by applying *locational skills.*

Locational Skills: How Is Information Found?

It is apparent that reference skills cannot be developed in isolation from locational skills. Knowing which reference or resource contains the answer to a question is only a part of solving a need; it is necessary to know how to locate the information within the correct resource. Locational skills can be roughly divided into two categories: library skills and book skills.

Teaching Children to Use the Library

The library card catalogue is a resource that children must learn to use. They need to know that the card catalogue is a file containing the title, author, and subject cards for every book in the library. They must also know how to find books through its use.

Various resources are available to help in planning activities that build pupil understanding of the card catalogue (Palovic and Goodman, 1968). An

(HRW photo by Russell Dian)

FIGURE 15.2   Children using the library

Children find books they need by looking them up in the library card catalogue.

excellent approach in Grade 2 or 3 for developing this necessary knowledge is to construct a simple card catalogue for the classroom library.

The books housed in the reading corner can each be noted by author, title, and subject on a 3 × 5 inch card. As a first step students can be asked to decide how the cards might be arranged for easy retrieval. Alphabetizing the cards by author's name is a handy technique and entirely satisfactory as a first step. Later students will discover that searching their card catalogue for an author is satisfactory only when the author of a book is known. Occasionally only a title is known. The suggestion should be made—hopefully by a student—that a second card, alphabetically filed by book title, might be added to the catalogue.

Subject cards can be added when students are ready for that kind of classification. The fact that several subject cards might be made for the same book is a significant discovery for children to make; this helps them understand the complexity of indexing. The suggestion can also be made—by the teacher, if necessary—that brief summaries or annotations added to the cards would be helpful to someone who finds an interesting title but wonders about the exact nature of the story or the difficulty of the book.

Using this approach, a fairly sophisticated card catalogue can be evolved by the children themselves by the fourth grade. Some children will then be ready to learn about the card catalogue in their school and public libraries. (Some children may be ready for this step as early as Grade 2. This sequence of steps illustrates only one possible approach. Other approaches, and especially other chronologies, will be appropriate in a variety of situations.)

Several resources are available to help teachers plan a unit on library skills (Palovic and Goodman, 1968). In connection with the card catalogue, intermediate-grade children should also be given instruction on these points:

1. Specific abbreviations are used in catalogue cards. For example: © *1964* represents copyright 1964; *96p illus* means a book is 96 pages in length and contains illustrations.
2. Cross-reference cards direct the user to other potentially useful sources of information.
3. Call numbers, listed in the card catalogue, are needed to find a book in the library.

As with reference materials, the best approach to teaching children how to use the card catalogue is to create a need for its use. Careful attention must be paid to the importance of prerequisite skills, such as alphabetic and classification skills.

UNDERSTANDING THE DEWEY DECIMAL SYSTEM

A second aspect of library locational skills is understanding the cataloguing system. One such is the Dewey Decimal System. Few people have memorized even the main categories of this system. That is not a goal of the instructional program. Rather, children should learn the function of the system and how it is organized. They should also learn how the system has been employed in their own libraries so that books of special interest can be located.

Dewey Decimal Classification System

000–099	General works
100–199	Philosophy
200–299	Religion
300–399	Social sciences
400–499	Language
500–599	Pure science
600–699	Applied science, or technology
700–799	The arts
800–899	Literature
900–999	History

Several discovery techniques might be employed in introducing the concept of a library classification scheme to children. For example, the books housed in the reading corner could be catalogued with a system devised by the class. Nonfiction and fiction books might be separated and then alphabetized by author. All books written by authors whose last name begins with A could be numbered (1A, 2A, 3A, and so on); the same numbering system would be used for books by authors whose names begin with B. Or books might be grouped by geographic location of setting, type of story, or even reading difficulty. The number assigned to a book (1A, 3B, and so on) would also be written on appropriate cards in the catalogue and would be noted on the spine of the book.

A presentation of the organization and function of the Dewey Decimal System by the classroom teacher or librarian might be just as meaningful as a discovery approach, provided children are later given an opportunity to study its application at firsthand. Typically, the major classifications and more commonly used subdivisions—such as fairy tales, reference volumes, and earth sciences—are introduced in the fourth grade. In later grades more specific categories can be presented.

USING THE PUBLIC LIBRARY

Children normally learn to use their school and classroom libraries with relative ease. Daily activities familarize children with these resources; the instructional program teaches them the skills needed to locate and use the materials the libraries contain. However, the objective of building lifelong reading habits requires that attention also be given to using the public library. It is human nature to avoid the unfamiliar, so the classroom teacher should introduce his students to the public library in order to increase the chance that they will utilize it, especially as adults.

The teacher should see that each child has a library card so that he can

(HRW photo by Russell Dian)

FIGURE 15.3   Using the public library

The public library should be a familiar place in each child's school routine where lifetime reading habits will begin.

borrow materials. The teacher can arrange for a class trip to the library, which might include a tour of the facilities and an opportunity to borrow a book, record, picture collection, or filmstrip. In conjunction with such a field trip a member of the public library staff might be invited to visit the classroom to make a presentation and answer questions.

Book Skills: Finding Information in Books

Most nonfiction books contain a number of useful features: a preface, foreword, or introduction, where the author or editor describes the purpose for writing the book; a table of contents; a list of illustrations, figures, and maps; various chapter, section, and subsection headings; a glossary; and an index or indexes. Children need to know the purpose and use of these parts of a book.

THE PREFACE, FOREWORD, OR INTRODUCTION GIVE THE READER INSIGHT

We often fail to recognize the importance of the preface, foreword, or introduction to a book. An attitude seems to prevail that the "important" part of a book begins on page one. But the preliminary message of the author or editor typically explains why the book was written and what unique contribution it makes to human knowledge. The preface usually explains the organizational scheme of the book and acknowledges people who contributed to the preparation of the book.

The teacher's task is primarily one of demonstrating the wealth of information contained in a preface. Perhaps he might read it to the class. The forewords of several similar books might be contrasted so as to determine what is unique about each volume. A follow-up assignment could be given in which annotations to various reference volumes are done on the basis of the information provided by the editors of a book.

THE TABLE OF CONTENTS PROVIDES AN OVERVIEW

In contrast to the personal message often conveyed by the author in a preface, a books' table of contents is a structured outline of its subject matter. The table of contents may enumerate only the chapter titles and page numbers on which each chapter begins. In other books the table of contents may also list the major sections or headings of each chapter. In either case the table of contents provides the reader with an overview of the book's contents and a general feeling for its organization.

By reading the introductory matter and studying the table of contents the efficient reader can quickly and accurately assess the appropriateness of a book to his needs. Naturally, youngsters must be led to make judgments about the usefulness of a book.

Beginning in Grade 1 the child must learn where to find a table of contents and how to interpret the information it contains. Gradually he must be shown the relation between chapters and units, the importance of chapter sequence, and how to identify where the needed information can be located.

LIST OF ILLUSTRATIONS, FIGURES, AND MAPS GIVEN EXACT LOCATION

A list of illustrations, figures, and maps is not always included in nonfiction or reference books. When given, however, it is normally found in the front of the book just after the table of contents. A reader may consult this listing to determine what sort of graphic information is contained in a book. He may feel that a history book should contain a variety of maps or that a book about airplanes must have photographs of different models to be useful to him.

A history textbook for the social studies class is likely to have such an illustration list. The teacher can demonstrate how to use it when the book is first introduced to the class. He might have several other books with similar listings on hand to demonstrate the use of this reference skill in a variety of resources.

CHAPTER, SECTION, AND SUBSECTION HEADINGS HELP ORGANIZE IDEAS

Another procedure for locating information is to use the headings an author has given to divisions in the book. Chapter, section, and subsection headings (organizers) are frequently arranged in outline fashion, with supporting ideas grouped as subsections under a main heading. Sections are then gathered into chapters and chapters into parts. This textbook, for example, has 19 chapters organized into seven parts. By being aware of the organization of a book a reader can use headings to identify where the information he needs is located.

The teacher can help students develop the habit of using headings or organizers by paging through several chapters of a book with them and pointing out the relation between sections. The headings might be written on a chalkboard in outline form. Later, children can outline parts of a book independently as a written assignment to gain practice in correctly relating the sections of a book.

Used in conjunction with skimming, organizers provide an excellent means for locating information in a book.

A GLOSSARY CLARIFIES WORD MEANING

The glossary serves much the same function as a dictionary, except that its contents are limited to entries taken from the book itself. Children with dictionary skills are able to use a glossary with only minimal additional instruction. The teacher's major tasks are demonstrating where the glossary can be found and providing practice in using this feature.

THE INDEX DIRECTS THE READER'S SEARCH

An index is an alphabetical list of names, subjects, events, and so on, together with page numbers. It is usually placed at the end of a book. By consulting the index a reader can locate exactly where the information that he wants is located in a book. Because of its utility the index is one of the most frequently used features of many reference volumes. An almanac, for example, would be most unwieldy without an index.

By the intermediate grades increased reading in the content areas will necessitate instruction on the use of an index. Instruction must begin with the simple and move to the more complex. At first, simply locating specific terms in the alphabetical index and noting a specific page number is appropriate. Later, using cross-references, identifying entries that might provide information on a topic, and employing multiple indexes in the same book can be undertaken. This exercise illustrates an activity index use:

Using an Index

Listed below are topics found in an index to a book on Egypt. Use the index to answer the questions that follow.

Alphabet, 31
Art, 15–17, 75, 76
  ancient, 43–45
  recent, 113–115
  in tombs, 45
Cairo, 13, 19–21, 25
  burning of (1952), 70
  government of, 140
Customs, 5, 57–59
Food, 48, 51

Islam, 99
Moslems, 95–98
  creed, 97
  laws of, 101
Nasser, Gamal Abdul, 117–121
  early life of, 117
  personality of, 123–125
Sports, 132–133
Villages, 17, 43, 83

On what page or pages in the book will you read about:

1. Islam? _____   5. Food? _____
2. Moslems? _____   6. Burning of Cairo? _____
3. Sports? _____   7. Customs? _____
4. Early life of Nasser? _____   8. Moslem laws? _____

How many pages are about:

1. Food? _____   3. Customs? _____
2. Ancient art? _____   4. Nasser? _____

GUIDE WORDS SERVE AS SIGNPOSTS

Guide words located at the top of a page in a dictionary, encyclopedia, or other reference volume indicate the first and last entries on that page. A reader can quickly determine whether a word or topic he is seeking will be found on a given page by determining whether it falls alphabetically between the guide words.

A child must know the alphabet and have some skill in alphabetizing before he can use guide words. Furthermore, he needs a demonstration of where to locate guide words and how to use them to quickly narrow his search for the correct page in a book.

Numerous opportunities for learning and practicing all the locational skills discussed here are contained in the daily activities of social studies, mathematics, science, and other content areas. Teachers can demonstrate the use of a glossary, for example, in connection with an American or state history text or reference book. The value of integrating reading instruction with specific content areas is nowhere more apparent than in teaching the skills of organizing information.

Organizing Information: How Is Information Remembered?

While a good many skills could be discussed under the heading *organizing information,* it is possible to treat only a few major topics here. These include:

1. outlining
2. taking notes
3. summarizing
4. making time lines.

Outlines Show the Relationship of Ideas

The ability to prepare an outline is a fundamental skill useful to many youngsters in organizing and writing a report. At the same time outlining is a complex task demanding careful instruction and guidance from the classroom teacher.

The first step in teaching outlining skills is to demonstrate how to use the headings of a well-organized factual or textbook. The teacher can place an outline of a selection on the board. After discussing the various elements of the selection, and how they are related to each other, the teacher should direct children to read for the purpose of noting an author's organization of main points and supporting detail. A follow-up discussion can then focus on how the author builds his case by relating ideas to major points. It can be shown that the skeletal framework of ideas contained in the teacher's outline on the board have been expanded by the author in sentence and paragraph form. Outlining is merely the reverse of the author's process; that is, identifying main ideas along with supporting detail and properly relating them to each other.

This introduction to outlining focuses children's attention on the organization of a selection. The teacher must also call children's attention to outline use of Roman and Arabic numbers, capital and small letters, and how points are grouped together by indenting them under a heading.

Armed with an understanding of how an outline is organized, and the mechanics of listing ideas in their proper relation, children are ready to try some outlining on their own.

Special care should be taken in selecting the first material to be outlined independently by children. First, it should be well organized. Second, it should have sections that are clearly marked by headings. Finally, it should be fairly brief—probably not more than four or five pages in length. A chapter or part of a social studies or science book is usually suitable.

Children can be asked to complete only the details of an outline that has been organized and developed for them through several levels. The following exercise illustrates this approach. The teacher can then gradually withdraw the amount of assistance provided. For example, in the exercise the number of points under each heading (A, B, C) is left for the child to determine. Next, the wording of each head is omitted so that only the number of headings is provided, and so forth. Through this strategy the child is gradually asked to provide more and more of the outline, until finally he can achieve the entire task by himself.

Procedure for Teaching Outlining Skills[1]

Directions: Provide children with an outline that is complete through the first three levels. Their task at this stage is to compare the outline with the text, noting form and the relation among elements of the chapter.

[1]The outlines presented here were prepared from Kenneth D. Wann, Henry J. Warman, and James K. Canfield. *Man and His Changing Culture* (Boston: Allyn & Bacon, Inc., 1967), pp. 108–128.

Chapter 4   Ancient Cultures in the River Valleys

I. The Tigris-Euphrates River Valley
   A. Conditions in the valley promoted settlement
      1. Rich soil (silt) was provided by the flooding rivers
      2. Rivers provided moisture for dry land
   B. The Sumerians were first to live in the valley
      1. Developed good water control system
      2. Irrigated dry land
      3. Built cities of sun-dried bricks
      4. Food surpluses led to specialization
      5. A way of writing was developed
      6. The Semites conquered the Sumerians
II. The Nile Flood Plain of Egypt
   A. Physical features of the region
      1. Little rainfall in Egypt
      2. Flooding covered land with silt
      3. The Nile River begins in mountains of central Africa.

The second step in this procedure is to provide children with an outline that contains labels for major sections and a list of the number of points to be found under each label. Children must provide the information that is missing from the outline.

Chapter 5   Cultural Gifts of the Ancient Greeks

I. Greek Lands
   A. Physical features
      1.
      2.
      3.
      4.
   B. Sources of food
      1.
      2.
      3.
II. A scattered nation
   A. Greek city-states
      1.
      2.
   B. Sparta
      1.
      2.

The third step is to provide children with an outline that contains only a list for major sections and subsections. The child must complete the information that has been omitted.

Chapter 6   Contributions of the Early Romans

I. The Italian Peninsula
   A.
      1.
      2.
   B.
      1.
      2.
II. The early history of Rome
   A.
      1.
      2.
   B.
      1.
      2.
      3.

Next the children can supply all of the labels for an outline. Only the form of the outline is given, with the number of points in each section indicated.

Chapter 7   Cultural Heritages from the Middle Ages

I.
   A.
      1.
      2.
      3.
   B.
      1.
      2.
      3.
II.

After the teacher leads children step by step through the elements of outlining, they should be ready to attempt an entire selection on their own.

Children who experience difficulty may be taken through this sequence again with more teacher guidance.

The teacher will also need to provide instruction on how to condense a sentence into a few words that still manage to convey an idea adequately. Discussion and illustration of the fact that some words can be omitted from a sentence to produce a "telegram style" can be undertaken. For example, an outline of complete sentences can be placed on the board. The teacher and class could then jointly erase or cross out all but the essential words. The revised outline is contrasted with the original sentences for clarity.

Note-taking Involves Reader Judgment

Taking notes requires that a student be able to choose the major ideas from a selection, decide what is worth recording, and state an author's ideas in a condensed but accurate form. Most note-taking is done to help a reader understand and recall information he has read. Since note-taking is an active process that requires a reader to restate an author's points, it can often help reading comprehension. Notes also provide a record of what has been read so that a written or oral report can be prepared.

Note-taking and outlining are similar in many ways. It therefore often makes sense to give instruction on the development of these skills at the same time. In the previous section a procedure was discussed for gradually building independence in outlining. The reader's task was primarily one of recognizing main ideas and supporting detail. Note-taking can be approached in much the same way. Initially the teacher might place notes on the board that he has taken while reading a selection. Following a discussion of the teacher's notes, children could be asked to read the same selection and note the main ideas. Follow-up discussion could focus on how one determines what part of an author's message to record. An outline of the same selection could be prepared and a comparison made between it and the notes taken. The similarity of outlining and note-taking should then become apparent.

As with most classroom activities, note-taking, especially for the purpose of preparing a report, is more meaningful and better received by the child if he feels a personal involvement in the project. Simply assigning a written report on the Civil War may provide practice in organizing and recording information, but the risk is run of the task becoming a dull, mechanical exercise. By using a child's personal interests the same practice can be provided, but in a setting that promotes more positive attitudes and a better chance for transfer of learning.

Summarizing Highlights Main Ideas

Anyone who has asked a child: "What is your book about?" or, "What happened in the movie you saw?" knows how difficult the task of summarizing can be. Many youngsters find it necessary to relate every detail in order to answer such a query. At the opposite extreme some children can summarize the most complex story in astonishingly few words: "It was about a horse." Or, "Everybody gets killed." One of the problems confronting the classroom teacher is leading children away from such extremes to the point where their summaries include only pertinent information, but in sufficient quantity to do a selection justice.

Outlining and note-taking are actually specialized forms of summarizing. Skill in selecting major points is required for each of these tasks. Placing ideas in proper relationships is also important when preparing an outline, taking notes, or writing a summary.

The child's first opportunity to summarize is provided early in the developmental reading program. For example, he may be asked in Grade 1 to recount the incidents from a story in his basal reader. Teachers are constantly refining the child's ability to summarize by discussing stories and daily events with him, and through their own examples.

Formal instruction might well take advantage of the close relation between summarizing and outlining/note-taking. For example, a chapter of a geography book might be outlined. Next the sections of the outline might be translated into sentence form, thus producing a summary of sorts. Notes taken on the same selection could be used to expand the summary where needed. Such a procedure would effectively demonstrate for the child how a summary is made up of the main points from a selection. It also illustrates the similarity of summarizing, outlining, and note-taking.

Time Lines Place Events in Order Graphically

The time line can be a highly useful device for organizing information. It is also a specialized means for summarizing information.

Children require help in learning to read time lines, and later in preparing them. We suggest the use of children's personal experiences as a meaningful introduction to time lines. For example, the teacher might introduce time lines by preparing one for the current school year. Special dates—such as holidays, vacations, and the beginning and ending of school—can be featured on the time line.

Each child might then make his own time line. He can begin with the present and block off as many years as he has lived. Each birthday marks a milestone on his time line. Other significant events—such as the birth of a younger sibling, memorable trips, major news events, and events with special personal meaning—can be noted.

The next step might involve changing the scale from one-year intervals to five-year intervals. Events prior to the child's birth might be added. Children can interview their parents and other relatives for this information.

The final step is applying the newly acquired skills needed for reading time lines to a textbook or newspaper article. Children can prepare time lines for U.S. history, for example, or read the time lines provided by the authors of their textbooks.

Reading Rate: The Effect Not the Cause of Efficient Reading

To be functional, reading skills must be applied efficiently. In this regard it is essential that reading rate be maximized. Chapter 5 contained a discussion of how reading rate must be adjusted to one's purpose for reading. It was also noted that difficult materials must be read more slowly because of the reader's unfamiliarity with concepts and vocabulary. Chapter 5 stated that all reading should be as rapid as one's skill and purpose for reading will permit. Nothing has yet been said about the means for increasing the rate of reading.

Commercial speed-reading courses are designed to increase one's reading rate. Many such courses accomplish this objective by teaching correct study habits and helping the learner practice these skills until a high degree of efficiency is attained. Frequently the SQ3R method (survey, question, read, recite, review), EVOKER strategy (explore, vocabulary, oral reading, key ideas, evaluate, recapitulate), or other approaches to reading a selection are taught. These commercial reading courses help someone become an active reader—

(Courtesy of Audio-Visual Research, Waseca, Minnesota, Wayne J. Photography)

FIGURE 15.4   Students using pacing machines

Rateometers, audiovisual reading pacers, are used by students to increase the speed of their reading.

one who previews what he intends to read, notes section headings, reads the first and last paragraphs of a chapter, and mentally predicts what a selection will contain. With this preparation reading becomes a process of verifying what one expects to read. The result is more rapid reading accompanied by satisfactory comprehension due to the active mental involvement of the reader. Classroom teachers should and usually do teach these techniques as part of the developmental reading program. The guided reading lesson provides for these steps, but sometimes they are "lost" on youngsters who see little need for such preparation. Legitimate speed-reading courses offer little that is new or unique; instead, they help the reader to make more efficient use of basic reading skills.

The popularity of speed-reading courses—and their success—is probably due largely to the high motivation and goal orientation of their students. Many adults and older students want to increase their reading rates to keep up with the demands of their jobs or studies. Research evidence indicates that the gains typically obtained in such courses are often eventually lost, as personal motivation subsides and regular practice ends. These findings indicate that the classroom teacher should begin early to promote rapid reading and continue practice over a long period of time. Only in this way can long-term gains in reading rate be realized.

The classroom teacher can borrow certain aspects of speed-reading courses and adapt them for classroom use. For example, most people do not read as rapidly as they can simply because they fall into the habit of reading slowly. Speed-reading courses provide practice in reading at a faster pace, one that more closely approximates the reader's true potential. Various commercial pacing machines are available for pushing the reader along at a given rate. These machines teach nothing in the way of new skills; they merely help the reader to realize his potential. Figure 15.4 shows readers using such a device.

A much cheaper and equally effective procedure than any teacher can use in the classroom is simply to provide practice sessions during which children are asked to focus their attention on reading rate. By providing the opportunity for children to consciously try to increase their reading speeds, marked success can often be gained. Each child should be given material to read that is written at his independent reading level. The teacher instructs the members of the class to consciously read faster than they normally do. At a signal the entire group begins simultaneously to read. The teacher stands at the front of the room where he can note the elapsed time and record each ten-second interval on the chalkboard. When a child completes his selection (usually one page of material of 200-500 words in length), he notes the last number the teacher has written on the board (a 6 would indicate that 6 ten-second intervals have elapsed). While other children are completing their selections he can calculate his reading speed. The number on the board multiplied by ten reveals approximately how many seconds it took the child to read his selection. The number of words in the selection are counted and divided by the number of minutes to get the average words read per minute.

For example, suppose a youngster read a selection of 300 words in 15 ten-second intervals. The total time required would be approximately 150 seconds (15 × 10 seconds per interval equals 150 seconds). By dividing 150 into 300 the number of words read per second is found to be 2. Multiplying this figure by 60 (the number of seconds in a minute), the number of words read per minute is found to be 120.

Step 1: 15 × 10 = 150
Step 2: 150)‾300‾ = 2
Step 3: 2 × 60 = 120 words per minute.

Each child could keep a chart of his own reading speed.

Comprehension questions can be asked by the teacher to make sure the child is actually reading the material and not just running his eyes over the page. This exercise can be practiced several times a week with an emphasis on surpassing the previous effort without sacrificing understanding of what is read. Materials of varied difficulty and content can be selected by the teacher to give a more accurate estimate of reading speed under several conditions and to provide practice in adjusting rate according to the type of material read. Children can often give themselves incentives if they know what to look for. A self-inventory on flexible reading, such as the following checklist, can be such a stimulus.

The act of trying to read faster frequently causes an increase in speed. Success with a more rapid rate proves to the child that he can speed up. Regular practice increases the chances that he will read more rapidly when he is not being timed.

Following a Study Strategy

These comments about reading rate should not mislead you, for rate is important only in relation to the purpose for reading. A reader adjusts his speed depending on the difficulty of the content and the reason for reading it. The reader should have some method of guidance, especially when he reads to study.

One of the more popular methods proposed for developing study habits is that of the SQ3R (survey, question, read, recall, review) already mentioned. Attempts to present the entire process and to have children follow this procedure frequently meet with difficulty, since children are impatient with activities that seem redundant. However, if reading assignments are consistently presented along the SQ3R lines, the procedure may become part of the child's skills due to repeated exposure to the model.

A survey of a section noting its headings, pictures and charts, and listing questions that may be answered in the section as a group activity will prepare children for reading and will provide an example of how to proceed when they are reading on their own. The same procedure with recall and review can be directed by the teacher in the early stages of developing this study strategy. After some time the actual stages can be identified and explicitly discussed and evaluated by the class.

My Reading Speed

	Never	Sometimes	Usually	Always	Undecided
1. I read easy books rapidly and with understanding.	——	——	——	——	——
2. When reading rapidly I look for main ideas.	——	——	——	——	——
3. Before reading I preview the material to see with what rate I will read.	——	——	——	——	——
4. I change reading rate from one selection to another as needed.	——	——	——	——	——
5. I skim when looking for a single fact, name, or number.	——	——	——	——	——
6. When skimming, I try a temporary meaning for a new word.	——	——	——	——	——
7. I read silently without moving my lips.	——	——	——	——	——
8. I read groups of words rather than one word at a time.	——	——	——	——	——
9. I do not look back at words I have already read.	——	——	——	——	——
10. I read without pointing with my finger.	——	——	——	——	——

The key elements of the SQ3R method appear to be setting purposes for reading and for reviewing what was read. These two aspects require stronger stress, and in some instances it may be more economical of time for the teacher to set purposes for reading and then to have the class set purposes for reading. To accomplish this they will have to survey—asking for recall (or whatever relates to the purpose of the content) will lead to reviewing what was read when the child realizes he has forgotten or overlooked content. Because there is evidence to suggest that recall is strongest for that material one looks for while reading, care must be taken to set purposes that shape the reading behavior in the desired direction.

Assessing Progress in Mastery of Library and Study Skills

When new library and study skills are introduced to children it is essential that feedback on student performance be given. The teacher must know who is ready to move ahead and who requires additional instruction. Misunderstandings must be caught before they are too well practiced to be readily overcome. As much as possible the feedback needs to be frequent. Informal measures are usually quite valuable in assessing library and study skills. They will be presented in the next section. Formal measures will be discussed later.

Informal Measures Provide Useful Information

One source of information on student progress that is available both immediately and on a daily basis is a written exercise such as those presented in this chapter. After teaching the use of guide words, for example, the teacher usually provides an opportunity for practice by means of an exercise. While children are doing the exercise the teacher can circulate among them to check their work and help with apparent difficulties. In a sense these are criterion-referenced tests, and the teacher can study the completed work of each child for errors and misunderstandings. Small instructional groups can also be formed on the basis of common needs. Children who demonstrate a readiness to move ahead can be given advanced work. This differentiation of instruction is possible only if the teacher is aware of each child's progress. By regarding daily written work as a source of diagnostic data the teacher can build awareness. A checklist similar to the one that follows can be used to keep track of observations and to divide the children into groups with similar needs

	Great difficulty with this	Making progress but still in need of additional growth	Has a grasp of all essential elements	Completely independent of all assistance
Student's Name				
Work Study Skills				
I. Organization Can the student do the following? a. Take notes b. Determine relationship between paragraphs				

	Great difficulty with this	Making progress but still in need of additional growth	Has a grasp of all essential elements	Completely independent of all assistance
c. Follow time sequences				
d. Outline single paragraphs				
e. Outline sections of a chapter				
f. Summarize single paragraphs				
g. Summarize larger units of material				
h. Make generalizations				
i. Draw conclusions				
j. Derive "drift" of unit from table of contents, topical headings, topic sentences, and so on				
II. Knowledge and use of reference materials				
Can the child do the following?				
a. Place words in alphabetical order				
b. Easily locate words in dictionary				
c. Use table of contents				
d. Use indexes of books easily and efficiently				
e. Apply the above skills in the use of encyclopedia				
f. Use library card catalogue				
g. Use the telephone directory				
h. Understand the purpose of footnotes and bibliographies				
i. Utilize the following sources to locate materials?				
1. Atlas				
2. World Almanac				
3. Glossary				
4. Appendix				
5. City directory				
6. Newspapers				
7. *Reader's Guide to Periodical Literature*				
8. *Who's Who*				
III. Following directions				
Can the student do the following?				
a. Follow one-step directions				
b. Follow steps in sequence				
c. See the relation between purposes and directions				
IV. Specialized skills				
Can the student accomplish the following graph and table skills?				
a. Understand how to use the calendar				
b. Interpret a table by reading across and down from given points				
c. Understand the purpose of lines and bars in graph measurement				

	Great difficulty with this	Making progress but still in need of additional growth	Has a grasp of all essential elements	Completely independent of all assistance
Can the student accomplish the following map and globe skills?				
a. Understand and interpret simple street or "landmark" type of maps				
b. Make practical use of a road map "key"				
c. Use an air map; understand such symbols as railroads, boundaries, rivers, mountains, and lakes				
d. Have the knowledge and ability to measure distance, area, and elevation, and locate certain points				
e. Indicate ability to interpret the following:				
1. Outline map				
2. Population map				
3. Crops map				
4. Elevation map				
5. Mineral production map				
6. Rainfall map				
V. Other specialized skills				
Can the student do the following?				
a. Understand the significance of pictorial aids				
b. Observe and infer from picture representations				
c. Read and interpret charts				
d. Read and interpret cartoons				
e. Read and interpret diagrams				
f. Read and interpret scales				
g. Read critically in content material				

Another source of information on pupil progress that has been mentioned in previous chapters is teacher observation. An alert teacher can gain insight into the skills and deficiencies of students by observing their behavior in the library, for example. Self-directed youngsters who consult the card catalogue for books concerning their personal interests contrast with those who must ask the teacher, librarian, or a friend where to look. Children who know which reference volume meets their need for information may be observed in the process of answering a question or solving a problem. The teacher can also gain valuable information about a youngster's progress when special projects are assigned in one of the content areas. Again, self-directed students may be observed going about the job of completing their assignments; those with skill deficiencies will need special assistance.

Occasionally a special task may be assigned specifically to serve as a test of students' library and study skills. A considerable amount of diagnostic information can be gained by this means. A "Treasure Hunt" can be created, for example, which requires students to locate pieces of information in various and scattered resources. All those who successfully complete the hunt can be recognized in some way (with a paper cutout of a treasure chest on their worksheets, for example). Those who have difficulty with the hunt may need help with library and study skills. An example of a treasure hunt is given below.

Treasure Hunt

Directions: Use whatever resources you need to answer the questions below. In addition to giving the answer, also describe where you found it.

1. Where and when was Charles Lindbergh born? _____
2. Where can you find a map that shows the amount of annual rainfall in Arizona? _____
3. What is the latest population figure reported for Denmark? _____ What year was the last census taken? _____
4. What magazine in our school library recently contained an article on sugar beets? _____
5. What is the name and author of a book that would help you improve your table manners? _____
6. What is the origin of the word *city?* _____
7. To whom did the author of *Rasmus and the Vagabond* dedicate his book? _____
8. What chapter of your science book contains information about evaporation? _____
9. How deep is the Grand Canyon? _____
10. How many daily newspapers are now published in New York City? What are their names? _____
11. What are the names of the books in our school library written by Marguerite Henry? _____
12. Does our school library have a picture of former President Richard M. Nixon that can be checked out? If so, where is it kept? _____
13. How many phonograph records does our school library contain? _____
14. What magazines are available in our reading corner? _____
15. What is the largest bird in the world? _____

A teacher-made test can provide useful information on students' library and study skills. Questions can be asked concerning a variety of reference volumes, or one skill can be assessed in depth.

The classroom teacher can systematize his assessment of students' skills somewhat by developing a checklist similar to that on page 356. The items on the check list guide the teacher in a search for pertinent information. Through observation, checking daily work, giving special assignments, and so forth a judgment can be made concerning each child's progress in various areas. Checklists can be prepared to focus intensively on specific skills or to cover a broad range of skills.

Children can be asked to assess their own progress with library and study skills. A self-inventory that focuses on study habits is provided below. The information obtained in such a questionnaire can assist the teacher in planning appropriate instructional activities.

Are You a Good Student?

Name _____ Date _____

Good students know *where* and *how* to study. Are you a good student? Answer these questions *yes* or *no*.

WHERE I STUDY   YES OR NO

1. I have a special place to study.   _____
2. My study area has pencils, paper, and other materials I need to
   study.   _____
3. My study area is quiet.   _____
4. I have plenty of light.   _____
5. I study at the same time and in the same place each day.   _____

HOW I STUDY

6. I ignore noises.   _____
7. I work by myself.   _____
8. My work is done on time.   _____
9. I do neat work.   _____
10. I use a dictionary when I need one.   _____

What is the one thing you need to work the hardest on to improve? _____

Assessing Growth with Formal Measures

Many achievement test batteries—such as the *Iowa Test of Basic Skills* and the *Stanford Achievement Battery*—include a section on study skills. Multiple-choice questions in these tests require the child to indicate which volume of a set of encyclopedias he would consult for information on Chile, for example. Other questions test his ability to use and interpret an index, read a table of contents, select the correct reference volume, use a dictionary, and generally apply the study skills described in this chapter.

Sample Achievement Test Items on Study Skills

Directions: Underline the word that would appear first if the four words below were arranged in alphabetical order.

A. 1. flying
    2. collar
    3. pale
    4. gym
B. 1. chime
    2. gold
    3. basin
    4. chip
C. 1. smoke
    2. slip
    3. sky
    4. shade

Directions: Answer the following questions by using the index provided. Underline the correct answer. If you cannot answer the question in this way, mark the fourth answer: "Not in index."

INDEX

Baseball, 24
Diving, 48, 55, 78
Football, 17–19, 25
Hockey. *See* Ice hockey
Ice hockey, 88
Ruth, Babe, early life of, 41
  records of, 44–45

A. What page tells about baseball?

1. 4   3. 41
2. 24   4. Not in index

B. What page might tell where Babe Ruth was born?

1. 44   3. 41
2. 44–45   4. Not in index

C. What page might give you the rules for playing tennis?

1. 9   3. 25
2. 41   4. Not in index

Directions: Answer the following questions by underlining an answer.

A. If you wanted to read about the life of Winston Churchill, which of these would you use?

1. an almanac
2. a dictionary

3. an encyclopedia
4. an atlas

B. If you wanted to know on what page of a history book the chapter on the Civil War began, where would you look?

1. in the index
2. in the preface

3. on the title page
4. in the table of contents

The classroom teacher can gain some understanding of general class needs and the progress being made by individual youngsters from achievement batteries. For example, a fifth-grade class that averages well above the national norms on spelling achievement and vocabulary, but drops appreciably below the norms on study skills, probably requires special attention in this area. In utilizing this information the teacher would first need to determine whether a few students greatly affected the class average or whether the whole group contributed to the situation. Depending on what is discovered, several alternatives might be appropriate. In the case of only a few students having low scores, immediate special grouping on the basis of need might be called for. Remedial instruction could be arranged for these students. A more widespread deficiency involving most youngsters in a classroom might require a special unit on study skills which includes almost the entire class.

The classroom teacher needs more specific information about students' performances than that he can get from average scores. Whether only a few or many students need special instruction, the pattern of responses that determine each child's test score is important. By intensively studying a child's achievement test answer sheet much diagnostic information can be obtained. Errors of a singular nature point the way for remedial instruction on that skill—selecting the correct resource, for example. Widely varied errors suggest a general deficiency in study skills, thus indicating an instructional program of another nature. The patterns of errors revealed by studying students' answer sheets provides the teacher with the evidence needed to group students for instruction, and also indicates where the instruction should begin.

SUMMARY

This chapter focused on how basic reading skills can be made functional. Library and study skills help the reader to meet personal needs for information by enabling him to select the correct reference, locate the information within the right resource, and organize the information he finds.

The teacher's role involves planning an instructional program that includes all necessary library and study skills in a sequence that facilitates effective learning. The teacher is also responsible for demonstrating the actual use of reference materials and skills. Children require an opportunity to apply and practice new skills to problems that are both real and interesting to them.

Children should know the dictionary and encyclopedia especially well. These resources can be introduced informally in the primary grades by having a class develop its own versions. Other reference volumes—such as an atlas, almanac, *Who's Who,* and the *Reader's Guide to Periodical Literature*—are more specialized in nature and can be introduced as students find a need for them.

Locational skills include knowledge of the library and of the parts of a book. Children should be introduced to the card catalogue and the Dewey Decimal System in the intermediate grades. They should also learn to use a table of contents, list of illustrations, chapter organizers, glossary, book index, and other special features of a book.

Outlining, note-taking, summarizing, and making time lines are skills which help the child organize and remember information.

Through daily assessment of progress the teacher determines how instruction should be differentiated according to individual needs. Informal and formal measures provide the teacher with the diagnostic information needed to properly adjust instruction.

Terms for Self-study

Dewey Decimal System
guide words
glossary

card catalogue
time line
SQ3R

Discussion Questions

1. How could a teacher take advantage of a child's interest in butterflies to teach a lesson on the use of a dictionary?
2. Why is it advantageous for a school or district to develop an overall plan for introducing and practicing study skills?

part VI

Individualizing Reading Instruction in the Classroom

In order to individualize reading instruction a teacher must have control of the various parts of the reading program. A plan must be developed for managing students, materials, and time. Several systems for teaching reading must be understood, as well as how to match individuals with the appropriate system. Materials for implementing the instructional program must be known along with ways to broaden and supplement the basic program according to the personal needs and interests of individual learners. This part of the book addresses these and related issues.

16

Organizing
for Instruction

Regina Clare sits at her desk one afternoon in early August. She is imagining the joy and challenges she will find in this classroom in a few weeks when the seats are filled with wiggling, restless children. At the moment a task that seems almost bewildering to Regina is organizing the children, books, desks, tables, and the host of other components of the reading program into a smooth-running, efficient pattern. The sheer logistics of assembling groups, planning and scheduling independent activities, and somehow individualizing instruction seem overwhelming.

This chapter offers suggestions for resolving organizational concerns, and will consider questions such as:

Why use groups if individualized instruction is the goal?
What kind of groups can I use in my classroom?
How do I set up reading groups?
How can children not working with me directly be occupied profitably?
What is a management system?
How can group and independent activities be combined?

Every teacher, experienced or not, must deal with the task of organizing children and materials for effective instruction. Easy solutions to problems of organization may satisfy the teacher who is not much concerned about differentiating instruction or meeting individual needs. For example, all children in a class can be given the same reading material, directed to stay on the same page all the rest of the children are reading, and do the same assignments. Organization becomes simple and routine with this approach, but differences among children are ignored. The more alert teacher will consider a variety of organizational schemes that permit children with varied needs, interests, and achievement levels to be better served.

This chapter addresses the issue of how reading instruction can be organized to facilitate individualization. Suggestions will be provided as to how independent activities can be planned and managed in a classroom of thirty or more children. Much of the discussion will relate to the effective use of groups, since outstanding teachers usually combine grouping and independent activities.

Grouping as a Means of Individualization

The advantages of independent work as a means of individualizing instruction are fairly obvious. Each child can be assigned a task that is especially designed for his needs. Not so obvious is the usefulness of grouping as a way of individualizing instruction. Yet for most teachers the effective use of groups will be their most important tool in differentiating instruction. Therefore let us first consider the teacher's more common response to individual needs—grouping. Next, various independent reading activities will be discussed.

Groups Are Comprised of Individuals with Varied Needs

In recent years the movement toward personalizing instruction in schools has sometimes given grouping a negative connotation. Teachers faced with the impracticality of managing a totally separate and different curriculum for every child have been placed in the uncomfortable position of using groups out of necessity, but often feeling guilty about doing so. In one sense this guilt has some basis in fact. Groups of children are comprised of individuals who are more different than alike. Yet this need not be a problem if groups are used simply as a way of scheduling time to insure that the teacher and children will meet regularly in something other than a mass setting. The teacher's attitude is crucial. If children in a group are regarded as identical or even similar in terms of instructional needs, grouped instruction can be a trap. If, however, the teacher remembers that every child in the group is an individual with a unique background and interests, grouping can facilitate differentiation of instruction.

Clearly the alternatives to grouped instruction are not altogether desirable as a single answer to organizational problems. Whole class instruction obviously lumps children together in a gross manner totally ignoring individual differences. Yet independent instruction by itself neglects the value of interaction among learners and neglects the fact that the development of communication skills, including reading, involves the sharing of ideas.

It seems that the issue is not whether grouping as such is valuable and useful, but rather when and how groups should be employed. The next section will address these important matters.

Grouping Practices

One of the tasks facing a teacher is grouping children so that individual needs can be met in the most effective way. Let's look at three ways this can be done:

1. achievement grouping
2. grouping by need
3. interest grouping

Each method has an important function in an effective reading program.

Georgia Talbot is an experienced teacher of nine- and ten-year olds who uses all three types of groups at various times. Early in the school year Georgia collects information about her students' reading performances from a combination of sources. Recognizing that not all the children can successfully read the same level of text for basic instruction, she decides to create *achievement groups.* These groups are comprised of children who read at nearly the same level, even though their skill needs are varied and different. In Georgia's classroom the children fall into roughly four groups:

1. those able to handle an advanced book (Level 20 of the basal series she uses)
2. those reading at their grade placement (Level 14)
3. those who are unable to read "at grade level" (Level 8)
4. the slowest learners who range from nonreaders to those who read at a low beginning level (Level 1–5).

Georgia recognizes that one important condition for effective reading instruction is matching the learner with reading materials that are neither too difficult, thereby frustrating him, nor too easy, therefore unchallenging. While actual skill instruction must be varied within each of the groups to provide for individual rates of growth on specific skills, the *achievement groups* enable Georgia to schedule time with groups of manageable size and to provide opportunities for practice reading in materials that are suited to each child's level of reading.

While Georgia's achievement groups are flexible, so that children can move from one group to another as this becomes appropriate, they remain fairly stable throughout the school year. The main reason for the stability of achievement groups is that children reading at roughly the same level will normally advance together in reading and in sharing stories within the same books, provided their individual needs are being met through differentiated skill assignments. If the teacher cares to individualize within groups to the greatest possible extent, the children in these groups need not share anything more than common reading experiences. Often children in an achievement group will profit from common skill instruction of a developmental or introductory nature, however.

When a child in any group does not advance at a rate similar to his fellow group members, reassignment to another group for basic instruction is called for. The key factor in making such shifts is determining that the difficulty level of the reading material being used with another group is more appropriate for the child than is the material being read in his present group. Skill needs cannot be satisfied by movement from achievement group to achievement group, since individuals within every group have unique skill needs.

Alert teachers such as Georgia make extensive use of another grouping pattern to avoid the shortcomings of achievement groups in meeting skill deficiencies, *need groups*. Georgia frequently pulls children from various achievement groups to work on a specific skill. In this way, children with similar *needs* form a short-lived group that may meet for only one session or at most for several sessions. Once the need has been satisfied, the skill group is disbanded. For example, efficient use of an index might constitute the focus of an especially formed skill group. Georgia would gather together children reading at Levels 20, 14, 8, and 1–5 who have misconceptions about the purpose and format of an index. Instruction is provided; children practice the skill until it is mastered; and then the group members return to their usual activities. Occasionally the entire class might be regarded as a need group when a skill is being reviewed or a general misunderstanding corrected. More often, skill groups will be rather small, perhaps having less than five members.

Georgia also places children into groups according to their *interests*. Regardless of the reading level, children enjoy and can profit from meeting with others who like to read mysteries, sports stories, or joke books, for example. Whether these are related to hobbies, themes growing out of social studies and science units, possible careers, or passing fads, interest groups stimulate reading, deepen and broaden subject areas, and motivate the slow reader. Group projects around common concerns can give all children a chance to participate and make a unique contribution to the class based on personal experiences and individual reading tastes. Achievement levels are forgotten in interest groups, and everyone in the group has a chance to succeed.

Because interests come and go—especially among children—Georgia reforms the interest groups often. In October the children form groups on: sports heroes, current events, horse stories, humor, and stories of fantasy. By mid-November only one group, the one on sports heroes, continues. The horse story group broadens its base to animal stories, thus attracting new members from various other groups. A new group forms around the theme of science fiction; humor is replaced by historical fiction; and fantasy gives way to myths

(HRW photo by Russell Dian)

Figure 16.1   A need group

Small groups can cooperate until a task is accomplished and then be disbanded.

and legends. Seldom do groups contain the same members from beginning to end of the year, although membership becomes firm while displays and reports are being prepared for sharing with the whole class.

The key to Georgia's use of groups is that all categories are employed at the same time. Depending on the day and the needs that she hopes to meet, the achievement, need, and interest groups might all operate at the same time. Because of the ongoing nature of a developmental reading program, achievement groups often form the backbone of the organizational scheme, especially for beginning teachers. However, this need not be the case. The point to keep in mind is that each type of grouping between students in the class makes a unique contribution to the reading program. No single grouping pattern is sufficient for effectively adjusting the reading program to individual needs.

Regardless of the basis for the various formations, good grouping has several important characteristics. First, groups must be *flexible*. Membership in any group should be based on the child's potential for benefiting from instruction. If membership in another group is more likely to tap his potential, immediate action should be taken to move the child to this other group. Second, groups—particularly short-term groups—must have *specific objectives*. This means that a specific task or set of tasks must be clearly outlined and activities oriented to the accomplishment of the task. Related to task orientation is a third aspect of good grouping—*termination* of groups that have achieved their purposes. Even long-term groups should be subjected to this criterion.

Groups must not be continued beyond the limits of their usefulness. Fourth, groups should be kept *small in size* whenever possible in order to maximize teacher interaction with each pupil. It is not possible or practical to define what is meant by small in this case. For some purposes four children comprise a large group; for other purposes ten children can be called a small group. Numbers are not the issue; the point is that groups should be small enough to maximize the opportunity for individualizing instruction.

A Plan for Meeting with Groups

Educational textbooks are sometimes criticized, as are methods courses, for an apparent failure to be specific. Prospective teachers badly want someone to describe exactly how to—in this case—group for instruction. The standard response to this request is that a recipe cannot be provided because different situations require vastly different solutions. Actually, there is much value—if not much satisfaction—in this stock reply. A textbook or methods instructor cannot anticipate every plausible circumstance and provide a list of surefire remedies.

At the risk of being misinterpreted, we will be specific with regard to grouping for instruction. Only by working effectively with groups can most teachers begin to differentiate instruction and thereby take the first halting step toward individualized instruction. The plan suggested here is only a starting point. Considerable adaptation and refinement must be part of its application. Despite these limitations, it is a useful and workable approach to the task of grouping for instruction.

Suppose the time of year is mid-August. The workshop before the opening of school is just getting underway. You have been assigned a third-grade class for this, your first year of teaching. You decide to group for reading instruction. How do you assign children to groups? How many groups should you have? What reading material should each child receive? In answering these questions the use of a controlled vocabulary system will be discussed. Other systems could be chosen, yet teachers often profit from the guidance provided with this approach.

Until the children arrive, you are limited to information that can be obtained at secondhand. If used properly, the cumulative record file, which most schools maintain on each child, is an excellent resource. You may have a chance to talk with the teacher or teachers who taught the youngsters in your class the previous year. Old workbooks and other samples of the children's work may be available. You can begin an anecdotal record file by entering the information gathered on each child in a notebook, with a full page or two reserved for each one. Included will be a summary of such data as standardized test scores, unusual attendance figures, the results of physical examinations, previous teachers' comments, and the reading level achieved the previous year.

It is best to regard all secondhand information of this sort as tentative.

Surprising spurts or setbacks can occur over a summer. Personalities and attitudes can undergo enormous changes. Each child should enter your class with a clean slate insofar as academic and social behavior is concerned. Be cautious about letting the information gathered prior to the beginning of the school year bias or prejudice your appraisal. Instead, let it serve to support or point up significant information you obtain for yourself during the school year.

A September Reading Program

No reading groups need be formed for the first two or three weeks of the school year. Permanent groups should never be formed, but relatively stable achievement groups can probably be identified after several weeks of school, during which you should be actively assessing student needs. Children can be interviewed individually for personal conferences. Brief discussions and informal chats to assess interests, language facility, and attitudes toward reading and school are most valuable for getting information about students. A series of paragraphs graded in terms of reading difficulty, called an informal reading inventory (see Chapter 6), can be given to each child. Questionnaires and checklists can be administered.

The school and classroom libraries ought to be fully used during this period. The children should be encouraged to read independently during this time of data-gathering. Books read by each child can be noted and entered in your ever-expanding notebook of pertinent observations and information. Library books can be brought to personal conferences for discussion and for oral reading by the children.

You might take this unstructured period as a time to begin a program for sharing books. A variety of appropriate activities were presented in Chapter 11. From the standpoint of diagnosis, oral and written book reports by children provide valuable information for the alert teacher. Comprehension, the ability to summarize, skill in noting significant detail, facility with verbal communication, and poise before a group are only a sample of the kinds of behaviors that can be observed and noted through children's sharing of books.

Many school systems administer achievement tests during the fall. The results of reading and study skills sections of these tests can provide additional information which is valuable to the teacher in establishing groups.

Occasionally a structured reading activity can be conducted by the teacher. For example, a skill-development lesson might be given with appropriate follow-up exercises.

On the basis of all the information gathered, trial reading groups can be established during the first month of school. Assignment of children to groups should be based primarily on the child's instructional reading level. The informal reading inventory (IRI) or cloze procedure, discussed in Chapter 6, can be used to indicate what level of material is most appropriate for each child. Preferably the material to be used for instruction is incorporated into this assessment. Other information gathered during the initial three or four weeks of assessment is especially valuable in supplementing these devices. Since any measuring device has limitations, evidence from other sources can be used as well to make initial placements.

It may be a good idea for inexperienced teachers to begin with two groups. Experienced teachers who are not accustomed to managing more than one group may also want to begin slowly. We suggest these two kinds of reading groups be formed initially: (1) children able to handle the grade-level text, and (2) children not able to handle the text. The main reason for this modest beginning is to protect the teacher. You may not be ready to administer the details of teaching more than two groups, even though more groups may seem necessary. Increased experience and familiarity with your class will gradually enable you to add a third and perhaps a fourth group. But two groups will provide you with the experience of planning independent activities for some children while directing a lesson for the remainder of the class.

Trial groups are recommended so that obvious errors in initial placement can be quickly corrected. Early in the school year it is a simple matter to move a child into a different group for several days to give him a trial. As the year progresses, changes can still be made—indeed should be made—but the initial gap between groups is widened every day. Therefore, whenever possible, experimentation with group placement should be conducted early in the school year for the most part.

Each group should be given reading texts according to its level. Often the same series is used with an entire class, and two different levels of books in the series are chosen to provide material near the instructional level of each group. In some cases, two separate series are used so that each group has a different basal. This latter plan enables each group to read "fresh" stories and avoids the common dilemma of what to do with a child who knows a story because he once heard another group of which he was not a member discuss it. The important point is that unless materials appropriate to the reading level of a group are located and used, much of the value of grouping for instruction is lost. Even at this early stage you will want to regroup children often into skill groups and interest groups in order to get a feel for this dimension of a balanced grouping program.

With only two achievement groups a perfect match between the instructional reading level of each child and the reading difficulty of materials is not possible. It is necessary to aim for the middle of a group, choosing materials that are not too far removed from any child's reading level. The extremely high- and low-achieving youngsters are obviously missed when this approach is used. As your expertness permits, additional grouping and individualization of instruction must be instituted. Suggestions for expansion of the grouping program will be discussed later in this chapter.

Meeting with Two Groups

A specific plan complete with illustrations of classroom activities cannot be presented in a text unless several assumptions are made. First, a reading period of approximately sixty minutes for basic instruction will be described.

Actual time allotments vary among various states and for each grade level. Again, you are reminded that considerable adaptation of this plan will be necessary before you employ it in your classroom. Second, children grouped in this manner must be capable of working independently. No magic spell can be cast to achieve this requirement. It is essential that clear and concise goals be established for children who are working independently. The goals or purposes should be readily available to the child on a chalkboard or a dittoed sheet.

When dividing your time among groups it is necessary to consider the number of children in each group. Larger groups will require more time, since each child will need and is entitled to an equal portion of your attention. It frequently happens that more capable students are deprived of an equal share of direct teacher supervision. Such youngsters usually work well on their own. And most teachers seem to identify with the youngsters who struggle at learning to read, occasionally to the neglect of more able students. Each child requires direction, even the very capable. Often it is these youngsters who are most retarded in reading—if achievement is compared to potential. Therefore, in dividing your instructional time you should consider the size of each reading group and make a genuine effort to work with all youngsters, not just those who obviously have problems.

To illustrate, here is a plan for meeting with two groups of comparable size. The total sixty minutes of instruction will be divided equally into two periods. You must schedule yourself with each group for about thirty minutes of activity and also plan thirty minutes of independent activity for each group. Figure 16.2 will help you visualize this assignment of time.

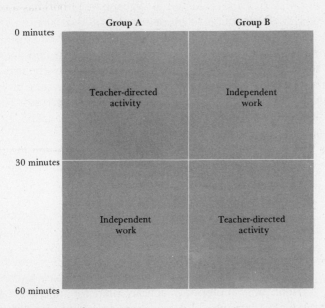

FIGURE 16.2   Meeting with two groups

This scheme represents one approach to organizing a reading period with two instructional groups.

Depending on what has transpired the previous day, various alternatives are possible. Suppose Group A has just completed the activities related to a story and is ready to move ahead to a new story. Group B, on the other hand, had completed a story the previous day, but has not completed several useful skill-building activities suggested by the teacher's guide and needed by the group. In this case the teacher might get Group B started on a worksheet he has prepared which requires the children to find descriptive phrases in the story and rewrite them in their own words. Since this activity will require only ten or so minutes for some youngsters, but the entire thirty minutes for a few, the teacher suggests that any spare time can be spent on free reading at the reading corner with the purpose of preparing a selection for oral reading.

Under teacher direction, Group A is given an opportunity to preview its new story and discuss the pictures, title, and general topic of the story. Several words are introduced by the teacher in sentences on the board, and the children are asked to apply their word-attack techniques to them. When he is satisfied that the group is ready to understand the story, the teacher directs the children to read for specific purposes. As the children of Group A are reading silently, the teacher can circulate among the children in Group B to check on their progress. Those experiencing difficulty can be aided and a note made on the special corrective instruction required by some children. Then, returning to Group A, the teacher has the children discuss the story. He checks their comprehension and tests their understanding of the new vocabulary. A workbook assignment can be given and Group A is left to work independently.

Returning to Group B, the teacher discusses the descriptive phrases the children found in the story. Each child gets to share some of his ideas and also compares the appropriateness of his responses to phrases that other children in the group share. The teacher can then collect the papers for further study and comment in order to individualize instruction where it is indicated. Next, the children might share their oral reading selections or immediately be regrouped for corrective instruction relative to the skill just used. Those needing no further instruction could go on to another activity—such as a reading game, a listening lesson, or a creative writing activity. To summarize, the teacher spends his time by:

1. starting Group B on the worksheet
2. previewing a new story with Group A
3. circulating among Group B, while Group A reads silently
4. discussing a story with Group A and assigning the workbook
5. discussing and correcting the seatwork with Group B
6. regrouping for immediate corrective instruction with Group B.

This very stylized plan gives a rough idea of how the teacher moves from group to group, and also illustrates the planning that is necessary to carry out such a scheme. Useful and appropriate actions both for independent and teacher-directed activities must be identified ahead of time. Teacher-developed materials should be ready and designed to meet the needs of the particular youngsters in Group *B*. The suggestions in the teacher's guide should be studied and appropriate activities utilized; other suggestions are to be rejected. Special instruction is immediately provided for members of a group who show evidence of confusion; those succeeding with the tasks are not required to sit through an extra lesson.

You may want to add a brief organizational period in this timetable prior to reading, and a brief summarization period afterward (*see* Figure 16.3). Only a few minutes are required to preview what activities are planned for the reading period before dividing into groups. Directions can be given then and questions answered in order to avoid confusion later. Again, it is important to have available a list of things to do and the goals or purposes so that students can refer to them easily. The brief summarization at the end of the reading period should be a positive experience for the children. With the help of your students try to point up the progress that has been made by emphasizing the successes of each group and occasionally of an individual child. You might also discuss occasionally why some activities were less than successful and decide with the class how to avoid such problems next time.

Frequently the amount of time allotted to a reading group should be adjusted according to the activity planned. For example, one group might be preparing a dramatization of a favorite story. In this case a twenty- or even thirty-minute period will be inadequate for making real headway. The teacher

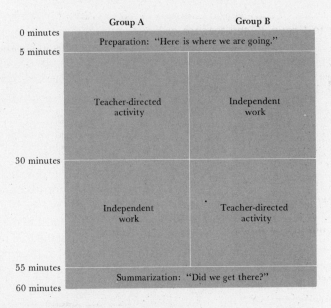

FIGURE 16.3   Adding preparation and summarization

A few minutes at the beginning of the reading period should be used to provide children with a sense of direction by clarifying the goals. A brief summarization near the end of the period can be helpful in evaluating progress toward stated goals.

who is flexible will simply extend the length of time given to this activity. If this means spending forty or fifty minutes with one group while the second group works independently, this should be done. By all means occassionally circulate among the independent workers to check their progress or start them on a new activity. You might even allow those who finish their work early to watch the rehearsal of the other group.

Another important policy—essential to running a smooth, efficient, and flexible reading period—is to permit interruptions by members of Group *A* when you are working with Group *B* and vice-versa. Some reasonable limit must be established, but a moratorium on questions from youngsters working independently is shortsighted. Given no opportunity to seek your help, a child having difficulty can soon disrupt a whole group or classroom. We suggest that children with questions be encouraged to stand quietly near you until you get a chance to help them. Then, while one youngster from the supervised group goes to the board or reads orally, you can turn to the child who is waiting and quickly provide the help that is needed. Any serious instructional problems in such circumstances must wait, but only by seeing and understanding the nature of a problem can you give the child something else to do and make a note to work with him individually on his problem.

Another possibility is to encourage assistance for a child with a problem by another member of the same group. More will be said about how children can help each other later in this chapter.

Expanding to Three Groups

You will soon want to consider adding a third reading group to challenge those youngsters who can handle reading material above the grade level. Two factors should determine when a third group will be formed:

1. Your ability to plan for and meet with an additional group.
2. Specific evidence that certain members of the class need other kinds of attention or activity.

Because each teacher will encounter his own special problems when grouping for instruction, no definite timetable can be given for expanding to more than two groups. Most teachers will want to experiment with a third group on a temporary basis. Appropriate reading materials and the membership of the third group can be decided by what happens during the trial period. The teacher can also discover how much of a burden is added to his workload by forming the third group (*see* Figure 16.4).

Dangers of Overgrouping

Because of special circumstances where one or several youngsters fall considerably beyond the scope of three groups, complete separation from a group may be required. A child reading material considerably more difficult

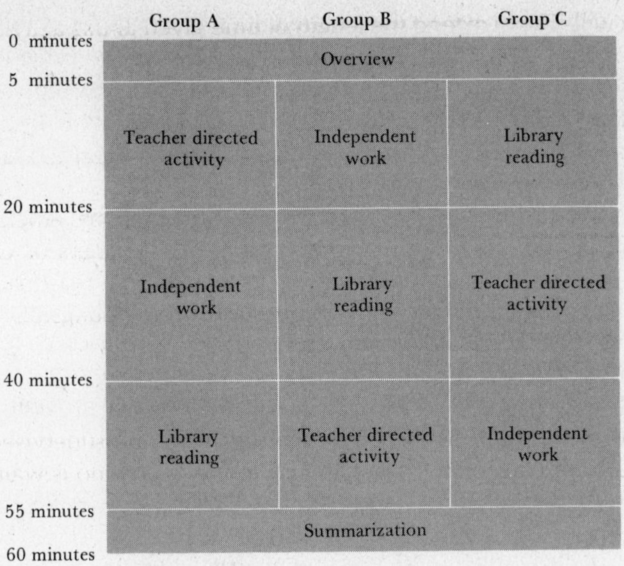

	Group A	Group B	Group C
0 minutes		Overview	
5 minutes	Teacher directed activity	Independent work	Library reading
20 minutes	Independent work	Library reading	Teacher directed activity
40 minutes	Library reading	Teacher directed activity	Independent work
55 minutes		Summarization	
60 minutes			

FIGURE 16.4   Meeting with three groups

With experience, the teacher can expand and refine the basic scheme for meeting with instructional groups.

than that read by his classmates will benefit very little from regular participation in group activities (occasional participation may be quite useful, however). Clearly, special provision must be made for such an exceptional youngster. At the other extreme, a child so severely retarded in reading achievement that participation in a grouped setting would be frustrating should be handled individually. It is hoped that a reading specialist can be asked to work with such a youngster. Expansion of the grouping plan to more than three groups will probably not be helpful in meeting the needs of such atypical learners.

Are more than three groups *ever* necessary? What is the largest number of groups a teacher can comfortably handle? It would be foolish to suggest that more and more groups enable the teacher to meet the needs of each child better. Three or four achievement groups should be adequate for most classrooms. Five or more achievement groups require so much preparation and scurrying about that only an exceptional teacher could operate effectively under such conditions. Teachers must be cautious about solving instructional problems with administrative juggling. Instead, a limited number of groups should be formed so that attention can be focused on individualizing instruction according to the varied needs of the children within each group. These guidelines for the number of groups do not apply to groups formed on the basis of skill need or interest. Such short-term groups can and should constantly vary in number and size.

Most teachers cannot tutor each child, nor do they want to teach only on a whole-class basis. A limited number of groups can be an aid to the teacher when arrangements are made for some sharing experiences for children. Too many groups defeat the purpose of grouping by requiring excessive time devoted to administration on the part of the teacher. The suggestion of two to four groups is intended only as a guide. The actual number of reading groups in a classroom is not significant; what matters is the individualization of instruction that occurs in the groups.

Individualizing Instruction within Groups

The point has been made several times in this chapter that grouping can facilitate individualized instruction. Grouping permits the classroom teacher to meet daily on a semipersonal basis with each child. Unless the individual children in a group are given differential treatment, however, grouped instruction is no better than whole-class instruction.

Differentiating Assignments

A number of techniques and instruments for gathering information on children's reading performance have already been mentioned. Included were formal reading tests, informal measures of reading, and teacher observations. Evidence for forming reading groups can be gathered with these tools. The same tools are vitally important for individualizing instruction within groups. For example, a basal reader test not only helps the teacher decide what a child's reading level is but also provides information on needed instruction. An informal reading inventory can be used to assess specific comprehension difficulties which require corrective instruction.

All information the teacher receives through observation, through test performance, or through written assignments is diagnostic data. The alert teacher translates such information into an instructional program based on the children's needs. Whenever an activity is undertaken by a reading group, the teacher can use the information required to differentiate instruction according to need. Youngsters in Group A who already possess a given skill—for example, matching sound and symbol—can be excused from a scheduled activity on that skill and can be given an appropriate alternative exercise. In many cases all youngsters in a group may need the instruction provided by the teacher. Occasionally only one or two youngsters will need assistance. Children can also be selected from various instructional groups and brought together for discussion and instruction. The ability to differentiate instruction as suggested here requires a knowledge of reading skills, the tools for assessing progress, a comprehensive record system that provides easy access to information on each child, and a teacher who is continually diagnosing.

Misuses of Grouping

Grouping is essential to good teaching. The practice is subject to some misuses, however, and these must be acknowledged and avoided. Some teachers, for example, use grouping as an excuse for regularly teaching a standard lesson to an entire group. In this case membership in a group causes children to lose their identities and thereby the pinpointing of their individual strengths and weaknesses.

Another serious misuse of reading groups occurs when the teacher mentally assigns each child to a status in a reading group and then assumes that same placement for each child in all other subjects. Trait differences—that is, differences within one individual—should caution us as to the dangers of this practice. The lowest-achieving child in a class during the reading period may be an excellent mathematician or speller.

Related to this danger of unfairly giving a child a low-achiever label is the old practice of seating children according to reading groups. We strongly recommend that youngsters be thoroughly mixed when seating plans are drawn. Some teachers unconsciously ignore one side of the room during a social studies discussion because the top reading group sits together on the opposite side. It is both unfair and educationally unsound to constantly identify a group of youngsters as a collective body, especially outside of the purpose for that group.

Still another misuse of grouping occurs when the teacher fails to break up groups occasionally or to combine groups for reading activities. The whole class ought to participate in an activity from time to time. A play or choral reading can offer excellent opportunities for whole-class participation.

Although personal taste dictates actual choices, we are opposed to giving reading groups names which have implied status. The Robins, Bluebirds, and Crows are labels frequently used as humorous examples. Why not use the name of the book being read or the name of a child in the group? While this seems a small matter, the stigma of group membership weighs heavily on some youngsters. The alert teacher will actively avoid contributing to this circumstance and seek to counteract it whenever possible.

Grouping is misused when all groups are not given adequate time. While the high-achieving group can and should work independently more often than other groups, this does not mean that teacher direction for the group is not needed. Indeed, with adequate supervision, capable youngsters can use their skills to make exceptional achievements. Left to themselves, they are likely to do only what is specifically assigned.

Children Should Also Work Independently

Our discussion of grouping places the teacher in a very prominent position. Much group instruction *does* center around activities the teacher plans and directs. Obviously, group activities can be developed and carried out without teacher direction, but the fact remains that one advantage of grouping is that the teacher can efficiently work with many children at the same time in this setting.

But it is also important to provide for *independent reading activities* in the classroom. In this case independent does not necessarily mean alone, but it certainly means without direct teacher supervision. Independent activities are important for several reasons. First, reading is fundamentally something that people do of their own volition throughout their lifetimes. It is through their own initiative and by their own self-discipline that they read for enjoyment, for information, or to solve a problem. Consequently, the more artificial the classroom situation in which a teacher directs reading, the less chance there is of building life-long reading habits. An independent situation controlled by the child himself probably leads to good future reading habits.

Another reason that independent reading activities are important is a very practical one: Grouped instruction is not possible unless the members of a class are capable of working independently. A teacher must be able to leave some children on their own for a period of time if the teacher is to work intensively with a reading group.

On a more general level, independent activities offer the child the opportunity to grow and mature as a person by making him responsible for his own accomplishments. While this important educational goal obviously cannot be reached in the reading program alone, there are unique opportunities during the reading period to contribute to a strong, healthy self-concept.

The Teacher's Role in Planning Independent Activities

Most teachers are greatly concerned about finding worthwhile activities that children can do independently. We are often asked how children working independently can be actively involved. More often, teachers ask: "How can I keep the rest of the class busy when I am working with a group?"

The teacher who wants only to keep children busy is missing an important opportunity. A healthy attitude toward independent work gives real emphasis to these pursuits. One of the major goals of reading instruction is making each child an independent reader—one who sets purposes for himself, organizes his resources, and carries a task through to completion. Only by carefully planning and conducting independent activities as an important aspect of the reading program can this goal be realized.

The first step in building independent work habits is deciding on appropriate activities. A worksheet assigned for the sole purpose of occupying children's time stands little chance of capturing their interest or enthusiasm. In such a case even the most responsible and mature learner gains nothing from the experience. A worksheet or activity selected because it ties in closely with a newly introduced skill comes much closer to being worthwhile. Children can be helped to see the importance of such a task and are much more likely to put forth real efforts to complete it.

A second factor to keep in mind is that frequently members of the same reading group are different and so do not need the same assignment for independent work. The worksheet related to a new skill is probably more valuable for some than for others. Occasionally the whole group *should* complete the same assignment. It is also possible to assign only part of a worksheet to some youngsters who require less drill, and then plan a different activity for the remainder of their independent work period. Only the teacher who knows the needs and abilities of his students can effectively differentiate assignments in this manner. The decisions involved in planning independent activities require that the teacher choose from a variety of alternatives.

Independent Activities Growing from a Reading Selection

One excellent type of independent activity relates directly to whatever reading selection the child has just completed. For example, the child can choose word pictures from the selection or prepare a section for oral reading. A group of children that has read the same narrative might prepare a dramatization based on the story. The selection can be studied for evidence proving certain statements true or false or for answering specific questions. Often a workbook or worksheet assignment can be found or developed by the teacher to further understanding of the narrative and promote analysis. Vocabulary items from the story can be used in sentences that alter the meaning of the words. A teacher's guide often contains numerous suggestions for such activities.

Independent activities can also lead the child to make immediate use of ideas gained from his reading. Individualized and recreational reading in particular ought to draw on such suggestions. An obvious, but highly worthwhile, activity is to pursue additional reading material on the same or related topics. The child might construct a model which summarizes or highlights events from a reading selection. Developing an outline of the story or making a comic or film strip based on the story's main events can also be valuable activities. A book or story can be publicized to other members of the class with a pupil-made poster, flyer, or map. Other individual projects include making a scrapbook, writing an original selection similar to the story that has been read, giving the story a different ending, or conducting an experiment.

Group projects, such as setting up a special display, can be undertaken. A radio broadcast, puppet show, or mural can be developed by a group. Often an appropriate excursion relating to the story can be planned and executed by a group with adult supervision. A quiz program on a selection can be a particularly effective group project.

Most of these activities may seem to be more appropriate for the intermediate than for the primary grades. However, with adjustment in the amount of teacher directions provided and the length of work periods, many of the same ideas can be effective with younger children as well.

Independent Activities that Give the Child a Choice

Some independent activities grow from the shared reading experiences children have in their groups. But other independent activities are "self-contained" in the sense that they stand on their own without reference to a story. Perhaps the greatest value of such activities is that they give the child a chance to make a choice. The following sections will describe some of these events.

Learning Centers Give the Child a Choice of Activities

Many teachers give their students a choice of independent activities by employing learning stations, or *learning centers*. Also called activity centers, these areas consist of designated places within a classroom where children may go to do a specific thing that is related to some concept or skill the teacher wishes the children to develop.

Learning centers are usually attractively set up to invite student involvement. Materials ranging from cardboard boxes to old window shades can be adapted in creative ways to encourage children to perform such interesting tasks as matching prefixes with their meaning, placing sentences into correct sequences, or performing literally hundreds of other reading-language-related work. Usually each center is separate from others and may even be sectioned off from the general classroom space by room dividers, bookcases, shower curtains, or other means.

While centers vary, they usually are based on certain common principles:

1. self-motivation
2. self-paced
3. self-selection
4. self-corrected.

To be sure, many teachers use centers prescriptively; that is, assigning some children to certain centers for appropriate practice of a skill. Nevertheless, centers provide children with many options and can be used to give them a choice of independent activities as well.

To the casual observer learning centers may appear to be haphazard and random in nature. Quite the opposite is true; centers are usually created with some specific objective or set of objectives in mind. All activities in the center are then designed to address that objective. By observing a child at a center, or studying the written results of his efforts at a center, teachers can identify skill needs, misunderstandings, and potential problems in a specific area. Used in this way, centers add a dimension to the informal diagnostic procedures available to the teacher.

Learning centers are usually popular with children because they make the learner an active participant. At one center used by a teacher in West Fargo, North Dakota, the child could spill a collection of five dice with letters printed on each side onto a table and then spell as many words as possible with the letters in three minutes. The child was required to write each word he spelled on a piece of paper and was challenged to improve his own record on subsequent tries. An egg-timer provided at the center added an air of urgency and accuracy was encouraged. The timing device motivated children to do better each time. Bonus points were earned for writing a sentence that illustrated the meaning of the words. Students recorded their scores on a tally sheet and placed their notes in a box so the teacher could review their progress. With this activity a child is active and has a chance to manipulate concrete objects he can touch and see.

Learning centers are also valuable for children with different learning styles because they are not limited by one approach that all must follow. With dozens of centers available at any time in a classroom, children can find those that suit their interests and particular learning modes. The very nature of centers arouses curiosity and promotes experimentation. It is also possible to create a range of centers from simple to difficult and from concrete to abstract.

Numerous resources are available to assist teachers in developing learning centers (Voight, 1971; Fisk, Lindgren, 1974; Don et al., 1973). It is important to regularly introduce new centers and revise old ones so as to keep interest high and topics current. Often, aides and volunteers can assist a busy teacher in creating and constructing learning centers. Teachers in several classrooms can also exchange centers to add variety. (*See* Figure 16.5.)

Cross-age Tutoring as a Means for Individualization

It is surprising how often techniques and methods are rediscovered in the never-ending search for better classroom procedures. What is discarded in one era sometimes resurfaces in another as an innovative practice. Cross-age tutoring is a classic example of how ideas recycle.

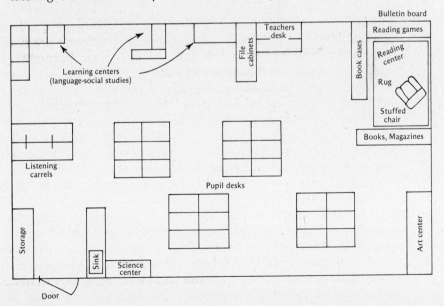

Figure 16.5

A classroom can be arranged to accommodate group, as well as independent, learning activities.

Simply defined, *cross-age tutoring* is having children teach other children. The familiar one-room rural school made extensive use of this technique decades ago when no other alternative was available to the teacher of grades 1–6 or 1–8. Rejected by many experts as recently as ten or fifteen years ago, as an example of teachers shuffling their responsibilities onto others, youth-tutoring-young programs are today seen as having special advantages for tutor and learner alike.

The value of cross-age tutoring makes it worth considering as a way to individualize instruction and provide meaningful independent learning activities.

Usually cross-age tutoring involves an older child working with a younger child. The older child assumes responsibility for teaching or reviewing some concept or skill that a teacher has determined the younger child needs. This does not rule out the possibility of same-age children working in a tutorial relationship, or even of having a younger child tutor an older one. Yet experience indicates that special considerations come into play in either of these latter arrangements.

The tutor—whether older, same age, or younger—must be well-prepared to serve his function successfully. This is the first value of tutoring. Children who might otherwise tend to loaf or even refuse to practice some skill can be easily motivated to master it if they know they will be teaching it to another child. If care is taken in matching tutor and learner, as a matter of fact, older, low-achieving children often profit enormously from the experience of tutoring a younger child. Freed from the stigma of doing "baby work," since he is preparing to teach a skill, he can and will work long periods mastering something well enough to teach it. A twelve-year-old boy, for example, can rehearse a Dr. Seuss story that he plans to share with his learner even though he could not justify to himself reading such an "easy" book on his own. The fact that this easy book is written at a level the boy can read successfully only with concerted effort is obscured by the tutoring program. Thus, needed reading practice is possible without loss of ego.

Tutoring is also valuable from the standpoint of the intense personal relationships it promotes. Working one-to-one, each child has close contact with another person on a regular basis. Emphasis is on a specific task where the chances for success are great. Competition with others is avoided. Cooperation is reinforced. Both tutor and learner come to respect each other and themselves in this kind of association when it works.

The ability of children to talk a common language is indisputable. A difficult task can often be explained by a child who sees it *as a child* and knows what makes it tough. Tutoring programs facilitate this type of exchange.

It is not always clear who benefits most from cross-age tutoring: the tutor or the learner. Evidently both can be happy winners. The tutor can build a strong self-concept of himself as a worthwhile individual with something to offer to others. The learner receives individual attention from someone who cares about him.

The teacher also benefits from a tutoring program in that additional human resources become available to meet individual needs better. Yet all is not profit, since some teacher time is required to meet with tutors and guide them in their work. Published accounts of successful tutoring programs indicate that an initial training program for tutors is advisable. Topics included in this training might range from how to reinforce the learner for correct responses to making flashcards. After initial training, tutors also require a teacher's time for general supervision to discuss specific problems, receive directions, provide feedback, and the like.

Dreyer (1973) suggests that teachers supervising a tutoring program should be prepared to:

have materials and assignments ready and available for the tutor

relate tutorial sessions to recent lessons through several kinds of activities

institute a spaced review system, thus providing tutors with a structured review method for each pupil

keep assignments within the time period and goals set by pupil and tutor

help tutor and pupil chart or otherwise record daily progress

assist tutors in developing motivation techniques—especially positive reinforcement

assign very specific tasks for tutors

teach tutors to make flashcards using the particular manuscript form the pupil recognizes

provide the necessary level of positive reinforcement to maintain enthusiasm and a conscientious attitude on the part of tutors.[1]

Despite the demands it places on a teacher, youth-tutoring-youth programs give the teacher another viable alternative for independent activities. Various other resources are available, if this brief description has stirred your interest. Gartner, Kohler and Riessman (1971) describe tutoring plans in great detail in *Children Teach Children,* as do Smith and Fay (1973) in *Getting People to Read.* Various magazine articles describe experiences teachers have had with tutoring (Dreyer, 1973; Zigler, 1971).

Independent Work Can Be Organized into Contracts

Reading teachers can borrow a practice that has been used in the teaching of social studies for many years for independent work—*contracting.* With this approach the teacher and child agree upon a certain quantity and quality of work. Specific objectives, means for reaching those objectives, and a certain length of time for the activity are usually spelled out in writing and "signed," much as a legal contract is signed, by both teacher and student. In some cases contracts are written for a certain letter grade if the teacher is required to give them. Often some product is developed by the child as a way of demonstrating the knowledge and skills he has learned while fulfilling his contract.

[1]Dreyer (1973), p.811.

To illustrate contracting let's visit the classroom of Don English, who teaches ten- and eleven-year-olds. Mary Yellowbird is a ten-year-old in Don's class who enjoys reading horse stories. Don believes Mary needs special instruction and practice in recognizing compound words, so he suggests in a conference that Mary and he agree on a contract that will focus on this skill. Don recognizes that a large part of the value of contracting lies in the motivation Mary will gain from designing much of her own program. He therefore identifies his concern and asks Mary to suggest how she might proceed. He suggests that her interest in horses be reflected in her learning program.

Mary decides on the following activities:

1. Make a list of fifteen compound words related to horses (for example, horseshoe)
2. Complete five worksheets on compound words.
3. Write a story about horses using at least fifteen compound words in a correct context.

A deadline is set for completing these activities (one week away) and Mary is ready to fulfill her contract. One copy of the contract is kept in Mr. English's folder, and one copy is kept by Mary.

Contracts prepared in this fashion can be designed jointly by the teacher and child to capitalize on unique learning styles. An active child, for example, can build a model or paint a mural to demonstrate competence. The great advantage of this approach is that the child assumes responsibility for his own learning. He decides how much he will do and how long it will take. Children can also work together on contracts when this is appropriate to their needs.

Teacher Aides Can Guide Independent Work

Most teachers have days when they seem to be needed in six places at one time. This is especially true if they are attempting to individualize instruction. One approach teachers seem to be turning to increasingly in order to meet the demands placed on their time is the use of teacher aides and volunteers.

Aides are valuable to the teacher in a number of ways. They can free the teacher from various routine tasks that require little or no training but consume inordinate amounts of time. Examples would be collecting milk money, taking attendance, mimeographing, typing, making reading games, cutting out bulletin board letters, correcting daily work, and so forth. Freed from these jobs, teachers are able to spend more time in planning, identifying, or creating appropriate materials, and in working directly with children.

Aides can also work individually with children or in small groups by supervising and guiding their efforts. Usually the teacher selects and structures the activities according to his judgment of the children's needs, and the aide carries out the task. For example, aides can write an experience story as it is dictated by children, listen to a child read orally, administer a test, play a reading game with children, read a book aloud, or organize a choral reading.

Tasks such as these require some training, but do not always need the teacher's skill. Other tasks require considerable training, but might also be appropriate for some aides. Examples are calculating readability levels of reading materials, recording oral reading miscues, explaining a phonic principle, or leading a discussion of a story with a group.

If aides are parent volunteers they can serve several other important functions. Parents who regularly participate in the school program come to understand and appreciate what a teacher is attempting to do in the classroom. They become a means for getting a complete and accurate picture of the school program to the community. Misunderstandings and fears regarding new techniques, materials, or procedures are often shortstopped by school volunteers who explain what is happening in school to concerned neighbors. Parents who speak the dialect of a region or subculture and understand the home environments of children can open up a two-way communication between teacher and children.

Perhaps the most important aspect of any teacher aide program is careful specification of expectations. Aides must have a clear understanding of what they are to do and how it should be accomplished. Training programs for aides can be of great help if certain tasks commonly assigned to them are discussed and the location of necessary supplies are identified. Aides should also be made aware of school policies that they must observe and enforce.

In a classroom that uses learning centers aides can provide a valuable service by supervising children as they move from center to center. Someone is often needed, for example, to resupply a center with materials or assist a child who experiences difficulty.

Many communities have a ready supply of volunteers that frequently is overlooked—senior citizens. Elderly and retired men and women often have time on their hands, as well as the desire to remain productive. It may be necessary to arrange transportation for some of these people, but the benefits derived by child and adult make the extra effort worthwhile. Senior citizens can read to children, listen to children read, supervise independent work, and perform other useful tasks within their physical limitations. And there is an added value for children in getting to know older people in this way, especially when the children's grandparents are far away or perhaps no longer living. Even homebound people may be willing to tape-record stories, cut out felt-board characters, and so on, if materials and directions are taken to them.

The national Right to Read effort seeks to overcome illiteracy in part by the use of volunteers. A 1973 statement by the International Reading Association describes how paraprofessionals should be selected, trained, and evaluated (*The Reading Teacher,* December 1973). An earlier, helpful IRA publication is *Handbook for the Volunteer Tutor* (Rauch, 1969).

Independent Activities Can Be Organized into a Kit

We have known teachers who gathered their independent learning activities together and organized them into a kit. While various schemes can be used, one approach is to group activities in the kit according to skills. All activities children can do independently and related to reading critically, for example, can be placed in a folder. Folders for various other skills are also developed, and the entire package is placed in a file drawer or box. Folders can be alphabetized by skill or arranged according to their order of presentation to children in the planned instructional program.

The activities in the kit might include worksheets and other paper-and-pencil tasks—such as crossword puzzles, riddles, and exercises from workbooks. Kits can also contain manipulative devices, and directions for activities that require more participation. Some teachers type each activity on a card called a Job Card, and give children the option of completing whichever "jobs" they choose. Obviously specific jobs can also be assigned by the teacher, as they are deemed appropriate.

A sample activity or job card is given here.

Job Card No. 51 Comprehension: Relationship of Cause and Effect

1. Read an adventure story
2. Tell something exciting that happened to the main character.
3. What caused this exciting thing to happen?
4. What was the outcome of this adventure?
5. What do you think the story character learned from this experience?[2]

Children enjoy adding their own ideas to a kit of this kind. Teachers can exchange ideas and adapt them to their programs. It is a good idea to have a range of difficulty within each skill area to accommodate children of various achievement levels.

Reading Games Are Excellent Independent Activities

Children respond especially well to reading games as another form of independent activity. Games are available commercially, and may involve reading directly or indirectly. At the very least, the directions for a game, the cards needed to play the game, and the playing board provide practice in reading. Some commercial games are designed specifically as reading games; others require extensive reading incidentally.

Many teachers develop their own reading games, or have aides and children make reading games the teacher has conceptualized. Basic game formats can be turned into literally dozens of skills activities. For example, dominoes (matching of tiles in a chain) can be turned into a reading game that

---

[1]*Language Arts Job Cards.* (Vancouver, British Columbia, Canada: B.C. Teacher's Federation Lesson Aids Service).

Gay Lea

requires the matching of: geometric shapes, letters, words, synonyms, antonyms, or homonyms.

Not only do games provide a pleasant respite from the usual classroom
routine they provide skill practice, encourage children to interact and learn
from each other, and appeal to several learning modes.

An example of a reading game is given below. You may want to see
Spache (1972); Cooper *et al.* (1972); Pratt (1960); and Wagner, Hosier (1970)
for suggestions on creating reading games.

Prefix Concentration

Directions:

1. Make a set of playing cards using 3" × 5" cards. Write a prefix on one card and the
   meaning of the prefix on another (for example, *pre* on one card and *before* on a
   second card). Make ten to twenty pairs of cards.
2. Two to four players sit around a table.
3. The cards are shuffled.
4. Place cards face down on a table in regular rows and columns.
5. Players take turns turning over two cards at a time. A match between a prefix and its
   meaning entitles the player to keep those cards and turn over two more. Cards not
   making a match are turned face down again in the same place, and the next player
   takes his turn.
6. Continue until all cards have been matched.
7. The player with the most pairs of cards is the winner.

Likened to concentration

Players turning over two cards in one turn that match
keep the pair and turn over two more cards.

The Ideal Independent Activity: Free-choice Reading

The best way to acquire most skills is to begin early and practice them
often. Champion athletes in sports ranging from golf to skiing acknowledge the
importance of practicing their skills regularly and often. Obviously, reading is

not a physical skill, but the parallel is illustrative. To become a proficient reader one must read—regularly and often.

Attitudes die hard and the attitude has persisted for a long time that free-choice reading is an occasional treat that should not be overdone lest children think school is all fun and no work. Little wonder that reading skills develop slowly and the reading habit fails to become internalized for children in this atmosphere. Happily many teachers and schools see the fallacy in that attitude. Nothing could be better for reading instruction than having children read materials they select and enjoy.

The ideal independent activity is simply having children read. A broad range of materials from magazines and comic books to encyclopedias and almanacs should be considered as appropriate fare. Opportunities for follow-up activities involving sharing of reading interests can also be regarded as excellent independent work.

Managing Grouped and Independent Activities

Taken separately, each of the previous sections of this chapter seem reasonably simple and workable. Viewed as a whole, the many parts may begin to look unmanageable. It is for that very reason that many teachers develop a traditional, "safe" organizational scheme which keeps children locked into a dull routine. Children not working directly under the teacher's supervision must sit quietly doing a battery of workbook or dittoed papers that will keep them busy and out of "trouble." Perhaps a brief discussion on managing a system with many disparate parts will help you feel more comfortable in giving the ideas described here a try in the classroom.

The key to running a multifaceted reading program is a sense of direction. The teacher must know where each activity is headed and how it contributes to the overall plan. This means quite simply that clear, achievable objectives must be identified for each component of the program. These objectives must be related to the broad goals of the reading program.

Individual tastes and beliefs will play a large part in determining how objectives will be stated. Behavioral objectives are a controversial topic, and we do not propose to resolve it here. Regardless of their form, however, when objectives are not clearly formulated, the many components of a reading program can easily get lost in activity for the sake of activity. Learning centers can proliferate, for example, without contributing in a significant way to improving reading performance on the part of the children.

Once objectives have been identified and activities, such as those discussed in this chapter, have been developed to lead to those objectives, the next task is to identify where each child stands with regard to each objective. A complete and workable record-keeping system is needed for this task. Some teachers develop a master plan with individual checklists for specific skill areas. They establish a file folder for each child and record progress on the various checklists. Each objective can be given a code and classroom activities can be keyed to that code. A learning center on using context clues, for example, might be identified as E4 to indicate Checklist E on Context Clues in the child's folder. The number 4 indicates that a specific subskill listed on the checklist, synonym clues, is featured in the learning center. By numbering the learning center (149) and noting this number on the checklist, the teacher has a simple cross-reference that identifies which activities treat a given skill (see Figure 16.6).

Whenever new skills are identified, they are simply added to the appropriate checklist, or a new checklist is created. When new learning activities are developed, the objectives are keyed to the code. In this way the teacher has a handy system for seeing that all activities contribute to the goals of the program.

Using the various sources of diagnostic information available, the teacher can identify which activities are appropriate for which children. All those who need practice with synonym type of context clues can be asked to visit center number 149, for example. Children needing help with skill A14 (finding roots of words) can be placed in a skill group for a review lesson.

FIGURE 16.5

Child's Name

Checklist E

Using Context Clues

Is able to use:
1. definition type of context clues
2. experience type of context clues
3. comparison type of context clues
4. synonym type of context clues
5. familiar expression type of context clues
6. summary type of context clues.

Learning Center 149

The purpose of this center is to provide practice in:
1. Using synonym type of context clues (E4)
2. Writing a creative ending to a story (G3)
3. Inferring the author's purpose (B8).

Many of the newer basal reading series have a management system that accomplishes the purposes just described. Teachers may want to key their learning activities to such a system or adapt the system to their own uses, depending on how they utilize the basal.

A management system for classroom instruction consists of:

1. a list of objectives (skills and attitudes) to be achieved
2. criterion tests or observation cues that match the objectives
3. a means for recording a child's performance on specific skills—a record that can be passed from teacher to teacher
4. a class plan sheet or a sorting technique for grouping those who need similar instruction and practice
5. a cross-reference chart and a file of materials that shows where in the classroom skills are taught and practiced; thus enabling the teacher to have immediate access to necessary lesson plans and practice materials.

Regardless of the system used, it is imperative that some management plan be designed if you want to conduct a reading program with many facets. Central to this effort is the importance of deciding what goals are to be pursued. With a large number of children and a variety of activities there are simply too many children and too many activities—too many variables—involved in a reading program to rely on your intuition alone. The alternative to a system of the kind described is to give every child the same program—hardly an attractive solution.

SUMMARY

Children with common instructional needs are frequently grouped together for reading. Differences among youngsters, as well as differences within the same youngster, prevent the creation of truly homogeneous groups.

Grouping within a classroom is essential for meeting the needs of the individual. Effective groups are flexible in membership, are formed to accomplish a specific task, are terminated when a task is completed, and are kept small in size. Information needed for forming effective groups must be gathered by a variety of means and on a continuing basis by the teacher.

This chapter presented a stylized plan for meeting with groups. During the first few weeks of school it was recommended that the teacher gather evidence on each child and encourage recreational reading. Teachers were urged to begin on a trial basis with two reading groups, splitting their time almost equally between the groups. Gradually it would be possible to add a third and perhaps a fourth group as the need arose and the teacher's ability permitted. Reading groups are not comprised of youngsters with identical needs, and therefore instruction within groups must be differentiated.

Children also require the opportunity to work independently. Some independent work can flow from a shared reading experience. Opportunities can be created to give children a choice and some variety in their independent work. These alternatives were described: learning centers, cross-age tutoring, learning contracts, teacher aides and volunteers, learning kits, and reading games.

The need for a management system in a classroom containing various learning opportunities was identified. One suggested management system was described in detail.

Terms for Self-study

need group   learning center
interest group   cross-age tutoring
achievement group   learning contract
independent activity

Discussion Questions

1. How can instructional groups help a teacher individualize reading instruction?
2. What is the value of giving children a choice among independent learning activities?

17

Instructional Systems

Some people think of teaching reading as teaching a book. That attitude confuses the materials that are used for instruction with the teaching methods employed. It is essential to know the difference between methods and materials in order to know what each contributes to an effective reading program. This chapter will help you understand that distinction.

You know that various instructional methods are used in the teaching of reading. The task of selecting and using one of these methods looms just over the horizon for you. You may know something about several methods, but be unable to tell how they differ from each other or how they work in the classroom. This chapter will help you understand the rationale underlying each instructional method.

Finally, you may wonder if one method can possibly fit the needs of all youngsters and, if not, how various methods can be effectively combined. This will also be treated.

In Chapter 17 you will find answers to such questions as:

What methods are used for teaching reading?
Which method is best?
What are the advantages and disadvantages of different approaches?

Can all children learn by the same method?
What is individualized reading?

Much like those in ancient times who quested the Holy Grail, educators have long searched for the best method of teaching reading. In recent times this search has spawned literally hundreds of investigations involving grand designs with hundreds of teachers and classrooms, as well as modest efforts within a single school or classroom. The major finding of practically every such investigation is that no one method of reading instruction is best for all children.

A considerable amount of evidence indicates that people learn in different ways. It is therefore not surprising that studies which compare teaching methods are typically inconclusive. Such studies often find a greater difference in achievement among learners taught by a single method than among those taught by different methods. Even when one teaching method is found to be equal to another, as measured by group achievement, when individual learners are compared, it is found that some youngsters do better with one method while others do better with the other. The same is true for children who do poorly; each method is relatively ineffective with some youngsters.

In the absence of clear evidence supporting the superiority of any one approach, we recommend that you make a careful study of the various approaches and select one you find useful as a starting point. Later in this chapter we will argue for the importance of combining features of several methods as your teaching experience makes this practical. But that discussion will be clearer after we have looked carefully at the various methods of teaching reading and considered the strengths and weaknesses of each.

Choosing an Instructional System You Prefer

Reading instruction must proceed according to some plan. Our analysis of the sometimes bewildering array of programs used in schools for reading instruction leads us to group them in to these four systems:[1]

1. controlled vocabulary approach
2. programmed approach
3. language experience approach
4. individualized approach.

None of these systems should be regarded as a cure-all; rather, each should be viewed as an instructional strategy with specific characteristics.

[1]The word *systems* is preferable to *methods* for two reasons: (1.) *methods* has been widely and inappropriately applied to materials and nonmethods, and therefore has incorrect connotations; and (2.) *systems* correctly implies a planned strategy for instruction with an underlying rationale.

Since individual youngsters have unique learning styles, one instructional system may be more appropriate than another for some children. The teacher has to adjust to the strengths and weaknesses of each system. A continued search for the *best method* of teaching reading appears to be a fruitless pursuit in light of the evidence already in hand. The key to effective reading instruction is evidently the teacher. The skillful teacher can create a successful reading program when permitted to teach with a system he endorses and understands.

The Controlled Vocabulary Approach

The controlled vocabulary approach is a highly structured system for teaching reading. The teacher is provided with a manual or guide that contains suggested procedures and activities; and the learner reads from a book which is carefully graded in terms of reading difficulty, and controlled from the standpoint of vocabulary, sentence length, sentence complexity, and sometimes story setting. Practice exercises are given in an accompanying workbook. In this system the presentation and reinforcement of skills are organized into a recommended sequence. In many programs supplementary and enrichment materials, as well as evaluation instruments, are available.

The controlled vocabulary approach seeks to avoid problems by controlling the teaching-learning situation. Systematic controls are placed on the materials the child uses in learning the complex act of reading, and specific directions are given to the teacher for planning learning activities. Each element in the scope and sequence of the total reading program is organized so that movement of the child through the system continually refines and broadens his skill in reading.

We prefer the label *controlled vocabulary approach* for two reasons:

1. the name focuses specifically on the distinctive aspect of the system
2. the more usual label, *basal reader program,* is so closely associated with specific commercial materials that numerous inappropriate connotations are unavoidable.

This discussion revolves around the teaching-learning principles that underlie the controlled vocabulary approach and the limitations of this system. The materials available in the typical basal program are discussed in Chapter 18.

Gerald Tinker, a teacher who uses the controlled vocabulary approach, groups students into two reading sections. One group uses the book designated by the publisher as being appropriate for Grade 4. The second group uses a book identified as a Grade 3 reader. No grade levels are indicated on the children's books, but the teacher's manual gives these grade designations because this is required by law in some states.

Gerald opens a typical lesson with his "top" group by building background for the story they are about to read. In addition to reviewing several ideas that are important to a story on bee-keeping, he introduces a number of new words and asks the children to apply their word recognition skills in

(OEO/VISTA photograph by Paul Conklin)

FIGURE 17.1   Discussing a story

When a teacher and students talk about a story they have read together, misunderstandings can be cleared up and difficulties can be eliminated.

identifying the pronunciation of each word. The children then read the story silently in order to answer several questions Gerald has written on the chalkboard.

The next day Gerald discusses the story with the children. Misunderstandings are identified, and several parts of the story are reread in order to clear up those difficulties. Next, Gerald introduces a skill following a procedure suggested in the teacher's guide. The skill is practiced in a chalkboard activity and the children complete an exercise in their workbooks on this skill. Several children who especially liked the story on bee-keeping go to the school library to locate a book the teacher's guide identifies for enrichment and extension of the topic. Other children in the group listen to a record that accompanies the reading series on a related topic.

This cycle is repeated with minor variations for subsequent stories in the reading series. The skills program is carefully related to the stories, and systematic review and practice of skills is provided for in the teacher's guide and ancillary materials. Gerald Tinker deviates from the plan as his judgment dictates, but for the most part he adheres to the structure and activities recommended by the system.

Rationale of the Controlled Vocabulary Approach

The controlled vocabulary approach is built on the premise that learning to read is a potentially difficult undertaking. The teacher, as well as the child, can easily experience difficulty and even failure with reading instruction. Consequently, the process of learning to read is analyzed, and the significant parts are organized into a logical, coherent series of lessons in this system.

1. *Content and setting should proceed from the known to the unknown.* The controlled vocabulary approach is based on a principle commonly accepted by educators: Proceed from the known to the unknown. The content and setting of controlled vocabulary stories reflect the same idea: Begin with what is familiar and/or interesting to the learner. Neighborhood scenes, with family and pets as the central characters, are frequently found in primary-grade controlled vocabulary stories. Fanciful and imaginative stories are common. The control of story content is intended to help the child learn to read by eliminating potentially troublesome factors, such as unfamiliar concepts and story characters.

2. *Vocabulary should be systematically repeated.* The principle of systematic repetition of words is another central element in the controlled vocabulary approach to reading. The rationale followed is that repeated exposure to a word is necessary for its mastery. In the controlled vocabulary approach a small number of new words is introduced in each story, and each new word is repeated a number of times to provide practice and reinforcement for the student.

3. *Reading selections should gradually grow more difficult.* The readability of stories in the controlled vocabulary approach is carefully graded to require more reading skill from story to story and from book to book. Sentence length and complexity, the number of characters in the story, and the length of stories all gradually increase. Stories gradually require more understanding of sequence and more inference on the part of the reader. The learner is asked to assume more sophisticated reading tasks, but he is led to do so in a systematic, controlled fashion.

4. *Reading skills should be systematically taught.* Reading skills are identified and taught with a high degree of organization and planning. The principles of continued practice and movement from the simple to the complex are also important in skill development. Workbook and suggested teacher-directed activities regularly introduce and reinforce reading skills. Finding the main idea is an example of a skill introduced early and developed in more difficult stories.

5. *A "complete" program is developed for teachers and leaders.* Materials are provided for the learner and the teacher. Teaching suggestions that have been developed by teams of reading experts, as well as tests and other evaluation tools, are provided for the teacher. References are given for supplementary and enrichment materials, such as filmstrips and reading games. Recently many of these materials have been included in the program itself.

The controlled vocabulary approach is not regarded by its proponents as a program that can teach all aspects of reading, but it is decidedly more complete and self-contained than any of the other systems for teaching reading.

Limitations of the Controlled Vocabulary Approach

1. *Today's children do not need such controls.* Some authorities have criticized the controlled vocabulary approach on the basis of the highly controlled nature of the program. They argue that present controlled vocabulary programs destroy rather than create an interest in learning to read. The critics point out that today's youngsters are sophisticated learners. Such criticisms are valid. Television has catapulted four-year-olds into space, under the sea, and into the heart of a living man; fourth-graders can watch the proceedings of Congress or the United Nations in color.

Technology, the critics argue, has further expanded the horizons of youngsters today by making transcontinental travel a common occurrence among many. Some children in Pittsburgh and Nashville stand a good chance of seeing Disneyland or the Astrodome before they are six years old. Families have more leisure time; rapid modes of transportation are available; and the means necessary for such travel are present.

2. *The language used in the stories is stilted and unnatural.* Although great strides have been made in recent years toward making the language of basal readers more like speech, the control and repetition dictated by a controlled vocabulary approach necessarily cause the language to be unnatural. Studies such as those by Strickland (1962) and Loban (1963) demonstrate that today's learner arrives in Grade 1 with astounding verbal facility. While estimates vary, the evidence currently available indicates that a six-year-old has a speaking vocabulary of at least 20,000 words. The six-year-old uses every form of sentence, including complex, compound, and complex-compound structures. Children's oral utterances have also increased in length.

It should be noted, however, that educators have sometimes incorrectly judged the interests and reactions of children. The "dry" stories of the primary-grade reading program may well be entirely satisfactory from the child's viewpoint. Repetition of a word may be more of a blessing than a bore to the youngster who struggles to decode each word he encounters.

The criticisms cited merit careful consideration, but one must not ignore the overwhelming success which controlled vocabulary programs have enjoyed.

3. *Educators misuse the system.* One criticism of the controlled vocabulary approach is directed more at misuse of the system than at the system itself. Despite cautions to the contrary, many educators regard the controlled vocabulary package as a total reading program. In some cases children do practically all of their reading in the graded reader and are not allowed to skip sections of the book. The workbook is regularly assigned without regard to individual need. Every suggested activity in the teacher's manual is followed. If the controlled vocabulary program has any responsibility for this misuse, it is largely indirect, since it *appears* to be a complete program.

4. *Reading is taught in a stylized manner unlike real-life reading.* Another disadvantage of the controlled vocabulary approach is that its structured nature makes reading instruction seem artificial when compared to the uncontrolled reading a child does for recreation or in other subjects. In this sense the controlled vocabulary approach does not present a realistic reading task; consequently, the important transfer of skills from the instructional program to application in everyday reading may be hampered. For example, seldom does the child begin reading a news item or directions for assembling a model airplane by studying the new vocabulary he will encounter. Yet the controlled vocabulary system introduces new words prior to reading as a regular procedure. Again, this criticism is not directed entirely at the system but at least partly at the manner in which teachers use it. Teachers' manuals often recommend that children be given the opportunity to practice reading skills in real-life settings. The apparent completeness of the controlled vocabulary approach may account in part for an unsatisfactory emphasis on the transfer of skills.

Vocabulary Can Be Controlled in Various Ways

Despite a great deal of similarity among all controlled vocabulary reading programs, distinct differences do exist. Basically the differences have to do with how the vocabulary used in stories is actually controlled. One approach is to control the vocabulary according to the sound-symbol association being introduced or practiced. A second approach is control through the spelling pattern being emphasized at any given stage. A third type of vocabulary control is based on word frequency.[2] In all these cases vocabulary control is exercised to add an element of logic and sequence to the instructional program.

[2]Word frequency is related to the number of times a word appears in oral or written context. Some words are more common than others; that is, they are used more often. Being familiar with words of high frequency enables a reader to recognize a greater percentage of the words he encounters. Some word lists are developed from tabulations of children's oral and written communications. Others are based on an analysis of the words used in popular basal reader programs.

The chapter on decoding (Chapter 9) described how each of these controls is employed to introduce word recognition strategies to beginning readers. It is worth looking again at those strategies, this time with attention to how the systems vary on the matter of vocabulary control so that you will be able to study reading programs available for use in your classroom with a clear understanding of how the programs are organized and why there are differences among them. Ultimately this will make you a better judge of what materials you wish to use if the controlled vocabulary approach appeals to you.

Phonic programs that begin with isolated sounds (for example, "the sound of the letter b") characterize the sound-symbol type of vocabulary control. Early learning tasks involve the reader in associating sound with individual letters and combinations of letters, blending sounds, and generally mastering the separate elements of the printed code. Some sound-symbol programs begin with consonants and then move to vowels, consonant clusters, vowel clusters, syllabication, and so forth. Others begin with vowels and follow another sequence. Stories included in these programs emphasize and illustrate whatever sound-symbol relationship the children are learning in the skills program (for example, one story may feature words with the letter w in beginning, medial, and ending positions).

So-called linguistic programs are organized around spelling patterns. Early learning tasks present the reader with words that are "regular" in pronunciation and follow some consonant-vowel arrangement. Stories present families of words that follow a pattern (for example, A fat rat sat on a mat). When one spelling pattern has been mastered, other patterns are introduced (for example, consonant-vowel-consonant-vowel, consonant-vowel-vowel-consonant).

Programs which use words of high frequency are not as easily identified as the other types of controlled vocabulary programs. There is nothing very distinct about stories that employ words such as will, run, boat, water, the, house, and so forth, except that no particular sound-symbol relationship is emphasized and no specific spelling pattern is followed. Words introduced initially are simply ones most children are expected to understand and use in their conversations. Typically the instructional program begins by teaching a body of sight words. The control exercised over vocabulary is primarily one of numbers. Each story introduces only a limited number of "new" words.

The Programmed Approach

First cousin to the controlled vocabulary approach is another system for teaching reading that carefully structures and sequences instruction: the programmed approach. Despite a number of similarities, we choose not to lump the programmed approach with the controlled vocabulary approach because of some distinct characteristics that will be discussed here.

Hilda Fortune teaches reading with the programmed approach. The materials for her system require the use of a machine—although not all programmed approaches involve machines. Hilda's program uses tape recorders. Each child goes to a listening post, where a cassette recorder, headphones, and a workbook are provided. The child puts the tape cartridge on which he is working into the recorder, puts on his headphones, and follows the directions of the narrator. The child is frequently asked by the voice on the tape to circle or underline one of three words printed on his workbook page, or to write a word in a blank. The narrator gives the child the correct answer, discusses why that answer is correct, and explains why other answers are incorrect. Proceeding step by step, the child works his way through the tape following the directions of the narrator and comparing his responses to those identified as correct.

The teacher is free during this listening time to walk around the room visiting each child as he works on his program. By noting the child's responses, the teacher can quickly identify progress, as well as difficulties, and plan her teaching accordingly. Mark may be jumped ahead several lessons; Susie may repeat a lesson, or begin a corrective sequence of lessons.

Rationale of the Programmed Approach

1. *Objectives are stated as observable behaviors.* Based on the work of behavioral psychologists, programmed instruction teaches by taking the student through a series of carefully planned steps, often in the form of statements or questions, culminating in some *predesignated terminal behavior.* For example, a beginning reader can be led through a step-by-step procedure into recognizing a family of words that rhyme with cat. Typically the terminal behavior is observable or behavioral. In this case the child would demonstrate his newly acquired skill or knowledge by correctly picking from a list of ten words the five that have the same spelling pattern as cat.

2. *The learner makes a response at each step.* Programmed instruction often requires a *series of responses* on the part of the learner. The steps in a program are arranged so that correct responses are practically certain. Clues are often provided to help the learner. For example, only the last two letters may be missing from the correct response to a question or statement in the program. As the program proceeds, the clues become fewer and the learner must provide more of the correct word or answer himself. Eventually the learner supplies an entire word without the benefit of prompts.

   This process of gradual clue withdrawal is referred to as *successive approximation;* and it is by a series of such approximations that the learner's behavior is "shaped."

3. *The learner receives immediate feedback and reinforcement.* Most programmed instruction provides *immediate feedback* to the learner concerning the correctness of his responses. After the learner supplies a response the teacher or program provides the correct answer for comparison with the learner's answer. Since each step is carefully designed to avoid incorrect

(Photo by Carl B. Smith)

FIGURE 17.2   Children at a listening table

A listening post, recorders, and headsets are used with this programmed approach to reading instruction.

responses, the learner is afforded *immediate* reinforcement. Proceeding a small step at a time, he can know his progress as it happens, and he is rewarded for each correct response. These features make learning efficient and provide real support for the programmed approach. An example of a programmed exercise is presented on pages 406 and 407.

4. *The learner works at his own pace.* Self-pacing is another important aspect of programmed instruction. Each learner can progress through a program at his own rate. The able learner is not held back by slower classmates, while very slow youngsters can take whatever time they need with each step, or "frame." With the programmed approach the slow learner makes as many correct responses as the bright student and suffers fewer failures than he would in a typical classroom setting.

5. *Programs focus on specific skills.* Programs are often written to develop specific skills and concepts. Since children work independently with pro-

grammed materials, the teacher can easily match the learner with a program that meets his individual needs. A youngster who experiences difficulty with short vowel sounds, for example, can be assigned to remedial work in a program suited specifically to this need. Children who are absent and might not otherwise be able to make up important lessons are able to do so with the programmed approach. The child simply begins where he left off before he was absent.

6. *Skills are sequenced carefully*. Perhaps most important, the programmed approach presents skills and concepts in a carefully organized, logically sequenced series of steps. Instructional goals are established ahead of time, and each step contributes to the eventual achievement of the objectives. Those responsible for developing programs are alert to possible confusion or errors, and anticipate them; and systematic research is conducted to guarantee that a program leads to the desired behavior.

Sample Program on Phonics

Directions: Place a piece of paper on the page below at the number one. Read the statement and write in the word you think fits. Next move your paper down to line number 2. Compare your answer with the correct answer. If you are correct, go on to line 3, repeating the procedure. If you are incorrect, go back to see why your answer was wrong. Then proceed to line 3.

One approach to the teaching of reading is by emphasizing sound-symbol associations. Often called phonics, in this approach the child is taught to decode by associating

1 a sound with a _____ .

---

2   symbol

Several strategies can be used to teach sound-symbol associations. Regardless
3 of the strategy, the approach emphasizing sound-symbol is called_____ .

---

4   phonics

One phonics approach teaches the child by beginning with individual letters
5 and the _____ associated with each letter.

---

6   sound

By practicing the sound-symbol association, the child learns automatic
7 responses that help him sound out words letter by _____ .

---

8   letter

9 Once the child has a sound for every letter he can sound
   out _____ .

10   words

11 This approach is called the synthetic approach to phonics. In the synthetic
   approach the child learns to associate individual letters and _____ .

12   sounds

13 Another approach has the child learn a small body of words at sight. Similarities among these words are then observed by the child. With this approach the child
   first reads whole _____

14   words

Limitations of the Programmed Approach

1. *Programmed learning can become monotonous.* Such pains are taken to
   eliminate the possibility that the student will make an incorrect response in
   programmed materials that little challenge or interest may remain for the
   learner. We have found that once the novelty of this approach has worn off
   students may find it monotonous.
2. *All students do the same work.* The step-by-step sequence of programmed
   materials tends to be extremely slow for most learners. The more able
   learner in particular may be bored by repetition of what to him is obvious.
   In a few programs an adjustment in sequence, often called *branching,*
   permits those who need less background to skip ahead and work at a faster
   rate. When branching is not provided, however, every student, fast or slow,
   goes through exactly the same steps. The argument that able students can
   pace themselves is not a satisfactory provision for individual needs.
3. *The teacher is less involved in instruction.* The interaction between teacher
   and child is not completely eliminated by the programmed approach.
   Indeed, freed from constant group work and paper correcting, the teacher
   may have more time for such interaction in a classroom using programmed
   materials. However, the impersonality of programmed instruction is an
   obvious limitation of this approach. Opportunities for discussion and

exchange of ideas are decidedly reduced. The teacher is less responsible for instruction and therefore may know less about the needs of individual children.

4. *Emphasis is placed on one correct answer.* At a time when many educators are urging greater freedom of thought and more creativity in the classroom the programmed approach, with its built-in emphasis on a single correct answer, may not be contributing much to our educational goals. Certainly, for example, interpretive and creative reading are worthy segments of an instructional program, yet it seems unlikely that programmed materials, as they are presently conceived, can effectively stimulate students in these areas of learning.

5. *Programs handicap poor readers.* Finally—and ironically—in most programmed approaches to the teaching of reading children must be able to read in order to respond. The child who has difficulty in reading is obviously at a disadvantage in such a program.

The Language Experience Approach

We have looked at two highly structured systems for the teaching of reading. The structure so evident in the controlled vocabulary and programmed approaches is pretty much one that is created by adults according to their ideas of how reading can best be broken down and sequenced into logical steps. In contrast, the language experience approach is tied directly to the child, his interests, and his needs. This is not to say that structure is absent in the language experience approach, or that adults do not have to exercise judgment about the order and content of instructional activities, for that would be inaccurate. But the language experience approach is clearly more child-centered and spontaneous than either of the systems we have discussed so far.

In connection with a Teacher Corps teacher training program in Grand Forks, North Dakota, one summer a group of children ranging in ages from six to thirteen attended a summer school. The Teacher Corps Interns were asked to think of ways to make a summer school program interesting and yet educational for children. The language experience approach was used extensively in the activities that were generated. We will describe several of these activities to illustrate how the approach works.

In a curriculum planning session the Interns decided that the community of Grand Forks offered several interesting possibilities for field trips. One of these was a potato-chip processing plant; the second was a railroad roundhouse. Planning was undertaken and arrangements made to visit those sites.

One morning two Interns gathered the twenty or so children around them to talk about how people in Grand Forks earn a living. Even the younger children had ideas on this subject. Farming and railroading were identified, along with many other occupations. Discussion focused first on what farmers grew in the Grand Forks area. Sugar beets, wheat, and potatoes were all mentioned. The children talked about ways that these crops are important to

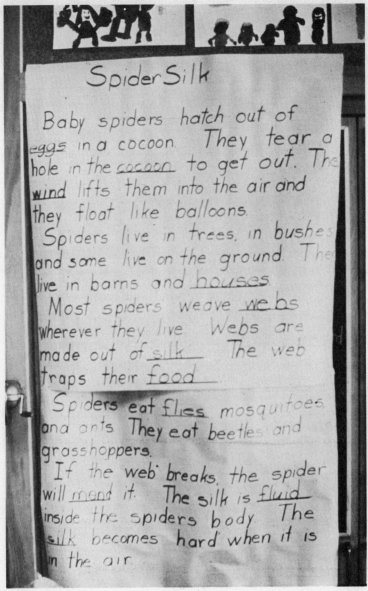

SpiderSilk

Baby spiders hatch out of eggs in a cocoon. They tear a hole in the cocoon to get out. The wind lifts them into the air and they float like balloons.

Spiders live in trees, in bushes and some live on the ground. They live in barns and houses.

Most spiders weave webs wherever they live. Webs are made out of silk. The web traps their food.

Spiders eat flies, mosquitoes and ants. They eat beetles and grasshoppers.

If the web breaks, the spider will mend it. The silk is fluid inside the spiders body. The silk becomes hard when it is in the air.

(Photo by Carl B. Smith)

FIGURE 17.3   An experience chart

Research and field trips are just two sources for experience charts written by a class.

our daily lives and how they are turned into foodstuffs. All the children discovered they had some idea as to how this was done, but many questions were left unanswered. The group generated a number of questions that were written on the chalkboard, including:

1. How are potato chips made?
2. Why do some potato chips taste like tacos?
3. How do potato chips get put into bags?

The possibility of visiting a potato-chip processing plant was raised and received with great enthusiasm. The next day a discussion was held about the field trip. The children were asked to develop a set of guidelines that would be followed during the trip. Small groups were formed and ideas written on paper. The entire group then discussed the ideas and agreed on these rules, which were written on the chalkboard:

1. No running or yelling.
2. Stay with your partner.
3. Listen to the teacher.
4. Don't touch things (they may be hot).
5. Remember to look for answers to our questions.

The group then reviewed the questions they had asked the previous day. These had been transferred to a chart-size tablet by an Intern and saved for just this purpose. Volunteers read each question aloud, and the discussion lead to the addition of several more:

4. What are the steps in making potato chips?
5. How are potatoes cut up to make potato chips?

The field trip was taken on the third day. A guide led the group through the plant, pointing out each operation in the process and answering questions after the tour. An Intern videotaped the potato-chip processing system with a portable backpack. Each person got a bag of potato chips as they returned to the bus.

When the group got back to school they discussed their trip, what they had seen, and how they felt about the tour over the next several days. The questions written on the chart were answered, and other ideas stimulated by the trip were discussed. All of this was tape-recorded for future reference.

With the teacher transcribing on the chalkboard, the group dictated a story about their field trip.

Our Trip to the Old Dutch Factory

We took a field trip to the Old Dutch Factory. The factory is hot. Potatoes get washed in a machine. A machine cuts the potatoes. Hot oil cooks them. We got a bag of potato chips to eat.

Older children who preferred to write their own stories were encouraged to do so. All drew pictures of some part of the field trip they wanted to remember. A brief caption was added to the pictures and they were displayed on a bulletin board under the title "Making Potato Chips."

The next day the videotape of the trip was viewed and the five questions were answered in writing on the chalkboard by the group. Several small groups were formed to pursue separate projects. Some of the older children prepared a narration to accompany the videotape. Another group wrote out in detail the steps involved in making potato chips. A third group wrote imaginative stories about "Peter Potato Gets Bagged."

Various follow-up activities over the next week further involved the children in writing and talking about potatoes, potato products, and food processing. Some children consulted encyclopedias and other reference books for information. Others wrote for brochures on potato farming. Each child developed a booklet containing copies of his own stories and descriptions, as well as mimeographed copies of group-produced stories.

Skill instruction involved some children in learning sight words from those used frequently in the stories (for example: process, machine, conveyor belt, and so on); others followed a sequence of ideas, reading critically and interpreting tables and graphs. The selections used for teaching these skills were for the most part ones written by the children themselves. Stories developed about the trip were cut into strips, with one sentence on each strip. Young children recreated the story by putting the sentences in order. Later, sentences were cut up so that individual words and phrases could be handled and recognized by the children.

A similar activity was undertaken several weeks later when a trip to the railroad roundhouse was planned. Stories were written for less ambitious projects as well. For example, a stroll around the neighborhood, making popcorn, visiting the principal's office, and making fudge—all proved to be experiences worth writing about.

Rationale for the Language Experience Approach

In the language experience approach reading takes its place as just one language skill that is essential in learning to communicate. Speaking, listening, reading, and writing form the foundation for the exchange of ideas and information. Both common sense and research evidence indicate the interdependence of these four language skills (Loban, 1963; Strickland, 1968).

1. *Good teaching begins with what is known to the child*. The oral language that a child brings to school is an excellent record of his past experiences. The child with numerous enriching activities in his background is likely to use language which accompanies such experiences. Other youngsters have less facility with language because of less adequate opportunity and stimulation. Reading instruction that utilizes the language of the child automatically builds on what is known. The children in the Teacher Corps summer school found meaning in the stories they read because they had shared the experience. In this way the child learns that what he thinks he can also say;

great!

what he says he can also write; and what he can write he can also read (Van Allen, 1963). The story belongs to the child. His background, his experiences, and his self-image are all employed in teaching him to read.

2. *Individualization is built in*. Because so little structure and systematic skill development are incorporated into the language experience approach the teacher must continually evaluate and diagnose the needs of students. While this method places a great deal of responsibility on the teacher, it also encourages careful assessment of each child, with the result that the opportunity for individualized instruction is maximized. One major strength of the language experience approach is that each learner progresses at an individual rate. His interests can lead him in many directions, and the freedom to explore promotes creativity.

3. *Skills are introduced as they are needed*. Skill development is conducted in a meaningful context through the language experience approach. Since no set sequence must be followed, the teacher can use ongoing activities to introduce and reinforce skills as they are needed. The primary advantage of such an arrangement is its emphasis on reasoning and the utilization of skills, as opposed to memorization.

4. *Reading is understood as one part of the communication process*. Especially important in this approach is the relation that is developed between the spoken word and its graphic form. In beginning reading the teacher writes out stories that usually come directly from the child's experiences. Introduced in this fashion, the child easily understands reading as a method of communication, with an exchange of meaning being the primary goal.

Limitations of the Language Experience Approach

1. *Heavy demands are made on the teacher*. The fundamental limitation of the language experience approach is the expertness on the part of the teacher required to make it operate. Because of the lack of structure and prepared materials, the classroom teacher assumes far more responsibility with this system than in the controlled vocabulary approach, for example. While the flexibility inherent in this plan makes the individualization of instruction more likely, it also raises the risk of creating a haphazard, incidental reading program.

2. *Skills may not be sequenced and practiced adequately*. The development of reading skills requires some organization in order to build readiness for subsequent skills. For example, following a sequence of events is a skill that depends on the ability to find main ideas and recognize transitions. Without instruction and practice on underlying skills, higher levels of competency are not attainable. A skillful teacher is capable of developing such a sequence for individual children. In order to instruct thirty individuals properly, however, superior ability and organization are required.

3. *Most materials must be made by the teacher*. The language experience approach does not eliminate the use of commercially prepared materials,

but it does place primary emphasis on teacher- or child-prepared materials. Again, this feature of the system maximizes the opportunity to individualize instruction, but it also places enormous demands on the teacher. With this system all the children do not use the same workbook, which must be regularly completed in spite of individual needs. Yet practice exercises are highly desirable for reinforcing skills and providing evidence of mastery. In the absence of a standardized workbook the teacher must develop or find appropriate materials. The same is true of books written with a desirable reading difficulty, or filmstrips helpful in supplementing a story.

4. *Vocabulary is not repeated*. Although not regarded as a limitation by some educators, the absence of structure with regard to vocabulary, sentence building, and concept development inherent in the language experience system may be troublesome for some youngsters. The planned repetition evidently required by some children in order to learn to recognize a word at sight is difficult to achieve with the language experience approach. The large number of words introduced by a variety of incidents children experience and write about places an additional burden on the learner. While research evidence indicates that even young children have a remarkable grasp of oral language, it is not clear whether the same assumption concerning language can be made for learning to read. It is likely that concepts or sentence structures that a child easily grasps in an oral setting become much more difficult when the tasks of decoding and interpreting written symbols are added to that of understanding.

Helpful References on the Language Experience Approach

Despite the length of our discussion we have really only scratched the surface of this approach to reading-language instruction. A number of references are devoted exclusively to describing the implementation and use of this system. You may want to consult McCracken and McCracken (1972), Stauffer (1970), Van Allen (1963), Veatch (1974), Hall (1970), or Lee and Allen (1963) for more extensive discussion of the topic.

The Individualized Approach

Since it is possible to adjust instruction to the unique needs of individuals with any of the systems we have already discussed, it is rather misleading to label a fourth approach as the individualized one. A more descriptive name would be the free-choice reading approach, since this label more accurately conveys the central element of the system. However, a large body of literature can be found under the heading individualized approach. We will employ this label, having pointed out that individualization as an instructional goal can be accomplished with any system.

As the name implies, the individualized approach teaches reading by permitting each pupil to progress at his own rate. Nearly all reading is done in books, magazines, or other material that the child selects. Conferences between the teacher and the child are held regularly to check progress and identify needs. Grouping is not the primary mode of instruction, although occasionally interest groups are formed. Most skill instruction is provided during the conference or in small groups that meet over a short period of time on the basis of need. Students often present book reports as a means of sharing their experiences with classmates.

Dorothy Sparks, a teacher who makes heavy use of the individualized approach in her fifth-year classroom, lets her students select any book they care to read from the extensive collection in the reading corner, from the school library, the visiting bookmobile, the city library, or their own personal libraries. Many of the books are paperbacks that have been purchased by the children through a book club the class belongs to. (See Appendix A for a listing of children's book clubs and addresses.)

Each morning during the scheduled reading period children read independently at their desks or in one of the comfortable spots that have been created around the room (for example, sitting on a pillow, lying on a rug, or sitting in an overstuffed chair in one corner of the room). Dorothy meets with one child at a time in a conference session at a table near the windows. Sitting next to the child, Dorothy gains an idea of what he is reading, what problems he is having, and how he feels about reading. Often her conferences involve a brief instructional acitivity. At other times a need is identified that is addressed later in a group setting, which includes other children having a similar need. Confer-

(HRW photo by Russell Dian)

FIGURE 17.4   An individualized approach to reading

Progress in reading can be checked by the teacher at regularly scheduled conferences.

ences vary in length, but generally last ten minutes. A conference is scheduled with each child at least once every other week and more often if requested by either the teacher or the child.

Rationale of the Individualized Approach

1. *The child's interests can be used to motivate him to read.* The idea behind the individualized approach is that, given the opportunity to pursue his own interests, the child will be eager and willing to read. This view is in contrast to that of several other systems which impose a series of stories, usually in the form of a graded reader, on the child. Self-selection of reading materials also provides the child with an opportunity to build a positive self-image by strengthening his ego. His interests and desires are an important part of the reading program. The close association between pleasant personal experiences and reading activities is a powerful factor in developing lifelong readers.

2. *Self-selection is characteristic of real-life reading activities.* A reading program based or self-selection closely matches the reading activities of a nonschool setting. Outside of school adults, as well as children, usually read only what they choose for recreation or information. School reading programs emphasizing assigned reading, follow-up discussions, and related skill activities do not resemble the reading demands of adult life. The strongest aspect of the individualized system may be that it bridges the gap between reading for school and reading for real-life purposes.

3. *Teacher and child meet on a personal basis.* Another outstanding feature of the individualized approach is the regular interaction that takes place between the teacher and learner. This arrangement not only facilitates instruction that meets the unique needs of each child but it also guarantees the child an undivided segment of the teacher's attention. As the teacher comes to understand the personality of each child, through such personal contacts, the child grows both emotionally and educationally.

4. *Opportunities occur to adjust to individual needs.* The teacher assumes a great deal of responsibility for organizing the instructional program in the individualized approach. From a positive standpoint the flexibility and freedom of such an arrangement enables the teacher to make whatever adjustments are necessary to individualize instruction. A premium is placed on being able to diagnose the needs of each student, and the opportunity to differentiate instruction is clearly available. Only the teacher's ability and the resources available to him limit the effectiveness of the instructional program.

The individualized system has much in common with the language experience approach. An important distinction between the two is the role of language production. Individualized reading depends primarily on prepared materials, such as library books, while in the language experience approach children prepare much of their own reading materials.

Limitations of the Individualized Approach

1. *Many demands are placed on the classroom teacher.* Although we have seen many teachers—both experienced and inexperienced—use the individualized approach successfully, there is no doubt that substantial demands are made on the teacher's time and energy. This system requires extensive planning, careful diagnosis and record-keeping, efficient organization, and a thorough understanding of the reading process. Unfortunately, not all teachers can measure up to these standards, and others are not willing to try. Those who want to make the system work must be prepared to put forth extra effort. To illustrate, few commercially prepared materials are ideally suited to the individualized approach. Those that are useful are usually not packaged and organized into a comprehensive program. The teacher must create a coherent plan by conceptualizing a skills program and locating instructional materials to support that program. The challenge and the reward of the individualized approach lies in its dependence on the teacher.

2. *Knowledge of children's literature is needed by the teacher.* The very nature of the individualized approach makes it important that the teacher be familiar with a wide variety of children's books and authors. This knowledge is necessary to carry on effective conferences and to help children locate appropriate reading materials. Even though self-selection of materials by the child is an important principle of this system, the teacher must guide and upgrade his reading tastes and interests.

3. *A large number and variety of books are required.* Some schools simply do not have sufficient numbers and varieties of books to implement the individualized reading system. To really provide each child with the opportunity to select reading materials on topics he enjoys, and at a reading level he can handle over a period of weeks and months, the school must have an average of twenty books per child. This standard requires a school of fifteen classrooms to have 3,000 books, not including textbooks and basal readers. In addition, a knowledgeable librarian who is available to students and teachers on a regular basis is also important to the success of the system. Obviously, one important limitation of this approach is the amount of resources necessary for its operation. Many schools do not meet these requirements and should be cautious about attempting to teach reading with this system if the needed personnel and materials are absent.

Combining Systems for Effective Instruction

We have presented four distinct approaches to the teaching of reading, each having unique strengths and weaknesses. Since no single system has been found superior for all children, it is important to match the learner with an appropriate instructional system.

We may appear to be suggesting that every classroom teacher must use all four systems to meet the needs of all his students. Actually, with some qualification, we are doing just that. The classroom teacher must initially select one system he endorses and understands. As his experience and expertness permit, he should supplement the chosen system with elements borrowed from other systems.

Typically, the cortrolled vocabulary approach is the system a teacher will employ when he first teaches. Because of its structure and suggested teaching activities, this is a useful system for the novice. At first many new teachers will no doubt follow the teacher's manual for a controlled vocabulary approach rather closely. The sequence of skillls and the variety of prepared materials which it offers are helpful to the beginning teacher. Soon, however, the teacher must begin to be selective in his use of suggested activities. The unique nature of his students dictate certain adjustments. The authors of the controlled vocabulary materials cannot anticipate the tremendous variety of teachers and students who will use their products. Consequently they aim their materials at the "average" learner, and usually admit that considerable adjustment will be necessary.

Eventually the teacher will be adding and altering ideas from the controlled vocabulary materials until they hardly resemble the original program. How long does this transition take? One cannot say exactly; some teachers achieve the break from close adherence to the system during or by the end of their first year, while others may follow the program rather closely for five or ten years.

A progression from the controlled vocabulary approach to the language experience approach seems quite natural. At one extreme is structure that approaches rigidity; at the opposite extreme is flexibility approaching randomness. Somewhere within this range the teacher must find a balance that suits his abilities and meets the needs of his class. From year to year the exact nature of the balance should vary, depending on the children being taught.

In addition, the teacher can incorporate in his program features of the individualized approach and the programmed approach, as they are appropriate. All children require the opportunity to read in a setting that corresponds to real life. Therefore, elements of the individualized approach are employed in an effective reading program. Occasional self-selection of materials and individual pupil-teacher conferences are two aspects of the individualized system which merit special use. At the same time, programmed materials, used judiciously, can be an invaluable aid to students who benefit from this type of presentation. For example, series of programs designed to teach specific spelling patterns are an excellent resource to have available in the classroom. The teacher can draw on such a collection as the need occurs.

Figure 17.5 illustrates how a teacher can begin with a controlled vocabulary approach and gradually expand his techniques to incorporate useful aspects of other systems. The move from a structured to a nonstructured reading program will correspondingly increase the amount of individualized instruction the child will receive.

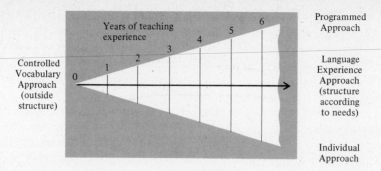

FIGURE 17.5   Combining instructional systems

As the teacher grows in experience he is able to move from the structure of the controlled vocabulary approach to a structure according to need, borrowing elements from various approaches.

SUMMARY

The search for one reading method that is best for all children has been fruitless. A more realistic approach is to recognize that individual learners benefit from different instructional systems.

There are four distinct systems of reading instruction:

1. the controlled vocabulary approach
2. the programmed approach
3. the language experience approach
4. the individualized approach.

The rationale and limitations of each system were discussed in the chapter in detail.

The controlled vocabulary approach is the most highly structured of the four systems. Constraints are placed on the vocabulary, sentence length, sentence complexity, and story setting in this system. The learner uses a textbook written at a specified difficulty level and a workbook containing practice exercises. The teacher is provided with a guide which contains teaching suggestions and activities. The careful control of all aspects of the system is designed to make learning tasks manageable for the child. The complexity of the tasks gradually increases as the learner grows in his ability to handle them. A major criticism of this approach is that such a high degree of control is unnecessary for today's sophisticated child.

The programmed approach teaches reading by taking the student through a series of highly organized, carefully planned steps. The learner makes an overt response at each step and obtains immediate knowledge of his success or failure. The child works at his own pace in such materials, and experiences almost constant success regardless of his ability. The major limitations of this system are its impersonal nature and its failure to provide for creative, divergent thinking.

The language experience approach builds the reading program around the child's own stories and interests. The interrelatedness of the language arts is emphasized by this system. Essentially the rationale of the approach is that what a child thinks he can say; what he says he can write; what he writes he can read. Early reading activities are based on stories created by the child. Later, books are used to stimulate and create activities which grow into language arts experiences. The major limitation of this system is its lack of structure in terms of skill development and sequence. In this approach the teacher must assume a large measure of responsibility for providing structure.

The individualized approach is essentially a reading program based on self-selection of library books. Each child selects his own reading materials, reads independently, and regularly meets individually with the teacher for discussion and skill activities. Personal interests and genuine ego involvement make motivation extremely high with this plan. For schools able to supply the enormous amount of material necessary to implement it, this system offers definite advantages. The major limitation of this approach lies in the amount of responsibility placed on the classroom teacher for planning and executing the system. In particular, the teacher must be capable of assessing and guiding a complete reading skills program for a whole class of children simultaneously.

Realistically, the beginning teacher is likely to use the highly structured controlled vocabulary approach until his knowledge and skill enable him to shift toward less structure, as in the language experience approach. Ideally, the best of each system is combined so that a teacher draws on the strengths of all systems.

Terms for Self-study

instructional systems
language experience approach
programmed approach
sound-symbol emphasis

controlled vocabulary approach
individualized approach
successive approximation

Discussion Questions

1. Why is it desirable for a teacher to adapt and deviate from the structure provided by the controlled vocabulary approach? How does teaching experience enter into making this adjustment?
2. In what sense is the language experience approach more child-centered than any of the other instructional systems?

18

Selecting
Materials for
Instruction

What books and materials will you use to teach reading? When you open the cabinets in your classroom, probably you will find a variety of books, charts, and games for use in the teaching of reading. After evaluating these materials you may find that you need others. If you are lucky, you may have a budget with which to purchase materials. Intelligent selection and use of teaching materials requires an evaluation of the specific needs of the children in your class.

As a teacher you need to know what kinds of instructional materials are available, where you can get additional information about them, when to use particular types, and how to choose appropriate materials for your students. Certainly there is no scarcity of books. Dozens of basic reading series have been published—many in the past few years—and thousands of supplementary items are produced each year. With this wealth of material and with an ever-increasing school budget, you must develop some guidelines to help in making selections. Answers to such questions as those below will aid you in evaluating instructional materials:

What is the difference between core reading materials and supplementary reading materials?

Are there books and materials to match your philosophy of teaching reading?

How does a teacher match materials with learners?
What criteria should be used in purchasing materials?

A knowledge of materials and guidelines for selecting them are priorities for every teacher of reading for two reasons: (1.) today's teacher has a significant voice in the selection of classroom materials, both on text selection committees and in the purchase of supplementary books for use in his own classroom; (2.) recently there has been an explosion of educational materials. How to sift the valuable from the less valuable becomes a decision the classroom teacher frequently has to make.

This chapter reviews the various kinds of materials, discusses their use for different types of students, and offers some principles for evaluating them. Materials are classified here as basic, or core, materials and supplementary. *Core materials* are those that carry the basic sequence of reading skills across several levels, or grades. *Supplementary materials* are library books, games, practice readers, enrichment readers, newspapers, and magazines which are used to reinforce, enrich, and personalize reading instruction.

Making Decisions about Materials

Instructional materials play an important role in teaching reading. But materials are only tools or means; they are not ends. They do not constitute a reading program, but they help to achieve a reading program. Since they are tools, decisions concerning the selection of materials should be based on how much they assist learners to achieve specific reading tasks.

How does a teacher know what materials to use? Here is a five-step plan:

1. Collect data to identify the needs of the students.
2. Develop an instructional plan based on needs.
3. Review materials that seem to fit the plan.
4. Use general criteria to evaluate materials.
5. Select materials to meet the needs of students.

How to identify the needs of students has been a continuing concern of this text. Chapter 18 specifically considers the criteria which a teacher can use to evaluate available instructional materials.

Ideally, the teacher will find and use materials that match the needs of the student perfectly. Actually, perfect matching is not always possible. Assessment techniques are not always accurate; commercial materials are not always available for specific needs; money may not be budgeted for desired products; or school policy may limit a teacher's authority to use materials other than those provided by the school's official curriculum committee. But the teacher should do his best to reconcile the needs of the student reader with the materials available. At times the teacher may find it necessary to improvise, to develop his own worksheets and exercises, and to ask the children to bring in their books and games.

Core Materials

Core materials are basic tools designed to give structure and a sense of sequence to reading skills. Most materials of this kind can be classified in one of the four systems for teaching reading, as was discussed in Chapter 17. Classification decisions between core and supplementary materials are not made arbitrarily, but are intended to give perspective and direction to this discussion. One caution is needed. A variety of approaches can be found in almost all core materials. Seldom does an author present a pure instructional system. He simply emphasizes one approach and brings in elements of others to offer an eclectic teaching program.

The Controlled Vocabulary System

The controlled vocabulary system offers a large quantity and variety of materials, due to the long history these materials have had and due to the subcategories of the controlled vocabulary system. The materials are presented here in three groups:

1. materials controlled by frequency of word use
2. sound-symbol materials
3. new alphabet materials.

This last category includes the initial teaching alphabet (ITA), Words in Color, and other unusual core materials that are related to the controlled vocabulary system.

Materials Controlled by Frequency of Word Use

Reading series that generally begin with vocabulary control based on the frequency of word use usually range from kindergarten through sixth- or eighth-grade volumes. Skill development ranges from readiness activities (skills and concepts needed prior to formal reading activity) to comprehension exercises using different kinds of expository selections. Between those two poles come word-recognition skills and meaning skills, arranged in a sequence that gradually builds the word stock and the skill complexity of the learner. The books and audio and visual aids that make up these series would fill a large closet and provide for a surprising number of different classroom activities. *Series r,* published by Macmillan, for example, has over 250 items available in its K–6 program.

Using only a few high frequency words in the stories has often been lampooned, especially the very first stories, when children can read only a dozen or so words. More recently, with the creative use of illustrations and the successful writing of children's authors, those early stories have sprung to life (see Figure 18.1, pages 424–425).

Try writing a story for use in the first semester of the first grade and see if you can do better than the published authors of such stories. For example, write a story using this set of limits:

1. Thirty-five words have been introduced. They are:

ride	said	I	apple
fast	you	can	get
see	balls	something	toys
and	wants	is	a
mother	red	dinner	go
look	chair	the	we
work	come	stop	surprise
at	here	pony	this
for	airplane	father	

2. Five new words may be introduced in this story. You may select any additional five one- or two-syllable words that are frequently used. You may use the names of people without counting them as new words.
3. Each of the five new words is to be repeated at least five times during the course of the story.
4. Describe the illustrations for each of the six-eight pages of the story. The pictures must support the story at this point.

To some degree the usable vocabulary determines the content of the story. This fact should indicate how to use most of the early reading selections. They are designed for practice in word and sentence recognition and for getting meaning from short selections. When an interesting or stimulating story does appear, the class should be encouraged to react to it and explore it. The higher the level, the more likely the stories are to have literary merit. In such instances—besides practice in word and sentence recognition—students work with higher reading skills such as analysis, evaluation, and synthesis.

A Complete Package of Materials

Though a large number of items is usually available with a controlled vocabulary series, only three items are defined here as core materials—a reader for the child, an activity book or workbook, and the teacher's guide. Some authorities object to the inclusion of a workbook in a reading package because it is sometimes misused as busy work for the child. Practically speaking, however, workbooks contain many valuable practice exercises. The teacher's guide is used to determine the objectives for a given story, what procedures the author recommends for teaching skills, and the kinds of practice activities the author believes will reinforce direct instruction by the teacher.

Bob likes little fish
and big fish.

FIGURE 18-1

Creative illustrations supplement a simple text which uses a few words over and over.

Criterion Tests

An attractive feature of most controlled vocabulary reading series is the testing program. Often tests are included that are specifically oriented to the skills treated in a unit or book. These tests can be used for readiness or entry purposes; or they can be utilized to check on performance following a unit of instruction; or both. For example, before learning to read a simple story in a preprimer a child learns how to "read" pictures. As a means of evaluating the student's sense of storytelling, a readiness test for preprimers might ask him to look at a series of pictures and put them in the proper sequence. Most reading

Bob likes to sit and fish.

Bob says,
"I like fish.
I like to sit
and fish."

47

(Courtesy Macmillan Publishing Co., Inc., New York)

series tests concentrate on a set of specific skills, and thus can be used as criteria for proceeding with instruction in new skills. Chapter 6 gives examples of criterion testing.

BOOKS FOR SPECIAL POPULATIONS

One principle used in constructing readers controlled by frequency of word use is that early reading should center on situations and characters with which the children can easily identify. The home and school are often used as a setting and young children as primary characters in the stories. Occasionally, series have been written to appeal to special populations. One such is the *Bank Street Readers,* named after the Bank Street College in New York City which experimented with the development of materials and demonstrated their use for some schools in the city. The beginning vocabulary of the Bank Street series reflects its difference from a typical reading program. In the list below you can see how story selections in the first grade have affected the vocabulary used by the Bank Street Readers as compared with the vocabulary from the Ginn 100 series, one of its contemporaries:

Bank Street Readers
Vocabulary 1:1 (samples)

boats	drill	policeman	snowplow
books	highways	potatoes	store
boxes	lunchroom	sea	train
car	mailman	sidewalk	truck
cat	plane	skates	tugboat

Ginn Reading Series
Vocabulary 1:1 (samples)

barn	ducks	mouse	quack
bunny	farm	paint	tree
cake	hen	party	turkey
candles	kitten	pets	wagon
cowboy	mill	plant	wheat

Use of Materials Controlled by Word Frequency

If the teacher, on the basis of an evaluation of the learning and environmental characteristics of his students, decides to use word-frequency materials he should choose a specific series of books based on the content of the stories and the difficulty level of the vocabulary. The gradual build up of vocabulary within the series makes it easy for a teacher to select a book to fit the instructional level of the child.

Created for use with both small and large groups, these materials provide for a structured and systematic approach to the teaching of reading, or for individual works, depending on the needs of the moment. The stories and vocabulary create an order and control that govern the general teaching procedures fairly well and guide the child in his daily progress toward reading.

Word skills and comprehension skills are often introduced inductively; that is, they are based on the content of the story and then reinforced through activities in the workbook or in the teacher's guide. For example, consider the sentence: Can the good goat get home safely?

Teacher's question: "Three words in that sentence are somewhat alike. What are they?"
Answer: "Good, goat, get."
Teacher's question: "Why are they alike?"
Answer: "All begin with the letter g."
Teacher's question: "Can you give another word that begins with the same sound?"

In this fashion the teacher uses the story to lead to an understanding of the sound represented by the consonant g. This does not imply that learning is restricted to an inductive approach. Word recognition skills, phonics skills, and comprehension skills are learned through a variety of techniques.

These techniques and the philosophy of the word-frequency method emphasize *meaning* and *thinking*. Much of the appeal of the method is in this emphasis and also in its opportunity for individualization. The sense of self-discovery and the emphasis on meaning give individual children latitude in which to be themselves, to be individual learners. A teacher must decide whether those characteristics match the characteristics of his students.

Sound-symbol Materials

Some materials designed for a contolled vocabulary system use phonics or linguistics to control the early vocabulary. As we have seen, in this approach children learn that there is a relation between the sounds within spoken words and the symbols used to spell the words. The symbol *b* is used to represent the sound one hears at the beginning of the words *bat, beggar,* and *bite*. This sound-symbol approach first identifies a sufficient number of sounds and symbols so that some words can be wholly constructed from the learned bits of sound. Once children learn a half-dozen consonant sounds with their appropriate symbols and the sound /a/ as in *bat,* they can decipher a number of words that make use only of those sounds. For example: *A cat can bat a rat.* By analysis and manipulation the child should be able to deal with any words that cannot go beyond those learned parts. *Pat the fat man* and *Dan ran fast past the cat* are words available for use in workbooks and readers. The vocabulary control rests on the words that fit the learned sound-symbols and their various combinations. Some readers in this group are called *phonics readers;* others are *linguistics readers*. From the appearance of the practice books, it may be difficult to distinguish one from the other.

Phonics Materials

A phonics program usually presents a number of time-honored rules concerning the spelling and related sounds of English words. Thus the silent "e" rule says that an e at the end of a one-syllable word usually indicates that the e is silent; and that the preceding vowel says its own name, or has a long vowel sound; for example, *state, pope, bite*.

Some programs, such as the one developed by the Economy Publishing Company, employ a large number of phonics rules. Initial activity in that phonics program centers on learning a single sound for each letter of the alphabet. Other phonics programs use only a few phonics rules.

Linguistics Materials

A linguistics program usually emphasizes the regularity and patterns within the English sound-spelling code. Instead of teaching the silent "e" rule, the linguistics reader might teach the consonant-vowel-consonant-vowel pattern (c-v-c-v)—such as *mate, pope, bite*—and contrast it to the consonant-vowel-consonant pattern (c-v-c)—such as *mat, pop, bit.* At this point there is no significant research evidence to indicate that either the linguistics program or the phonics program is superior.[1] There *is* some evidence to indicate that sound-symbol materials in general help children to score high on standardized achievement tests in reading, although this issue has been hotly debated among educators (Chall, 1967).

Linguistics readers are probably more diverse in appearance and construction than any other group of readers. The content varies considerably from a highly repetitive spelling-pattern approach (Charles Merrill Company) to fun-filled stories about frogs, puppies, and toy soldiers. The Merrill series does not use pictures; in another series an illustration appears on every page. Merrill produces a series that emphasizes spelling patterns and visual differences—that is, spelling differences, within the same general pattern of consonant-vowel-consonant (c-v-c). *Bad* represents a different word than *Dad* because the first letter is different. A sample page from Reader 1 is:

Nat on a Mat

A fat cat sat on a mat.
The fat cat is Nat.
Pat the mat, fat cat.
Is the mat on Nat?
Nat is on the mat.

Series r (Macmillan Publishing Company) stresses the need for *natural language* in beginning stories—language that children recognize as language that people speak. *Series r* builds its sound-spelling generalizations through teachers guides and children's workbooks. Thus the benefits of both natural language and sound-spelling patterns are preserved.

Use of Sound-symbol Materials

The content of sound-symbol materials should be judged on its environmental and motivational effects, as was suggested for word-frequency materials. The teacher must decide whether the child needs to be led systematically through a careful sequence of word-analysis techniques in order for him to read independently. Because of their highly structured exercises, the sound-symbol materials usually are easy to follow, and the child can see his progress

[1]Linguistics is used here in the manner of Bloomfield and Barnhart (1961), and Fries (1962), who focused almost exclusively on phonemics and the structural patterns in English words.

almost daily. The teacher, too, may find it easier to assess specific skills with sound-symbol materials, because the tasks are clearly defined and the criteria for evaluation are easily identified, at least in the early stages. Can the child match the symbol and sound (a with /ă/)? Can he blend the symbols to produce the complete word sound (cat says /kăt/)?

For the auditory learner sound-symbol materials have the obvious advantage of making use of known sounds (speech) to lead him to read visual symbols. For example, the child is asked to note the similarity in the sounds in the middle of the words bat, mad, ran. Then he is shown that the middle sound is spelled with a. This training in relating sound and symbol will help the auditory learner to analyze words until they become part of his automatic reading vocabulary.

New Alphabet Materials

Though both phonics materials and linguistics materials emphasize the regularity of the English sound-symbol relations, there are some evident exceptions to the rules and patterns. For that reason a number of new alphabet approaches have been developed to assure greater consistency in sound-symbol relations and to make it simpler for beginning readers to decode written symbols.

The initial teaching alphabet (ITA), Words in Color, Unifon, and a diacritical marking system all attempt to simplify the sound-symbol relations of English. New alphabet materials are viewed by their creators as an initial means for introducing the child to a fundamental process in conquering the symbols on a page—that is, decoding the symbols into the sounds they represent. Since they are aimed primarily at this initial segment of the reading program, some teachers do not define them as core materials. Yet they can be the basic materials used to begin training in reading. In the case of ITA the materials extend throughout the entire first-grade program and into the second grade. Both ITA and Unifon create new symbols so that each of the forty-plus sounds of the English language has its own distinctive sign. Some of those symbols are the traditional letters of the alphabet (see Figure 18.2).

The diacritical marking system uses stories from a traditional reading series and imprints diacritical marks above the vowels and difficult consonants in order to simplify the sound-symbol relations.

Words in Color stands apart from the other materials that we have mentioned in this section. Developed by Caleb Gaeteno, inventor of the Cuisinaire Color Rods used in teaching mathematics, Words in Color uses only standard alphabet symbols. Words in Color materials also attempt to get the child to respond initially to a single symbol for each of the sounds of English. Instead of an alphabet symbol, however, the child is initially shown a color that represents a sound. He is told to say /ă/, as in at, whenever he sees white; /p/, as in pat, when he sees red; /t/, as in tap, when he sees yellow; /i/, as in it, when he sees blue; /k/, as in cat, when he sees fuchsia, and so on with other colors. Charts containing forty-four columns of color are used to elicit specific sounds.

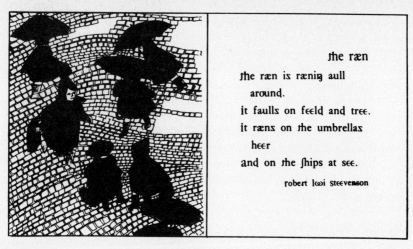

ſhe ræn

ſhe ræn is ræniŋ aull
around.
it faulls on feeld and tree.
it ræns on ſhe umbrellas
heer
and on ſhe ſhips at see.

robert lꙍi steevenſon

FIGURE 18.2 An ITA storybook

From *Poems*, Albert J. Mazurkiewicz and Harold J. Tanyzer, consultants. © copyright 1965 Initial Teaching Alphabet Publication, Inc. Reprinted by permission of the publisher.

Every time the teacher points to a color the children respond with a corresponding sound.

As soon as the child has learned to respond to the strips of color with the appropriate sound, he is taught to blend sounds into words and to look at the printed symbol on the chalkboard and in little black-and-white paperback exercise books and readers. The materials carry the learner through the equivalent of approximately one semester. The charts are placed around the classroom for reference, while the child takes up other materials in order to learn additional reading skills.

Use of New Alphabet Materials

Research indicates that the new alphabet materials are as successful or more successful than other materials in teaching reading. Bond and Dykstra (1967) suggest that some of this success may be due to the teacher's interest and enthusiasm for what is new.

Because of their emphasis on sound-symbol relations these materials may be used in the same general ways as sound-symbol materials. Some teachers recommend using ITA and Words in Color for slower learners, because initially all the words presented are regular and students are not confronted with confusing spelling irregularities.

The Language Experience Approach

No one set of materials fits the language experience method, as defined in this text. In a sense the teacher and the child develop their own reading materials. After the initial dictation of stories, the teacher has to select materials which foster the development of children's skills in listening, speaking, and writing, as well as reading, since this system stresses the interdependence of all the communication skills.

The Encyclopedia Brittanica Corporation publishes a series of guides for teachers and pupil materials for the development of experiences and stories. These materials are written by R. Van Allen, whose name is closely associated with the language experience approach as a result of his research and his book on the system (D. Lee and R. V. Allen, 1963).

The experience story enables students to build initial reading habits, learn to identify some words, and begin to discuss their experiences as possible subjects for stories. They consider such questions as: "What are stories?" "Where do they come from?" "How are they put together?" Having gone through the process of creating stories of their own, beginning readers soon learn to answer these questions inductively and begin to appreciate how stories in books are organized and prepared for their enjoyment. This technique combines listening, discussing, and reading in the child's initial activities.

Once students see the relation between speech and the creation of a book, teachers may introduce a phonics or other word-analysis activity to continue practice in word analysis and to point out the relations between the sound of a word and its spelling.

The Sounds of Language (Holt, Rinehart and Winston, 1967) features stories and poems that make the student conscious of language, words, and the delight he can have with language if he knows some of its music and nuances. This series also contains many activities for speaking and writing about the stories children have heard or read (see Figure 18.3).

The last major activity in the language experience approach is reading a wide variety of selections and reacting orally or in writing. Thus the teacher keeps on hand a large supply of the books children can read for enjoyment. Written summaries, reactions, and creative compositions may follow from individual reading. These compositions, in turn, become materials to be shared, exchanged, read aloud, or posted for students to read at their leisure.

Use of Materials in the Language Experience Approach

The experience story is a fairly personal one. It must be the child's own story. Pictures and books can be stimulants, but the language and vocabulary on the paper should belong to an individual.

The language experience system has particular applicability for students who need to be stimulated to use language, or who need to feel that their language has value. For example, the system may motivate a child who seems afraid to speak in class because he comes from a less verbal environment than some of the other children.

In a mountain school in West Virginia we watched youngsters tell stories with obvious enjoyment, and then exchange written versions of the stories. The

So Many Monkeys

Learning sequence: a) Silent reading,
b) choral reading, and *possibly* c) language analysis.

Monkey Monkey Moo!

Shall we buy a few?

Yellow monkeys,

Purple monkeys,

Monkeys red and blue.

Singular and plural

Be a monkey, do!

Who's a monkey, who?

He's a monkey,

She's a monkey,

You're a monkey, too!

Contractions and pronouns

Invite the children to read
this poem to themselves.
Then quickly read it aloud
together. Have fun with it.
And don't be surprised if
children go about calling
each other monkeys for a
while. If you're in the
mood, analyze the lan-
guage. And don't forget
the word cards.

by Marion Edey and Dorothy Grider,
picture by Kelly Oechsli

79

FIGURE 18.3   A basal reader page

From *Sounds Around the Clock,* a Sounds of
Language series, Bill Martin, Jr., ed. © copy-
right 1970. Reprinted by special permission of
Holt, Rinehart and Winston, Inc.

Reading and language learning can be fun for children and teachers, as is seen in this page from a basal
reader.

children read each others' work and asked their neighbors for help with words they did not recognize. The teacher confided that students in the past had usually been uninterested in reading and had not fared well with it. But once she helped children to use their own language and to dictate their favorite stories, they approached reading enthusiastically and their skills improved noticeably. These children put their stories together into a hand-bound book. They began to read both the county newspaper and stories by writers from Appalachia.

Schools or teachers using a language experience system usually set up a series of reading skills they want children to develop. The ebb and flow of classroom interest, however, often alter the schedule of the program so that students do not always develop skills in the exact order in which they were listed. This kind of freedom promotes a wide use of creative energy, but places a great burden on the teacher who must see that specific skills are learned and that appropriate materials are used.

For this reason the teacher should acquaint himself with a wide variety of instructional materials that fit into an independent skills program and provide many stimuli to communication. He must also know where to find and how to select books on many topics wirtten at various levels, so that all members of the class can read, discuss, and write on subjects that interest them at a level suited to their ability.

The Individualized System

The individualized system as defined in this text is probably the most difficult approach for the beginning reading teacher. One reason for this is the large number of books per pupil required to carry on an individualized reading program, as we have learned. What was said about selection of materials for the language experience approach applies equally here. In cooperation with the school and local librarians, the teacher must make a selection of books for the classroom and for the library that will stimulate children to learn through the interest they have in the books available to them (Wheeler, 1973).

Use of Materials in the Individualized System

Finding materials that interest students does not usually pose a problem in an individualized approach. Some publishers are now producing kits that can be used in an individualized system. The Random House Pacesetters, for example, offer a series of graded, high-interest stories with word exercises and comprehension questions to be answered by the child after he has read a selection of his choice. The skills and exercises proceed in a developmental fashion. Record sheets and check tests give the student and teacher some indication of progress.

Some teachers find it helpful to build a file of tearsheets from workbooks, organized according to specific skills. As the teacher sees a need for skill development or practice by a particular student, he can pull the file for that skill and have the student work out an appropriate exercise. The POWER reading system published by Winston Press provides a comprehensive skills program that works well with a file drawer plan.

In a truly individualized system more materials are needed than in any of the other systems described in this book. In fact, all of the materials mentioned for the other systems should be available for spot use with the individualized approach. A skilled, experienced teacher is needed in order to teach individualized reading, for he must be able to analyze test data, diagnose problems, plan personalized programs, and help students select materials appropriate for them.

The teacher must realize that he has considerable opportunity to individualize through a typical basal reader. Most teachers will want to use the objectives or the index in the teacher's guide as a means for adjusting to individual student needs.

The Programmed Instruction System

Programmed instruction system material is put together in the form of very short problems, usually boxed off in frames (*see* Figure 18.4).

Programmed reading exercises may be given by machine, in which case

FIGURE 18.4   A programmed reader

Reproduced from *Programmed Reading*, Bk. 8, by C.D. Buchanan and N.W. Sullivan. Copyright © 1963 by Sullivan Associates, with permission of The McGraw-Hill Book Company.

In programmed texts the student can check his response at once by uncovering the answer column on the left.

answers are recorded electronically or mechanically (Atkinson and Fletcher, 1972). More commonly, however, programmed reading exercises are given in a series of paperbound books. Each page is divided into frames, and a column at the left-hand side of the page contains the correct responses. A piece of cardboard, a *slide,* covers the answer column until it is slipped down to reveal the correct response. The McGraw-Hill programmed reading series is an example of this kind of approach. This series moves from teaching the alphabet and the sound-symbol relations into getting facts and main ideas from short paragraphs.

Use of Materials in the Programmed System

The reading programs thus far developed with the principles of programmed instruction are not broad enough to be used as the only material for teaching reading. They are sometimes used as the skills base for individualized reading or for the language experience system. Because of the nature of the materials, programmed readers include only short paragraph type of exercises at the end of the sequence of skills. Programmed reading can often be helpful in a class where there is a wide variety of abilites. After observing the status of the children the teacher can place each child in a section where he can develop the skills he needs. The teacher and the child then confer from time to time to evaluate progress. Since programmed material is worked on privately and at an individual pace, the teacher should provide opportunities for the children using the materials to share ideas, stories, and oral reading.

Supplementary Materials[2]

In addition to core materials the teacher of reading has available a variety of supplementary aids, books, and worksheets. These are used to give added practice, correct deficiencies, or to enrich reading instruction. They can serve as illustrative devices, means of motivation, and as organizers. They can serve the student by stimulating his interest, giving him additional practice in a needed skill, or providing him with emotional experiences that may not be a part of the core materials. A teacher's preferences and teaching style determine how many materials related to the basic program he will use. The following pages describe some typical related materials and how they may be used as part of the core materials.

The Big Book

For the first couple of months the first-grade teacher may use a big book to introduce each day's lesson. The big book is a chart-size reproduction of one or

---

[2]For a comprehensive survey of the use of supplementary materials *see* B. Callaway and O. T. Jarvis. "Programs and Materials Used in Reading Instruction: A Survey," *Elementary English* (April 1972), 49, pp. 578–581.

more of the preprimers. With it the teacher demonstrates how to look at a story and how to read it. The children then turn to their own small books and read them as was demonstrated.

Charts

Many kinds of charts are published—for example, picture stories, phonics rules, and vocabulary lists—for different purposes. Word-analysis charts are useful for group drill and can be utilized as a permanent reference if they are placed around the room. Figure 18.5 shows how one teacher made her own phonics chart.

Audiovisual Devices

Many basic reading programs include records and tapes which provide songs and stories as background for the reading selections. Filmstrips and movies also form part of the material designed to make a lesson attractive and to motivate the child. The modern elementary school classroom can easily use a tape recorder, record player, and/or slide projector as standard equipment. Audiovisual materials are available in quantity and are useful for a change of pace, motivation, reinforcement, and providing repetitive practice exercises.

Materials for Independent Work

Core materials in reading instruction are designed to provide a basic structure of skills needed so that the child can read efficiently. Materials for independent work differ from the core materials in several ways:

1. They usually are not concerned with introducing all of the skills essential for a mature reader.
2. The materials usually call for short-term activities and do not carry over several years, as is the case with most core materials.
3. The content may be fanciful or different, as opposed to the predictable and traditional content of core materials.
4. The materials are often called supplemental, as opposed to basic or core materials.

There are many categories of materials for independent work, including audiovisual materials, supplementary books, reading kits, games, workbooks, and teaching machines.

Using Audiovisual Materials

Almost all new schools are equipped with built-in screens, speakers, dimmer switches, and storage areas for valuable machinery and equipment. Teachers are finding that audiovisual equipment can be used to motivate

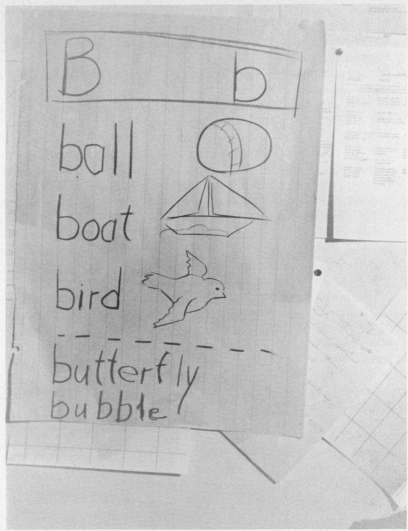

(Photo by Carl B. Smith)

FIGURE 18.5   A phonics chart

Phonics charts may be constructed by the teacher for special demonstrations.

students; and school boards are discovering that such equipment makes learning much more exciting for children. The overhead projector and tape recorder may soon be in use in every classroom in the country. Filmstrip projectors, movie projectors, and videotapes will be available to any classroom teacher who wants to use them to enhance learning. Many of these devices are specifically designed to teach reading skills.

Sets of overhead projection transparencies, for example, teach the sound-symbol relation, phonics generalizations, and sight vocabulary. Filmstrips can be had for almost any phase of learning to read, including comprehension activities with cartoons and copy that resemble those of a basic reader. Audiotapes for use on a standard tape recorder, like records, are available for reviewing sounds, building vocabulary, developing experiences, and listening to stories read by professionals.

Movies develop concepts about how to read for facts, how to organize what is read, and how to get the main idea. Others are designed to prepare the child for a teaching system; for example, many publishers have produced movies showing how children use their books and techniques. A recent development is the use of filmloops, or cartridges of film, which are usually limited to a single concept. They can be snapped into a small projector without threading the film into the machine and do not require rewinding (see Figure 18.6). When used in a study carrel and flashed on the wall of the carrel, the filmloop serves as a handy and interesting device for individual concept building or story preparation. Catalogues are available from many companies, and teachers can find new products reviewed in magazines—such as *The Instructor, The Grade Teacher,* and *K-Eight.*

Audiovisual equipment can be used for group or independent work. More and more schools are setting up audiovisual areas in the classroom. Besides their motivational values, audiovisual devices create strong sensory images, often a valuable technique where strength of impression and repetition are needed in order to develop language skills, such as vocabulary and automatic recognition of words.

Using Laboratories and Kits

One of the most popular items for independent study has been the reading kit, or reading laboratory; for example, the SRA Reading Lab, and the POWER

FIGURE 18.6   A filmloop projector

Filmloop cartridges, usually limited to one subject or concept, are easy to use in the classroom.

(A product of Bell & Howell Audio Visual Products Division)

FIGURE 18.7   A reading kit

The POWER reading laboratory from Winston Press works well when there are students in a class who need a variety of skills.

(HRW photograph by Russell Dian)

Reading System (Winston Press). Many publishers produce reading kits made up of a package of reading selections, response sheets, answer sheets, and score cards. The reading selections, which are quite short, are graded from easy to difficult and are printed on individaul cards or in little booklets. Sometimes colored stripes are used to distinguish levels of difficulty within the same kit. A student's reading level is determined by means of a test. He is then told to begin his work with the kit at a place where the selections match his reading level. He reads the short selections one by one, answers the vocabulary and comprehension questions after each selection, and scores his own paper from the answer sheet provided. This exercise provides the learner with practice in reading and in answering certain kinds of questions, usually having to do with finding facts and giving synonyms for words. Each task is relatively short; progress is noted on a personal record chart and by the color of the stripe on the selection. The theory is that the student's skill is developed through practice by gradually increasing the level of difficulty of his materials.

Motivation and practice seem to be the major values in the use of these kits. The materials are designed for independent work and thus are one answer for some teachers who ask: "What practice work can I give the children when there is a wide variety of reading levels in the class?" (*see* Figure 18.7). Some kits have diagnostic aids for the teacher. With criterion tests and specific skills focus, they help identify skills deficiencies and provide specific skills practice for children.

Using Games

A visitor to an elementary school class once asked a youngster what helped him most in learning to read. "I learn my words better when I play the word games," he said.

All kinds of games are available for the teacher of reading, from word cards to manipulative devices aimed at improving perception through coordination activities. The book entitled *Spice* (Instructor Publications, 1957) lists games and activities for language arts instruction. Card games and bingo games of all kinds help develop sight words and recognition of sounds. Puzzles, tracing materials, and blocks with words on them are other popular devices for the game or activity corner of the classroom.

These items are often available on a shelf or table for use when the children have finished other work. The teacher explains how each can be utilized and encourages students to practice vocabulary sounds, phrases, or sentences by playing the games. The sense of competition created by games indicates their motivational force on youngsters. Since boys develop reading problems twice as often as girls (Strang, 1969), and since they tend to like games, it is worth encouraging practice in reading skills by whatever means are available.

Using Enrichment Materials

Reading incentive programs, practice readers, and stories for both girls and boys are available at reading levels from Grades 1 through 12. Some publishers—Garrard, Harr-Wagner, and Steck-Vaughan—specialize in high-interest books written at a variety of reading levels. Macmillan has a broad spectrum of Solo Books, K–8, specifically written to match the reading levels of those ages.

Some teachers use book clubs to get books into the hands of their pupils on a regular basis. Scholastic Press, Pflaum Publishing Company, and Grolier, Inc., among others, offer paperback books to children through classroom purchase plans. This arrangement has the advantage of placing books in the children's homes, but it should not be the sole means of providing additional books for the reading program. The teacher and the school librarian, working together, can form an effective book selection committee for any given group of children. The reading teacher should remind the librarian of the incentive and motivational books that are available, and identify the reading levels found in the class.

Using Supplementary Workbooks

Most of the materials described for a basic system of reading instruction come with a workbook or a practice book. The textbook publisher's catalogue will reveal that many other workbooks are published along with the basic materials. These workbooks may simply contain additional drill exercises on a given skill. The teacher introduces a skill, and the child makes some responses to indicate that he has acquired the concept. Reading skills particularly need to be practiced until they become habitual. For that reason supplementary practice books, used on an individual basis in class or at home, may offer many benefits to the child. Some publishers, such as Continental Press, sell workbook programs on ditto masters. The teacher can then select the exercise that provides needed drill and duplicate as many copies as are needed.

Some teachers build files of practice exercises and pull out the appropriate skill sheets as a child needs them. It is important that supplementary workbooks be chosen to fulfill specific needs and be selected on the basis of their ability to deliver that skill.

Evaluating Materials

Books and other instructional aids are used to promote learning. In selecting them, therefore, the purchaser must ask: "Do these materials achieve what is needed in this school?" Some recent materials carry a description of the specific performances that the exercises are designed to achieve. A statement of performance objectives should help considerably in a teacher's evaluation of materials.

From an instructional point of view materials should be developed by first looking at the educational objective, or the task the child should be able to perform, and then working back from that point. Can you follow the logic of building one exercise on another until the objective is reached? Practice materials should exhibit that kind of logic.

Instructional facilities today are changing to encourage greater individualization. Classrooms have ceased to be four bare walls enclosing thirty-five chairs. Study carrels, room dividers, learning centers, library centers, and collapsible walls encourage the teacher to break the whole-group instruction habit and plan learning programs that meet individaul needs.

Diagnosis permits the matching of learner and materials. Hopefully, the good teacher makes that match. To do so, though, means becoming well acquainted with reading behavior and with materials (Quilling and Otto, 1971).

Keeping abreast of materials can be an overwhelming job unless the teacher uses some selected techniques for updating his knowledge. Reading the monthly columns on new materials in the *Reading Teacher* (International Reading Association) and in *Elementary English* (National Council of Teachers of English), visiting exhibits at conventions, and getting on publishers' mailing lists are some simple ways of staying current with new materials.

Guidelines for Evaluating Materials

Most of the research on early reading is actually a study of materials and not of systems or teaching strategies. The U.S. Office of Education study of first-grade reading often pits one set of materials against another. The materials are found to be quite similar in many respects: In general they use highly structured lessons, a gradual vocabulary stockpile, and stories that show a similar view of home and school. Even the teaching strategies and internal rewards for students are similar. It is not surprising, then, that Bond and Dykstra (1967) conclude that the teacher seems to be the key to differences in performance—not the method or the materials. Do not be misled by this statement, for certainly some materials are better than others, and some methods are more appropriate than others for specific students. The teacher carries on a continuous search for attractive and efficient materials. Publishers give considerable attention to improving materials and applying research evidence when type size, column width, and number and kinds of illustrations are chosen (Tinker, 1965). How else could a teacher find appropriate books for his classroom? When selecting books, the teacher should evaluate these general areas:

1. instructional techniques
2. content
3. format
4. classroom effectiveness

Under each of these areas questions similar to the ones listed below should be asked to see if the proposed materials seem worthy of use. For the person who has many items to review, a more objective comparison from item to item could be made by creating a checklist from the questions that follow.

Guiding Principle

The first rule in evaluating instructional materials is: *Evaluate materials in terms of your own instructional objectives.* Before looking at materials, the teacher must determine precisely what the materials are supposed to do. It is unwise to try to select materials for instruction before a teacher has described how a child should perform when he has finished the course of instruction. If, for example, a teacher is selecting supplementary independent materials for Grade 1 that give the child practice in using short-vowel words (consonant-vowel-consonant pattern) and give him enjoyment at the same time, three criteria can aid the search:

1. Do the materials supplement the first-grade series?
2. Do they provide practice in reading short-vowel words?
3. Do they emphasize the fun of reading?

With these questions in mind the teacher may decide that some of the Dr. Seuss nonsense books or similarly light-hearted books suit the purpose. Once he has identified a body of materials as fitting the learning tasks to be achieved, then the teacher can ask questions about the instructional psychology, the content, and the format of the materials.[3] Sample questions are given below.

[3]E.P.I.E. (Educational Products Information Exchange) provides a bulletin and a continuing review of educational products. Your school system may be a subscriber.

General

1. Do the materials claim to do what you expect the children to learn to do; for example, get the main idea of a paragraph?

INSTRUCTIONAL VALUES

2. Do the materials fit the population?
    Is the reading level appropriate? Is the pace of instruction satisfactory (fast, slow)? Do materials appeal to special cultural aspects of the population (setting, illustrations, vocabulary)?
3. Do the materials have clearly defined performance objectives?
    Did the authors know where they were headed?
4. Can a child work his way through a series of experiences and arrive at the stated objectives?
    Do the tasks truly lead him to competency in analyzing short-vowel words?
5. Are the instructional tasks arranged in logical order, or organized so that the structure is evident?
6. Can the teacher and the child get clear direction from the student's materials and the teacher's guide?
7. Are the means to evaluate progress indicated for the child and the teacher?

Content Principles

8. Does the general story content fit the population?
    Can the children identify with the action and enjoy the story?

9. Does the content provide a variety of reading experiences in keeping with the objectives of the program?
10. Does the content include motivational and interest factors suitable to the age and culture of the population?
11. Does content lead to appreciation of literature and a lifelong interest in reading?
12. Is the skills development logical or based on recent research?

Format Principles

13. Are the materials sufficiently attractive for their purpose?
    Is the type easily read by the prospective learner? Are the illustrations clear and stimulating? Are there enough illustrations?

14. Are different typographical techniques used to help the reader?
    Are there a variety of headings, use of italics, and variation of margins?

Utility Principles

15. Are the materials durable?
    How long will they last in the hands of a child?

16. Are the materials easy to handle?
    Will they lie flat for reading and writing?

17. Is the cost commensurate with the instructional value they provide?
    Will another, less expensive item produce the same effect on the learner?

SUMMARY

Materials for reading instruction are classified into two major categories—core materials and supplementary materials. Core materials are those that carry the major skills and content. Supplementary materials are those that aid the teacher in his presentations or the student in his independent study.

Core materials are described in four major groups, representing examples of books and materials used in each of the four systems of reading instruction: the controlled vocabulary system, the language experience system, the programmed learning system, and the individualized reading system. The controlled vocabulary system has more materials available than the other three systems combined.

The large quantity of materials available today, both core and supplementary, makes selection difficult. Guidelines for evaluating reading materials are listed under criteria for:

1. instructional techniques
2. content
3. format
4. classroom effectiveness.

All materials must first be judged on whether they can achieve the teacher's instructional objectives; that is, to teach at appropriate levels, to meet specific skills needs, and to provide continuing motivation for the child.

Terms for Self-Study

core materials	readability
supplementary materials	new alphabet materials
sound-symbol materials	reading kits

Discussion Questions

1. Upon taking a new assignment in a school, how does a teacher get a realistic view of what materials are available for use?
2. In a practical way, how would a teacher match the characteristics of children with the characteristics of available books?
3. Assuming that the basic or core materials were already purchased, how would you spend an allotted $300.00 in supplementary materials money?

part VII

Putting It Together

The last act, the final chapter—to put it all together. Theories and practices have been reviewed. Now each individual needs to decide how he will judge himself as a reading teacher. This part of the book attempts to help in that analysis and that projection.

19

Evaluating Progress

In Chapter 1 we described a particular first-grade classroom. The teacher, Regina Clare, organized her class and worked from an attitude that enabled her to react systematically to the needs of individuals. She worked with groups in various centers of activity and had records on each child to show where they might need or want directions that were slightly different from others. After four or five months of working in that environment it is appropriate for her to ask: "How am I doing?"

How does a teacher review and evaluate reading instruction—whether teaching goes on in a continuous progress environment or in a more traditional setting? Part of the answer comes from pupil performance, part from teacher performance, and part comes from the attitudes and feelings that exist among them. Those performances and those attitudes are specific things; they are behaviors that Regina Clare thought were important in her view of reading.

A Personal Definition

Throughout this book we have used a model of reading that enables a teacher to act on the specific needs of children who are trying to improve their performances. To determine needs, we have emphasized the need for teachers to define reading in terms they can work with. That personal definition is important, because it directs a teacher's planning and observation of children's reading. Think for a moment about the aspects of reading that you have dealt

447

with in this text and those that you have seen in classrooms you have visited. Could you now begin to define reading in a way that helps you to teach children, to observe their strengths and weaknesses, to lead them to new learning, and to provide practice that is appropriate for their needs? If you haven't done it earlier, now is the time to formulate your definition of reading instruction. In this chapter we will remind you of some aspects of reading instruction discussed in this text. By means of that review, we can formulate the kinds of questions and procedures that Regina Clare, for example, needs to determine her success.

Background

The importance of the reader's experience cannot be overstressed. A reader thinks with his background forming a foundation for whatever he is reading. When he reads out loud, for example, he sometimes uses words that are different from the ones on the printed page because his mind races ahead and speaks words that are more familiar than are those of the author. Since the child's language is integral to his experience, the teacher respects and tries to build on that language, alerting the child to its power and to the ways that language is reflected in print. His background supplies the reader with energy, attention, and purpose, since it includes all the emotional overtones that his previous experience suggests he apply to the subject and the situation. Those background experiences must color all the cognitive categories that you include in a definition of reading instruction.

Cognitive Factors

Any reading program or set of materials used in a reading program will include word skills, comprehension skills, and creative activities. The Harris-Smith model in this text includes those categories and develops them in a logically consistent sequence from simple to complex. This model provides a cognitive picture of how the reader works on the printed page to build the kind of understanding that suits his purpose. The model also makes it possible to observe the reader and make judgments concerning his strengths and weaknesses. It is designed to promote diagnostic-prescriptive teaching.

Each chapter in this text has shown examples of typical classroom activities using terminology most frequently found in classroom practice materials. At the same time we have indicated where those activities fit into the Harris-Smith model. The chapter headings refer to typical activities that are used in daily teaching and in children's basic textbooks. A combination of the model and the chapter headings is a two-handed tool that gives insight into the act of reading and also shows ways that teachers can help children to learn and practice.

Working with Children

A teacher's definition of reading must be translated into action. It not only directs the teacher's thinking about the kinds of activities to engage in but also guides his observations of children's work. The definition becomes a framework for diagnostic teaching. At each stage of the child's development the teacher uses the definition to observe and to push forward to more effective reading. (This would be a good place for you to compare your present definition with the one that you wrote when you first began to read this text.)

Getting Started

Language experience stories constitute an effective means of showing children the relation between speech and print and of emphasizing communication. Along with that activity, auditory and visual discrimination skills can be developed. This text emphasized the importance of environmental factors in teaching initial auditory and visual skills.

Reading Vocabulary

This textbook also suggested teaching a small body of sight words as an early step in actual reading instruction. Through visual memory the child learns to associate a printed symbol with its counterpart in the spoken language. In most cases the words he initially learns to read are ones of great personal importance—his name and the names of familiar objects, people, and places. He dictates language-experience stories about events that occur in school, at home, and on the playground. Thus the children are able to read a story in a book immediately. Those sight words and their experience story activity give children success in a printed language format.

Decoding

Almost immediately the child also begins to learn a strategy for decoding word symbols. When he has learned to recognize several words with the same initial letter at sight, the teacher calls his attention to the similarity among the words. From that point a systematic decoding program (phonics or linguistics) can be taught. The child gradually learns to generalize about the sound-symbol associations found in the words he can read. That constitutes a major step in enabling him to read independently.

Meaning is not neglected during these early days of reading instruction. The teacher constantly checks the understanding the child brings to the printed symbols and provides instruction to assure that meaning is present.

While instruction on decoding continues, the scope of the instructional program broadens. Additional techniques for recognizing words are taught; comprehension is emphasized, as the content of what is read becomes more difficult and more complex; oral reading skills are taught; and the child's reading interests are strengthened and expanded.

Becoming Independent

The child must become independent in his ability to recognize words. Therefore, expanding the child's sight vocabulary continues to be a teaching objective. Until a word is recognized instantly it must be analyzed each time it is met. Some words can be broken into familiar parts; others must be reduced to syllables or even phonemic elements. The efficient reader has these skills at his disposal. He is also able to use context clues in conjunction with word analysis to quickly unlock words not recognized at sight. The child learns a battery of word recognition skills in the primary reading stage.

Getting the Meaning

Even at the primary level the child is asked to read increasingly more difficult material. At first he need do little more than add up the author's thoughts to understand the message contained on the printed page. Later he must follow more complex logic, restructure broken sequence, recognize sarcasm, and generally apply higher thought processes as he reads. In other words, the reader must be able to apply his thinking skills during the act of reading. In order to comprehend a written message the reader must have background experiences, real or vicarious in nature, that permit him to associate meaning with the printed word correctly. His language skills, including vocabulary and grammar, must be equal to the task of correctly interpreting the author's thoughts. He must be able to adjust his reading for different purposes and according to the kind of material. Comprehension is the payoff in reading.

The primary reading skills also include oral reading. On many occasions an audience depends for information on someone who is reading orally. Consequently, the reading program must teach the skills necessary for effective oral reading. The teacher can also use oral reading as a means for assessing reading problems. This textbook suggests that teachers regularly read aloud to their students.

Building Interests

The teacher must expand children's reading interests by introducing them to new ideas and topics. As children develop an interest in books they should be led to set personal standards for judging what they will read. They require instruction in the principles of literary analysis in order to increase their appreciation of what they read.

Higher competencies in reading are not delayed until a given date or grade level. It is not crucial that all primary reading skills be handled at a specified degree of sophistication before a higher-level skill (such as study skills) be introduced. In the general sequence of reading skills, the higher competencies of critical and creative reading, reading in the content fields, and study skills normally follow the primary reading skills. That traditional sequence results from a need to set grade level priorities. It should in no way limit what teachers and children can do.

Reading Critically and Creatively

Nowhere is the dependence of a higher-order ability on one of lower order more apparent than in the areas of critical and creative reading. Without a solid foundation in reading comprehension the child is ill-equipped to take on a critical reading task. Critical reading has been identified in this text as those reading-thinking skills that enable the reader to apply criteria to a selection and make judgments about it. In this process the skills of analysis, inference, and evaluation are crucial. Creative reading involves integrating the reading experience into the knowledge and thinking of the reader, and producing a response that is unique to the individual. The skills of synthesis and application are basic. The teacher is responsible for leading the child to read critically and creatively.

Reading for Information

In school a child reads history and science books, follows mathematical problems, understands geography concepts, and so forth. The teacher is responsible for helping a child adjust his reading to the style, format, organization, and difficulty of expository materials.

Children also use reading as a tool when they apply their library and study skills. They must be familiar with standard reference volumes, know how to locate information in a library or given volume, and be able to organize information to solve a problem or answer a question. The teacher must demonstrate the use of these skills and provide children with the opportunity to use them in realistic situations. The close relationship between reading in the content fields and library-study skills makes it highly desirable to integrate the instruction provided in these areas.

Teacher Self-evaluation

"Have I been a successful teacher?" Obviously there is no simple way to decide the answer to such a complex question. Information from a variety of sources is needed to provide a satisfactory answer.

Evidence concerning the success of the reading program can be gathered from the results of children's performance on criterion tests, the number of children needing special remedial instruction outside the classrcom, the attitude of children toward reading class, the quality of daily workbook assignments, and dozens of other sources. This text cannot begin to present an adequate discussion of the total evaluation of teaching. However, it is possible to describe several simple but useful means for teacher self-evaluation. Included will be interaction analysis, closed-circuit television, introspective means, library usage, and student growth.

Classroom Interaction

During a discussion about a reading passage, students must be alert and thinking. The nature of comprehension operations requires interaction. The discussion period should be characterized by verbal exchanges, and that means at least as much pupil talk as teacher talk. During the reading period a teacher could have a colleague observe and record who is speaking at every ten-second interval. A simple tally of teacher talk and student talk would quickly reveal whether students were active in the discussion. That's a start in measuring interaction.

Flanders (1965), Amidon (1967), and others have developed procedures for assessing the nature of classroom interaction. Somewhat over-simplified, the interaction-analysis technique requires that an observer classify the types of activities in a classroom according to *who is speaking* (for example: teacher, student, or no one), the *nature of the talk* (for example: lecture, giving directions, or taking directions), and the *nature of the interaction* (for example: acceptance of feelings, praise or encouragement, criticism, or acceptance and use of ideas of students).

Interaction analysis can be an effective tool for appraising a teaching-learning situation. Interpretation of the results involves some subjectivity, but generally reveals the degree of teacher dominance in classroom activities and the kind of intellectual tasks that children are asked to perform. From the standpoint of reading instruction it is essential that children have numerous opportunities to talk, react, debate, and share. Insofar as the type of thinking that is taking place, higher-level tasks—such as interpretation and synthesis—are preferable to memorization or simple recall. An analysis of the type of interaction found in the classroom can provide feedback on how well the teacher is following good instructional principles. It is simple and highly desirable for the classroom teacher to tape record his lessons and conduct an interaction analysis of his teaching.

Videotaping

Videotape can be a helpful tool for self-evaluation of teaching. The opportunity to see a lesson as an observer has several advantages. First, the teacher can focus on different aspects of the teaching situation and see the same lesson a number of times. Second, with the press of teaching responsibilities removed, the teacher can observe his behavior with a degree of detachment not possible while a lesson is in progress. For example, the number of students participating in a discussion can be noted or the adequacy of a phonics lesson can be checked. This technique enables the teacher to personally judge his performance and effectively plan a program of self-improvement.

Introspection and Surveys

Teachers are constantly in the process of evaluating their performances by introspective means. As a lesson proceeds, for example, the amount of attention exhibited by the class is noted and serves as feedback for self-evaluation. Teachers have many daily opportunities for introspective self-evaluation. The sensitive and concerned teacher depends heavily on this useful approach to evaluation.

A more systematic approach to introspective evaluation is by means of checklists, such as the one that follows. The items on a checklist can vary from straightforward questions, requiring little or no subjective judgment (for example: "Are reading skills presented so that one specific skill is developed in a lesson?"), to very subjective questions requiring much self-analysis (for example: "Are follow-up activities constructed so as to contain a balanced program of written and oral responses?"). The greatest value of such checklists is that many aspects of the reading program are explored which might otherwise be forgotten or ignored. Introspection is highly suspectible to self-delusion. The teacher who wants to be completely satisfied can rationalize and explain away nearly any negative aspect of his teaching. The teacher intent on objective self-evaluation can learn much about himself from introspection.

Teacher Self-evaluation of the Reading Program[1]

LOOKING AT MY CLASSROOM

I. Are there evidences of my reading program around the room?
  A. Charts
    1. Primary
      Are there experience charts?
      Are there charts relating to specific reading lessons?
      Are there vocabulary charts?
      Are there sound charts?
        Teacher made?
        Pupil made?
      Are there attractively arranged displays of pupil language efforts?
    2. Intermediate
      Are there charts to guide development of writing and speaking skills?
       Example: paragraphs, reports, letters
      Are there pupil-teacher-made summaries?
       Example: social studies, science, health
      Are there charts to develop word meanings and concepts?
      Are there charts to illustrate principles of word analysis?
      Are there attractively arranged displays of pupil effort?
  B. Additional materials for independent reading
    1. Are there books of varying levels related to *different topics* and of diverse types (textbooks, biographies, travel books, stories, and so on) attractively arranged and easily available to children?

[1]Prepared by John E. Connelly. Reading Center, State University College, Fredonia, New York.

2. What provision do I make in my planning for:
   a. helping children develop an interest in independent reading?
   b. building cooperatively general but meaningful purposes for this reading?
   c. sharing the ideas, information, and enjoyment children gain from this activity?

II. Does my classroom environment lend itself to individual and group work in reading?
  A. Is there a library or reading corner which:
    1. displays books in an enticing manner?
    2. provides space for book reviews, book information, and pupil comments?
    3. provides a comfortable reading in terms of chairs, tables, adequate lighting?
  B. Is the room so arranged that the group working with the teacher:
    1. is compact enough to enable all to hear without using a loud voice?
    2. is far enough from those working independently so that it is not disturbing to the others?
    3. has sufficient space to work comfortably?
    4. is planned so that graphic materials used by the teacher are readily visible to all members of the group?
    5. is planned so the teacher has writing space available if the situation demands additional visual material?

LOOKING AT MY CLASS

I. Is each person in my room at a proper reading level?
  A. Have I accurately assessed each child's instructional reading level and independent reading level through:
    1. studying the reading record card?
    2. analyzing objective test results?
    3. reading former teacher reports?
    4. administering needed informal inventories?
  B. Have I utilized the above information in planning:
    1. other language activities?
    2. social studies?
    3. science, health, safety?
    4. mathematics?

II. How have I provided for the group working independently?
  A. Are the independent activities:
    1. reading or language centered?
    2. differentiated according to pupil abilities?
    3. related to previously taught reading skills?
    4. the result of a directed reading activity follow-up?
    5. an outgrowth of independent reading?
    6. so constructed that there is an identifiable learning purpose in them?

LOOKING AT THE LESSON

I. Are my directed reading activities (developmental reading lessons) a strong part of my reading program?
  A. Are the introductory phases planned so that they include:
    1. definite, precise, specific, attainable teacher purposes?
    2. adequate (neither too little nor too much) readiness in terms of theme, background knowledge, vocabulary, and concepts?

3. necessary vocabulary presentation in context?
4. a check of individual pupil mastery of needed concepts and vocabulary?
5. challenging, interest-provoking, attainable purposes set for the individuals in the group?
6. silent reading to achieve purposes set?
7. a culminating activity in oral or written form?
8. an appropriate length of time for the particular group?
9. suitable distribution of time among the various elements of such a lesson?

B. Are follow-up lessons constructed to contain:
1. teacher-guided pupil recall of purposes?
2. activities appropriate to purposes set and material read?
3. opportunities for use of vocabulary and concepts introduced in the original presentation?
4. carefully constructed, preplanned questions, statements, or challenges to stimulate pupil reaction to material?
5. a balanced program of written and oral responses?
6. approaches other than question and answer?
7. provision for ample opportunities for pupil self-evaluation and teacher-pupil evaluation?
8. reasonable time for these activities?

C. Are reading skills presented so that:
1. one specific skill is developed in a lesson?
2. children are helped to discover principles and generalizations *for themselves?*
3. children are helped to understand how and when the skill is applied in reading material?
4. sufficient practice items are used with the group?
5. individual written practice follows the group presentation?
6. situations are provided in which the skill is applied?
7. the proper amount of time is devoted to each phase?

II. Are oral reading activities given their proper place in the total program?

A. Are oral reading activities planned so that:
1. the time devoted to oral reading is minor in scope and used for a specific purpose?
2. of those included, a major portion involves:
   a an audience situation in which only the person reading has the book?
   b. reading to prove a point?
   c. reading to find a point of information?
   d. choral speaking?
   e. sharing poetry?
   f. dramatizations?

Use of Libraries

The finest reading instruction with regard to skill development, materials, tests, and the like might well be regarded as a failure if the children do not read widely for information and recreation.

The number of books read by a class per week provides an excellent index of how successful the reading program has been in stimulating reading. More careful analysis might contrast fiction with nonfiction circulation. These and other factors might be helpful in determining what aspects of the total reading program need attention. But unless simple circulation figures indicate a healthy flow of books into the hands of children, more fundamental issues should be considered first.

The use of libraries is probably one of the best estimates available as to what attitudes toward reading are being nurtured in the reading program. Interests and tastes in reading can also be assessed by noting the types of books being read by the children.

Student Progress

While it would be foolish to base teacher self-evaluation solely on the reading achievement of students, some insight into the quality of instruction can be gained by studying student progress. Various means can be used to make such a comparison. For example, the year-end gain in raw score points for reading could be noted on criterion tests that match the reading skills taught. Informal measures would also reveal progress. Suppose the child who could not use an index at the beginning of the school year can accurately compete an exercise on the use of an index at the end of the year. Growth of this sort is concrete evidence of teacher effectiveness. Systematic evaluation would require that evidence be gathered for all children in a class on a variety of reading skills. Nonetheless, mastery of a skill on an informal measure is excellent proof of progress.

A teacher who actually teaches diagnostically would have records of children's progress in any number of forms that could be used for evidence of growth. A check on skills mastered late in the school year could be compared with a similar checklist completed in September. The number and types of books read for pleasure per week by each child early and late in the school year could be contrasted. Teacher-made tests and basal reader tests can provide similar information regarding student growth.

The Importance of the Teacher

It is obvious from even this simplified description that the reading process is extremely complex and is full of situations in which performance can go awry. In view of this complexity the teacher's task takes on special importance.

We have suggested that a classroom teacher can effectively discharge his responsibilities for teaching reading by approaching the reading process diagnostically. He must organize the various reading skills into some logical sequence. He must then systematically determine where each learner stands in the sequence. He needs diagnostic tools and techniques to gather this information. But, perhaps most of all, the teacher must have an attitude that causes him to approach every classroom activity with a diagnostic point of view. He must be constantly on the alert for useful feedback; he must watch for patterns of behavior that indicate an instructional need; he should classify information and relate it to his conception (or model) of the reading act. Without such an approach the task of teaching reading can be overwhelming.

Focus on Joy

No better motto could be placed above a reading teacher's door than:

"HE FOCUSES ON JOY!"

The teacher who creates an atmosphere that leads to joy through reading has certainly achieved the highest priority. That joy cannot be achieved without progress toward reading competence. In the final analysis the most positive self-evaluation rests with the statement: "I helped the children to joy through reading."

Discussion Question

1. Can you define reading and demonstrate how your definition will guide you in observing, organizing, and developing attitudes?

Appendixes

Appendix A   Children's Book Clubs

The availability of books is an extremely important factor in whether children develop the habit of reading. When children themselves own books they are easily accessible. The book clubs listed here can help the teacher place books within easy reach of every child.

American Heritage Junior Library, 336 West Center Street, Marion, Ohio.

Arrow Book Club, Scholastic Book Services, 904 Sylvan Avenue, Englewood Cliffs, New Jersey 07632 (Ages 9–11)

Beginning Reader's Program 575 Lexington Avenue, New York, New York 10021.

The Bookplan, 921 Washington Avenue, Brooklyn, New York 11225 (Ages 8 months–11 years).

Catholic Children's Book Club, 260 Summit Avenue, St. Paul, Minnesota (Ages 6–16).

Dell Paperback Books, Educational Sales Department, 1 Dag Hammarskjold Plaza, 245 East 47th Street, New York, New York 10017.

Junior Literary Guild, 177 Park Avenue, New York, New York 10017 (Ages 5–16).

Lucky Book Club, Scholastic Book Services, 904 Sylvan Ave., Englewood Cliffs, New Jersey 07632 (Ages 7–9).

Parents' Magazine Book Club for Little Listeners and Beginning Readers, 52 Vanderbilt Avenue, New York, New York 10017 (Ages 3–8).

See Saw Book Club, Scholastic Book Services, 904 Sylvan Avenue, Englewood Cliffs, New Jersey 07632 (Ages 5–7).

Teen Age Book Club, Scholastic Book Services, 904 Sylvan Avenue, Englewood Cliffs, New Jersey 07632 (Ages 12–14).

Weekly Reader Children's Book Club, Education Center, 1250 Fairwood Avenue, Columbus, Ohio 43216 (Ages 4–10).

Young America Book Club, 1250 Fairwood Avenue, Columbus, Ohio 43216
(Ages 10–14).

Young Folks Book Club, 1376 Coney Island, Brooklyn, New York 11230.

Young People's Book Club, 226 North Cass Avenue, Westmont, Illinois 60559
(Ages 4–10).

Young Readers of America (Division of Book-of-the-Month Club), 345 Hudson
Street, New York, New York 10014 (Ages 9–14).

Appendix B   Newspapers and Magazines for Children

Newspapers and magazines for children can stimulate interest in reading.
Teachers should encourage parents and relatives to give subscriptions as long-
lasting and worthwhile gifts.

American Forests, 1319-18th Street, N.W., Washington, D.C. 20036.

American Girl, 830 Third Avenue, New York, New York 10022.

Boy's Life, New Brunswick, New Jersey 08902.

Calling All Girls, Better Reading Foundation, Inc., 52 Vanderbilt Avenue, New
York, New York 10017.

Child Life, 1100 Waterway Boulevard, Indianapolis, Indiana 46202.

Children's Digest, 52 Vanderbilt Avenue, New York, New York 10017.

Cricket, P.O. Box 100, LaSalle, Illinois 61301.

Highlights for Children, 2300 West 5th Avenue, Columbus, Ohio 43216.

Humpty Dumpty's Magazine, 52 Vanderbilt Avenue, New York, New York
10017.

Jack and Jill, Box 528, Indianapolis, Indiana 46202.

Kids, 747 Third Avenue, New York, New York 10017.

My Weekly Reader, 245 Long Hill Road, Middletown, Connecticut 06457.

National Geographic and *National Geographic School Bulletin,* 17th and M
Streets, N.W., Washington, D.C. 20036.

Ranger Rick's Nature Magazine, National Wildlife Federation, 1412 16th St.,
N.W., Washington, D.C. 20036.

Scholastic Magazines, 50 West 44th Street, New York, New York 10036.

Science Digest, 244 West 57th Street, New York, New York 10019.

Sprint, 902 Sylvan Avenue, Englewood Cliffs, New Jersey 07632.

World Traveler, Box 3618, Washington, D.C. 20007.

Appendix C   Selection Aids for Children's Books

American Library Association. *Caldecott Medal Books* (Chicago, Ill. 60611: 50
East Huron Street).

Annual, annotated brochure of award-winning picture books.

————. *For Storytellers and Storytelling: Bibliographies, materials, and
Resource Aids* (Chicago, Ill.: 50 East Huron Street, 1968).

Includes versions of stories expressed in other art forms—such as
poetry, dance, music, the cinema, and recordings.

American Library Association. *Newbery Medal Books*. Chicago, Ill. 60611: 50 East Huron Street,

> Annual brochure listing Newbery Award books with occasional annotations.

Arbuthnot, May Hill, and Zena Sutherland. *Children and Books* (Glenview, Ill.: Scott, Foresman and Company, 1972).

> Reviews books for children by main characters and plots, and suggests ways of using some of them for reading aloud and storytelling. Discusses illustrations and illustrators of children's books and criteria for judging illustrations, and lists extensive reference materials at the end of each chapter.

Association for Childhood Education International. *A Bibliography of Books for Children* (Washington, D.C. 20016: 3615 Wisconsin Avenue, N.W., rev. ed. 1968).

> An annotated bibliography of over 1,500 books for children of ages 2–12. Includes author and title index, and a reference books section.

Brewton, John E., and Sara W. Brewton, comps., *Index to Children's Poetry* (Chicago, Ill.: The H. W. Wilson Company, 1954, 2d suppl. 1965).

> A title, subject, author, and first line index to poetry in collections for children and youth. Information about the poems is given in the title entries, with cross-references to 130 books of poetry. This listing gives author(s), name of book, approximate price, a very brief summary, and the suggested grade level for the book.

Eastman, Mary H. *Index to Fairy Tales, Myths, and Legends* (Boston, Mass.: Faxon, 1926, 1st suppl., 1952).

> Lists fairy tales, myths, legends, and stories in alphabetical order by title, with location or author. Author or book title is also listed in a second section with date of publication, publisher, and approximate price.

Gaver, Mary, ed. *Elementary School Library Collection: A Guide to Books and Other Media* (Newark, N.J.: Bro-Dart Foundation, 1968, suppl. 1969, suppl. 1973).

> Lists and annotates basic print and nonprint materials in classifications of reference materials, nonfiction, fiction, easy books, periodicals, and professional tools for the teachers. Contains an author, title, subject index with a graded listing, a classified listing of audiovisual materials, a list of large print materials, and a directory of publishers.

Gillespie, John T., and Diana L. Lembo. *Introducing Books: A Guide for the Middle Grades* (New York, N.Y.: R. R. Bowker Company, 1180 Avenue of the Americas, 1970).

> A book talk manual for the educator to use with ages 8 through 12. Eighty-eight books are concisely described and analyzed for use as book talks. Suggests themes (and related book and nonbook follow up) that reflect needs and concerns of the intermediate group's growing social and ethical awareness: family, friends, physical problems, values, adult roles, reading for fun.

Green, Ellin. *Stories: A List of Stories to Tell and to Read Aloud* (New York, N.Y.: New York Public Library, 1965).

> Divided into two main parts: list of stories to be told; stories and poems to read aloud. Another section includes a list of recordings by well-known storytellers or authors reading from their own works. Name and subject indexes.

Guilfoile, Elizabeth. *Books for Beginning Readers*
————, *One Hundred More Books for Beginning Readers*. (Champaign, Ill.: National Council Teacher of English, 1962).

> Discusses useful books and indexes them by author, title, illustrator, publisher, date of publication, and appropriate grade level.

Heller, Freida M. *I Can Read It Myself* (Columbus, Ohio: Ohio State University, 1965).

> Independent reading for primary grades listed from easiest to more difficult. Includes a publishers' directory. Self-explanatory titles of the bibliography sections are: "I'm Just Beginning to Read by Myself"; "I'm Reading a Little Better", "Now I Can Read Real Good."

Hodges, Elizabeth D., comp. and ed. *Books for Elementary School Libraries; An initial collection* (Chicago, Ill.: American Library Association, 50 East Huron Street, 1969).

> Over 3,000 books, catalogued by subject, with brief descriptive annotations and complete bibliographic information; K–8.

Huck, Charlotte S. *Children's Literature in the Elementary School* (New York, N.Y.: Holt, Rinehart and Winston, 3rd ed. 1976).

> Reviews current and historical books for children by subject matter; and helps children, teachers, and librarians build a frame of reference for book selection. Gives guidelines for children's literature program in school and library and details audiovisual supplements. Author, publisher, and title index and subject index are included, as well as publishers' addresses, book selection aids, a pronunciation guide for children's book authors, and a listing of children's book awards.

Huus, Helen. *Children's Books to Enrich the Social Studies: For The Elementary Grades* Washington, D.C.: National Council for the Social Studies, rev. ed. 1966.

> A major topic is presented, such as "Times Past," with subtopics, such as "The First Settlements, Toward Independence," under which the books are listed by title, author, illustrator, publisher, city of publication, year of publication and appropriate grade level, with a brief paragraph summarizing the content.

Keating, Charlotte Matthews. *Building Bridges of Understanding* (Tucson, Ariz.: Palo Verde Publishing Co., 1967).

> Lists fully annotated ethnic stories to help children gain insights into the contribution of different ethnic and religious groups: Blacks, American Indians, Spanish-speaking, Chinese-Americans, Japanese-Americans, Hawaiians, Jews, and others. Arranged by author under each subject. Preschool to high school.

Kingman, Lee, ed. *Newbery and Caldecott Medal Books, 1956–1965*. (Boston, Mass.: Horn Books, 1965).

An update of children's award-winning books (*see* Mahoney and Field reference below).

Larrick, Nancy, *A Parent's Guide to Children's Reading* (Garden City, N.Y. 11530: Doubleday & Company, 4th rev. ed. 1975).

A handbook for parents, with an extensive annotated bibliography.

Larrick, Nancy. *A Teacher's Guide to Children's Books*. (Columbus, Ohio 43216: Charles E. Merril Books, 1300 Alum Creek Drive, 1960).

A book on children's literature with annotated bibliographies.

Mahoney, B. E., and Elinor Whitney Field, eds. *Newbery Medal Books, 1922– 1955,* (Boston, Mass.: Horn Books, 1955).

Presents brief comments about each year's Newbery Medal winner, given for exceptional children's books, with a short excerpt from the book, a biographical note about the author or other qualified person, the author's paper of acceptance, and illustrations from some books.

Mahoney, B. E., Louise P. Latimer, and Beulah Folmsbree, eds. *Illustrators of Children's Books, 1744–1945* (Boston, Mass.: Horn Books, 1947).

———. *Illustrators of Children's Books: 1946–1956*

——— *Illustrators of Children's Books, 1957–1966.*

Describes the history and development of the use of illustrations in children's books. Includes illustrators from many countries, and describes various procedures used for printing illustrations. Also includes a bibliography of illustrators and authors.

Miller, Bertha Mahoney, and Elinor W. Field, eds. *Caldecott Medal Books: 1938–1957* (Boston, Mass. Horn Books, 1957).

Complete data on each medal-winning book and its illustrators from the beginning of the award to 1957. Includes name of author, book note concerning artist's technique, the artist's acceptance paper, and a biographical paper for each winner. Teachers will appreciate the value of distinctive art examples that are available for use by and with children.

New York Public Library Committee. *Children's Books Suggested as Holiday Gifts*. (New York, N.Y. 10018: Library Sales Office, 5th Avenue and 42nd Street, 1968).

An annotated bibliography of books of the year.

Perkins, Flossie L. *Book and Non-book Media: Bibliography of Selection Aids* (Champaign, Ill.: National Council of Teachers of English, 1970).

An annotated selection aid of book and nonbook media with emphasis on school library materials. Items are listed by title with complete bibliographical data for ordering.

Rollins, Charlemae. *We Build Together: A Reader's Guide to Negro Life and Literature for Elementary and High School Use*. Champaign, Ill.: National Council of Teachers of English, 1967).

Lists many books now available that show blacks honestly and not as a steryotyped people. For all age groups except adult. Includes annotated bibliography on biography, poetry, folklore, history, picture books, fiction, and nonfiction. Directory of publishers.

Shor, Rachel and Estelle A. Fidell, eds. *Children's Catalog* (Chicago, Ill.: The H. H. Wilson Company, 11th ed. 1966, with four annual supplements).

> Designed to serve as a basic selection aid for elementary schools. Done in three parts: classified (subdivided by Dewey Classification, fiction, easy books, and story collections) with full bibliographical data for each book, plus an annotation and excerpts from review(s); author, title, subject, and analytical indexes; directory of publishers and distributors.

Spache, George. *Good Reading for Poor Readers* (Champaign, Ill.: Garrard Publishing Company, 1974).

> Describes the "psychological interaction of a child and a story." Lists trade and library books, and also adopted and simplified materials, textbooks, workbooks, games, magazines, newspapers, series books, and book clubs, with suggested grade levels.

Sragow, Jean. *Best Books for Children* New York, N.Y. 10036: R. R. Bowker Company, 1180 Avenue of the Americas.

> Annual, annotated bibliography for kindergarten–Grade 12, arranged by grades and subjects.

Appendix D   Illustrative Instructional Activities

The instructional activities presented in this appendix are intended to illustrate how the classroom teacher can encourage children's use and refinement of various reading-thinking skills. The specific activities offered illustrate rather than exhaust the options open to the teacher. By adjusting and adapting these ideas and by striking out in new directions which these ideas only suggest, the creative teacher can develop any number of exciting, enjoyable, and challenging instructional activities. We recommend that you return to the chapters and sections of this text which deal with a certain aspect of reading to refresh your understanding of how a suggested activity promotes development in an area. References to aid you in this regard are given with each activity.

Mastery of most reading skills requires practice over a considerable period of time (often months or even years). Completion of the suggestions offered here will not automatically lead to children's success in learning to read or even to mastery of one component of reading. Used intelligently, however, activities such as those that follow can provide children with opportunities to apply and practice the reading-thinking act in a variety of settings through concrete applications.

Be careful to guard against these activities becoming ends in themselves; they are only a means to an end.

Comprehension Including Critical and Creative Reading

These activities are intended to help children learn, practice, and apply various thinking operations to the reading act.

Have children read part way through a story or book, stopping at some predesignated point. (All children can read the same or different material, as you prefer.) Discuss the characters and events as they have developed up to that point. Make a special effort to help children identify the conflict involved in the story they have read ("What problem do the characters try to solve in the story?"). Ask the children to predict different ways the story might end. Seek explanations for the endings they suggest. Encourage children to consider the personalities of the characters and how these will affect the outcome, the likelihood of unusual intervening events, and so forth.

Ask each child to write on paper the ending he finds most plausible, with a brief rationale for the answer given. Have each child seal the predicted ending in an envelope with his name on the front; collect the envelopes and keep them in a safe place for later reference.

After finishing the book or story have each child open his own envelope and share his prediction by reading it aloud if he is willing. Discuss the predictions made and what clues children used in making the forecast. Identify clues in the story that were missed initially but seem more important with the advantage of hindsight.

Repeat the process later with another story, encouraging children to apply the insights they gained from their first attempts at predicting outcomes. Be sure to point out that more than one ending is plausible for most stories.

This activity will be most successful when used with groups of children because of the interaction this involves. However, it can be used with individuals in a conference setting. Advanced readers in the upper grades will normally profit most from this activity because they can better deal with the personalities and events in a story. Younger children can and should engage in activities of this type, but the analysis they are expected to perform must be adjusted to their level of sophistication.

As a follow-up activity in predicting outcomes, cut popular comic strips from the daily newspaper. Snip off the last frame of each strip. Have children read the first three frames and draw the final frame, including dialogue. They can then compare their endings to the original. No answer should be considered wrong; however, some will probably be quite similar to the original which will indicate the child's ability to predict the outcome. Use simple comics with beginning readers; more complex ones with primary and advanced readers.

Refer to Chapter 5, "Reading Comprehension: Cognitive and Affective Factors," for a discussion of the principles these activities address.

Have children draw vertical lines on a piece of paper to form five columns. Label the columns *Who, What, When, Where,* and *Why.* Demonstrate how to put relevant information in each column using a well-known fairy tale or fable for purposes of illustration (for example, story of "Jack and the Bean Stalk").

Who	What	When	Where	Why
Jack	Trades cow for magic beans	One afternoon	In the village	To become rich

Have children fill in the columns using information from a story they have just read. Discuss the children's responses.

This activity is appropriate for readers at all stages of development and can be used with groups or individuals.

Refer to Chapter 5, "Reading Comprehension: Cognitive and Affective Factors," for a discussion of the principles this activity addresses.

Locate and clip short articles from children's magazines or the daily newspaper. Remove the title or headline from the articles. Put the articles in one envelope and the titles or headlines in a second envelope. Invite children to spill the contents of the two envelopes on a table, read the articles, and locate and match the correct title or headline with the article. Normally four or five articles are enough to avoid mere guesswork, but more can be added to make this task more difficult. Roman numerals or letters on the backs of the pieces can provide feedback on whether the task has been done correctly.

Advanced students can be asked to write their own titles or headlines for comparison with the original.

This activity is most appropriate for a child working alone. By adjusting the difficulty of the articles, the activity can be made appropriate for all but the beginning reader.

Refer to Chapter 5, "Reading Comprehension: Cognitive and Affective Factors," for a discussion of the principles this activity addresses.

Write a statement of fact and a statement of opinion on the chalkboard about some game the children enjoy playing outdoors. For example: If the game is basketball, this statement of fact could be used: "A regulation basketball hoop is ten feet above the ground." This statement of opinion could be used: "Basketball is more fun than baseball." Ask the children to identify which statement is fact. Point out that statements of fact can be verified (in this case by a rule book), but statements of opinion are based on personal preference or belief. Invite the children to generate additional statements about the game you have chosen. Have children classify these as fact or opinion, and tell why the classification was made.

Have children make a bulletin board display with the title "Fact or

Opinion?'' Divide the board into halves. On one side the children can post newspaper articles with statements of fact underlined. On the second side other newspaper articles can be posted with statements of opinion underlined. Create teams and award points for each correct example posted during a three-day period by the members of that team. The team receiving the most points might develop an exercise on distinguising fact from opinion for other children to complete.

These activities are appropriate for readers at all stages of development. Even beginning readers can and should have experience with critical thought. As presented here, these activities are appropriate for groups of children, but they could be adapted for independent work.

Refer to Chapter 12, ''Critical Reading,'' for a discussion of the principles these activities address.

Have children develop a parody on an advertisement frequently seen on television. Suggest that some feature of the ad be exaggerated or altered by the children to create a humorous variation. Arrange to have each child (or group) present the parody to the class. Discuss each presentation, paying particular attention to the feature selected for alteration. Have children identify who the ad is intended to persuade and how the appeal is made. Study the language used in the ad. Experiment with advertising language by substituting synonyms for words that are actually used. (For example: ''fragrant'' may be replaced by ''smell'' in a room freshener ad.)

As a follow-up activity have the children develop an advertising campaign for some imaginary product, employing techniques often used in commercial advertising.

These activities are most appropriate for advanced readers working in a group setting.

Refer to Chapter 12, ''Critical Reading,'' and Chapter 13, ''Creative Reading,'' for a discussion of the principles these activities address.

Word Recognition

These activities are intended to help children learn, apply, and practice a variety of techniques for recognizing words.

Collect a variety of discarded magazines and catalogues. Let children each select two or three that have special personal appeal. Instruct children to page through the material for the purpose of cutting out pictures of scenes or objects they would like to read about. Have children paste the pictures they choose on a large piece of butcher paper or tagboard.

At this point a number of alternatives exist. Beginning readers can be helped to label the pictures they select. At various odd moments during the next few days children can then be asked to tell why they selected their pictures and can read the printed labels.

Primary-level readers can be helped to find books or stories related to the pictures they selected. When the children have finished each book or story they can write the author and title, along with several words they found interesting or challenging, beneath the appropriate picture. Again, odd moments of the school day can be used to have children share their posters with others, giving brief comments about the book or story. Special attention can be given to the words selected.

This activity is designed for beginning readers and for those who are reading at the primary level. Children can work alone on this task or in small groups. In either case, sharing as described above benefits all children in the class.

Refer to Chapter 8, "Visual Memory of Words," or Chapter 9, "Decoding Word Symbols," for a discussion of the principles this activity addresses.

Show children how a crossword puzzle works. Discuss how such puzzles are probably created. The whole class can develop a simple crossword puzzle on the chalkboard with the teacher's guidance. Have children make their own crossword puzzles around some familiar theme (a season of the year, a popular book, a sport, and so on). Let the children exchange and solve the puzzles.

With younger children you may find it desirable to provide a crossword puzzle that you have already begun to make. The children can then build additional word squares and clues around those items you used as a starting point.

More advanced readers may be interested in trying to do commerically prepared crossword puzzles, such as those carried by most daily newspapers. Teams of children may have greater success with harder puzzles than they would working individually.

With an adjustment in the difficulty of words and clues used, this activity is appropriate for all readers, with the exception of beginners.

Refer to Chapter 10, "Word Recognition—A Strategy" (and Chapter 4, "Reading Comprehension: Experiential and Language Factors"), for a discussion of the principles this activity addresses.

Bingo, as you probably know, involves a caller, or leader; Bingo cards; and a collection of tiles, or pieces, that are pulled from a pile one at a time and read aloud by the caller. A tile tells players which column to look in and gives a number the player must match. The player covers a square that matches what the caller announces. The goal is a series of five matches that form a straight line (vertically, horizontally, or diagonally). This variation on Bingo, called

Winky, substitutes information on the Bingo cards and tiles for the numbers, making it a reading game. All other aspects of the game remain identical to Bingo. Make a set of Winky cards (whatever number you need). Each card should have twenty-five places arranged in a 5 × 5 column and row grid as illustrated:

W	I	N	K	Y
		FREE		

Depending on the age and reading ability of the children who will play the game, various options exist for completing the Winky cards. For example: Consonant letters can be written in the places. Beginning readers could then play Winky by finding the letter in a column that corresponds to the beginning (or ending) sound of a word written on a tile, pulled and read aloud by the caller. In this way auditory discrimination is practiced. If letters are written in the columns, the game could give practice with visual discrimination. For example: the caller can pull and hold up a large letter card. The children then find and match that letter in a certain column. Numerous other possibilities can be developed for games played with letters of the alphabet.

The squares can also be filled with words. At a very easy level children can match words pulled by the caller. Variations can be introduced that turn Winky into a game for practicing context clues (For example: "In column W, cover a word that fits the blank in this sentence: I _____ to the store.")

Winky can be turned into a prefix or suffix game. Here the caller pulls a prefix, such as *un,* and instructs players to cover a word in a specific column that can be formed with the prefix *un.* As a related task the child can be required to write the word with the prefix in a sentence on a separate sheet of paper.

Winky can be turned into a comprehension game by putting the names of characters from a basal textbook in the places. The leader then pulls tiles containing descriptions of the characters. For example: "In column K, cover the name of a character who has trouble with the weather."

By varying the content of the Winky cards and the nature of the directions given by the caller, this game can offer a host of interesting possibilities for reading activities. Children can easily make many of these games themselves.

This activity is most appropriate for beginning readers and those reading at the primary level. It is obviously a group activity.

Refer to Chapter 7, "Visual and Auditory Discrimination and Perception," Chapter 8, "Visual Memory of Words," Chapter 9, "Decoding Word Symbols," and Chapter 10, "Word Recognition—a Strategy," for a discussion of the principles this activity addresses.

The familiar game of tick-tack-toe can be turned into any number of interesting and worthwhile reading games. For example: a large block of nine squares is drawn and a word card turned face down in each square.

Before a player can place either a cross or circle in that square he must turn over the card and read the word aloud (and use it in a sentence, if you like).

This activity is appropriate for beginning readers and must involve two children.

Refer to Chapter 8, "Visual Memory of Words," for a discussion of the principles this activity addresses.

As a variation, the words written on cards can be ones frequently used in compound words—for example: *some, earth, every, where*. The player must create a compound word using the word on the card. Make it more challenging by requiring the player to create two compound words containing the base word on his second turn, three compound words on the third turn, and so on.

Refer to Chapter 10, "Word Recognition—a Strategy," for a discussion of the principles this activity addresses.

Have children cut an article from a daily newspaper. Ask each child in the group to find a word in the article that contains a prefix. Discuss the meaning of that prefix and how removing the prefix would affect the meaning of the sentence. Challenge children to see how many other prefixes they can find in the same article. List all words found on the chalkboard.

As a follow-up activity develop a poster which lists common prefixes, the usual meaning of the prefixes, and examples of the prefix in use.

This can be either a group or an individual activity. It is most appropriate for those who are reading at the primary level or for more advanced readers, if more uncommon affixes are used.

Refer to Chapter 10, "Word Recognition—a Strategy," for a discussion of the principles these activities address.

Clip pictures of a variety of common objects from old magazines and catalogues. Mount each picture on a 3 × 5 index card. These cards can be used with beginning readers to practice auditory discrimination. Have children sort the cards into groups of words that begin with the same sound. Later, when initial sounds have been mastered, the cards can be sorted by ending sounds, and then according to vowel sounds.

Children can be helped to check their own efforts at grouping if you write the word on the back of the card. When they have finished sorting the pictures they simply turn the cards over to see if they have grouped words beginning with *b* together, for example, or have grouped words ending with *p* together, or words with a short *a* together (this would require that vowel sounds be marked long or short). Having the words on the back of the card also makes them useful for building sight vocabulary. The association of the printed symbol *cat* with a picture of a cat may eventually help beginning readers learn to recognize the word.

The index cards can also be used to practice alphabetizing. As a start simply have children put the cards in order according to the first letter of the word. Later, words that begin with the same letter can be put in order according to the second letter of the word, and so on.

Children can do these activities while they are working alone. The activities are most appropriate for beginning readers.

Refer to Chapter 7, "Visual and Auditory Discrimination and Perception," and Chapter 9, "Decoding Word Symbols," for a discussion of the principles these activities address.

Have children write a new or interesting or appealing word on an index card (computer cards also work well). When the child is able to recognize the word and use it in a sentence, the card can be put into a pack marked "Words I know." Challenge each child to add a word a day to his packet. Occasionally pair up children for a review of words in the packet. Any word that has been forgotten is removed from the packet and studied until it is "known" again.

More advanced readers can use this same activity as a device for increasing vocabulary. In addition to saying the word aloud and using it in a sentence, they can be asked to give one or more meanings for the word, as well as synonyms and antonyms.

Refer to Chapter 10, "Word Recognition—a Strategy," for a discussion of the principles this activity addresses.

Ditto or mimeograph copies of experience stories the children have written or dictated themselves, but delete every tenth word leaving a blank. Have children fill in the blanks using the context of the story and the sentence to determine what is missing.

With older children creative writing stories can be reproduced in the same way with every fifth word deleted. Encourage children to discuss their answers, comparing particular instances where they each supplied different words for a blank.

These activities are most appropriate for children who are working alone. Readers at all stages of development can profit from such activities.

Refer to Chapter 10, ''Word Recognition—a Strategy,'' (and Chapter 4, ''Reading Comprehension: Experiential and Language Factors'') for a discussion of the principles these activities address.

Content Reading

These activities are intended to help children learn, apply, and practice reading skills in the content areas. Refer to Chapter 14, ''Teaching Reading for Life,'' for a discussion of the principles these activities address.

Let children decide whether they would prefer to work in a group that will explore math, physical science, biological science, history, geography, economics, health, music, or art. Form groups that honor the preferences as closely as possible. Give each group the task of developing two lists of words: One is to include technical words that are important to the content and process of the field they are studying (for example: steppe, plateau, tree line, and so on in geography); two is to include words that have a special meaning in the field they are studying and a different meaning in general conversation (for example: beat, harmony, swing, and so on in music).

The groups can begin the search for words by consulting their textbooks. Encyclopedias and other reference books can also be consulted. The final product of each group's efforts should be two lists of words in alphabetical order with examples of the words in sentences.

This activity is appropriate for advanced readers.

Involve the children in original research in one of the social sciences. Identify the kinds of questions a sociologist, political scientist, or historian might ask about children in a given school, for example. Arrange for students to interview other children in the school for the purpose of testing an hypothesis or reaching a generalization. Have children organize and study the information gathered from such interviews. End the experience with a report in written or oral form summarizing the findings.

Possible areas of exploration could include: the television viewing habits of children in different grade levels, the mobility of children and families in the school, career goals of elementary school children, political loyalties of ten-year-olds, how children earn and spend money, population trends in the neighborhood, how teachers happened to become teachers, customs and ceremonies practiced by the families, and so forth.

This activity is appropriate for advanced readers.

Write out study guides for the children to help them focus on important issues, key words, and subtle relationships as they read a text or reference in a content area. Make the questions and tasks as personalized and relevant to the children's interests and backgrounds as possible. (For example: "In the section on the causes of the Civil War, three points we discussed in class are made. What are they?")

This activity is appropriate for primary level and advanced level readers.

Provide children with a skeletal outline of material they have been assigned to read. Have them take notes by filling in the parts of the outline that are left blank.

This activity is appropriate for advanced readers.

Put material that is difficult for some children to read on audiotape. Those who wish to can listen to the tape and follow along in their books, or can simply acquire the information through listening. More capable readers can help make tapes for those needing this type help.

This activity is appropriate for primary level and advanced level readers.

Study Skills

These activities are intended to help children learn, practice, and apply reference and study skills. Refer to Chapter 15, "Library and Study Skills," for a discussion of the principles such activities address.

Develop a grid that lists random letters of the alphabet at the top and topics the children like to read and talk about along the side.

A sample grid might be:

	B	P	N	E	W
Dogs					
Horses					
Mysteries					
Outer space					
Rocks					
Dinosaurs					
Music					

Challenge the children to find a nonfiction book in the library whose title or whose author's last name begins with the letter of the alphabet given at the top of the column, and whose main topic corresponds to the subject on the left. Allow a certain length of time in the school library (for example: thirty minutes) to work on this task. (Probably no one will fill all the spaces; some squares may even be impossible to fill.) Five points can be earned by filling in one of the squares with a title or author not reported by anyone else. Three points can be earned if only one other person reports the same information. One point is earned for all other correct responses. The person with the highest point total wins. (*Suggestion:* Stagger the thirty-minute periods in the library throughout the day so that resources are not overburdened.)

Vary this activity by changing the topics and using different letters of the alphabet. You might also limit the source of data to the encyclopedia, almanac, atlas, or other reference volume, and then vary the task accordingly. For example: If an atlas is used, the topics might become rivers, countries, cities of at least 100,000 in population, mountain ranges, and so on. Children can also work in teams on such a task to promote peer instruction and interaction.

These activities are appropriate for advanced readers.

Give each child a mock travel voucher for your general area (the amount can vary, but should permit extensive travel—$500 or so). Explain that each person is to plan a trip by automobile to whatever location(s) in the area they would like to visit, given the time and money needed (up to the limit specified). Set these conditions:

1. Gasoline costs $.65 per gallon.
2. The automobile gets twenty miles per gallon.
3. All admission fees must be included in the budget.
4. Food and overnight expenses must be figured at thirty dollars per day.

The child's task is to plot his route on a road map, prepare a day-by-day itinerary, and describe in brief the sights and attractions he intends to see. A budget showing how the funds have been distributed should also be presented by the child.

As an extension of this activity each child could correspond with officials in various cities and request brochures, detailed maps, public transportation schedules, and so on for the purpose of making a display of his trip. Each child could also write an imaginary log of the trip, bringing in characters, imaginary problems, and heroic actions taken to overcome the obstacles encountered. These written accounts could be bound into a volume that can be placed in the reading corner.

These activities are appropriate for advanced readers.

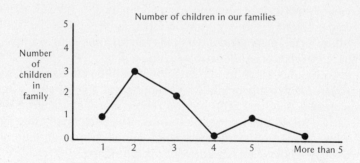

Number of children in our families

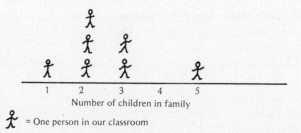

Number of children in our families

FIGURE A.1

Gather some basic information from the children about themselves and their families. For example: Ask about the number of children in the family, the number of aunts they have, the number of uncles they have, the number of pets at home, the type of pets and other information that is easily remembered. Have the children help you express this information in the form of graphs and charts on the chalkboard. An example of a graph and one of a chart is given in Figure A.1 on page 474.

Help the children identify questions they would like to survey. Assign the task of gathering responses to the questions and then making a chart or graph to present the results to each question. Encourage children to go beyond the limits of their own classroom. They might survey neighbors, consult the sports pages of the daily newspaper, call merchants on the telephone, and so on for information.

These activities are appropriate for primary level readers.

Set up a cooking center in the classroom. Display a variety of cookbooks or make selected recipes available in a card file. Encourage children to locate a recipe that appeals to them, bring the necessary supplies to school, and make the dish. (This can also be a homework assignment.) Be sure to remind the children about safe use of a hot stove, knives, and other equipment.

A similar activity can be developed around directions for assembling model autos, model animals, model airplanes, and the like, which are available at any hobby center.

As a variation, children can write their own recipes or directions for playing a game, making a gift, or finding a treasure hidden in the classroom. Others in the class can try to follow these written directions.

Such activities are appropriate for primary level and advanced level readers.

Have the children bring parts or all of their hobbies to school. Give each child an opportunity to tell about how he became interested in the hobby, when and what he likes to do with it, and how it has changed over time. Ask children to think about how they would help a person get started who wanted to pursue the same hobby. Instruct children to develop a general outline for a hobby that would guide them in helping a beginner. Have children share the results. Offer suggestions for improvement. Have children add details to the general sections of the outline. Post the final products on a bulletin board.

This activity is appropriate for most children in Grades 3 to 5 and for advanced readers.

Give the children a list of ten words with instructions to locate the page in the dictionary where each is defined. Make a game of seeing who can find and record the page numbers first.

This activity is appropriate for all children who can use a dictionary.

Invite the children to imagine that they are going to join an expedition that intends to explore a newly discovered river in South America. This river is thought to begin high in the Andes and flow into the Amazon River. Discuss and speculate about what such an adventure would be like.

Ask the children to decide what equipment they would need if their expedition were to be taken by helicopter to the mouth of the river. Instruct them to develop a list of necessary items, the weight and cost of the items, and where they could be obtained. Make catalogues and telephone books available to the children, and give them several days to work on the task.

Have children share their findings. They can compare their lists for the purpose of deciding which items are absolutely necessary and which are not. If a parent or other person in the community is experienced in wilderness survival techniques invite them to visit with the children and lead a discussion. Encourage interested children to read fictional and nonfictional accounts of people and expeditions that have survived extreme conditions.

This activity is most appropriate for advanced readers but can also be adapted for primary grades.

Selected Bibliography*

Altick, Richard. *Preface to Critical Reading.* New York: Holt, Rinehart and Winston, Inc., 1969 (Chapter 12).

Amble, Bruce R., and Francis J. Kelly. "Phrase Reading Development Training with Fourth Grade Students: An Experimental and Comparative Study," *Journal of Reading Behavior,* II, no. 1 (Winter 1970), 85–97 (Chapter 10).

Amidon, Edmund, and John Hough. *Interaction Analysis: Theory, Research and Application.* Reading, Mass.: Addison Wesley, 1967 (Chapter 19).

Arbuthnot, May Hill. *Children and Books.* Chicago: Scott, Foresman and Company, 1972 (Chapter 11).

Ashton-Warner, Sylvia. *Teacher.* New York: Simon and Schuster, 1963 (Chapters 8, 10).

Atkinson, Richard C., and John D. Fletcher. "Teaching Children to Read with a Computer." *The Reading Teacher* (January 1972), 319–327 (Chapter 18).

Austin, Mary, and Coleman Morrison. *The First R: The Harvard Report on Reading in Elementary Schools.* New York: The Macmillan Company, 1963 (Chapter 12).

Bailey, Mildred H. "The Utility of Phonics Generalizations in Grades One through Six" *The Reading Teacher,* XX (February 1967), 413–418 (Chapter 9).

Baratz, Joan C., and Roger W. Shuy. *Teaching Black Children to Read.* Washington, D.C.: Center for Applied Linguistics, 1969.

Barrett, Thomas. "Taxonomy of Reading Comprehension," *Reading 360 Monograph.* Lexington, Mass.: Ginn and Company, 1972 (Chapter 5).

Barrett, Thomas C. "Visual Discrimination Tasks as Predictors of First Grade Reading Achievement," *The Reading Teacher,* XVIII (January 1965), 276–282 (Chapter 7).

Bateman, B. "Reading: A Controversial View, Research and Rationale," *Curriculum Bulletin,* XXIII (1967), 1–41 (Chapter 7).

Beaucamp, Wilbur L. "A Preliminary Experimental Study of Techniques in the Mastery of Subject Matter in Elementary Physical Science," *Supplementary Education Monograph,* No. 24. Chicago: University of Chicago Press, (1925), 47–87 (Chapter 5).

*Chapter references that follow some listings are recommended for specific parts of the book where they are particularly applicable. When no such chapter reference appears, the material is for general reading.

Betts, Emmett A. *Handbook on Corrective Reading.* Chicago: Wheeler Publishing Co., 1956.

————. "Structure in the Reading Program," *Elementary English,* XLII (March 1965), 238–242.

Biskin, Donald, and Kenneth Hoskisson. "Moral Development through Children's Literature," *The Elementary School Journal,* LXXV (December 1974), 152–157 (Chapter 5).

Bissett, Donald J. *The Amount and Effect of Recreational Reading in Selected Fifth Grade Classrooms.* Ph.D. dissertation, Reading and Language Arts Center; Syracuse, N.Y.: Syracuse University, 1969 (Chapter 11).

Bloom, Benjamin S., ed. *Taxonomy of Educational Objectives Handbook* I: *Cognitive Domain.* New York: David McKay Company, Inc., 1956.

Bloomfield, Leonard, and Clarence L. Barnhart. *Let's Read: A Linguistic Approach.* Detroit: Wayne State University Press, 1961 (Chapter 9).

Bond, Guy L., and Robert Dykstra. "The Cooperative Research Program in First Grade Reading Instruction," *Reading Research Quarterly,* II, no. 4 (Summer 1967) (Chapters 7, 9, 18).

Bormuth, John. "Cloze Tests and Reading Comprehension," *Reading Research Quarterly,* IV, no. 3 (Spring 1969), 359–367 (Chapters 4, 6).

Bormuth, John R. *Cloze Tests as Measures of Readability and Comprehension Ability.* Bloomington, Ind.: Indiana University, Ed.D. dissertation, 1962 (Chapter 10).

Brady, Larry M. *How Stated Purposes for Reading Affect Reading Comprehension Scores of Fifth Grade Students in a Midwestern Suburban School District.* Grand Forks, N. Dak.: University of North Dakota, Unpublished Ed.D. dissertation, 1974 (Chapter 5).

Braun, Carl. "Interest-loading and Modality Effects on Textual Response Acquisition," *Reading Research Quarterly,* IV, no. 3 (Spring 1969), 428–444 (Chapter 8).

Brink, Carolyn. *Caddie Woodlawn,* illustrated by Kate Seredy. New York: Macmillan Company, 1936 (Chapter 11).

Bruner, Jerome. *The Process of Education.* Cambridge, Mass.: Harvard University Press, 1960.

Burger, I. Victor, T.A. Cohen, and P. Bisgaler. *Bringing Children and Books Together.* New York: Library Club of America, 1956 (Chapter 11).

Burnett, Richard W. "The Classroom Teacher as a Diagnostician," *Reading Diagnosis and Evaluation,* XIII, Part 4. Newark, Del.: Proceedings of the Thirteenth Annual Convention of the International Reading Association (1970).

Buros, Oscar K., ed. *Seventh Mental Measurements Yearbook.* Highland Park, N.J.: Gryphon Press, 1972 (Chapter 6).

Buros, Oscar. *Reading Tests and Reviews.* Highland Park, N.J.: Gryphon Press, 1969 (Chapter 6).

Burton, Virginia Lee. *Mike Mulligan and His Steam Shovel.* Boston, Mass.: Houghton Mifflin, 1939 (Chapter 11).

Buswell, Guy T., and William H. Wheeler. *The Silent Reading Hour.* Chicago, Ill.: Wheeler Publishing Company, 1923.

Callaway, Byron, and Oscar T. Jarvis. "Program and Materials Used in Reading Instruction: A Survey," *Elementary English,* XLIX (April 1972), 578–581 (Chapter 18).

Carroll, James L. "A Visual Memory Scale (VMS) Designed to Measure Short-term Visual Recognition Memory in Five and Six-year Old Children," *Psychology in the Schools,* IX (April 1972), 152–158 (Chapter 8).

Carver, Ronald P. "A Critical Review of Mathemagenic Behaviors and the Effect of Questions upon the Retention of Prose Materials," *Journal of Reading Behavior*, IV (Spring 1972), 93–119.

Casteel, Doyle J., and Robert J. Stahl. *Value Clarification in the Classroom: A Primer.* Pacific Palisades, Calif.: Goodyear Publishing Company, 1975 (Chapter 5).

Chall, Jeanne. *Learning to Read: The Great Debate.* New York: McGraw-Hill, Inc., 1967 (Chapters 9, 18).

Clymer, Theodore. "The Utility of Phonic Generalizations in the Primary Grades," *The Reading Teacher*, XVI (January 1963), 252–258 (Chapter 9).

Coleman, James C. "Perceptual Retardation in Reading Disability Cases," *Journal of Educational Psychology*, XLIV (December 1953), 497–503 (Chapter 7).

Cooper, David, et al. *Decision Making for the Diagnostic Teacher.* New York: Holt, Rinehart and Winston, Inc., 1972 (Chapters 8, 16).

Cordts, Anna D. *Phonics for the Reading Teacher.* New York: Holt, Rinehart and Winston, Inc., 1956 (Chapter 9).

Coulter, Myron L. "Verbal Problem Solving in the Intermediate Grades," *Reading and Inquiry.* Newark, Del.: IRA Conference Proceedings, X (1965), 303–306.

Covington, M.V. "Some Experimental Evidence on Teaching for Creative Understanding," *The Reading Teacher*, XX (February 1967), 390–396 (Chapter 12).

Crary, Helen L., and Robert W. Ridgway. "Relationships between Visual Form Perception Abilities and Reading Achievement in the Intermediate Grades," *Journal of Experimental Education*, XL, no. 1 (Fall 1971), 17–22 (Chapter 7).

Crosby, Muriel, ed. *Reading Ladders for Human Relations*, 4th ed. Washington, D.C.: American Council on Education, 1963 (Chapter 11).

D'Angelo, Edward. "Critical Thinking in Reading," *Elementary English*, XLVIII, no. 8 (December 1971), 946–950 (Chapter 12).

Davis, Frederick B. "Psychometric Research on Comprehension in Reading," *Reading Research Quarterly*, VII, no. 4 (Summer 1972), 628–678 (Chapters 4, 5).

————. "Research in Comprehension in Reading," *Reading Research Quarterly*, III, no. 4 (Summer 1968), 499–545 (Chapter 5).

Davis, Ira C., John Burnett, Wayne E. Gross, and L. Benton Prichard. *Science 3, Discovery and Progress.* New York: Holt, Rinehart and Winston, Inc., 1965 (Chapter 14).

Dawson, Mildred A. "Children's Literature—Lodestone in Children's Books," *Changing Concepts of Reading Instruction*, VI (1961), 183–186 (Chapter 11).

Dawson, Mildred A., and Henry Bamman. *Fundamentals of Basic Reading Instruction.* New York: David McKay Company, Inc., 1959 (Chapter 10).

DeBoer, John. "Teaching Critical Reading," *Critical Reading*, King, Wolf, and Ellinger, eds. Philadelphia: J.B. Lippincott Company, 1967 (Chapter 12).

Deighton, Lee C. "Flow of Thought Through an English Sentence," *Vistas in Reading*, IRA Conference Proceedings, XI, Part I (1966), 322–326 (Chapter 4).

Deutsch, Martin. "Early Social Environment: Its Influence on School Adaptation," *The School Dropout.* Daniel Schreiber, ed. Washington, D.C.: National Educational Association, 1964 (Chapter 7).

Distad, H.W. "A Study of the Reading Performance of Pupils under Different Conditions on Different Types of Materials," *Journal of Educational Research*, XVIII (April 1927), 247–248 (Chapter 5).

Dolch, E.W. *The Basic Sight Word Test.* Champaign, Ill.: Garrard Publishing Company, 1942 (Chapter 8).

Don, Sue, *et al. Individualizing Reading Instruction with Learning Stations and Centers.* Evansville, Ind.: Riverside Learning Associates, Inc., 1973 (Chapter 16).

Downing, John A. *The Initial Teaching Alphabet Reading Experiment.* Chicago: Scott, Foresman and Company, 1964 (Chapter 9).

Downing, John A., Daphne Cartwright, Barbara Jones, and William Latham. "Methodological Problems in the British i.t.a. Research," *Reading Research Quarterly,* 3 (Fall 1967), 85–100 (Chapter 9).

Draper, Arthur G., and Gerald H. Moeller. "We Think with Words," *Phi Delta Kappan,* LII (April 1971), 482–484 (Chapters 8, 14).

Dreyer, Hal B. "Rx for Pupil Tutoring Programs," *The Reading Teacher,* XXVI, no. 8 (May 1973), 810–813 (Chapter 16).

Duker, Sam. "Basics in Critical Listening," *English Journal,* LXI (November 1962), 565–567 (Chapter 7).

Durkin, Dolores. *Children Who Read Early.* New York: Teachers College Press, Columbia University, 1966 (Chapters 7, 11).

————. *Phonics and the Teaching of Reading.* New York: Teachers College Press, Columbia University, 1965 (Chapter 10).

Durrell, Donald D. *Durrell Analysis of Reading Difficulty.* New York: Harcourt Brace Jovanovich, Inc., 1955 (Chapter 6).

————. *Improving Reading Instruction.* New York: World Publishing Company, 1956.

Durrell, Donald, and Helen A. Murphy. "The Auditory Discrimination Factor in Reading Readiness and Reading Disability," *Education,* LXXIII (May 1953), 556–560 (Chapter 7).

————. "Auditory Discrimination Abilities and Beginning Reading Achievement," *Reading Research Quarterly,* I, no. 3 (Spring 1966), 5–34 (Chapter 7).

Dykstra, Robert. "Classroom Implications of the First Grade Reading Studies," *College Reading Association,* IX (Fall 1968), 53–59 (Chapters 7, 9).

————. "Summary of the Second Phase of the Cooperative Research Program in Primary Reading Instruction," *Reading Research Quarterly,* 4 (Fall 1968), 49–70.

————. "The Use of Reading Readiness Tests for Prediction and Diagnosis: A Critique," *The Evaluation of Children's Reading Achievement,* Thomas Barrett, ed. Newark, N.J.: International Reading Association, 1967 (Perspectives in Reading Series).

Eastman, P.D. *Cat in the Hat Dictionary.* New York: Random House, Inc., 1964 (Chapter 15).

Elkind, David, Margaret Larson, and William Van Doorninck. "Perceptual, Decentration, Learning and Performance in Slow and Average Readers," *Journal of Educational Psychology,* LXVI (February 1965), 50–56 (Chapter 7).

Emans, Robert. "History of Phonics," *Elementary English,* LV (May 1958), 602–608 (Chapter 10).

————. "The Usefulness of Phonics Generalizations above the Primary Grades," *The Reading Teacher* (February 1967), 419–425 (Chapter 9).

————. "The Usefulness of Word Pronunciation Rules." Speech at AERA Convention. Chicago, Ill., 1966 (Chapter 9).

Farley, Walter. *The Black Stallion.* New York: Random House, Inc., 1941 (Chapter 11).

Farr, Roger, and Nicholas Anastasiow. *Review of Reading Readiness Tests.* Newark, Del.: International Reading Association, 1969 (Chapter 6).

Fillmer, H. Thompson. "Professional Reading Activities for Paraprofessionals," *The Reading Teacher,* XXVI, no. 8 (May 1973), 806–809 (Chapter 16).

Fisk, Lori, and Henry Clay Lindgren. *Learning Centers.* Glen Ridge, N.J.: Exceptional Press, 1974 (Chapter 16).

Flanders, Ned A. *Teacher Influence, Pupil Attitudes and Achievement.* Washington, D.C.: U.S. Department of Health, Education and Welfare, Superintendent of Documents, Catalog no. F.S. 5.225: 25040, 1965 (Chapter 19).

Flesch, Rudolf. *Why Johnny Can't Read and What You Can Do about It.* New York: Harper & Row, Publishers, 1955 (Chapter 12).

Forbes, Esther. *Johnny Tremain,* illustrated by Lynn Ward. Boston: Houghton Mifflin Company, 1944 (Chapter 11).

Fries, Charles C. *Linguistics and Reading.* New York: Holt, Rinehart and Winston, Inc., 1962 (Chapters 8, 9).

Fry, Edward. "Teaching a Basic Reading Vocabulary," *Elementary English,* XXXIV (November 1957), 38–42 (Chapter 8).

Gagné, Robert M., and William J. Gephart, in collaboration with Eleanor J. Gibson. "Perceptual Learning in Educational Situations," *Learning Research and School Subjects.* Bloomington, Ind.: Phi Delta Kappa, 1968.

Gartner, Alan, Mary Kohler, and Frank Riessman. *Children Teach Children.* New York: Harper and Row, Inc., 1971 (Chapter 16).

Gates, Arthur I., and Walter H. MacGinitie. *Gates-MacGinitie Reading Tests.* New York: Teachers College Press, Columbia University, 1964 (Chapter 6).

Gates, Arthur I., and David H. Russell. "Types of Materials, Vocabulary Burden, Word Analysis and Other Factors in Beginning Reading" *Elementary School Journal,* XXXIX (September 1938), 27–35.

Georgiou, Constantine. *Children and Their Literature.* Englewood Cliffs, N.J.: Prentice-Hall, Inc., 1969 (Chapter 11).

Gibson, Eleanor J. "Perceptual Learning," *Annual Review of Psychology,* XIV (1963), 29–56 (Chapter 7).

————. "Perceptual Learning in Educational Situation," *Learning Research and School Subjects,* Robert M. Gagné and William J. Gephart, eds. Itasca, Ill.: F.E. Peacock Publishers, Inc., 1968, pp. 61–86 (Chapter 7).

Gibson, Eleanor J., James J. Gibson, Anne D. Pick, and Harry Osser. "A Developmental Study of the Discrimination of Letter-like Forms," *Journal of Comparative and Physiological Psychology,* 55, (November 1962), 897–906 (Chapter 7).

Gilmore, J.V. *Gilmore Oral Reading Test.* New York: Harcourt Brace Jovanovich, Inc., 1952 (Chapter 6).

Glutman, Lila R., and Paul Rozin. "Teaching Reading by Use of a Syllabary," VIII, no. 4 (Summer 1973). Newark, Del.: International Reading Association, pp. 447–483 (Chapters 9, 10).

Goodman, Kenneth S. "Analysis of Oral Reading Miscues: Applied Psycholinguistics," *Reading Research Quarterly,* V, no. 1 (Fall 1969), 9–30 (Chapter 6).

————. "A Communicative Theory of the Reading Curriculum," *Elementary English,* XL (March 1963), 290–298 (Chapter 4).

————. "Dialect Barriers to Reading Comprehension," *Reading and Inquiry,* IRA Conference Proceedings, X (1965), 240–242 (Chapter 4).

Goodman, Kenneth, *et al. Choosing Materials to Teach Reading.* Detroit, Mich.: Wayne State University Press, 1966 (Chapter 18).

Goodman, Yetta M., and Carolyn L. Burke. *Reading Miscue Inventory.* New York: Macmillan Publishing Co., Inc., 1972 (Chapter 6).

Goudey, Charles. "Reading—Directed or Not?" *Elementary School Journal,* LX (February 1970), 245–247 (Chapter 5).

Gray, William S. *Gray Oral Reading Test.* Indianapolis, Ind.: Bobbs-Merrill Company, Inc., 1963 (Chapter 6).

Guilford, J.P. "The Three Faces of Intellect," *American Psychologist,* XIV (1959), 469–479 (Chapter 5).

Guszak, Frank J. "Questioning Strategies of Elementary Teachers in Relation to Comprehension," Speech given at IRA Conference in Boston, Massachusetts, April 1968 (Chapter 5).

Hackett, Alice. *Seventy Years of Best Sellers: 1895-1965.* New York: R.R. Bowker Company, 1967 (Chapter 11).

Hall, Mary Anne. *Teaching Reading as a Language Experience.* Columbus, Ohio: Charles E. Merrill Co., 1970 (Chapter 17).

Hall, Robert A., Jr. *Linguistics and Your Language.* New York: Doubleday Anchor, 1960 (Chapter 9).

Hammill, Donald. "Training Visual Perceptual Processes," *Journal of Learning Disabilities,* V (November 1972), 552–559 (Chapter 7).

Harris, Albert J. *How to Increase Reading Ability.* New York: David McKay Company, Inc., 1975.

Harris, Larry A. "A Study of Altruism," *Elementary School Journal,* LXVIII (December 1967), 135–141 (Chapter 5).

————. *A Study of the Rate of Acquisition and Retention of Interest-loaded Words by Low Socioeconomic Kindergarten Children.* Unpublished Ph.D. dissertation, University of Minnesota, 1967 (Chapter 11).

Harris, Larry A., and Carl B. Smith. *Reading Instruction through Diagnostic Teaching,* New York: Holt, Rinehart and Winston, Inc., 1972.

Hay, J., and C. Wingo. *Reading with Phonics.* New York: J.B. Lippincott Company, 1960 (Chapter 9).

Hedges, William D., and Veralee B. Hardin. "Effects of a Perceptualmotor Program on Achievement of First Graders," *Educational Leadership Research Supplement,* XXX (December 1972), 249–253 (Chapter 7).

Heilman, Arthur. *Phonics in Proper Perspective,* 2d. ed. Columbus, Ohio: Charles E. Merrill Publishing Company, 1967 (Chapter 9).

Heilman, Arthur W. *Principles and Practices of Teaching Reading.* Columbus, Ohio: Charles E. Merrill Publishing Company, 1967 (Chapter 12).

Henry, Marguerite. *Born to Trot.* Chicago, Ill.: Rand McNally & Company, 1950 (Chapter 11).

Hildreth, G.H., and N.L. Griffiths. *Metropolitan Readiness Tests.* New York: Harcourt Brace Jovanovich, Inc., 1965 (Metropolitan Readiness Test Series), (Chapter 6).

Hislop, Margaret J., and Ethel M. King. "Application of Phonic Generalization by Beginning Readers," *The Journal of Educational Research,* LXVI (May-June 1973), 405–412 (Chapter 9).

Hoskisson, Kenneth. "The Many Facets of Assisted Reading," *Elementary English,* LII, no. 3 (March 1975), 312–315 (Chapter 4).

————. "Should Parents Teach Their Children to Read?," *Elementary English,* LI (February 1974), 295–299 (Chapter 4).

Huck, Charlotte S. *Children's Literature in the Elementary School,* 3rd ed. New York: Holt, Rinehart and Winston, Inc., 1976 (Chapter 11).

Huhkins, F.P., and P. Shapiro. "Teaching Critical Thinking in Elementary Social Studies," *Education,* LXXXVIII (September-October 1967), 68–71 (Chapter 12).

Hunt, Mabel Leigh. *Ladycake Farm,* illustrated by Clotilde Embree Funk. Philadelphia, Penna.: J.B. Lippincott Company, 1952 (Chapter 13).

Hurd, Edith Thacher. *Engine, Engine #9.* New York: Lothrop, Lee and Shepard Company, Inc., 1961 (Chapter 11).

Huus, Helen. "Developing Interest and Taste in Literature in the Elementary Grades," *Reading as an Intellectual Activity,* VIII (1963), 46–50 (Chapter 11).

Ilg, Frances L., and Louise Bates Ames. *School Readiness: Behavior Tests Used at the Gesell Institute.* New York: Harper & Row, Publishers, 1965 (Chapter 7).

International Reading Association. "Paraprofessionals and Reading," *The Reading Teacher,* XXVII, no. 3 (December 1973), 337. Handbook of Committee on Paraprofessionals and Reading (Chapter 16).

Ives, Sumner. "Some Notes on Syntax and Meaning," *The Reading Teacher,* XVIII (December 1964), 179–183 (Chapter 4).

Jennings, Frank. *This Is Reading.* New York: Teachers College Press, Columbia University, 1965.

Kaplan, Sandra Nina, *et al. Change for Children: Ideas and Activities for Individualizing Learning.* Pacific Palisades, Calif.: Goodyear Publishing Company, Inc., 1973 (Chapter 16).

Karlsen, Bjorn, Richard Madden, and Eric F. Gardner. *Stanford Diagnostic Reading Test.* New York: Harcourt Brace Jovanovich, Inc., 1966 (Chapter 6).

Kasdon, Lawrence M. "Oral Versus Silent-oral Diagnosis." Paper presented at IRA Conference Proceedings, Boston, Mass., May 1968 (Chapter 6).

Katz, Phyllis, and Martin Deutsch. *Visual and Auditory Efficiency and Its Relationship to Reading in Children.* Cooperative Research Project No. 1099. Washington, D.C.: Office of Education, Department of Health, Education and Welfare, 1963 (Ch. 7).

Keedy, Mervin L., Leslie K. Swight, Charles W. Nelson, John Schlvep, and Paul A. Anderson. *Exploring Elementary Mathematics,* V. New York: Holt, Rinehart and Winston, Inc., 1970, 252–253 (Chapter 14).

Kelly, Madden, Gardner, and Rudman. *Stanford Achievement Test.* New York: Harcourt Brace Jovanovich, Inc., 1964 (Chapter 6).

King, Martha L., Bernice D. Ellinger, and Willavene Wolf, eds. *Critical Reading.* Philadelphia, Penna.: J.B. Lippincott Company, 1967 (Chapter 12).

Kingston, Albert J., Wendell W. Weaver, and Leslie E. Figo. "Experiments in Children's Perceptions of Words and Word Boundaries," *Investigations Relating to Mature Reading,* Frank P. Greene, ed., *Twenty-first Yearbook of the National Reading Conference,* 1972, 91–99 (Chapter 8).

Kjelgaard, Jim. *Big Red.* New York: Holiday House, 1945 (Chapter 11).

Kohlberg, Lawrence. "Stage and Sequence: The Cognitive Developmental Approach to Socialization," *Handbook of Socialization Theory and Research,* D. Goslin, ed. Chicago, Ill.: Rand McNally & Company, 1969 (Chapter 5).

Krathwohl, David R., *et al. Taxonomy of Education Objectives, Handbook II: The Affective Domain.* New York: David McKay Company, Inc., 1964.

Kumin, Maxine W. *The Beach Before Breakfast.* New York: G.P. Putnam's Sons, 1964 (Chapter 13).

Kunitz, S.J., and H. Haycraft, eds. *Junior Book of Authors*. New York: H.W. Wilson Co., 1951 (Chapter 15).

Labov, William. "Some Sources of Reading Problems for Negro Speakers of Nonstandard English," *New Directions in Elementary English*, A. Frazier, ed. Champaign, Ill.: National Council of Teachers of English, 1967, 140–167.

Labov, William, and Clarence Robins. "A Note on the Relation of Reading Failure to Peer-group Status in Urban Ghettos," *Linguistic-Cultural Differences and American Education. The Florida FL Reporter*, VII, no. 1 (Spring, Summer 1969), 66–67.

Laird, Charlton. *The Miracle of Language*. New York: World Publishing Company, 1953.

Lamb, Pose. *Guiding Children's Language Learning*. Dubuque, Iowa: William C. Brown Company, Publishers, 1967.

——————. *Linguistics in Proper Perspective*. Columbus, Ohio: Charles E. Merrill Publishing Company, 1968 (Chapter 9).

Larrick, Nancy. *A Parents' Guide to Children's Reading*. New York: Doubleday & Company, Inc., 1975 (Chapter 11).

Lee, Doris M., and R.V. Allen. *Learning to Read through Experience*. New York: Appleton-Century-Crofts, 1963 (Chapter 17).

Lefevre, Carl A. *Linguistics and the Teaching of Reading*. New York: McGraw-Hill Book Company, 1964 (Chapters 7, 8).

——————. "Reading by Patterns: A Psycholinguistic Remedial Tutorial Program for Young Adults," *Investigations Relating to Mature Reading*, Frank Green, ed., *Twenty-first Yearbook of the National Reading Conference*, 1972, 228–236 (Chapter 4).

Lippet, Peggy, and John E. Lohman. "Cross Age Relationships—An Educational Resource," *Children*, 12, no. 3 (May-June 1965), 113–117 (Chapter 16).

Loban, Walter. *The Language of Elementary School Children*. Champaign, Ill.: National Council of Teachers of English Research Report No. 1, 1963 (Chapter 17).

McCloskey, Robert. *Homer Price*. New York: The Viking Press, 1951 (Chapter 11).

McCracken, Robert A., and Marlene J. McCracken. *Reading Is Only the Tiger's Tail*. San Rafael, Calif.: Leswing Press, 1972 (Chapter 17).

McCullough, Constance M. *McCullough Word Analysis Tests*. Boston, Mass.: Ginn and Company, 1963 (Chapter 6).

——————. "Recognition of Context Clues in Reading," *Elementary English Review*, XXII (January 1945), 1–5 (Chapter 10).

——————. "Responses of Elementary School Children to Common Types of Reading Comprehension Questions," *Journal of Educational Research*, LI (September 1957), 65–70 (Chapter 12).

McDowell, E.E. III, and R.A. Youth. "Effects of Discrimination Pretraining upon Intralist Similarity Phenomenon in Developing Beginning Reading Skills," *Perceptual and Motor Skills*, XXXVI (June 1973), 1039–1045 (Chapter 8).

Marsh, R.W. "The London i.t.a. Experiment: A Rejoinder," *Reading Research Quarterly*, 4 (Fall 1968), 120–123 (Chapter 9).

Mason, George. "A Second Report on Word Confusion: Sequence and Duration of Instruction in the Mislearning of Words," *Journal of Reading Behavior*, 3, no. 4 (Fall 1970–1971). Milwaukee, Wisc.: National Reading Conference, Inc., 41–46 (Chapter 10).

Mathews, Mitford M. *Teaching to Read: Historically Considered*. Chicago, Ill.: The University of Chicago Press, 1966.

Mattleman, Marciene. "Beginning an Activity-centered Classroom," *The Reading Teacher*, XXV, no. 5 (February 1972), 424–429 (Chapter 16).

May, Frank B. *Teaching Language as Communication to Children*. Columbus, Ohio: Charles E. Merrill Publishing Company, 1967.

Meehan, Trinita. *The Effects of Instruction Based on Elements of Critical Reading upon the Questioning Patterns of Pre-service Teachers*. Bloomington, Ind.: Indiana University, unpublished Ed.D. dissertation, 1970 (Chapters 12, 14).

Monroe, Marion, and W. Cabell Greet. *My Little Pictionary*. Chicago, Ill.: Scott, Foresman and Company, 1964 (Chapter 15).

Muehl, Siegman, and Ethel M. King. "Recent Research in Visual Discrimination: Significance for Beginning Reading," *Vistas in Reading*, IRA Conference Proceedings, XI, Part 1 (1966), 434–439 (Chapters 7, 8).

Nardelli, Robert R. "Some Aspects of Creative Reading," *Journal of Educational Research*, L (March 1957), 495–508 (Chapter 12).

Naylor, Marilyn. "Reading Instruction through the Multi-station Approach," *The Reading Teacher*, XXIV, no. 8 (May 1971), 757–761 (Chapter 16).

Nodine, C.F., and J.V. Hardt. "Role of Letter-position Cues in Learning to Read Words," *Journal of Educational Psychology*, LXI (January 1970), 10–15 (Chapter 7).

North, Sterling. *Rascal*. New York: E.P. Dutton and Co., Inc., 1963 (Chapter 11).

O'Brien, Jack. *Silver Chief: Dog of the North*. New York: Holt, Rinehart and Winston Inc., 1933 (Chapter 11).

Oliver, Peter R., Jacquelyn M. Nelson, and John Downing. "Differentiation of Grapheme-phoneme Units as a Function of Orthography,' *Journal of Educational Psychology*, LXIII (October 1972), 487–492 (Chapter 7).

Palovic, Lora, and Elizabeth B. Goodman. *The Elementary School Library in Action*. West Nyack, N.Y.: Parker Publishing Co., Inc., 1968 (Chapter 15).

Peoster, Minnie. *A Descriptive Analysis of Beginning Reading, Combining Language Experience, Story Writing, and Linguistic Principles*. Bloomington, Ind.: Indiana University, unpublished Ed.D. dissertation, 1970.

Piaget, Jean. *The Language and Thought of the Child*, 3d. ed. New York: The Humanities Press, Inc., 1959, 288 (Chapter 2).

————. *The Origins of Intelligence in Children*, Margaret Cook, trans. New York: International Universities Press, 1952 (Chapter 7).

Piaget, Jean, and B. Inhelder. *The Child's Conception of Space*, F.J. Langdon and J.L. Lunzer, trans. New York: The Humanities Press, Inc., 1956 (Chapter 7).

Platts, Sister Mary E., Rose Marguerite, and Esther Shumaker. *Spice*. Benton Harbor, Mich.: Educational Service, Inc., 1960 (Chapters 8, 16).

Powell, William R. "Reappraising the Criteria for Interpreting Informal Inventories," Paper presented at the thirteenth annual convention of the International Reading Association, Boston, Mass., 1968 (Chapter 6).

Preston, Ralph C. *Teaching Social Studies in the Elementary School*. New York: Holt, Rinehart and Winston, Inc., 1968.

Quandt, Ivan. *Self-concept and Reading*. Newark, Del.: International Reading Association, 1974.

Quilling, Mary, and Wayne Otto. "Evaluation of an Objective Based Curriculum in Reading," *The Journal of Educational Research*, LXV, no. 1 (September 1971), 15–18 (Chapter 18).

Raim, Joan. "Rolling Out the Welcome Mat to Tutors," *The Reading Teacher*, XXVI, no. 7 (April 1973), 696–701 (Chapter 16).

Rankin, E.F., and J.W. Culhane. "Comparable Cloze and Multiple- choice Comprehension Test Scores," *Journal of Reading,* 13 (1969), 193–198 (Chapter 6).

Raths, Louis E., Merrill Harmin, and Sidney B. Simon. *Values and Teaching: Working with Values in the Classroom.* Columbus, Ohio: Charles E. Merrill Publishing Company, 1966 (Chapter 5).

Rauch, Sidney J. *Handbook for the Volunteer Tutor.* Newark, Del.: International Reading Association, 1969 (Chapter 16).

Rawlings, Marjorie Kinnan. *The Yearling.* New York: Charles Scribner's Sons, 1944 (Chapter 11).

Robinson, Helen M. "Developing Critical Readers," *Dimensions of Critical Reading,* Russell G. Stauffer, ed., XI (1964), 1–11. Newark, N.J.: University of Delaware, Proceedings of the Annual Education and Reading Conferences (Chapter 12).

————. "Visual and Auditory Modalities Related to Methods for Beginning Reading," *Reading Research Quarterly,* 8 (Fall 1972), 7–39 (Chapter 7).

Roe, Anne. *Making of a Scientist.* New York: Apollo Editions, Inc., 1961 (Chapter 11).

Rosenberg, Phillip E. "Audiologic Correlates," *"Dyslexia" Diagnosis and Treatment of Reading Disorders,* Arthur Keeney and Virginia Keeney, eds. St. Louis, Mo.: The C.V. Mosby Company, 1968, 53–59 (Chapter 7).

Rosenshine, Barak, and Norma Furst. "Research in Teacher Performance Criteria," *Research in Teacher Education,* B.O. Smith, ed. Englewood Cliffs, N.J.: Prentice Hall, Inc., 1971, 37–72 (Chapter 2).

Rosenthal, Robert, and Lenore Jacobson. *Pygmalion in the Classroom.* New York: Holt, Rinehart and Winston, Inc., 1968 (Chapter 11).

Russell, David Harris. *Children's Thinking.* Boston, Mass.: Ginn and Company, 1956 (Chapter 5).

Russell, David H., and Etta E. Karp. *Reading Aids through the Grades.* New York: Columbia University, Teachers College Press, 1951 (Chapter 8).

Sanders, N. *Classroom Questions, What Kinds?* New York: Harper & Row Publishers, 1966 (Chapter 5).

Schack, Vita G. "A Quick Phonics Readiness Check for Retarded Readers," *Elementary English,* XXXIX (October 1962), 584–586 (Chapter 9).

Schneider, Herman, and Nina Schneider. *Science in Our World.* Boston, Mass.: D.C. Heath, 1968 (Chapter 14).

Seashore, R.H., and L. Eckerson. "The Measurement of Individual Differences in General English Vocabulary," *Journal of Educational Psychology,* 31 (January 1940), 14–38 (Chapter 8).

Sebesta, Sam L. "Literature in the Elementary School." Speech given at International Reading Association Conference Proceedings in Boston, Mass., April 1968 (Chapter 11).

Severson, Eileen E. "The Teaching of Reading-study Skills in Biology," *The American Biology Teacher,* XXV (March 1963), 203–204 (Chapter 14).

Shores, J. Harlan. "Reading of Science for Two Separate Purposes as Perceived by Sixth Grade Students and Able Adult Readers," *Elementary English,* XXXVII (November 1960), 461–468 (Chapter 5).

Shotwell, Louisa R. *Roosevelt Grady.* Cleveland, Ohio: The World Publishing Company, 1963 (Chapter 11).

Shuy, Roger W. "Bonnie and Clyde Tactics in English Teaching," *Linguistics Cultural Differences and American Education. The Florida FL Reporter.* VII, no. 1 (Spring, Summer 1969), 81 (Chapter 4).

Silbiger, Francene, and Daniel Woolf. "Perceptual Difficulties Associated with Reading

Disability." *College Reading Association Proceedings*, VI (Fall 1965), 98–102 (Chapter 7).

Silvaroli, Nicholas J., and Warren H. Wheelock. "An Investigation of Auditory Discrimination Training for Beginning Readers," *The Reading Teacher*, XX (December 1966), 247–251 (Chapter 7).

Simons, Herbert D. "Reading Comprehension: The Need for a New Perspective," *Reading Research Quarterly*, VI, no. 3 (Spring 1971), 338–363 (Chapter 5).

Smith, Carl. "The Double Vowel and Linguistic Research," *The Reading Teacher*, XVIX, no. 7 (April 1966), 512–514 (Chapter 9).

————. *How to Read and Succeed*. New York: Essandess Special Edition, 1967 (Chapter 9).

————. "Tadpoles Make the Nicest Frogs," *Bulletin of the School of Education,* Indiana University, XLV, no. 6 (November 1969), 113–125 (Chapter 14).

Smith, Carl B., and Mary C. Austin. "Conducting a National Study of Title I Reading Programs," *Reading Research Quarterly*, IV, no. 3 (Spring 1969), 323–341.

Smith, Carl, and Leo C. Fay. *Getting People to Read*. New York: Delacorte Press, 1973 (Chapter 16).

Smith, Dora V. *Selected Essays*. New York: The Macmillan Company, 1964 (Chapter 11).

Smith, E. Brooks, Kenneth S. Goodman, and Robert Meredith. *Language and Thinking in the Elementary School*. New York: Holt, Rinehart and Winston, Inc., 1970 (Chapter 4).

Smith, Frank. *Comprehension and Learning*. New York: Holt, Rinehart and Winston, Inc., 1975 (Chapters 4, 5).

————. *Psycholinguistics and Reading*. New York: Holt, Rinehart and Winston, Inc., 1973 (Chapters 4, 5).

Smith, Nila Banton. *American Reading Instruction*. Newark, Del.: International Reading Association, 1965.

————. *Reading Instruction for Today's Children*. Englewood Cliffs, N.J.: Prentice-Hall, Inc., 1963 (Chapter 10).

Smith, Richard J., and Thomas C. Barrett. *Teaching Reading in the Middle Grades*. Reading, Mass.: Addison-Wesley, 1974 (Chapter 5).

Sochor, E. Elona. "Literal and Critical Reading in Social Studies," *Journal of Experimental Education*, XXVII (September 1958), 49–56 (Chapter 14).

Spache, Evelyn B. *Reading Activities for Child Involvement*. Boston, Mass.: Allyn and Bacon, Inc., 1976 (Chapter 16).

Spache, George. *Good Books for Poor Readers*. Champaign, Ill.: Garrard Publishing Company, 1974 (Chapter 11).

Spache, G.D. *Spache Diagnostic Reading Scales*. Monterey, Calif.: California Test Bureau, Del Monte Research Park, 1963 (Chapter 6).

Sperry, Armstrong. *Call It Courage*. New York: The Macmillan Company, 1940 (Chapter 11).

Spitzer, H.T., in collaboration with Ernest Horn, Maude McBroom, H.A. Green, and E.F. Lindquist. *Iowa Every-Pupil Test of Basic Skills*. Boston, Mass.: Houghton Mifflin Company, 1964 (Chapter 6).

Spodek, Bernard. "Developing Social Science Concepts in the Kindergarten," *A Look at Continuity in the School Program. 1958 Yearbook,* Association for Supervision and Curriculum Development. Washington, D.C.: National Education Association (Chapter 11).

Stauffer, Russell G. *The Language-experience Approach to the Teaching of Reading*. New York: Harper & Row, Publishers, 1970 (Chapter 17).

————. "Reading as a Cognitive Process," *Elementary English*, XLIV (April 1967), 342–348.

Stephens, Lillian S. *The Teacher's Guide to Open Education*. New York: Holt, Rinehart and Winston, Inc., 1974 (Chapter 16).

Stone, Clarence R. "Measuring Difficulty of Primary Reading Material: A Constructive Criticism of Spache's Measure," *Elementary School Journal*, 57 (October 1956), 36–41 (Chapter 8).

Stone, David R., and Vilda Bartschi. "A Basic Word List from Basal Readers," *Elementary English*, XL (April 1963), 420–427 (Chapter 8).

Strang, Ruth. *Diagnostic Teaching of Reading*. New York: McGraw-Hill Book Company, 1969 (Chapters 4, 11).

————. *Reading Diagnosis and Remediation*. Eric/Crier Reading Review Series. Newark, Del.: International Reading Association, 1968 (Chapter 7).

Stratemeyer, C.G., and H.L. Smith, Jr. *Frog Fun*. Evanston, Ill.: Harper & Row, Publishers, 1963 (Chapter 14).

Strickland, Ruth. "Building on What We Know." An address to the International Reading Association Convention, Boston, Mass., 1968 (Chapter 17).

————. *The Language of Elementary School Children: Its Relationship to the Language of Reading Textbooks and the Quality of Reading of Selected Children*, Bulletin of the School of Education. Bloomington, Ind.: Indiana University, July 1962 (Chapter 17).

————. *The Language Arts in the Elementary School*. Lexington, Mass.: D.C. Heath and Company, 1969.

Taba, Hilda. *Thought Processes and Teaching Strategies in Elementary School Social Studies*, American Educational Research Association paper presented in Chicago, Ill., February 13, 1963 (Chapter 11).

Thompson, Bertha Boya. "A Longitudinal Study of Auditory Discrimination," *Journal of Educational Research*, LVI (March 1963), 376–378 (Chapter 7).

Tiedt, Iris M., and Sidney W. Tiedt. *Contemporary English in the Elementary School*. Englewood Cliffs, N.J.: Prentice-Hall, Inc., 1974.

Tiegs, E.W., and W.W. Clark. *California Reading Tests*. Monterey, Calif.: California Test Bureau, 1963 (Chapter 6).

Tinker, M., and C. McCullough. *Teaching Elementary Reading*. New York: Appleton-Century-Crofts, 1962 (Chapter 10).

Tinker, Miles A. *Bases for Effective Reading*. Minneapolis, Minn.: University of Minnesota Press, 1965 (Chapter 18).

Torrance, E. Paul. "Introduction," *360 Reading Series* Boston, Mass.: Ginn and Company, 1969 (Chapter 15).

Van Allen, Roach, and Dorris M. Lee. *Learning to Read through Experience*. New York: Appleton-Century-Crofts, 1963 (Chapter 17).

Veatch, Jeanette. *Individualizing Your Reading Program*. New York: G.P. Putnam's Sons, 1959.

Veatch, Jeannette, et al. *Key Words to Reading: The Language Experience Approach Begins*. Columbus, Ohio: Charles E. Merrill Publishing Company, 1973 (Chapter 17).

Vernon, M.D. *Backwardness in Reading*. London: Cambridge University Press, 1960 (Chapter 7).

————. "The Perceptual Process in Reading," *The Reading Teacher*, XIII (October 1959), 2–8 (Chapter 7).

Voight, Ralph Claude. *Invitation to Learning* I: *The Learning Center Handbook*. Washington, D.C.: Acropolis Books Ltd., 1974 (Chapter 16).

————. *Invitation to Learning* II: *Center Teaching with Instructional Depth*. Washington, D.C.: Acropolis Books Ltd., 1974 (Chapter 16).

Wagner, Guy, and Max Hosier. *Reading Games*. New York: The Macmillan Company, 1970 (Chapter 16).

Wallen, Carl J. "Independent Activities: A Necessity, Not a Frill." *The Reading Teacher*, XXVII, no. 3 (December 1973), 257–262 (Chapter 16).

Ward, Lynd. *The Biggest Bear*. Boston, Mass.: Houghton Mifflin Company, 1952 (Chapter 11).

Wardeberg, Helen. "The Art of Questioning," mimeograph. Ithaca, N.Y.: Cornell University, 1969 (Chapter 12).

Wardhaugh, Ronald. "Linguistics and Reading," *Teacher's Resource Book—Series r*, by Carl B. Smith and Ronald Wardhaugh. New York: The Macmillan Company, 1975, 32–44 (Chapter 9).

Weintraub, Samuel. "Children's Reading Interests," *The Reading Teacher*, XXII (April 1969), 655–659 (Chapter 11).

Wepman, J.M. "Auditory Discrimination, Speech, and Reading," *Elementary School Journal*, LX (March 1960), 325–333 (Chapter 7).

Wheeler, Alan H. "A Systematic Design for Individualizing Reading," *Elementary English*, L, no. 3 (March 1973), 445–449 (Chapter 18).

White, E.B. *Charlotte's Web*. New York: Harper & Row, Publishers, 1952 (Chapter 11).

Wilson, Robert M., and Linda B. Gambrell. "Contracting—One Way to Individualize," *Elementary English*, L, no. 3 (March 1973), 427–429 + (Chapter 16).

Wolf, Willavene, Martha L. King, and Charlotte S. Huck. "Teaching Critical Reading to Elementary School Children," *The Reading Research Quarterly*, III, no. 4 (Summer 1968), 435–498 (Chapter 12).

Yates, Elizabeth. *Mountain Born*. New York: Coward-McCann, Inc., 1943 (Chapter 11).

York, Jean. "Instructional Materials," *Elementary English*, XLIX, no. 8 (December 1972), 1196–1204 (Chapter 18).

Zigler, Edward. "Learning from Children," *Childhood Education*, XLVIII, no. 1 (October 1971), 8–11 (Chapter 16).

Index*

*Items in bold face are defined on the page or pages indicated.